Being an
Anthropologist

Being an Anthropologist

Anthropologist

Fieldwork in Eleven Cultures

Edited by

George D. Spindler

Stanford University

HOLT, RINEHART AND WINSTON, INC.

New York Chicago San Francisco Atlanta
Dallas Montreal Toronto London Sydney

*This book is dedicated to the people with whom
anthropologists work and live in the field and to
students who would like to know how it goes there.*

Copyright © 1970 by Holt, Rinehart and Winston, Inc.
All rights reserved
Library of Congress Catalog Card Number: 74–108848
SBN: 03–081105–8
Printed in the United States of America
1   2   3   4   5   6   7   8   9

Preface

Anthropologists undergo self-expansion and enlarge their range of perceptions and sensitivities when they do fieldwork. The changes in personal values, self-feelings, and attitudes toward others are often profound. Anthropology differs from its peer disciplines in the methods employed in the field and the questions asked. Being an anthropologist in the field usually requires a drastic adaptation to someone else's way of life and an adoption of the other's point of view. *Being an Anthropologist* is a report of how thirteen anthropologists, and other members of their families, made this adaptation in eleven different cultures.[1] Each of these cultures is described under a title in the series *Case Studies in Cultural Anthropology* and was selected purposely from this series. Methods of data collection and analysis are discussed, but the major purpose declared during the planning of this book was to describe the anthropologist's personal adaptation to the field experience.

[1] We acknowledge the distinctions currently made between culture and society and their various ramifications. We use the term *culture* in this preface and in the title of this book in the sense of *cultural system*, including ideational and behavioral patterns, structural alignments, membership and social interaction, and ecological interrelationships as we develop the concept in *Culture in Process* (Alan R. Beals with George and Louise Spindler, Holt, Rinehart and Winston, Inc., 1967).

This book is a contribution toward filling a gap in the methodological literature of anthropology, but is intended mainly as a help to students (and others) who want to understand anthropology and anthropologists. These chapters furnish a dimension of experience, observation, and reaction that is usually left out of ethnographies and that is rarely reported elsewhere in the literature,[2] but that is essential to an understanding of the ways of life that have been studied and the way in which anthropologists study them. Experience, perception, and interpretation occur in a kaleidoscopic relationship to all events past and present in the experience of the observer-interpreter. There can be no "culture," "social system," or "community" in the absolute, transcendental sense. There is culture, social system, and community as perceived and interpreted. Unless the observer is psychotic, the ethnography is never relative only and wholly to the observer. But all ethnographies are partly personal documents, balanced by strivings for objectivity. Attempts are frequently made, by experienced as well as inexperienced fieldworkers, to be dispassionate observers. To be truly dispassionate in a human community would be inhuman—a profound bias that does not enhance objectivity. A great stride toward objectivity is taken when personal involvement is acknowledged, for once acknowledged it can be recognized, to some extent controlled, and even utilized as a source of valuable data and insight. Ultimately we may understand the use of human perception, feeling, and experience as scientific instrumentation appropriate to the study of human life.

Every ethnography is unique, just as every ethnographer, every field site, every day, every event is unique. An ethnography is a report and interpretation of events that never again will be repeated, that occurred in a time forever gone. But the classes of events, the categories of behavior, are repeated endlessly. By moving through the events assembled for us in ethnographies to the ethnographer and his experience and back to the assembled events, we can gain some insight into the nature of those categories. When we do this we find the personal adaptation and involvements of the anthropologist in the field to be significant influences on not only the reporting and interpretation of events but upon the events themselves. Fieldwork is a complex transaction. Interpretation of data gathered in the field adds another dimension of complexity.

To help the reader see the relationships among personal experience, observations, and interpretations, we have made every effort to personalize the chapters in this book and their authors. The latter has been more difficult than the former. Our colleagues are modest. Nevertheless, some of the most significant relationships are apparent, and there are tantalizing hints of many more, at deeper levels of awareness and influence.

The effort, partly, at least, successful, to personalize field experience, should

---

[2] See Recommended Reading for annotated, relevant references.

not mislead the reader. The disciplined aspects of anthropological fieldwork appear in these chapters, but they are given second place.

The chapters in this book are written by anthropologists selected for differences in theoretical position, age, time of fieldwork, and the location and nature of their field experience. It was anticipated that there would be sharp differences in approach represented in this range that would be reflected in the chapters in this book. This did not turn out to be true. The social situations encountered, the problems of entrée, of establishing rapport, adjusting to strange environments, handling one's presentation of self, managing the interactions between self and others of varying identity, striving for objectivity with rules for collection, of data and their interpretation, keeping one's balance with the excruciating ethical problems of becoming friends with people in order to observe them at close and meaningful range—these categories of experience appear again and again. Personal reactions vary in intensity and there is inevitable self-doubt and anxiety aroused in situations where one gathers the most essential data from fortuitous informal contacts. But usually there is deep emotional satisfaction in fieldwork. Nostalgia for friends and places where one lived and worked, the great meaningfulness of the field experience, and the personal experiences associated with it are persistent themes in these chapters. This is not always true for the anthropologist in the field. It is true for these anthropologists in this book and the field experiences they report.

These studies have all been used for good purposes. They produced observations and interpretations of human life that broadened horizons, that helped break down barriers between human groups, that helped to reduce the death-dealing propensity of humans to dichotomize the human population into *we* and *they*. These chapters and the case studies that they represent help to humanize the human view. This is, as we see it, one of the fundamental tasks of anthropology. In this perspective, anthropology as a way of life and as a value system serves a most idealistic purpose.

G. D. S.

Contents

Editor's Note

This book can be read profitably for itself, but since each chapter is a report of fieldwork that resulted in a case study in the series, *Case Studies in Cultural Anthropology*, they are best read in conjunction with the case studies. We hope that by joining the results of fieldwork with reports of the process of fieldwork it will be possible for students to learn more effectively about anthropology, anthropologists, and the ways of life they study. We hope this not only results in a better intellectual understanding of social and cultural systems but also makes a contribution to a way of thinking that is crucial, it seems to us, in human affairs in our world today.

The *Case Studies in Cultural Anthropology* series is published by Holt, Rinehart and Winston and is edited by George and Louise Spindler. The term "case study" was originally selected rather than "ethnography" to avoid the connotations of formality and completeness usually evoked by the latter term. The first case studies were published in 1960, after several years of experimentation and exploration of instructional needs in the teaching of anthropology by the editors. The series maximizes cultural diversity. Each case study is the unique product of an anthropologist's experience with a unique way of life. Yet, reading several case studies leads the student to the conviction that there are universal categories of experience and adaptation underlying the diversity and uniqueness. The case studies are intended as primary instructional material, to be used as both a source of generalizations about human life, through inductive analysis and interpretation, and as documentation and extension of established generalizations.

The map on page xiv locates the sites of the case studies in this volume, indicated by the numbers given below. Certain major geographical areas not represented at all in this volume, but for which there are case studies, are represented in other publications on field methods in the series *Studies in Anthropological Methods*, also edited by the Spindlers.

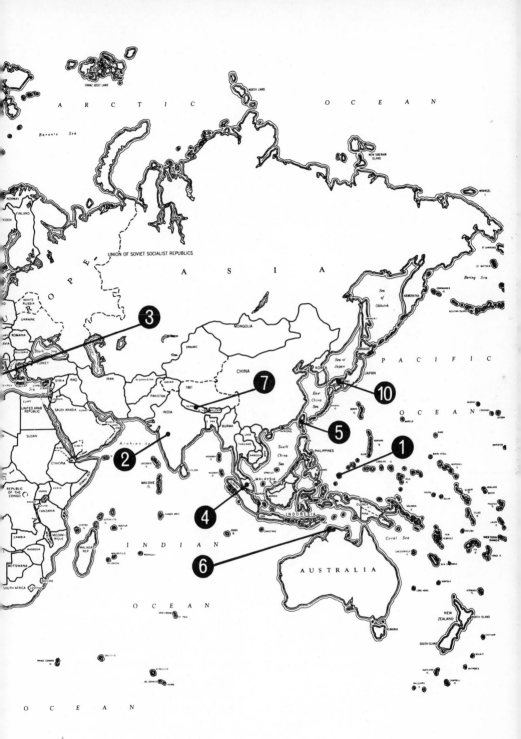

1

PALAUAN JOURNAL

HOMER G. BARNETT
University of Oregon

Related Case Study: **Being a Palauan**

Anthropologists often speak of the desirability of keeping a diary for each day in the field. Many do, but few publish them. Homer Barnett's selections from his own journal, kept while he was doing fieldwork on Palau, are of particular value. They not only show the nature of such a diary, but also illustrate the events that make up fieldwork from day to day.

His journal illustrates that much fieldwork consists of waiting for things to happen, being friendly, receptive, and present. The approach is low key, and nonthreatening. The role of the participant observer becomes clear. He is something more than an honored guest and something less than one of the people. It is clear that he is able to see what is going on because he is present, though not always really participating as a full member of the group. Even in the intimacy of his relationship with the people there is some distance between him and his informants. This is always true, but here in this journal we can see the nature of this distance clearly. To be invited to all the places he went and to all of the affairs he participated in as guest, he had to be attractive, trusted, and available. This does not make Homer Barnett a Palauan.

But at the same time he was accepted as an elder brother by one of his closest assistants. This relationship was of great significance. Homer Barnett was, therefore, inside and outside the Palauan system simultaneously. This is usually the anthropologist's position. "Palauan Journal" makes this clear.

The Author

Homer Barnett was born in Bisbee, Arizona. He began his anthropological career with archeological fieldwork near Taft, California, in 1932. In

Homer Barnett and Azu.

1934 and again during 1935–1936 he did fieldwork among Indian tribes, first in southwestern Oregon and then among the Salish of British Columbia. Later he did fieldwork among the Klamath, Yurok, the Tsimshian, and the Yakima, all Northwest Coast people. He has long had a special interest in the Pacific Islands. In 1947–1948 he lived in a Palauan village, in 1952–1953 he visited Fiji and New Caledonia, in 1955 Netherlands New Guinea, in 1961 Australian New Guinea, in 1962 the Solomon Islands, and in 1966–1968 Australia. As Staff Anthropologist for the U.S. Government's Trust Territory of the Pacific Islands, he visited all the major island groups of American Micronesia with extended revisits to Palau to deal with special problems arising from Palauan adaptations to changing conditions. He has also been an adviser to the Netherlands New Guinea government on its native welfare programs and a member of the Research Council of the South Pacific Commission, a body of social scientists that recommends studies of native and administrative needs as traditional patterns are modified through contact with alien cultures and demands. He is a Professor of Anthropology at the University of Oregon where he has taught since 1939. In 1961 he was President of the Society for Applied Anthropology. He has written many articles on cultural process and is particularly well known for his book, *Innovation: the Basis of Cultural Change*, first published in 1953. His books also include *Palauan Society, Anthropology in Administration, Indian Shakers,* and *The Coast Salish of British Columbia.*

He explains how he came into anthropology:

I wandered into anthropology at the University of California in Berkeley as a graduate student. My undergraduate years were spent at Stanford, where no course on the subject was given at the time. I knew what I wanted to do and be, but I didn't know the name of it. I knew that I wanted to understand people, all people, because I came from a part of the country where race prejudice was rampant and at times violent. The closest I could get to this at Stanford was in philosophy and in courses on Russian and Chinese literature. Then, after five years of knocking around the world as a seaman on various freighters, I reluctantly decided to become a teacher, a high school teacher. That was in 1932 when the economic bottom had fallen out of everything and I came to the happy conclusion that I would rather starve as a student than as an unsuccessful salesman of subscriptions to the *San Francisco Chronicle*. During a semester of boredom in the curriculum for teacher aspirants at the University of California, I combed through the catalogue of courses and made up my mind to go all the way and try one called "Primitive Society." That did it. From then on anthropology has been not only my vocation but my avocation. I feel myself lucky in that I cannot and do not want to distinguish between the two. I have been playing at my work and working at my play ever since.

G. D. S.

Preface

From August 23, 1947 until May 21, 1948 Allan Murphy, a graduate student, hereafter usually referred to as Al, and I lived in a small village in the northern part of the Palau Islands. At that time the U.S. Navy administered the islands under a civilian code of law. Ulimang, the hamlet in which we lived, was one of five in the district of Ngarard, the others being Ahol, Ngbuked, Alap, and Geklau.

Our basic problem was to learn the Palauan language. Charlie Simmons was the only Palauan—his father was German—who could speak English, and he was in the employ of the administration at the capital in Koror as an interpreter and factotum. He was loaned to us for the first week of our residence in Ulimang. Beyond that assistance, we had only a minimal English-Palauan word and phrase list; no grammar of the language.

The narrative that follows consists of excerpts from the journal that I kept. The entries relate my day-by-day experiences and reactions to life in Ulimang. Necessarily they are much condensed. In addition to the journal, I recorded

Azu's father.

Lagoon near Ulimang.

detailed ethnographic data in notebooks. In the interests of conserving space and the reader's patience, the entire record of some days and cross references to my notebooks have been deleted. In several places I have entered parenthetic statements to inform the reader about omitted data relevant to the subject matter included. The names of persons have been altered. Other than these changes, the excerpts are printed as they were written. Let the prepositions fall where they may.

August 23 We were taken from Koror to Ngarard by two Navy vessels. We landed somewhat upriver at a house in the hamlet of Ngbuked. Our interpreter, Charlie Simmons, told us to remain in the boat until the chief of Ngbuked was summoned. When he arrived we shook hands and, after some conversation between him and Charlie, we went ashore. The young men who were to carry our heavy gear were fishing, so it was decided that the chief, Charlie, Al, and I should go on to Ulimang and send men for our equipment later. We ascended a low central crest along a wide, cleared pathway through Ngbuked, the chief of the village in the lead. Houses, some of them of the old-type construction, were irregularly spaced off the pathway that over most of its length through the hamlet was paved with stones. On the top of the rise was a men's clubhouse, in about the center of the hamlet. At one end there was a siren. Charlie sounded it three times—the call for an assembly of the people of Ulimang, of which Charlie is a chief.

After about twenty-five minutes we arrived at Ulimang, on the east coast. A middle-aged man came to meet us. We sat on a high bench on the edge of the school grounds while he sat on the ground in front of us. After a short talk we proceeded to the schoolhouse where we were to stay until other arrangements could be made. On the way to Ulimang a few women in doorways spoke to the two chiefs as we passed, but I was impressed by the apparent lack of curiosity about us. Even the children seemed indifferent. Heads were not hanging out of doorways; none apparently appeared from cover. People did not follow or congregate around us. There were several children playing on the broad sandy schoolyard, but they remained where they were, and only came near some time after we had stopped and two more chiefs from nearby villages arrived to greet us.

For the rest of the afternoon, until about 4:30, we sat with the chiefs while they chatted. In the meantime, school boys and girls were sent to get such pieces of our equipment as they could carry. By 5:00 I was getting rather hungry, and was undecided as to what to do. Finally Charlie explained that the first chief of the district, whom we had met in Koror, had sent a message saying that we were to arrive on the following day, and that the people had intended getting a feast ready for us then. As it was, food was being prepared but it would be late in coming. It did arrive after dark, brought by two women on trays carried on their heads. The school teacher had lighted a lamp on our table in the school-

Author's house in Palau.

room building. He helped set the food before us. We ate alone while the Palauans sat outside talking. After we had eaten we joined them. Charlie asked whether we wanted food brought to us each day, or whether we wanted a girl or a boy assigned to help us prepare our food. I explained that we would do our own cooking and most of our other domestic chores.

Before eating we went to see a house nearby. It was being built by a young man, Kai by name, for his own use, but it was offered to us. It was quite suitable and I was pleased at our good luck, but I tried to make it plain to Charlie that we did not want to take it at the inconvenience of the owner. I was assured that he had enough room in another house just back of the one that we would occupy,

Old-type house.

which did not convince me, and I was determined to compensate him in some way.

August 24 The canned foods that we have brought with us are mostly the so-called C rations issued by the military government for its personnel. They are, I trust, nutritious, but they are nonetheless tasteless. I have realized over the past month in passing through Guam and Koror that one of my personal needs is for American-style fresh vegetables—carrots and cabbage exempted. I could add fresh beef, but that is out of reason, because here there is only fish, which I must learn to like. I think I will start a vegetable garden. If it succeeds that would amaze no one more than myself.

August 27 No progress has been made toward getting settled in our house. Monday afternoon Charlie told us we could move in yesterday. We got packed in the morning, but no one came for our baggage, and since we are regarded as chiefs it would be beneath their expectations of us to transport our own effects. This attitude has its advantages but it belongs to another situation. If the people continue to regard us as sahibs the social distance thereby created will deny us the participation that is essential to our purposes. I am referred to and addressed as "Doctor," which may set up still another barrier. This stems from the auspices of the military government, from which I want to disassociate myself as much as possible. Charlie told me earlier that the Ulimang people were notified in advance by the officials in Koror that a "Doctor Somebody" would be coming to live in their village.

Yesterday I gave a package of mints to the oldest girl among about twenty children playing on the schoolground. The rest displayed no eagerness or curiosity about it, even the smallest of them, aged three to five years. The girl to whom I gave the mints walked around with them for awhile and all the children continued to play as they had done before. Finally, after fifteen or twenty minutes they all sat in the shade and the girl proceeded to divide the candy among them, the others sitting in a ring about her. I gave the same girl a package of mints today under the same conditions, and the same thing happened. The children, all of whom seem to be residents of this village, play most of the day on the schoolgrounds. They pay no attention to us, and remain at the opposite corner from us. This is presumably their normal habit. However, I am beginning to suspect that they, as well as the adults of this village, have been told to ignore us, or at least not to bother us.

August 28 One of the school teachers came to ask for help with his English, beginning tomorrow night. I welcomed this as I have hoped to get as much from the teachers as I know they are hoping to get from us. This particular teacher, Pelew, is eager to learn English, not only for the advantage it will give him in dealing with Americans, but because he must teach his pupils how to read, write, and speak it. His command of it now is minimal. He knows the Japanese language—which was the one used in the schools that he attended before the Americans arrived—and he owns a Japanese-English dictionary. Using that he has taught himself about all he knows of English. Working with him, and using that dictionary, I hope to build my Palauan vocabulary.

This afternoon Charlie suggested that we visit Ngbuked and Alap, partly to show us around, and partly because the second chief of Ngarard, who lives in Alap, wanted to give us some oranges in response, I suppose, to the gift of the six cigars which I sent to him yesterday.

August 29 We moved into our house today. On the way we met a rather small young man wearing blue trunks, shoes, and a junior navy officer's cap. His dress was altogether strange by comparison with the other people we have met. In a rather authoritative tone he asked the others if the stuff that they were carrying was ours. The boy who was pushing the cart with some baggage in it said yes and made a gesture offering him the job. All laughed except him. He refused and looked rather angrily at me when I smiled. I was afraid I had made a mistake until one of the men said, "He a little crazy." I kept my eye on him until we got into the house.

Charlie and two other chiefs were already there sitting on our kitchen floor when we arrived. The young men who had helped with the moving sat in what was to be our dining room, while the "Crazy One" joined us in the kitchen. Throughout the time he was present he identified himself with the chiefs, and even overreached them. He made free with the second chief's betel, despite the latter's unobtrusive and fatherly objection. I laid two cartons of cigarettes and about a dozen spools of colored thread on the floor and told Charlie they were for the men and women who had made the house ready for us earlier during the week. Then I set out another and indicated that a package should go to each one for this morning's work. The chiefs proceeded to enumerate the individual men who had helped, and laid out packages of cigarettes by villages. The "Crazy One" took a bold part in this distribution, passing the cigarettes to those who were to get them and repeating the words of the chiefs. Once or twice a remark was made to him by one of the three chiefs, and the other men smiled or laughed. Finally, the second chief told the young men to go, and had to request and repeat his request directly but quietly for the "Crazy One" to leave also.

August 30 We continued intermittently with our household chores through the day. Time goes fast and we seem to accomplish very little, the principal reason being that someone drops by, we invite him in, give him cigarettes, and try to extend our vocabulary and improve our pronunciation. Naturally this is time-consuming. We are anxious also to build goodwill and to be accepted casually. We want the people to come to us rather than the other way around until later on.

September 2 Yesterday was the first day of school. Today as I passed the schoolground where the children were playing, those who are from other villages and who had not yet been near me stood up, faced me, stiffened their arms at their sides, bowed, and said, "Good morning, Sir." Upon our first acquaintance, chiefs have also bowed slightly to me. They have also raised their right hand in salutation. They have ceased to do this, or do it only hesitantly, apparently in response to my rather offhand, inconsistent attention to it myself. I notice that the children in this village have ceased to raise their hands to me and also to come to attention upon meeting me. I believe that if I had demanded it by my attitude, they would have continued the formality. We are certainly no longer lacking in attention by the children nor the adults. Practically everyone who passes our house—and there are many, for we are on the common path leading from the village center to the bathing and watering place—peers in as he passes by. Sometimes a whole group will do the same. We have practically no privacy, and there are scarcely fifteen minutes when someone is not trying to get a glimpse of us.

None of the teachers can speak even fair English, and they do not know many basic words such as "learn," "means," and the like. I have tried to use charades, my limited Palauan, their limited English, and several Japanese-English dictionaries and phrase books to explain and to be explained to by them. It is on occasions such as these that one is impressed with the really fundamental character of "the meaning of meaning." You soon reach the point beyond which explaining seems impossible.

September 4   I have scarcely moved from the house for two days. Pelew has been here for the past two nights and we have stayed up until 12:00 working on English and Palauan. People continued to bring us bits of food. Kai brought us a fish last night. Pelew had already given us one. Masas, one of the older school boys, brought us two eggs tonight. It has been mainly these three who have brought us food, perhaps because we are neighbors. As yet I do not even know who lives at the other end of the village, because I have been so occupied with those who live near us.

September 7   This afternoon the second chief came to see me bearing gifts— three oranges, three fish, and a chicken. The chicken is so skinny it would be pointless to eat it now, so I set to work to pen it up and feed it for awhile. The chief is jolly, and made a joke which I took to mean that if I used the chicken as a lure others would be drawn to it and I would thereby have a flock. He talked on and I nodded, only partly guessing what he was saying, but I gathered that he wanted to tell me that he would have a carpenter here to build our outhouse—a little matter that has concerned me for some time.

September 8   Al and I hoed the weeds out of a patch of ground in the backyard of our house—the beginning of a garden. Both activities, the outhouse building and the hoeing, were regarded rather humorously by many passers-by. They think, I believe, that trying to raise a garden in our backyard is a silly business of white men. And our pale skin, our larvae-like appearance in shorts probably adds to their amusement. Our chicken has been a source of curiosity for the children and the quiet amusement of several adults. I have penned it in a screened enclosure under the house. Both the pen and the use of the space under the floor is strange to the people. Native chickens run free, and no use at all is made of the area under the elevated floor of the house.

September 9   About 4:30 this afternoon a young man came to ask whether I had a "picture engine." I guessed he meant a camera. And so he did, because he wanted me to take a picture of himself and of Kai's wife and their baby. I was happy to have our cameras introduced in this way; that is, by request. We had not so far brought them out. I took the picture, then suggested one of Kai, then one of the whole family in front of their house.

September 11   There was considerable activity all day. I set our motion picture camera at our front window about noontime, focused it on the section of the path in front of our door, and took a strip of pictures of every passer-by until 4:00 P.M.

September 12 Kai appeared about 3:00 P.M., eager to teach us Palauan. He is very bright and helpful. He stayed until 6:00; then was back again at 8:00. About 9:00 Masas and one of his young friends came by as they have been doing, and we did some more language study to mutual advantage. We got to bed at 11:30, which has come to be normal.

September 16 This has been a very full day, so much so that I have had little time to myself. The Ngbuked chief came as we were washing breakfast dishes around 9:00. He brought a stalk of bananas and three small chickens. I gave him three cigars and a package of cigarettes. He stayed for a full two hours, sitting on the kitchen floor with us. I brought out the recording machine and the motion picture camera for the first time. He asked about the generator that we have not uncrated and that everybody has supposed is for a lighting plant. Actually it is to generate electricity for our steel wire recorder. He wanted to know whether I am Catholic or Protestant and when I replied Protestant he was jubilant—and seemed distressed and puzzled when I added that Murphy is a Catholic. I gathered that he could not understand our living together. Anyway, he invited me to church services in Ngbuked Sunday after next and asked me to bring the camera.

September 17 Isuwut came early and worked all day on our generator. He was able to get it started, but it was difficult. I have my doubts, as I always have had, about its utility. I tried to give Isuwut 50 cents, but he refused. We also asked him in to have lunch but he refused. I urged him, but he said he was not hungry. Apparently none of them will eat with us. Even Charlie, who is otherwise accustomed to associating with Germans, Japanese, and Americans, has been reluctant to do so when other Palauans are present.

September 25 I visited the school today. I went there to set my watch by the school clock, but found that it is set by the sun. I sat in the sixth grade class. They were trying to write English sentences, using "house" and "see" and were having a difficult time. The pupils rise when the teacher enters the room, but otherwise the proceedings are quite informal, though the teacher's attitude is stern and abrupt. The teacher had his class sing for me. The song was the *Star-Spangled Banner*—I think!

October 9 It rained rather hard for an hour again this morning. Yesterday afternoon I decided to transplant some of my house-raised tomato plants, and to set out two or three dozen onions. Our corn has survived—it is 8 or 9 inches high. The pole beans are higher. Melons and squash are doing well. No lettuce has ever showed above ground. Thin hairlike blades of onions have appeared but have died, probably due to lack of water. Three radishes have survived.

October 10 The Ngbuked chief invited me to join the Protestants for the opening of a new church building in Ngerchelong, which is about two and one half hours' walk from here. I declined because I do not want to become closely identified with that or any other element in the community.

October 12   Kai took us out to the reef this morning at low tide. Since it is Sunday and his coconut oil plant was not operating, he was agreeable to the suggestion of our taking pictures of him spearfishing. He was in fact a willing and enthusiastic actor before the movie camera.

October 20   We spent most of the day getting our gasoline engine and our recording machine in operation. We have it set up about 50 yards from the house. By the time the operation was completed we had an interested and a dumbfounded audience, which had collected to observe the activity. We picked up their conversation and played it back to them. For the first time they got the idea, and then Kai explained it all. At the end a small boy wanted to sing a song and did. I asked that the school children come to our house to have their songs recorded.

October 22   The recording experiment with the school children was an unhappy failure. The gasoline engine seemed to run well enough, but there was a pulsation in the current. The songs were badly distorted, due in part to the rise and fall of current intensity—like a lopsided phonograph record. After several attempts to adjust the machine we abandoned the experiment and, much to my disappointment and embarrassment, sent the children back to school.

October 23   We spent the whole morning repairing an air rifle belonging to an old man of Alap. We had previously fixed his flashlight and given him batteries for it. Other people seem to regard our association with him as a little ridiculous. Kai refers to him to me as "Mr. Murphy's Friend" and laughs. The old fellow, whose name is Ackul, has no social position and does not seem to fit well with his society. He repeatedly says that Palau is bad, and that he admires Americans.

October 24   I spent two hours this morning with Pelew at school. He suggested this the night before and I was happy for the chance. This should dispense with so much night study and also keep me in touch with what is going on at the school.

October 25   We set out for Ngbuked about 10:00 A.M. On the way we stopped at Kai's coconut oil plant where all of his helpers (five of them) were sitting around discussing financial matters. We spent a couple of hours talking with them since they had nothing better to do it seemed. Their supply of coconuts was exhausted, and since it was Saturday they were quitting work at noon anyway. We had a very profitable language lesson.

November 2   We returned from our monthly trip to Koror for supplies last night. While there, I borrowed a combination Palauan-German and German-Palauan dictionary from the Protestant missionary. He loaned us a New Testament so we can collate the Palauan translation of St. Luke. He also gave us some printed Sunday school lessons in Palauan. These are very helpful.

November 7 The work on the new office buildings continued today. The older men set up the foundation posts for the new store also. The work proceeded very leisurely. At any one time about half of the men were sitting around talking among themselves and heckling the others who were working. In the meantime, the young men were energetically putting up a new house for the first chief of the district. They worked much more rapidly, and few sat around; in fact, very few at one time. They worked until dusk, and by then had completed the roof and half of the walls of the building. I spent the morning between these two jobs, taking pictures, listening, and observing. During the afternoon I wrote several letters to get them off on the boat that is expected tomorrow. Al and I are planning on taking this boat to Kayangle (an island to the north), stay overnight, and return Sunday, with Kai as our guide. Kai suggested it and it is a good opportunity for us.

November 8 In spite of the threat of rain and prospects of an unproductive trip, Kai and I went to Kayangle. Al decided to stay home. Our boat trip was more pleasant than I had expected. We did have a heavy sea for a distance of perhaps 10 miles just before reaching the Kayangle lagoon.

We arrived just after dark and were put up in a small vacant house, which probably is reserved for such occasions. A cot was brought for me and a mattress, mat, pillow, and blanket for both of us. We were brought food—fish, taro, and a kind of squash in coconut milk. After eating, Kai rather diffidently asked if I wanted to attend a dance. We went about 9:00 P.M. to an old building on the edge of the village. It apparently is a young people's recreation hall. Several boys and girls and also some young married men and women were there. A few of them danced in couples to some dismal records on an old phonograph. *Red Wing* was one of them. It was popular in the States when I was a teenager. I noticed that it was not unusual for two boys to dance together, even while girls sat around on the floor against the walls. I suppose this has been copied from our army personnel, because during the war there were soldiers stationed on the island.

After awhile Kai told a young man I would like to see one of the native women's dances called a *ngloik*. The women, and some boys on each end, lined up and, led by the young man standing in front of them, they sang and danced. The singing was in a confusion of languages including Palauan, Japanese, and English—very little of it entirely Palauan. There were a succession of dances and songs set off by intervals during which all of the dancers marked time, so to speak, with a relaxed forward kick, to a time count called by the leader who said: "Left, right, left, right,"—without regard to the named foot, however. This continued for perhaps one-half hour, after which they returned to the couple-type dancing. I asked Kai whether *ngloiks* were danced in Ulimang and he said no. Finally, he told me that the head chief of the district had prohibited them—which seems to account for the fact that several young people from Ulimang were on the same boat with us and attended the dance.

Men's clubhouse.

November 9   We were up early and walked around the southern end of the island. I saw an excellent speciman of the old-type canoe, placed under a well-constructed canoe shed, and a good, new rowboat. Also, I saw two old-style men's clubhouses, of which I obtained pictures. Our boat left for home at 9:30 A.M. but we did not arrive until 5:00 because of mechanical difficulties. Murphy reported that the young men's group had completed most of the work on the head chief's house by noon Saturday and then had a rather wild celebration—drunken arguments, threats with knives, and so forth. He thought that the anticipation of this was the reason why the head chief and Kai wanted to get us out of the village. This proved to be correct, because Kai came over about 9:00 P.M. and when the subject was raised he volunteered that he wanted to get us away from the village. He had seen an accumulation of liquor and expected trouble. He is getting rather confidential, and I think our trip to Kayangle broke some ice.

November 11   The second chief of Geklau invited me to visit him, saying that he would send a boat for me. I also had some small talk with a dynamic and sympathetic man of my age who lives near the Ngbuked men's clubhouse.

Interior of clubhouse.

He invited me to visit him, too. He speaks clearly and forcefully and is easier to understand than many others. I attribute some of this cordiality and other expressions of friendliness to my trip to Kayangle. It is my impression that this adventure served the purpose for which I had hoped, namely, to establish a closer bond between us and the ordinary people.

Kai came over in the late afternoon to put some bamboo shelving in our kitchen area. As usual the occasion turned out to be a language lesson. He is insisting, and rightly so, on my learning the vernacular as well as the more "classical" or stilted expressions found in dictionaries. With his acting ability and ingenuity these sessions are entertaining as well as instructive.

November 13 I was awakened about 3:00 A.M. because I was cold. I continued to doze until about 4:00, during which time the wind increased and the rain, which had begun about 10:00 P.M. last night, continued. By 4:30 there was a strong wind from the west, so much so that the curtain on our west window was flapping vigorously and the rain was coming in. By 5:00, Al and I were fully awake and concluded that we were in for a typhoon. We got up at 5:30, dressed, and prepared for breakfast. The wind and rain came in gusts. The violence reached a high point about 10:00 A.M. when a corner of our house lifted slightly off its foundation. We retreated to one part of one room to keep dry. Kai was busy nailing sheet iron covers over our windows and setting braces across our doors. By 11:00 his wife and others across the way became concerned about a heavy cluster of nuts swaying over our house. Kai and his brother-in-law came to tell us we had better go to the latter's house. We did, and sat there until 2:30 in the afternoon when I proposed to go home and eat. During this time there were several slack intervals, but no real abatement. There were strong gusts until 5:00 P.M., after which the storm began to subside, though it continued to rain until much later.

During the storm many young men made the village circuit—partly to help, partly out of excitement and curiosity. Considerable damage was done. Three coconut tree tops were broken off in our immediate vicinity. Many banana trees were blown down. Two houses in Ulimang collapsed; also one in Ngbuked, as well as the building at the end of the dock there.

November 21   I spent the morning sitting with and watching a group of older men building the new office. As always, there was an almost continuous stream of talk of one sort or another—everybody had something to say, everybody had some advice to give, everybody kibitzed. There was a lot of raillery and horseplay. All laughed at the jokes of others, and there were a lot of them.

November 23   This Sunday has been a very busy and a very long day. We started out at 10:30 in the morning with our cameras, intending to get some pictures for the record and at the same time to treat some of the people to pictures of themselves. We arrived at the Ngbuked men's clubhouse at 12:00, where the Protestant congregation was assembled. I supposed that the services were nearly over, so Al and I sat outside. Soon a boy was sent by the chief to ask us to come in; the services were just about to start. We stayed for them and afterwards took several pictures of members of the congregation. We continued our circuit of the district, finding almost every house closed.

December 1   Yesterday in talking with three of the older men I had several pertinent questions put to me: Why did the war occur; why did the Palauans get involved in it; why are we Americans here and not the Japanese; why do I want to study the Palauan people? These questions were asked in a perfectly friendly way. I felt rather helpless.

December 8   After watching activities around the store for a time, Al and I went to sketch the Ngbuked clubhouse. We spent the morning there but got little done because we became involved in a conversation with two men, one old and the other fairly young. The latter is a woodcarver who was taught his craft by the Japanese. He talked for some time about Japanese oppression. So did the old man. Both of them, like many others, seemed to delight in recounting the superior war exploits of the Americans over the Japanese. The old man excitedly described Palauan warfare, and also told us about the prostitutes who used to live in clubhouses with the young men.

December 11   Al and I returned to the Ngbuked clubhouse this morning to complete our sketching of it. We found that preparations were under way beside it for a turtle feast. The turtle was cooked by 11:00, so I had some of it at their invitation. Also some of the tapioca liquor which one of the men brought. I thought this was again an expression of their confidence in me because the making and the drinking of this liquor is forbidden by the administration.

December 17 The Catholic missionary who lives in Koror dropped in to see us unexpectedly at 4:30 this afternoon. He is making the rounds of the villages in preparation for Christmas services. He invited us to a prayer meeting and a children's catechism in the clubhouse here this evening. Both Al and I attended.

December 18 Just in the past few days I have noticed a change in the attitude of the people toward us. Or at least I think I do. Mingling as we have with them so regularly, they take us more for granted. They are less self-conscious, and there is no interruption in the proceedings, whatever they might be, when we arrive. No special attention is given to us. They are not so camera shy as they were in the beginning either—at least the men are not. The kids congregate around us as before but less out of curiosity than in friendliness.

December 19 The men from four of the villages of the district gathered at the Alap clubhouse to repair damages caused by the storm. All of them sewed nipa leaf patching, sitting in the shade on the platform in front of the clubhouse. Murphy sewed some too, which pleased the others. We came home at noon, and Al went back to work with the men and stayed until 4:30. He and I are invited to a completion feast tomorrow.

December 24 The blustery weather continued through the morning. I made a tour of the villages to check on activities, but was soon discouraged by the rain. I asked Kai if anything had been planned to celebrate Christmas and he said no, that a person had to go either to Koror or to Ngerchelong where there were to be services. Al and I have heard rumors, however, that native dances will be held here, either tomorrow or on New Year's. The Protestants are planning to go to Ngerchelong, and one of them asked me to accompany them. I refused, thinking that maybe something more interesting was going to be held here and that they were again trying to lure me away so I could not witness it. It now appears that I was wrong, but it is too late to switch, because I invited Kai to dinner tomorrow.

December 25 Kai appeared early, all dressed up, with his hair oiled and plastered down. He had promised to make noodles, which he had learned to do from the Japanese. He also wanted to watch our biscuit-making and other preparations. Instead, Rdor, his brother-in-law from across the path, brought noodles and stayed to watch and to help. Kai and I killed and plucked a chicken; Rdor cleaned it. The four of us had a gay time while dinner was being prepared—Al doing all the cooking. We were ready to eat by 3:00. Still I had seen nothing of Kai's wife, Emei, so I asked about her. She had gone to her taro field. It still did not occur to me that she was not to eat with us. It took a minute for me to grasp this—which I should have known, for Emei would not eat with Kai and me when I went to his house about 8:00 P.M. last Saturday before the family had eaten and was invited to stay for a meal. Emei and the children went in the other room and ate there. Families do not eat together when a guest is present, I know; but I thought that with this family it would be different.

December 27   It was a beautiful moonlit night and I could not go to sleep. I thought I heard singing in the distance. I fell asleep and awakened at 3:00 A.M. and again thought I heard music so I got up and walked along the beach. The tide was out, and the moon was high. It was just right for a dance and I believe that one was going but I could not locate it.

December 29   In the afternoon, beginning at 2:00, Al and I attended a district court session. Two of the village chiefs served as judges. There were four cases: A young man recently returned from Guam had beaten on a high-ranking man's door late at night; another man was charged with something that was not clear to me—and I am not certain it was clear to him either; three young school teachers were severely reprimanded for being drunk and showing off; and another man wanted to divorce his wife. This last case developed into a discussion between all concerned, and it was only secondarily a court case. It took a long time to argue that one through. Court was not over until 5:30.

January 1   Today Kai gave a dinner for Al and me. I had asked him to let me watch him cook it, but when I went to his house this morning at 9:30 everything was finished. Kai was not there. Emei said he was visiting. Their two girls, Doska and Iska, and their young son Azu were dressed in their finest— the girls wearing dresses that Emei had made from cloth that my wife sent for them.

Kai, his brother-in-law, Rdor, and one of his oil plant partners appeared about noon. They had planned that we were to eat outside so our tables were borrowed and set up under trees near the beach just back of our house. The men threw up a coconut leaf screen to hide us from the view of passers-by. It soon began to rain so we had to move into the house. Kai drew our blinds and closed our doors, the reason for the secrecy, I guessed, being that they did not want to be seen eating with us. The only other reason I could think of was that they did not want people seeing them giving us rum. Maybe they just wanted a private party, and knew that passing drunks would barge in; for as we were sitting many of them went by, yelling and staggering in an exaggerated fashion as they often do, and looking for any and everyone to call on. We kept very quiet until they had gone away. Finally, Rdor made a tentative gesture to eat—I judged to get Al and me started, for as it turned out they ate practically nothing. They left immediately after we had finished. I was disconcerted and even disgusted when I discovered that they lost no time eating the remains of the food which they took with them to Kai's house. I cannot explain this unless it is due to a reserve that is so deeply ingrained that they cannot shed it. There was nothing hostile in their behavior.

January 2   While Al and I were sitting on the bench at one corner of the schoolgrounds with Kai and two other men the "Crazy One" marched across the grounds and straight up to me. He took my feet, abruptly looked at the soles of my shoes, then briskly did the same with Al. Then he shouted at Al, accusing him of going around at night and doing something—it was not clear what. Then he went to the school building to tell the constable about it. We all took it hilariously. Later the constable came to apologize.

January 3 We went to Ngerchelong for a *kledaol*, which is a display of native dances and a feast. It was a two and one-half hour walk. There were several other Americans there, all of them officials and their wives who had come from Koror by boat. So was Reklai, the head chief of all the districts. After dinner with our compatriots I slipped away to a clubhouse on the outskirts of Ngerchelong where the young people were having fun. They were presenting skits and practicing the dances to be held tomorrow. I sat with Reklai in the front row, practically at the feet of the performers. I stayed until midnight, although Reklai repeatedly asked if I did not want to go to bed and apologized for the quality of the performances. It was just another example of their feeling that we cannot appreciate their inferior customs. I was determined not to leave, however, even if I did create an element of unease on their part.

January 12 The Ulimang head chief came by and invited me to his house at noon. I could not make out what the occasion was to be, and waited until a boy came to tell me that all was ready. By then I had seen all sorts of people going in the direction of his house carrying foods and pots, and I knew that a feast was going to be held. It still did not dawn on me that this was to be an *oraul*. While we were eating I noticed a plate being passed around and a man with a paper and pencil putting down the names of people who placed money in it. I asked the man next to me what this was about, and was told it was to help the chief pay for his new house. I then volunteered to contribute—to the astonishment of all—especially when I said $5. With that things began to perk up, and I was invited to go, right away, to another *oraul* in Ngbuked, to be given by one of the men who was sitting at our table. At 1:30 we started to walk to Ngbuked, which takes about one-half hour. I did not contribute to this man's *oraul*, because I could not see how I could gain by participating in all of these affairs and I could see how I could go broke. Anyway I ate again, a little, and sat around trying to understand the conversation until about 5:00 P.M.

January 14 I strolled to the schoolgrounds about 10:00 A.M. to see what was going on and found a meeting of some of the headmen and the young men's work group leaders in session. The discussion was about plans and work procedures, and also about food preparation for the coming *kledaol* on the 24th and 25th. This one is to be given in honor of the American administrative officials in Koror, along with the members of Pelelieu village, which is a kind of a brother community to Ulimang.

January 16 The women practiced their dances for the *kledaol* literally all night. They were singing when I woke up at 7:00 this morning. The men stopped at 10:00 last night. In going to practice they take bundles of goods—pillows, blankets, and food for their babies (which they also take with them) if not for themselves. The young people clearly object to so much work and the other demands on their time, but without any show of anger—in a joking way, but it is serious. Kai said there is too much work going on and no money coming in. He said that play on Saturday and Sunday is fine, but not dancing every night. Obviously the practicing is necessary because the people are no longer accustomed to dancing. They have to practice in order to put on a good show when the visitors arrive. They have to work at it because it is no longer fun.

January 26   After dinner Al and I went to the school where more dancing was to be held. The show started about 9:00. Al and I had front-center seats, along with the district chiefs and the head chief of Pelelieu. The dances of last night were repeated with more encores; and with different *shibais* presented. The latter were excellent amateur performances which the Palauans learned to stage from the Japanese. The evening was so cold that I could not stay for the finish. At 2:00 A.M. after one of the chiefs suggested that we could go if we felt like it, I left and went to bed. Al stayed along with the chiefs, until the party broke up, at 4:00 A.M.

January 27   As some of us were sitting around one corner of the schoolground waiting for a meeting with the chiefs to begin, the constable, who was among those assembled, explained that the cement monument in that corner was put up in 1928 to provide a niche for Tenuhega's (the Japanese Emperor) picture, and that every morning the school children had to bow toward it. The tree that stands nearby was planted at the same time. The constable talked much about events during the war, especially about American planes attacking. He also said that he thought it would be a good idea for the people of the district to plant a tree in memory of me, like the one for Tenuhega!

I wanted to see what was going on in other villages so I took the opportunity to give the carpenter who had worked on our house a good hammer. Kai noticed Al and I leaving our house and asked if he could go along. It turned out to be a very profitable trip. As we passed Tuman's house he came out to greet us. He was very talkative, and soon began to complain, or to explain, that all this business of the *kledaol* was "without purpose" and that most people dislike it. Kai agreed with him. They feel that the expense is too great, the work of providing food and of practicing dances is a waste of time and effort. It also leaves the Ngarard people broke. They said that the young people are timid and afraid to object to the older conservative ones because they would be called bad, unprincipled, and irresponsible. The young people look forward to the time when the oldsters die and their customs go with them.

January 29   I spent most of the morning at the school with Pelew. Daob, another teacher, listened to our conversation. He has been much more friendly during the past week, much more human than he usually is. It may have something to do with his putting more trust in us. The day after the *kledaol* I made a point of congratulating him on his performance in the *shibais* for two reasons: because they were very well acted, especially by him, and secondly to allay any anxiety he and others might have with respect to our witnessing the *shibais*. It was obvious that many people were uncertain how we were going to take two of them in particular: one displayed the Japanese flag, the other the beheading of two American airmen downed by the Japanese. At the time of the performances both the Ulimang and the Pelelieu chief made a point of explaining to me that all of this was just play-acting. Daob did the same, first to Al and later to me. Other people have taken the trouble to make the explanation, including the constable.

January 31 I went to the Alap clubhouse where I found an old man by the name of Aregon and another whose name I do not yet know. I talked with them—or they talked at me—for about two hours. They spoke of many things, mostly those occasioned by the presence here of the Americans, the Spanish, the Germans, and the Japanese. They recounted the now familiar stories about abuses by Japanese soldiers and the American war superiority; and as is always the case they laughed in telling about Japanese cruelty to them. I have never seen an expression of hatred on their faces. I did notice that Rdor showed sorrow when speaking of the death of his children due to Japanese negligence. I have encountered only head-shaking and joking about all of it even when they tell of the Japanese beating and robbing them.

I was told that soon an *oraul* would be held in the clubhouse here by a few chiefs to get money to pay the carpenter to put in the floor. And of course I was invited to attend. They also said they wanted to paint the inside of the clubhouse—with my paint, that is. Aregon told me briefly about the stories portrayed on a few of the beams of the clubhouse. He wants me to wait until his brother Tura comes back from Ngerchelong before we begin seriously writing down the stories that are pictured on the walls and facade of the clubhouse. He suggested that he and I go to another old clubhouse where the carvings are better preserved so he could show them to me, but I was getting hungry so I came home. On the way I again stopped to observe the man building the fish trap, and asked him to make a model for me.

Al walked to Ahol this afternoon. He wanted to see what goes on there on Saturdays, suspecting that young people go there to have their fun where they cannot be so easily observed by us. We have suspected that something or some things go on at night about which we are told nothing. Last night this end of the village was completely deserted as far as I could determine. No one was home, and there were no lights on in the houses. This is very unusual. We suspected some kind of a party in either Ngbuked or Alap. If it had not been so dark we would have taken a walk to explore late this evening, but it did not seem worthwhile especially because rain was threatening.

February 1 This morning at 10:00 Kai suggested that we go to the cemetery. Why, I am not quite sure, except that Emei wanted her picture taken there. We picked up her younger brother and a woman in another house who also wanted her picture taken. A noticeable attitude was their entirely secular behavior toward the graves and in their talk about the dead. There was no hush, no avoidance, no sentimental regard. I took pictures of the graves and head stones.

February 6   I paid a call on Ackul, "Mister Murphy's Friend." He has been busy trying to get a wife in Ngerchelong. He launched into this without prompting and told me the trouble that he is having. The woman or her people want too much money for her. However, he is going back tomorrow and thinks that a bargain can be made. He said he would bring his wife to see us.

Just in the past month I have noticed a decided improvement in my mastery of this language. Until recently it has been mostly disconnected words, but now I can build and understand sentences. The striking thing about this is the suddenness with which it has happened. Secretly I had almost given up hope that I would ever be able to learn to really *speak* the language, although I did understand it fairly well.

February 10   I went in search of Sakau, wanting a haircut. His shop is in his home. He sent his son to get two green coconuts so that we could have a refreshing drink. In the meantime he carefully washed all his accessories. He gave me a good haircut and razor trim—all around the eyes, including my eyebrows, the temple hairline, and up my nose. It was undoubtedly the most thorough haircut I ever had. His razor was quite dull and he damned it as Japanese, and of course praised one of American manufacture that he had seen in Koror. He talked quite a bit, mostly dissatisfied talk about community work still to come, but also about Palauan customs which encourage wealth differences between the people.

February 17   For several days I have been hinting to Nira, the second chief of our district, that I would like to accompany a party of Ulimang people due to go to Ahol to negotiate a financial settlement occasioned by the death of the wife of a chief of that village. He has been noncommittal until around noon today when he sent word that we would leave in a couple of hours. Upon arrival in Ahol our party went directly to the clubhouse. No one was there at the time, but a boy was sent by Nira for Mega, the deceased woman's husband. He came immediately and Nira apologized for having arrived a day in advance of schedule, explaining that I wished to see what was to go on and that I wanted to stay overnight. They talked about this for awhile, then Mega excused himself saying that he had many things to attend to. A few other men appeared by the time darkness fell, including several from Ulimang. I took a walk to see what was going on and to get a little relaxation, returning about dusk. Soon after that food was brought to us on individual trays. In the meantime women arrived and their children seated themselves at the opposite end of the clubhouse from the men. They were served food, and slept in the clubhouse, as we did, that night.

There was much talk after dinner and we finally settled into our bedding about midnight. Four kerosene lamps hung down the middle of the clubhouse, and they remained lighted all night. The sleepers began to arise at daybreak. I was among the last, getting up about 6:30. This, again, is an example of how little these people sleep during the night. They do take naps during the daytime, but they often sleep only a few hours at night.

February 18   Rash, one of the Ngbuked chiefs, suggested that he and I look for water to wash our faces, so we went to the bathing spot some distance away. He bathed, I just washed. The rest of the people evidently did not even get wet. Since I knew it would be some time before breakfast I took my tin cup, some Nescafe, and canned heat tablets out of my bag and went to the beach to make coffee for myself. I walked down the beach to a place where a turtle was being cut up for the feast, but I was not very hospitably received, so I went back through the village to the clubhouse. I arrived there about 9:00 to find that food was being served and others were waiting for me. That was the beginning of a very long day, most of it spent in a cramped sitting position listening to hours of low-keyed talk about who owed whom what.

February 20   Aleman, a chief of Ngbuked, dropped by this morning, bringing four eggs, and obviously seeking cigarettes. I gave him a package, and then hinted that I would be very pleased to have the broken bead of Palauan money that he showed me last Sunday. He gladly gave it to me, taking it out of his handbag, and even volunteered to look for a better piece. He was reluctant only to let me have the *broken* one. He wants to have a whole piece taken to the States. Asked the value of this bead, he said that if it were whole it would be worth about $30; in Japanese times perhaps $50. It can be perforated, can still be used to buy goods, but it would be worth perhaps only a few dollars among Palauans.

I wrote notes after Aleman left for a couple of hours and then I decided to make the circuit through the villages with the ultimate objective of seeing Nira. I wanted to appeal to him to let me know when things such as funerals are going to happen. It has been rather aggravating that, in accordance with native protocol, no one but a chief informs us of what is going on or what is expected to occur that is out of the ordinary.

I also stopped at the house of Saig to see the new baby. She is seventeen days old and is the one that I more or less named at Saig's request. I chose the name Jane because it is relatively easy for Palauans to pronounce.

February 22   Masas did not appear for instruction in English today, as I had hoped he would not, and I spent the day alone. It gave me an opportunity to collect my thoughts about the information I have been getting on clans and property, and to formulate some questions about it. After dinner I went over to Kai's house and we had another session about it. Now that I have the general idea and know some of the kinship terms, I am making headway, but many details remain to be cleared up. It is a very complicated situation.

February 25   I went in search of Nira this morning. He had previously asked me if I had any tar patching for the nail holes in his tin roof. It happened that I had, so I took a can of it to him. He was grateful and invited me to have lunch. While this was being prepared I again told him that I would like very much to know when something important was planned. I explained that I was attempting to write the "truth" about Palauan customs to take back to America, and that in order to do this I wanted to see things for myself and not depend on rumors and "lies." He was genuinely sympathetic, but said that some occasions, such as a funeral, were private family matters, and that only members of the family could invite outsiders, and even then only the family heads really have this privilege.

February 27   I visited Rash this morning to give him the same pep talk that I gave to Nira about advising me and inviting me to parties and ceremonies —after thanking him for the trip to Ahol. He too seemed agreeable, but did not elaborate his answer as much as Nira did. He asked if I had been to an *oraul* (forgetting that I had gone to two of them with him). I think he had in mind that one was even at that moment just about to start in the little hamlet of Kale, which is just a few minutes' walk from here. I told him that I would like to get some genealogies from him. He agreed, saying that we could do it next Sunday. Then he began to explain about the ratings of Ngbuked families. Aleman joined us and we had some light talk about old customs. Soon Aleman left, saying he was going to Kale. When I asked why, he said that he had "some business" over there. "Some business!"

I should be more patient with these people, at least as patient as they are with me. They have been very generous with their time, and have invited me to participate with them in most of their group activities. In spite of my unde-niable charm and tact, I must nonetheless be a nuisance at times, and only their good nature prevents them from expressing irritation with my incessant prying into their private affairs.

March 6   I returned from Koror with Goss, a government official. He was going to Nemat to supervise the election of a new chief there, and he invited me to go with him. We arrived about 8:30 P.M. and were taken to the clubhouse, where two cots with mosquito nets were already set up for Goss and myself; bedrolls and mats were brought for the rest of the party. The election was to take place the next day, Sunday, so there was nothing to do but talk. We all went to bed about 12:00, but the gnats were so bad that most of the Palauans left the clubhouse and went to the beach where they built smudges.

March 7   We were up early, in fact shortly after daybreak, for Goss had to catch the boat at 1:00. After breakfast the election was held—if it can be called that. Under the direction of Goss all the externals of a secret ballot were there, but the proceedings were an obvious farce because the outcome had been pre-determined by the Palauan style of behind-the-scenes political maneuvering, the basic features of which are not confined to the Palauan islands. Goss was de-jected and not a little annoyed.

March 10   This morning I passed the home of Saig, whose wife had a baby on February 6. She was sitting in the doorway with nothing on but her pants, and was not at all embarrassed when I asked her how the baby was. She is the first woman who has not tried hastily to cover her upper body when Al or I appear. She was just as casual the other time I stopped to see the baby, though then she was partly covered with a ragged dress. Most women are embarrassed even to nurse children in my presence. Emei has several times hastily taken her breast from her baby when I have unexpectedly appeared. A few women on the Koror boat have gone ahead with their nursing in a half-concealed way when I have been near them in the cabin.

March 13   Emei told me this morning that Risa, an elderly woman of about sixty, came to her home last night and waited for me so she could tell me about old Palauan birth customs. Emei had asked her to do this. A little later I met Risa on the path in front of our house and we set a time for me to go to her house tonight. She talked freely and easily. She, like many others, knows about Kubary (a German ethnologist) and praises his knowledge of Palauan language and customs. She knows a few German words herself she said, and then proceeded to sing *The Kaiser is a Good Man*—to the tune of *God Save the King*.

March 16   About 7:00 this evening Risa came to see me and whispered that a young woman living nearby had given birth, but that the placenta had failed to appear. She had been sent by the chiefs to see if I could help. I put two aspirin tablets in my pocket and followed her to a small house in one room of which the sick woman lay with several older women sitting close by. The other room was crowded with men. The sick woman had a headache and a slight fever, so I offered the tablets saying that there was nothing else that I could do. Some of those present were obviously skeptical. I found it almost impossible to explain to them that although I am a "doctor" I really am not.

March 19   The women's work group cleared the trails to the cemetery and around the clubhouse. I approached them with my movie camera and asked if I could take pictures of them at work. I was agreeably surprised, for they were quite willing, only showing embarrassment about stooping over with their backsides to the camera. Risa was especially helpful, and even made an old-fashioned hat of banana leaves, such as women used to wear in the fields, and put it on for my benefit. Many of the women sang as they worked. I was with them for an hour or more, after which I came back to the clubhouse and talked with three old women for awhile. They too were very friendly. One of them asked if I could get some dye for her graying hair. She explained that the Japanese women dyed their hair and that the Palauan women copy them.

March 22   I scarcely got out of my chair today from 8:30 in the morning until 2:00 this afternoon. While I was still writing notes after breakfast, Tura dropped in. He wanted a pair of spectacles. Last week I gave a pair to Rdor. (I brought fifteen pairs, having bought them at Woolworth's before I left.) The word that I have them spread rapidly. Several of the people really need glasses and this is the only way they can get them. I pumped Tura for an hour, and when his brother arrived I began on him. Soon another man showed up. I steered the talk to religion and Tura told some myths and described shamanistic practices. He shied away from contemporary religious beliefs. When this seemed to end in an impasse we turned to family histories and to kinship terminology.

March 26   About 9:00 A.M. I took Risa a package of cigarettes in return for a fish she brought me last night. She told me a child had died earlier in the morning in Alap. This was sudden news to me, so I got busy and asked the child's relatives if I could attend the funeral. All said that it would be O.K. I went to Alap with several of them around 10:00, and spent the rest of the day watching the funeral rites. Later I questioned Emei and Risa about what I had seen and about the relationships of the child to the people who were present.

April 8   Tura stuck his head in our doorway early this morning. He had been "on business" to Kale, and was hotfooting it to Ngerchelong. I am sure by now that he is an active member of *modekne* (a nativistic cult that was suppressed by the Japanese and is at present actively discouraged by the American health authorities). He seems forever to be going around the island visiting people. He and the old man who was with him warmed to my attempts to talk about Palauan religion, and I think Tura is about ready to tell me more about his "business." He said he would be back to see me on Saturday.

April 12   Rash called on me and stayed for an hour. I gave him a cigarette lighter, and questioned him about the elaborate ceremony for the woman and her newborn that has been going on for the last four days. He said that it was the "real Palauan way," but that few families follow the custom today. He added that the full treatment given this woman was mainly because the people wanted me to see it and that Nira had urged that it be done. I think, however, that Risa was the real mainspring.

Ackul came by early this morning to say that he had come from Niwal, that the money for the marriage of his daughter there was ready, and that he must now get food together for the feast. I am going to Niwal with him. He says "the business part" of the marriage ceremony will take place on Thursday. He was on his way to Geklau to buy coconuts, betel, and other feast goods. Plans for his own marriage are stalled. He thinks the woman and her relatives are just "playing with" him.

April 17   I was sick with dysentery for the three days I was in Niwal with Ackul, and did not do much besides watch the marriage proceedings. We were supposed to leave last night but no boat was available. I was fed up with the place, and with fish, and wanted to come home, but went to bed early, as I did every night, and waited for this morning. We were supposed to leave at dawn, but still no boat was available, and the hours dragged on. Finally, Ackul borrowed a canoe with an out-rigger and the five in our party from Ulimang boarded it for home.

April 22   This evening I walked through the villages. It was a beautiful night with a full moon. Many people work on nights like this. Women were carrying baskets of taro from their plots to Alap. Torong was sewing roof thatching by a dim light. I stayed for awhile with him and a man who was visiting him. They wanted to know about the American school system. We talked, as I have so often with almost all of the older people, about the Negroes in America. I also had the pleasure of hearing Torong explain to his friend why they are black and why Al and I are white—the biblical story.

April 29   I decided to make a frontal attack on the *modekne* business, so I went to Nira's house with a little gift for his wife. Esube, another high-ranking man, was there, as was Nira's adopted son. At what I thought was the proper moment I told Nira that I would like to attend a meeting of the *modekne*. The request startled both of the older men, but after the first shock they said I could not attend a meeting because none are being held, but maybe I could talk with someone, whereupon Nira called his son to his side and whispered to him. The boy left and soon returned with word that it would be O.K. When did I want to talk? I said this afternoon. The name of the informant was not mentioned, but I guessed that it was Tura, and this turned out to be right. Nira took me to the clubhouse where Tura was waiting alone. Having sanctioned our meeting, Nira left. Tura was quite willing to talk, but very hush-hush. He spoke so quietly that I could hardly hear him at times. He is a firm believer in the cult, and he gave me a subjective account of it, mentioning only those features he knew I would approve of. It was nonetheless a most informative session, filling the gaps in what I already knew about the cult.

May 3   I found Kai in an informative mood, and plied him with questions on land inheritance and related subjects. He was interested in the map of plot ownership that I had drawn up. He supplemented it with corrections of the boundaries in a way that indicated to me that he knew what he was doing. He said he knew about these lands and their ownership because he has bought coconuts from the owners.

May 9   We were invited to Masas' home for a meal. It was one of the farewell variety and came at an odd hour for us. We were invited at 10:00 A.M. "to talk and visit." Food was served soon after we arrived, and there was a great quantity of it. Masas wrapped the remains of our meal in banana leaves and took them to our house. It would have been undignified for us to carry them.

May 10   We were invited to another "little dinner" at noon in the house of Kari. I must say that this meal was the worst that I have encountered—five boiled eggs, all of them so rancid that they could not be hard-boiled, along with some boiled taro. I did my best with it. I also tasted some *wassa*, which is the salted, boiled-down essence of fish. I have often seen the stuff but had not eaten any. It looks like axle grease, and it must taste worse.

May 12   We were invited to another festivity at 4:00 P.M., this time a feast given by Saig in celebration of the birth of his daughter, Jane. We again had lots of food, altogether too much; but all of us have thought that Al and I would be leaving the day after tomorrow. This morning our travel orders arrived, and the date of our departure is now set for May 21. This gives us some needed time, but it is anticlimatic.

May 18   It is becoming more difficult by the day to get anything but snatches of information, here and there. All have our departure on their minds and they inevitably direct discussions to that subject. They want to know about our proposed trip, and then about America. They thereby turn the tables on me, and I become the informant. As a consequence of this and various other things, including farewell dinners, this week has been enjoyable but not very productive. . . .

Epilogue

Shortly after Murphy and I completed our research in Palau I wrote a monograph which I called *Palauan Society: A Study of Contemporary Native Life in the Palau Islands*. It had a dual purpose. One was to provide information for the guidance of American officials whose responsibility it was to administer the affairs of the island population as a whole. This was an important but not an overriding consideration, because the Office of Naval Research, through the National Academy of Sciences, had sponsored, partially financed, and materially facilitated our research for whatever practical benefit the administrative officials could derive from it. Our observations and inquiries were not specified or controlled by the Navy. From the outset it was understood that they were to be in the nature of "pure" research. In consequence, *Palauan Society* could serve its second purpose, which was "to fill the gap in our scientific knowledge of the area that was closed to investigation for many years by the Japanese" (Preface, p. iii). In other words, it was intended to be an ethnographic account comparable to hundreds of others written by anthropologists describing other ethnic groups, primarily for fellow members of their profession. It is objective and analytical. In it Palauan custom is identified and described in ways that are customary among anthropologists. Things, beliefs, and behaviors were selected and assigned to such standardized conceptual realms as subsistence, kinship, religion, birth, marriage, and death. The data presented in this systematic fashion were drawn almost entirely from the impersonal record of numerous observations and responses to inquiries contained in my notebooks by the usual method of classifying, indexing, interrelating, and generalizing from them.

As well as can be determined, *Palauan Society* has served its purposes adequately, though not beyond the degree expected. Yet even at the time of writing it I knew that a good half of the picture of Palauan life was missing for the practical-minded administrator as well as for the anthropological theorist. In common with other books of its kind it lacks vitality. It does not tell the reader what it means to live like a Palauan. It does not present his view of what anthropologists call his culture, or how he lives by or with it. It gives only glimpses of a commonplace observation in Ulimang; namely, that Palauans usually live according to the rules of custom because it is to their advantage to do so, but with the ever-present temptation to either break them or manipulate them to satisfy their personal needs and ambitions, just as Americans and every other people do; and that conformance is characterized by individual variations about a norm that may or may not be explicit, just as it is elsewhere. It is this dimension of understanding the Palauans which is recorded, however sketchily, in the Journal. The microscopic detail in that record is the analogue of the macroscopic forms and categories that were abstracted and summarized from my notebooks. In it I endeavored to describe to myself how it felt to try to live and think like a Palauan, as well as what it meant to them personally insofar as I could ascertain this by the means indicated in the excerpts above.

Being a Palauan is very much a product of the Journal, and is thus an analogue of *Palauan Society*. As is stated in its Introduction (p. 3),

An effort has been made throughout to convey an understanding of Palauan society and culture by presenting the Palauan view of the world in terms of the author's understanding of how the Palauan sees and comprehends what goes on around him. The objective, then, has been to delineate a way of life as free from the anthropologist's conventionalized structuring of it as possible, in the hope of communicating what it means to live and die in a small village in Palau.

It is egocentric. It attempts to depict the individual's apperception of the Palauan universe; his confrontation and interaction with things and people as he conceives them to be; his comprehension of and behavior with respect to what we call accidents, typhoons, Americans, births, deaths, his father, his foster father, his elders, his chief, his gods, and his soul. The orientation and emphasis is on being and doing, on the continuity of events and personalities over time and as they interact at the moment.

Anthropologists have spent a great deal of time, especially since 1950, arguing about which of these approaches is "real," valid, or most productive. At present the argument often takes the form of an opposition between what are termed the "emic" and the "etic" interpretations, the "insider's" versus the "outsider's" view, based upon the distinction in linguistic analysis between phonemes and phonetics. In my opinion neither of these interpretations is adequate by itself to enable us to understand a people or to explain their behaviors. Moreover, they cannot be cleanly separated. They overlap and interpenetrate, and where they do not they are complementary. Sometimes a skillful ethnographer can weave them into the fabric of one description, but it is not easy and usually not professionally acceptable. The alternative, given the desire on the part of the ethnologist, is to present the two dimensions separately and to link them, knowing fully well that neither can be completely divorced from the other. This is why I welcomed the opportunity to write *Being a Palauan*, and now to relate it to *Palauan Society* and to the personal encounters with Palauan beliefs and behaviors that are recorded in the Journal.

The case study is not, and should not be as personal as is the Journal. Still, they are comparable in tone and orientation, and there are deliberate linkages between them. The opening paragraphs of the case study, for example, describe one of the many tantrums of Azu, who is the same little boy mentioned by that name in the Journal, and one of whose fits of temper I recorded on motion picture film as well as in deleted portions of the Journal. Similarly for the frequent references to his father and mother, Kai and Emei, whom I regarded not only as good friends but as voluntary research assistants. In fact, my intimate acquaintance with this family, and the entrée into the community which it provided, convinced me that I could and should write something like *Being a Palauan*. Kai spoke of me to others as his elder brother. He treated me as such and I was so accepted by other residents of Ngarard. This was neither as false nor as difficult as it might be in other societies because the establishment of fictive kinships is a Palauan custom. It gave me a place in their social system, in addition to the one I inevitably was assigned as a prestigious outsider and a privileged associate of their chiefs. In both roles I was something of a showpiece, especially after I learned to speak the language fairly well and (unwittingly) used "big" words—those found in German-Palauan dictionaries and habitually used only by elderly men. In true Palauan style the people of our district delighted in exhibiting me to visitors from elsewhere, beaming when I spoke to them as if to say "See what *we* have!" Above all, what convinced me that I knew the Palauans well enough to write the case study was that I learned to appreciate and engage their sense of humor. It is often said that this is one of the most esoteric and elusive aspects of any people's culture. There is evidence enough in the Journal that the Palauans like to joke, and some indications that they often do it about events and circumstances which many Americans would regard as misfortunes to oneself or to others. It may be added that much of their humor would be considered to be banal, contrived, crass, or childish by many Americans. The point is that if one gets to know them well enough, it turns out that many Palauans feel the same way about the merriment of some of their countrymen. In other words Palauans, like Americans, are comically as well as socially stratified.

It would be misleading to leave the impression that I believe I became a Palauan. That would have been impossible even if I had cherished the hope. It is obvious in several of the Journal excerpts—and it is intended to be—that there were areas of belief and behavior to which I remained a stranger and others about which I learned only through an aggressive suspicion. The most that can be claimed is that I temporarily and moderately successfully straddled two ways of life.

Like many other ethnographic accounts, neither *Palauan Society* nor *Being a Palauan* has much to say about how the data for them were collected. Although it should not be so, anthropologists generally expect their colleagues to take their field methods for granted; and it is true that most procedures in data collection are so well known and routinized that professional readers do, rightly or wrongly, expect that they have been employed. The same readers will readily recognize research strategies and techniques in the excerpts from the Journal—

among them what are commonly referred to as gaining entree, identification of purpose, establishment of rapport, the use of key informants, surveying or cross-sectioning the universe of custom, role-playing, the repetition of observations and queries, and genealogical charting. These techniques and others are implicit in the excerpts above. In fact, the latter were selected for that reason. Other contributors to this volume on method will no doubt formally present and illustrate some of them by reference to their own case studies. It might be worthwhile for the nonprofessional reader to reverse this tactic and to identify the methods that are embodied in relevant excerpts from the Journal.

It should not be overlooked that keeping a journal is itself a research device which may be variously employed or not employed at all. Some ethnologists make of it an impersonal record of daily events comparable to a ship's log. It is evident that for me *Palauan Journal* was something more. It was a means of regularly thinking over each day's events and planning for those ahead. It thus provided a subjective measure of accomplishment. But it was also a therapeutic device which enabled me to systematically talk to myself, to quietly explode, and to privately confess my frustrations, anxieties, and failures.

The Journal ends abruptly, in the original as in the last excerpt. This is a reflection of the state of the research as well as my state of mind. I left Ulimang knowing that the investigation was incomplete and that it was likely to remain so. No group study ever has an end as long as the group exists because it is always changing, especially in the modern world. Being a Palauan today is not the same life experience that it was in 1948. Partly for this reason and partly for others, some of the younger Americanized generation have expressed doubts that it ever was what it seemed to me twenty years ago. Admitting that there is always some justification for such disagreement, and anticipating that it will be expressed by people who read what is written about them, is part of being an anthropologist.

2

GOPALPUR, 1958-1960

ALAN R. BEALS
University of California at Riverside

Related Case Study: **Gopalpur: A South Indian Village**

Alan Beals shows us the difference between being an uninvolved observer and a participant observer as he describes how he became a member of the community of Gopalpur rather than a "Redman" from Bombay. Alan and Constance Beals became members of their community in a way that many anthropologists aspire to but few achieve.

He also describes the problems of household management that sometimes loom so large that the anthropologist does not really get his fieldwork done. He comments on learning a new language. He says something that is well known but often not practiced—that the fastest way to learn a foreign language is to be isolated with and dependent upon people who speak only that language. He discusses also the taking of notes and keeping of a diary, and the fallacy that a camera and tape recorder will do one's recording in the field.

But the most important message in Beals' paper is what "participation" means to him. It means that at some point one ceases being a remote observer and becomes involved. With involvement come conflicts. This chapter makes the process of involvement exceptionally clear.

Alan Beals also makes clear the personal meaning of the fieldwork experience when in discussing his return to the civilization of the United States with his wife, Constance, and his child, Robin (born in India), he says poignantly, "We could never forget that we had once lived in a world that had not yet gone mad."

Alan Beals says of the involvement problem, "I think the point is that a dispassionate observer cannot exist since such an observer distorts the data by behaving in an inhuman manner. The solution would seem to be to participate, but to try to limit one's passion and involvement to the minimum expected by the community" (personal communication).

This is precisely the fine line that the anthropologist must draw in his self-management in the field; to be involved and yet detached but not dispassionate.

The Author

This is how Alan R. Beals describes his coming into anthropology:

Until my senior year in college, I had relatively little interest in anthropology. In the seventh grade, I wrote a paper justifying Mexico's nationalization of the petroleum industry, and from that time, my goal in life was to save the world—using the techniques of crusading journalism. In college, possibly as a result of prolonged association with my father, an anthropologist named Ralph L. Beals, I developed sufficient interest in anthropology to take several courses. My father agreed to this reluctantly, but refused to permit me to take any of his courses. In the summer of my sophomore year, having nothing better to do, I participated in an archeological investigation being conducted by A. E. Treganza. This experience impressed me with the value of the scientific method and I came to believe that, if the world was to be saved at all, it would be saved through knowledge, not through journalism.

In 1948, after graduation, and with my father's reluctant agreement, I entered graduate school at Berkeley. I had originally planned to go to Harvard in order to escape my father's influence, but when he introduced me to Clyde Kluckhohn, I realized there was no escape and switched to Berkeley on the grounds that it was cheaper and warmer. After receiving my degree in 1954, I was drafted into the United States Army and converted into a research psychologist. In 1956, I went to Stanford and remained there until 1968 when I was made Chairman of the Department of Anthropology at the University of California at Riverside.

My fieldwork in South India was carried out in 1952–1953, 1959–1960, and 1966. The results of this fieldwork have been published in a number of articles and in a small book called *Gopalpur*. With the collaboration of George and Louise Spindler I have published a textbook, *Culture in Process*, and with Bernard J. Siegel, a theoretical discussion of conflict, *Divisiveness and Social Conflict*.

G. D. S.

Getting There

In 1952, when I was living near Bangalore in the village of Namhalli, I used to buy *bidis* (cigarettes) across the street in Sab Jan's store. When I made my purchases, we often exchanged homely bits of advice and rural wisdom. One of Sab Jan's contributions to this educational effort was: "The Hindus believe

The ethnographer's hair must be cut short before visiting the local missionaries for tea. Despite all precautions local missionaries and government officials were often scandalized by our behavior.

that there are many roads to Heaven, we [Muslims and Christians] know that there is only one straight road." For a time, I agreed with Sab Jan. Surely there is one right way to do everything, and surely one of the troubles with Hindus is an insufficient concern with the true truth, the straight and narrow, and the one and only.

On the other side of the coin, one of the troubles with those brought up within the Judeo-Christian religious traditions is an overconcern with the shortest distance, the right way and the absolute truth. When I came to

A formal portrait to be hung in the living room next to the family "God-photos." The smiles were considered undignified and Kanamma's sari is too high.

Namhalli, I believed that all modernizing or urbanizing communities would tend to move through a series of regular and predictible changes. The family would become smaller, there would be more dependence upon a cash economy, there would be more kinds of jobs, and so on. Assuming the existence of a single straight road to urbanization, I was concerned with the channels of communication and other forces moving the village of Namhalli onward and upward.

After I had lived in Namhalli for several months, my relatively enormous height won me a place on the village volleyball team. As a member of the team and in various other capacities as well, I became familiar with many of the villages surrounding Namhalli. All of these villages, particularly those which had volleyball teams, were modern, but they were all different. In some villages families were becoming smaller; in some villages they were becoming larger. Some had become totally dependent upon cash; others still bartered goods for grain. In some there had been a multiplication of occupations; others had become more and more specialized. After I had returned to the United States and had begun to consider my experience in Namhalli, I realized that nothing was more important for an understanding of rural India than an understanding of the differences I had noticed between neighboring villages.

It was this idea, crystallized out of earlier experience, which formed the basis for the study of Gopalpur that my wife Constance and I would carry out between September 1958 and March 1960. For this, my second fieldtrip and Constance's first, I wanted to work in Gulbarga District in Northern Mysore State. The region was 100 miles away from the nearest modern city and, having been until recently a part of the kingdom of Hyderabad, it had been little influenced by the modern world. Here, in a traditional region unafflicted by rapid change, it should be possible to obtain an accurate picture of the kinds of differences and similarities normally existing between villages. To make my research proposal concrete, I planned to compare irrigated (rice agriculture) villages with unirrigated (millet agriculture) villages. Since the question of the difference between irrigated and unirrigated agriculture had been much agitated in the literature of anthropology, it was possible to produce a list of references emphasizing the theoretical importance of the research problem. The proposal appealed to the National Science Foundation and I was given an $11,000 research grant.

A former student arranged an appointment for me as Honorary Visiting Reader at Osmania University in Hyderabad. This elite connection with Osmania University was of great importance in securing visas and in arranging for assistance from influential persons in Gulbarga District. On the other hand, it is difficult for people to help you when they do not understand what you are doing, and we were largely unsuccessful in convincing important people in Hyderabad and Gulbarga that there was any value whatsoever in studying small villages. It was generally expected that we would obtain a large cool house, fill it with servants, and sit on the veranda drinking cool drinks and considering the servant problem, tropical diseases, and the unbearable heat. One distinguished member of the nobility of Old Hyderabad became incensed with us when she learned that Constance had failed to bring badminton rackets from the United States.

In Gulbarga, the English-speaking intellectual elite was so tiny that our desire to live elsewhere than in town provoked anger and frustration. A wealthy landlord ordered us to live in his village and threatened to retaliate if we failed to do so. The local missionaries warned us that we would soon die of malaria and other diseases. Government officials wondered what we could possibly be studying that they did not already know about: "Just tell me what you want to know, and I'll answer all your questions." Constance, who had been suffering from some kind of mild illness, began to feel worse and worse. The doctor in Gulbarga examined her. She was suffering from homesickness. Serious consequences might result if I subjected a delicate foreign lady to harsh conditions.

All the same, Constance did not seem to be exceptionally sick. Perhaps she was only suffering from "culture shock." We decided to go ahead and find a village. We obtained letters to the local officials of Yadgiri, one of the few irrigated regions in Gulbarga District. Soon we had established ourselves in the mosquito-filled Traveller's Bungalow at Yadgiri. Constance was quarreling with the caretakers in a vain attempt to get good food at reasonable prices, and I was conducting involved negotiations with the local government official (Tahsildar). The Tahsildar felt that Yadgiri Tahsil would be unhealthy for us. In fact, the Assistant Commissioner had just recently died of malaria. I pointed out that my wife was ill, that we could not simply wander from place to place, and that Yadgiri Tahsil seemed ideal for my purposes.

The Tahsildar had a letter from the Commissioner. He would have to find us a village. We waited. It seemed that our affairs were not of very high priority. Repeatedly I made the dusty walk to the Tahsildar's office to find out why the jeep had not come as promised. Each day something had come up and the jeep had been sent elsewhere. When the jeep finally came, it took us to Minaspur.

Minaspur is a large village containing thousands of people. Just outside the village is an attractive bungalow located on the shores of a deep and beautiful lake. Below the lake stretch thousands of acres of irrigated rice land. The family that owned the land and the village would make us comfortable. Like Rama and Sita in the forest, Constance and I would enjoy the utmost delights. I turned to the Tahsildar and to the wealthy, powerful, hospitable landlords of Minaspur: "What a pity that I speak Kanarese and the people of Minaspur speak Telegu; what a pity that the American Government has ordered me to study a small village instead of a large one."

We returned in glum silence to Yadgiri. After several days of impatient waiting, I managed to track down the Tahsildar: "Never mind bringing the jeep, we shall go out on the bus and find a village." I had put the Tahsildar in an impossible position. He could not allow a distinguished visitor to ride a bus like a common peasant; on the other hand, he knew of no place to take me. "We have found the perfect village for you;" said the Tahsildar, "the jeep will come by at 9:00 tomorrow." For several days the jeep failed to appear and I had difficulty tracking down the Tahsildar. One day at noon, the jeep appeared. The Gauda[1] of Gopalpur was in the back seat.

Gopalpur seemed perfect. It filled the specifications I had given the Tahsildar. It had irrigated land, it was some distance from the road, it contained less than 500 people, it was close to an unirrigated village, and everyone spoke Kanarese. Besides this, Gopalpur was only 2 miles from a large village containing a dispensary. In the Gauda's garden was a vacant house that he would be glad to lend us. In our present state of mind the garden seemed perfect. It was fenced, which would keep people from bothering us. There was an outdoor sitting room

---

[1] A kind of headman.

shaded by sacred nim trees. There was a shallow irrigation well filled with clear water. A stream flowed across one edge of the garden.

Survival

In 1952, on the way to India, I asked a distinguished British anthropologist to tell me his secret of success in doing fieldwork. His response was "Never accept free housing and always carry a supply of marmalade." To Gopalpur we brought stoves, cooking utensils, typewriters, and other equipment we were sure would not be available. Our plan was to live totally without servants, depending upon locally available food supplies and vitamin tablets. As soon as we had arrived in the garden house, I unpacked our equipment and began getting the stove ready to boil water. The Gauda, his servants, and some twenty important persons from the village gathered around to watch the lighting of the primus stove and to give me such helpful advice as they could. With an air of great coolness, I began assembling the parts. Accustomed to carrying out the business of living in complete privacy, the steady flow of advice soon broke my nerve. My hands began to tremble, my face flushed, and the stove became more and more obdurate. After hours of tinkering, the stove came to life. With an air of confidence, Kanamma (Mrs. Connie) seized a pan and went to the creek to obtain water. With a quick glance at the other ladies to see what they were doing, she dug a shallow hole in the sand, waited for the dust to settle and began to scoop water into her pan. Somehow, the water trickled away between her fingers and the little water that reached the pan turned out to be full of dirt. A seven-year-old child came over and filled Kanamma's pan.

In a surprisingly short time, we were painfully aware that we had achieved an almost legendary reputation for incompetence. We could not get water, we could not make fire. We seemed totally unable to get food or prepare it properly once we had it. Already exhausted by such simple tasks as getting water, Kanamma was in no shape to scrounge around for foodstuffs or to endure the routines of cookery that involved six to eight hours of hard work on the part of highly skilled local women.

Within a few days, we were begging the Gauda to find us a servant. The Gauda greeted our request with consternation. Servants were hard to find and he was reluctant to part with any of his own. Besides he felt responsible for the well-being of the people in the village and he was well aware of the fact that Europeans customarily beat and kicked their servants. On the other hand, there was Tamma (Beals 1965: 67–68). Although Tamma was supposedly working for the Gauda, he was lazy and insolent. Lately he had been caught helping himself to tamarind from the Gauda's tree.

The Gauda told us to pay Tamma 18 to 20 rupees per month (less than $5) and to keep him working day and night so he could not sneak off and sleep with his wife. At odd times throughout the day, the Gauda would appear in

Grinding grain and preparing foodstuffs takes many hours each day.

the garden: "Where is Tamma? Why is he not working?" Actually, Tamma was working: At 9:00, he had gone 2 miles away to the village of Yelher to buy some meat for lunch. He had arrived at that village at 9:30 and stopped at a relative's house to rest. The relatives had urged him to stay and eat. People had gathered about him and interviewed him concerning the behavior of the strange foreigners in Gopalpur. The missionaries had sent for him, given him some tea, and a package of jello to give to us. By 12:30, the Sabaru (plural[1] of Sahib, meaning distinguished foreigner) was storming about the house demanding to be fed. Tamma returned to face the combined wrath of the Kanamma, the Sabaru, and the Gauda. The great people are always scolding their servants for no particular reason. Servants are the people who understand the business of being servants, the great people do not understand the problem and their advice is not to be listened to. Tamma had faced indignation all of his life. He weathered the storm gravely and quietly.

In time, Tamma and Kanamma developed a kind of secret language. Tamma's free spirit appealed to Kanamma. She raised his pay beyond 20 rupees. The Gauda and others remonstrated with the Sabaru. The Sabaru refused to discuss

[1] The plural form is always used in respectful address.

the matter with Kanamma. The Sabaru refused to kick or beat Tamma. It was felt that the Sabaru lacked the force and dignity required to maintain a smoothly running household. Still with Tamma's aid, Kanamma managed to obtain small quantities of meat and vegetables. There was almost always a pot of something vaguely resembling lamb stew simmering on the primus stove and there was usually rice to go with it. Later, Kanamma discovered the Bombay Store and the market in Yadgiri and there were weekly trips to obtain carrots, potatoes, and the inevitable marmalade.

But Kanamma was still sick. Almost every day she had a slight temperature which the Sabaru assured her was psychological. Gathering together her failing strength, Kanamma took Tamma in town and walked the 2 miles to the bus stop. An obliging conductor, in defiance of government regulations against overcrowding, allowed Kanamma and Tamma to squeeze onto the bus. For thirty minutes while the bus negotiated the seemingly interminable trip to Yadgiri, Kanamma and Tamma endured bone-wracking misery. From the bus station, they walked a mile to the hospital. At the hospital was an attractive young woman doctor who had been trained in the United States. There seemed to be a good chance that she could diagnose the mysterious tropical illness that had baffled doctors in Hyderabad and Gulbarga. "You are pregnant," said the lady doctor. "Impossible," said Kanamma reposing complete faith in the marvels of modern contraceptive techniques. Tests were performed. Again, the tedious trip to Yadgiri was repeated. Kanamma had been pregnant for four months. In fact, the worst part of her pregnancy was over. A few vitamin tablets would cure her illness completely. Kanamma announced the news to the old ladies of Gopalpur. "Of course," they said, "we noticed right away."

Friends and Enemies

In 1952, the Sabaru was a poverty stricken student. Seeing his youth and helplessness, the "educated class" in Namhalli, composed as it was of young men the Sabaru's age, had welcomed him and taught him about their village. They were able to practice their English and to learn many things about urban life. People around Bangalore were familiar with Europeans and, by and large, they liked them. In Gopalpur, things were different. People had seen few foreigners. Those they had seen, they had seen as members of an under class in the city of Bombay. In Bombay, the light-skinned Marathi and Gujerati speakers referred to people from Mysore as black people. They were considered unwelcome immigrants subject to violence and oppression. Only a few years ago, the Government of India had invaded Hyderabad State and made Gulbarga district a part of Mysore. People in Gopalpur felt like a conquered people.

The Sabaru was a foreigner, a Redman, a Bombay person. He spoke Kanarese like an official of the new and not yet accepted Government of Mysore. The foreigners had already taken most of the wealth of India. Perhaps the Sabaru had come back for something the English forgot when they left. Perhaps the Sabaru would drop an atomic bomb on the village. He might even carry the village to America on an airplane. He might conscript people for the American army. He might steal and eat young children as the missionaries apparently did. Perhaps he intended to level the village and construct a landing field for the American invaders.

Isolated in the garden house, the activities of Sabaru and Kanamma seemed more and more mysterious. The Sabaru, having read somewhere that you should start fieldwork by mapping the village and taking a census, began striding up and down the village streets measuring and taking notes. People came up to ask him what he was doing. When he replied, they shook their heads sadly, "He can't talk our language." The Sabaru became sullen and irritable. Back at the garden house, Kanamma flared out angrily at the Gauda. She was tired of his constant advice about how to cook, how to keep house, and how to dress. Relationships with the Gauda began to be strained.

After a month or two in the garden house, word came that the Commissioner himself was coming to find out if we were comfortable. Minor government officials invaded the village. The Village Level Worker, a stranger to the village, appeared and set everyone to work without pay digging drainage ditches, smoothing the streets, and generally creating an appearance of vast and successful village development activities. The Commissioner came. He interviewed us. He was satisfied. The government had done its part.

Next week, the Gauda came to the garden house. He was sorry, but we would have to leave. It was time to store the harvested grain in the garden house. The Sabaru refused to leave. The Gauda's cattle broke into the garden and ate the Sabaru's vegetables. The Sabaru threatened to write an angry letter to the Commissioner. There was hard bargaining. A house might become available if the Sabaru agreed to fire Tamma and hire Tamma's disagreeable cousin instead. The Gauda filled one room with grain. Sabaru and Kanamma defended the remaining room. We would have to leave the village. Tamma told the Sabaru that there were indeed plenty of empty houses. The Sabaru offered to pay rent. People said, "In Bombay, you Red people make us pay 100 rupees a month for houses no bigger than a packing crate." The Sabaru offered 10 rupees.

There was a large house in the center of the village. It was dark and old. The ceiling was beginning to rot and there was a steady rain of twigs, scorpions, mud, and carbon from old fires. There were rat holes in the floor large enough to accommodate a large cat. The owner of the house was an old woman who lived just outside the front door in a small hut with her one surviving teenage son. The other six children had died. Thus, the house had acquired its reputation and fallen empty.

Tamma and his friends, the Shepherd, and the Confidence Man began to clean up the house. Lime for whitewash had to be brought from a town 25 miles away. While Sabaru and Kanamma fought off the nameless horrors of the decaying house, Tamma and his friends disappeared for days on end collecting the materials required to make the house livable. Neighbor ladies brought in samples of their cookery. A crowd of people who had ignored us while we lived protected in the garden appeared to request shirts and other gifts. Missionaries generally had old clothing to distribute and people felt dishonored if their requests were refused. They demanded their rights. Tempers flared. We said we were poor. We said we did not have any old clothing. Finally, we drove everyone out and locked the door.

For an outrageous sum, the Confidence Man brought special wear-resistant mud and spread it on the floor. The Sabaru obtained some Wafarin rat poison from a supplier in Poona. The rats died in their holes filling the house with the odor of their decay. The Confidence Man rented a cart and brought special clay to spread on the roof and render it proof against the rain. The day Kanamma returned from the hospital with her baby, the monsoon would strike, and, as water spouted from the roof, we would discover the true value of his labors. The landlady insisted on tying her buffalo in our living room. All night long we could hear it chewing, moaning, and stamping its feet. Kanamma drove the buffalo outside while the landlady wept and expostulated.

We offered to buy milk from the landlady. She was delighted and sold us several buckets of water before we angrily cancelled her contract. Tamma installed himself in our kitchen where he was frequently visited by the Shepherd and the Confidence Man. The landlady visited daily to complain about her husband who had taken a second wife and was living on the opposite side of the village. At times, the husband would appear and attempt to remove grain from its hiding place in our living room. He and the landlady would scream at each other. He would accuse her of killing her children. She would burst into tears. Later, Kanamma would comfort her and listen once again to her tale of woe.

Another neighbor, an elegant lady dressed in silk and bedecked with jewelry, brought milk for Kanamma and little gifts of food, usually flat cakes of unleavened bread heaped with a fiery mixture of spinach and chili. In the evening, Tamma would spirit the food away to his family. We discovered that Kanamma's friend was the mistress of a number of important people. She had a husband who lived in another village. Sometimes he would appear, loaded with marihuana, and beg her to return to him.

As we bought salt in the village store and as we carried out our widening search for eggs and milk, we gradually began to acquire friends and supporters. Although nobody profited very much from our presence, a large number of people were beginning to see us as a valuable resource. They became friendly. Even their relatives became friendly, so that when the Sabaru went out into the fields of ripening grain, people began to call to him and to offer him the delicacies of the fields. There were sugar-filled stalks of cane, strange and inedible fruits pressed upon the Sabaru by smiling children, there was fresh-roasted grain. The Sabaru began to have special friends out in the fields. There was Little

When our landlady's buffalo died, the leatherworkers refused to remove the carcass on the grounds that such work was unsuitable for Christians. When the stench became untenable a group of Gopalpur men removed the carcass gingerly without touching it.

Brother who smiled at him and explained the mechanics of his agriculture. Little Brother took the Sabaru 4 miles away to his distant field and prepared a lavish portion of roasted grain and brown sugar. He told the Sabaru how people in the village were trying to kill himself and his brothers. He told how they had attacked his house and how his older brother had killed one of the attackers and been sent away to jail. The Sabaru discovered that the Farmer caste was divided between two hostile families and that each family had claimed a life and was daily threatening to take another. The Saltmaker caste, of which Tamma was a member, was similarly divided, and so was the Shepherd caste. The rival groups were divided into two factions that daily threatened to split the village. In time, it was discovered that most of our friends were in a single faction (Beals 1965: 70–74).

The enemy faction, "the partners," were engaged in collectively farming some land belonging to the Gauda. Each year the Gauda auctioned this land to one of the factions and their competitive bidding was a delight to the Gauda. When the Sabaru approached the fields belonging to the partners, they waved him away. When the Sabaru attempted to take pictures, they covered their heads with their blankets. Sometimes, they told him to leave the village. The leaders of the enemy faction were the "Thug," the "Crook," and Tamma's relative, the "Untouchable." We believed that these men were allied with the Gauda against us.

The Untouchable's chief goal in life appeared to be to secure Tamma's job for his younger brother. The Untouchable and the Crook plotted endlessly to bring this about. Sometimes, they would welcome the Sabaru to their houses and gradually bring the conversation around to the absolute necessity of firing Tamma. Eventually, the Crook and the Thug gave Tamma a good drubbing with their staffs (Beals 1965: 69–74). The Sabaru brought a policeman into the village and had everyone sign a paper promising that there would be no further violence.

The enmity of the partners was upsetting. It did not square with the mystical notion of "establishing rapport." To me, this meant being on friendly terms with everybody. Certainly, getting involved in local disputes was a poor way to do fieldwork, yet we had become involved before we knew what was happening and there now seemed no way out. Sometimes, particularly when there was a festival, even the partners would become friendly. They would invite the Sabaru to their houses, feed him, and give him pancakelike festival delicacies to take home. "At last," we would say to ourselves, "the magic of anthropology is working and rapport is established." A few days later, a new-found friend would begin demanding a shirt in the most offensive manner possible and the dream of rapport would collapse.

In Namhalli, I had been surrounded by a protective ring of educated people. They were prepared to treat me as an equal and to establish the kind of friendship most valued by Americans. Such egalitarian relationships were virtually unknown in Gopalpur. The Sabaru was a person of high status, and his great wealth and power could never be forgotten. On the other hand, a kind of mutual respect developed and, while relationships were not always warm and friendly, they were always close and intense. In retrospect, the ideal rapport that I thought I had had in Namhalli seemed shallow and impersonal. The continual three-cornered duel among the Sabaru, Tamma, and the Untouchable was close and personal. We learned each other's weak spots and we set clever little traps for each other. There would be a time when we missed our enemies almost as much as we missed our friends. Somehow we became involved in Gopalpur in a way that had been impossible in Namhalli.

In Gopalpur, people had come to forget that we were honored guests and had come to treat us in much the way that they treated each other. This kind of treatment carries real dangers. Being involved, we had to choose sides in village quarrels. In 1952, I had refused to play a role in disputes. I had stood unmoved when the village women tearfully begged me to intervene to prevent violence. I had watched children playing in the forbidden milkweeds and said nothing to their mothers. In Namhalli, I was an audience, a dispassionate observer. In Gopalpur everything was different. I was in the center of village conflicts. When I saw children tormenting a calf, I scolded them and sent them packing.

Somehow it seemed that from the very beginning people in Gopalpur were unwilling to let us play a dispassionate role. They were unaccustomed to

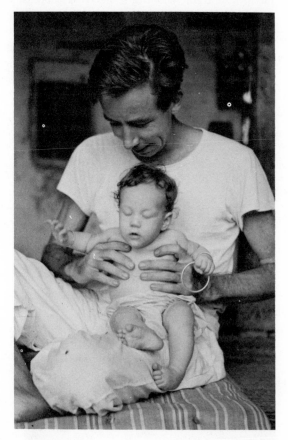

Father and daughter.

strangers and they would not let us remain strangers. We began our fieldwork as people always do, cast in the role of child or idiot. At first, proper behavior was not expected from us. Later, as we learned about the village, we were subjected to social sanctions that we at first interpreted as disrespect. When we failed to behave properly, people told us what they thought of us. This applied with special force to our treatment of our baby, Robin. She was not to be allowed to cry; she was not to eat foods regarded as dangerous; and she had to have a rather costly naming ceremony. We were forced to become properly behaving human beings.

Except under extraordinary circumstances, there will always be a kind of clear plastic film separating the fieldworker from the rest of the community. The fieldworker does not fully understand the motives of others, he may in fact come to display a kind of paranoia arising in the fact that he knows that he is a center of attention, but is not sure why. The fieldworker who behaves like a mechanical man, who treats others as subjects, or who coldly calculates the degree of friendship to be extended in each case, is going to appear less than human. People will be puzzled and dismayed by his behavior. Certain kinds of information are available to the dispassionate observer. He is not likely to make enemies or to become involved in disputes. On the other hand, he may have a considerable impact simply because his behavior is impossible to understand or

Robin's bath, a public event.

predict. Perhaps the ideal fieldworker would be a person who learned to behave in a natural and predictible manner, involved but not strongly involved. For our part, we came to feel at home in Gopalpur. Even today we can remember each friend and each enemy as well as we remember our friends and enemies at home. We were a part of the community, and we shall never forget it.

Field Assistants

We employed a number of persons whom we expected to help us out in one way or another. A good field assistant can give instructions concerning the proper ways of behaving and speaking; he can collect many kinds of information; he can type field notes; and he can serve as a channel by means of which people find out what the fieldworker is like and what he is really up to. A bad field assistant may serve as a barrier between the fieldworker and the people he is studying. He may slow the learning of language and custom by his excessive eagerness to translate and explain, and he may repeat unflattering tales about his employer. In the Gopalpur region, there were few English-speaking people available, and those who did speak English did not speak it well. Field assistants who could type or speak or who had social science training had to be brought from outside. In India, such persons are usually unfamiliar with ways of living in small communities and they have little knowledge of local dialects and customs. Very often, educated persons have their own ideas about what villagers are like and they may prefer to inform the fieldworker of these prejudices rather than try to collect concrete information.

Our first field assistant was a Brahmin youth who spoke perfect English, had finished high school, and had been raised in a nearby village. He was what I have come to think of as a "natural ethnographer." He was interested in talking to people, he had a sense of the value of the work, and he seemed to understand what we were trying to accomplish. Others had perceived his value and within a few months, he left for a job as fireman for the railroad.

The next field assistant to appear had a Master's Degree in one of the social sciences and no taste for fieldwork. There were hot words and he left the village for good. The Indian government, feeling that its own people should be trained in the mysteries of fieldwork, suggested that a government-employed anthropologist be sent to work with us. Since we respected the idea that we should contribute to the development of anthropology in India, we eagerly agreed. The person who arrived was a senior professional who had already spent more than a decade engaged in fieldwork and who knew a great deal more about it than we did. Such a person could scarcely be used as a field assistant, and in the end, the government anthropologist carried out a separate project in another village. In general, since anthropology is a highly individualistic discipline, it seems unlikely that a trained anthropologist would ever make a useful field assistant. He is going to want to pursue his own research problems in his own way.

Reluctantly and with a sense of desperation, we decided to try hiring one of the "hospital people." The hospital people were Christians and, while they played a vital role in the region, many people suspected that they were of low caste. They were suspected of making lower caste people "uppity" by converting them to Christianity after which they would refuse to remove dead animals from the village streets. The young man we hired turned out to be conscientious and, despite a few early reverses, was successful in integrating himself into the life of the village. Since he came from a family of hospital technicians, he had some scientific training. Our best field assistants were young, educated, and unemployed. They had definite statuses in the region (they were known quantities to the people of Gopalpur) and could establish effective working relationships. For example, our Brahmin assistant was the son of a respected village accountant and our Christian assistant had relatives who played a public role in a hospital that people from Gopalpur had visited. Men who had been referred to us by local men of influence, such as the missionaries and the Tahsildar, were anxious to perform well so the news would filter back to their patrons.

Our first inclination in using field assistants was to use them as companion-interpreters. This prevented direct communication with anyone and delayed our learning of Kanarese. Because routine operations like census-taking went far better when I was not around, the field assistants began to work alone collecting statistics or writing out documents in Kanarese. Under the circumstances existing in Gopalpur, the field assistants had a high level of training in their own culture and a low level of training in social science. For Constance and myself, the situation was reversed, we were untrained in the local culture and highly trained in social science. The ideal solution seemed to be to find for each person the thing that he could do best and set him to work doing it. The fact that we were each collecting information more or less independently provided a variety of views of Gopalpur rather than just one.

Learning the Language

In Namhalli, where I worked earlier, many of the young men had been to school and spoke fluent English. I had learned some Kanarese, but it was never very fluent and it had always seemed more convenient to have things translated into English. In Gopalpur, where it proved difficult to find persons with an adequate knowledge of English, it became almost impossible to accomplish anything without a fluent knowledge of Kanarese. Counting the year and a half spent in Bangalore and six months in Gopalpur, it took me two years to begin to be able to converse. Once I began to use Kanarese, I found myself using it exclusively, even with my field assistants, though there were still many specialized terms that I did not readily understand.

In this learning process, regular language lessons seemed of little value and I came to regret the time that I had spent studying Kanarese grammar. The grammar that I learned was that of Sanskrit and Latin and had little relevance to the way in which people actually formed sentences. The final breakthrough seemed to be due to two things: isolation from persons who could speak English and the transcribing of field notes in Kanarese. If I had to do it over again, I would go alone to a place where nobody spoke English and I would arrange for the constant companionship of an uneducated young man between the ages of nine and fifteen. As soon as I could ask simple questions like, "What is that?," I would begin asking them and carefully writing down both the questions and the answers. After each interview, I would practice reading back the material to my companion and I would try to form simple sentences like, "That is a tree." Isolated in a strange place, unable to talk, unable to ask for food, one is placed under the same pressures that confront a child learning a language. There is no choice but to learn and learn quickly.

This simple sink or swim method of learning languages has been known to anthropologists for years. It was advocated by Leonard Bloomfield and Bronislaw Malinowski, to say nothing of Robinson Crusoe. Why I failed to put it into practice and why so many other anthropologists fail to put it into practice is a mystery, for it is a means of acquiring adequate language skills within a few months. As an English planter wrote in 1871:

> I trust I have now sufficiently indicated what every one should do in learning a new language, and that is that he should learn it exactly by the same method he unconsciously pursued when learning his own. This seems such a very obvious and natural conclusion to come to, that I am really almost ashamed of writing on the subject at all. But perhaps it would be more to the point to say that I am almost ashamed to have occasion to enforce propositions which are, after all, nothing but the veriest truisms. To carry out, however, my intentions of writing for all classes, it is necessary, as I have before observed, to enunciate, as clearly as possible, facts which have been known for thousands of years, but which are not widely enough known to be universally acted on. And that these facts which I am now repeating are not sufficiently known, I have had much and frequent occasion to know; for how many have I seen labouring at the oar, and how many more resigning for ever the hope of learning a language which might have been acquired without thought or exertion, if the proper method only had been pursued at the outset! (Elliot 1871: 260–262).

Taking Notes

When the anthropologist writes things down, he is developing documents that he plans to use later as a basis for any conclusion he might draw about the community he is studying. One of our regrets concerning the 1960 fieldwork in Gopalpur was that we did not have a motion picture camera or a tape recorder. We attempted to remedy this defect on a later fieldtrip, but we found that even with equipment available, we did not make as much use of it as we expected to. Not only are film and tape expensive and hard to get in out-of-the-way places, but the analysis of filmed and tape recorded materials is difficult. A body of filmed or taped materials leaves the fieldworker still facing the task of reducing quantities of material to a size that he can conveniently handle.

Written notes remain the primary means of recording observations and interviews. They are essential even when tapes and motion pictures are used. One of the appropriate forms that notes should take is that of a diary or journal. Here, Kanamma proved to be an excellent journal keeper and her journals provide a good part of the background for this chapter. My own journal is full of gaps. In retrospect, I see that an ideal journal is a kind of record of the fieldworker's attempts at proper behavior. Each action of the fieldworker is an experiment in which the fieldworker attempts to exhibit proper behavior. If he succeeds, he is rewarded with information or assistance; if he fails he is punished with ridicule or rejection. A record of the fieldworker's fumbling attempts to perform correctly in another culture would be of the greatest value. Without such a document, it is difficult to explain in later writings how the fieldworker came to know the things he thinks he knows. Often the final account is written as if there never was a fieldworker; this, despite the fact that the basis of the reliance placed in ethnographic accounts is the prolonged firsthand contact of the fieldworker and the people around him.

Notes should be taken continuously during the day and typed in duplicate or triplicate as soon as possible. Each sheet of paper should have the place, date, fieldworker's initials, and page number on it. Copies should be stored in different places. As the journal or notes are typed, materials omitted from the handwritten copy can be added along with commentary. If copies of field notes are mailed home periodically, it becomes practically impossible to lose them.

Often it seems desirable to write down everything that happens, but even a motion picture camera cannot be everywhere at once. The goal of finding out everything or writing down everything degenerates into the unplanned collection of random information. Sometimes, the lack of planning provides an opportunity for the uncontrolled expression of the fieldworker's unconscious biases and hypotheses.

Research Problems and Tactics

The overall goal of fieldwork is to find out what is going on in some particular place. Much of the formal and informal interviewing and observation carried out by the fieldworker, his assistants, and his major informants is dedicated to that purpose. Since the various members of the field team are, in the end, human, much of what they record will reflect bias. In Gopalpur, we tried to correct this by involving as many people as possible in our work. We collected verbatim interviews in Kanarese. We listed all of the households in the village and made a point of visiting households selected at random from the list. We tried to formulate biases in concrete terms as theoretical propositions subject to rigorous testing through the application of specific research procedures such as questionnaires and sample surveys.

Definite studies aimed at answering particular questions can achieve a much higher level of accuracy and rigor than can casual observation and interviewing. Yet, there are two kinds of accuracy. One derives from a kind of general knowledge about what is going on in the community and one derives from the application of formal methods. It is never clear whether it is best to learn more and more about less and less or less and less about more and more. Our intensive research in Gopalpur and in the surrounding region revolved around a single major question: "How many similarities and differences between neighboring communities can be explained?"

Similarities and Differences

The plan of the original research proposal involved an intensive comparison of one unirrigated village and one irrigated village. This was to be followed by a survey study of a sizable number of neighboring villages designed to determine the extent to which the differences between the two intensively studied villages could be explained in terms of irrigated and unirrigated agriculture. By studying neighboring villages, I hoped to hold constant historical and geographical factors related to differences in kinds of agriculture. With over 100 acres of irrigated rice lands, Gopalpur appeared to be a good choice for our irrigated village. The village of Gannapur, just a mile away, totally lacked irrigated agriculture. It seemed, then, that a comparison of the two villages would provide the basic information we needed.

We began work with the intensive study of Gopalpur. At the outset it was clear that Gopalpur possessed a number of unique attributes. It was a small village, larger than a hamlet, but still dependent upon neighboring communities for a variety of goods and services. The shape of Gopalpur's boundary was such that it included a variety of soil types and conditions. There were cheap, sandy, unirrigated fields, costly unirrigated black soil fields, rice fields, and a few acres of irrigated garden lands. Another difference between Gopalpur and other villages lay in the particular assortment of kinds of people living there. Since there was a source of salt-water near the village, there were a number of salt-makers. A segregated colony of stoneworkers had formed in order to take advantage of an outcropping of granite on the South side of the village. Presumably, each of these groups brought its own customs and practices into the village. The arrangement of particular groups and kinds of people gave Gopalpur its own unique pattern of social arrangements.

The village boundary, itself a product of interaction among neighboring villages, circumscribed a variety of ecological and other environmental conditions that were unique. The assortment of castes within the village could be attributed in part to the nature of the environment and in part to a "founder effect," produced by the kinds of people who came to the village in the first place. Other factors, such as distance from the road, distance from the town of Yadgiri, and general accessibility could also be supposed to exert an influence toward the development of unique qualities in the village. Counteracting in some degree all of these tendencies toward differentiation were a host of factors tending to make Gopalpur similar to other communities. These mainly centered about ties and relationships between Gopalpur and other villages and towns. These ties and relationships involved the more or less uniform influence of the government officials and influential persons of the region upon all villages; the influence of trade relationships and economic ties; the influence of intervillage visiting and marital relationships; and the influence of pilgrimage centers, markets, and towns.

As we began to understand these things about Gopalpur and Gannapur, we began to formulate questions that would enable us to get at important features of other communities and of the region as a whole. These questions involved two general approaches: one was a detailed set of enquiries which could be made in a number of villages; the other was a series of specialized studies of the manner in which Gopalpur and Gannapur fitted into the general cultural and social arrangements of the region. Information about particular villages could be obtained through government records stored in the town of Yadgiri and through on the spot interviewing of persons in other villages. Since many of our questions concerned specialized knowledge not available to the man of the street, our interviewing ultimately took the form of group interviews involving the leaders of the different villages and their associates.

For each village we collected statistical information concerning acreages of lands of various types, numbers of people and animals, and kinds of castes present. A small sample of people in each village were asked where different items were purchased, how long it took to reach the nearest bus stop or market, and where various standard services were obtained. We visited village school teachers, if there was a school, and found out how many students were enrolled. We wandered through each village and noted the quality and number of its temples, schools, and other public buildings. We found out what sorts of cooperative activities were carried out and what sorts of crimes and conflicts tended to occur. We found out how often government officials visited each village and what they did when they came. We tried to find out how many families in each village owned large acreages of land.

Since it seemed likely that irrigated villages would have a greater incidence of malaria and other water-borne diseases than unirrigated villages, we attempted to obtain relevant statistics from the local hospitals and medical practitioners. The director of one large hospital felt that we were attempting to find out whether or not patients in certain castes were receiving favored treatment and refused us information. To the extent that we were able to get information from hospitals, it turned out that most patients came from nearby communities. The only thing that could be demonstrated was that most sick people lived near the hospital. This meant that the only way to get good information on the distribution of disease types in the local area would have been to sample a series of villages at random and subject large numbers of people to medical examinations.

This would have been expensive even if adequately trained medical personnel had been available.

Government officials proved easier to deal with. The deputy superintendent of police provided a list of villages and a record of all arrests made in each one. The Tahsildar made available maps, survey records, censuses, and other official materials. Records of land ownership and cropping practices presented complex problems. The land records of Yadgiri had originally been set up by Brahmins from Maharashtra who used Marathi and a secret record-keeping language of their own. When the region was a part of Hyderabad, Muslim officials amended the accounts using a version of Hindi and the Arabic script. Officials from Mysore State and English-speaking Tahsildars and deputy commissioners had kept parts of the records in Kanarese and English. Thus, the copying of government records became a major task and a great deal was lost in translation. In many cases, the records were erroneous to begin with. This was particularly true of estimates of acreages planted in different crops. These acreages were listed by village headmen who were chiefly concerned with seeing that each crop census was not too different from the crop census before. None of them had the time or the inclination to actually conduct a census; if they had, most farmers would not have been able to give accurate information. In the end we were able to compare official statistics with statistics that we collected in the individual villages.

In some cases, for example, when it comes to estimating how far a village is from the paved road or how many acres it contains, it is possible to obtain figures that are quite accurate. It is a special perversity of nature that accurate figures are often not useful figures. What we want to know when we measure the distance of a village from the road is, "How difficult is it to travel from the village to the road?" The figures do not describe the creeks that have to be forded, the sandy stretches that make jeep and cart travel impossible, or the muddy fields that cannot be crossed during the rainy season. Useful figures often have to be derived from gross and inaccurate estimates: "How long does it take to get from the village to the road?" The village level worker can provide accurate records showing how often he visited each village. A truer, but less accurate measure, of his impact is to ask people, "How often does the village level worker visit the village and who does he talk to when he comes?" Figures concerning the total land acreage reveal nothing about soil types or the kinds of crops that are grown, yet if one wants to know how many acres of sandy soil there are in a particular village it is necessary to rely upon vague estimates. Here again, the imperfect data is more useful than the accurate data because information about soils and crops provide a summary of the ecological conditions characteristic of each village.

If we want to know whether or not there is a relationship between modernization and per capita income, we find that direct measures of these things are not available. People do not think in terms of annual income and do not report their annual income accurately when they do know it. Indirect measures such as number of persons per acre, number of animals owned, kinds of houses, or frequency of such supplementary occupations as carpentry, priestcraft, and basketweaving must be used. Measuring the degree of modern influence is even more difficult. Does it consist of the ownership of flashlights, glassware, and aluminum cooking pots? Does it consist of the use of chemical fertilizers, new kinds of seed, or insecticides? Does it consist of schools and literacy rates? Does it consist of a wealthy landlord who owns a tractor, jeep, or an American plow? Does it consist of the number of people who have gone off to find jobs in Bombay? If being modern is regarded as a state of mind, the best way to test modernity might be through an attitude questionnaire. To administer an attitude questionnaire, it would be necessary to draw a random sample from each of the villages being considered. This would cost over $1000 in Yadgiri Tahsil.

The collection of statistics only tells a part of the story of similarities and differences between villages. To understand the role of marriage in the creation or disruption of intervillage ties, it is good to know how marriages are arranged, what happens when a wedding takes place, and how the relatives interact after the ceremony. This means traveling with the wedding procession to another village; accepting proferred hospitality without worrying too much about germs; and observing, photographing, and taking notes. When one is a wealthy and fantastic foreigner, there are other problems: questions about the United States; dense crowds of children with huge round eyes; special uncomfortable bug-infested chairs; and worst of all, the compulsory second or third helping.

A periodic trip to the Sunday market, 4 miles away, to examine dried-up onions and dusty ready-made clothing provides abundant material on the interaction of people from different villages. On the road back, the sun seems to set a good half hour earlier than usual and the last mile of the journey involves blundering about in the dark amidst razor-sharp sorghum stalks all the while hoping that the distant light is Gopalpur and not some bandit's campfire or other supernatural manifestation. Travel after dark was enlivened further by a rumor that gangs of men were roaming the neighborhood searching for persons to be sacrificially buried alive under a large irrigation tank then being constructed.

During the hot season, young men travel ceaselessly from village to village to participate in wrestling bouts. Almost every other village has an annual festival. Sometimes we would borrow a cart from the Gauda and the ladies would ride in style. Usually, it was a matter of a two- or three-hour walk toward the end of the day and a night spent watching a drama or wrestling match. At dawn, the Gopalpur contingent, starving and exhausted, would wander back to collapse in the shade of a veranda or under a distant mango tree until the time arrived for the next night's festivity. This might be another wrestling match, a wedding, or perhaps a party out in the fields where people could sing religious songs all night and pass a pipe loaded with marihuana from hand to hand. Particularly during the hot season, when intervillage festivities were at their height, field journals would fall further and further behind and sometimes be limited to comments like, "Sabaru slept all day."

In time, our incessant party-going would give us a picture of a range of devices which served to maintain interaction among neighboring villages. This interaction (through marriage, economic relationships, participation in ceremonial, sometimes angry confrontations at wrestling matches) was the vehicle which served to maintain a common culture throughout the region, despite a host of ecological and historical factors supporting the emergence of important differences among the different villages of the region.

Getting Back

Suddenly, just as it seemed that we were really beginning to get some work done, it was time to return to the United States. While in the field, we thought often of home. We thought of rare beef steak, shower baths, and the joys of being once again among people we could really understand. When we got on board the jet airplane that was to carry us to San Francisco, the plane was a sea of cold, washed-out faces. People looked at our baby as if they thought it would poison them. Not one person picked the baby up, admired, or talked to her. The plane lurched skyward at terrifying speed and we clutched each other, convinced that doom was upon us.

In San Francisco, the baby took one look at her grandmother and burst into tears. We could not understand why people were so distant, so hard to reach, or why they talked and moved so quickly. We were a little frightened at the sight of so many white faces and we could not understand why no one stared at us, brushed against us, or admired our baby.

We could not understand the gabble of voices on the television set. When we could understand people, they seemed to be telling lies. The trust and warmth seemed to have gone out of life to be replaced by coldness and inhumanity. People seemed to have no contact with reality. All of the natural human processes—eating, sleeping together, quarreling, even playing—seemed to be divorced from earth and flesh. Nowhere could we hear the soft lowing of cattle or the distant piping of the shepherd boy. Simple pleasures, like sitting under the nim tree at evening and gossiping with the neighbors, did not exist.

Where in Gopalpur there was a feeling of stability, timelessness, and adaptation to nature, even the houses and buildings in the United States seemed to express instability, sterility, and a kind of opposition to nature. Everyone seemed to be rushing toward the mystical doom of atomic destruction, all the while pretending that nothing was the matter. We had returned to civilization. We were suffering from culture shock. In time we would get used to it. We would never forget that once we lived in a world that had not yet gone mad.

Findings

Our original research proposal involved a contrast between irrigated and unirrigated villages. We found that life was not that simple. Each separate village of the thirty villages we studied contained a different assortment of crops and varieties of land. Rice agriculture turned out to be of far less importance than did the possession of the heavy black loam referred to locally as "black cotton soil." On this soil it was often possible to grow two crops a year. In the fall, practically without benefit of rainfall, people could plant and grow the sweet sorghum upon which they depended for their daily bread and for fodder for their cattle.

Where the black soil was absent, villages were small in size. The people in them were poor and they spent months each year working as laborers in other villages. Where there was abundant black soil, large landlords controlled the land and there were many poor people in the villages. Where there was a mixture of kinds of soils, villages were of medium size; most people, as in Gopalpur, owned agricultural land, and there were many blacksmiths, carpenters, and other specialists catering to these middle-class farmers.

Thrust willy-nilly into the storm center of contending parties in the village, we found ourselves gathering more and more material about conflict. We found that in many villages, people denied the existence of conflict, while in other villages it was impossible to avoid being subjected to play-by-play, blow-by-blow descriptions of the thefts, quarrels, fights, and riots that had taken place in the past. Village size and the particular arrangement of different castes in each village seemed to have a great deal to do with the emergence of conflict. Villages that were engaged in conflict usually engaged in such public demonstrations of unity as building schoolhouses, holding festivals, or maintaining drama companies.

Since the common pattern of marriage consists of bringing in women from other villages, it seemed likely to us that a great force for maintaining the similarities between villages was the raising of children in each village by women who had been raised in a variety of different villages. We became interested in child-training. Questionnaires were administered to most of the mothers in Gopalpur. Kanamma and one of the field assistants spent long hours observing children as they played in the village streets. The Sabaru investigated kinship terminologies, trying to discover the manner in which marriages with father's sister's daughter, mother's brother's daughter, and sister's daughter maintained ties between villages. The Sabaru's findings turned out to be quite different from those of specialists in the field of Dravidian kinship and "cross-cousin" marriage and the Sabaru was left wondering if everyone was out of step but him.

In the end, although we found out a good deal about child-raising, conflict, kinship, and the similarities and differences among communities, we found ourselves with more questions than answers. On our return, we discovered that a revolution was taking place in the methods of collecting anthropological data. People were asking sharp questions about the kinds of informal observation and interviewing that we had carried out. Such fields as linguistics, computer programming, and statistics were contributing new and more precise ways of working. We became aware of a host of new techniques that we might have used in the field. We decided to return to Gopalpur in 1966 and try to find out what village conflicts were really about. (Some earlier ideas about conflict in Namhalli can be found in Beals and Siegel [1966].)

Between ourselves and in discussions with our colleagues, we wondered if we had done the right thing in Gopalpur. In many ways, we had failed to achieve what we set out to achieve. We had failed to attain the kind of "rapport" that we read about in the textbooks. To our shame, we had gotten involved in local conflicts. Somehow, we had not been as scientific as we should have been. Had we captured any truth or had we vainly impressed our own prejudices upon our subject matter? A letter came: "While I was reading your book, I thought that I was in my native village. It brought me several sweet memories. . . ." Perhaps it was worth it after all.

References

Beals, Alan R., 1962, *Gopalpur: A South Indian Village*. New York: Holt, Rinehart and Winston, Inc.

Beals, Alan R., and Bernard J. Siegel, 1966, *Divisiveness and Social Conflict, an Antropological Approach*. Stanford, Calif.: Stanford University Press.

Elliot, Robert H., 1871, *The Experiences of a Planter in the Jungles of Mysore*, Vol. II. London: Chapman and Hall.

3

FIELDWORK IN MALTA

JEREMY BOISSEVAIN
University of Amsterdam

Related Case Study: **Hal-Farrug: A Village in Malta**

Jeremy Boissevain takes us step by step through the sequence of events
leading to and through his fieldwork in Hal-Farrug. The preliminary
stages of getting to Malta, seeing people and filling out documents, finding
a village, then settling in a family of four in improvised quarters, and the
initial fieldwork contacts with the people, give us an intimate and useful
view of events that are rarely reported in the ethnographic literature. Of
particular importance to an understanding of the anthropologist's work
in the field is the description of the problem villagers had deciding what
he was and why he was in Hal-Farrug. This is always a problem and one
that is frequently underestimated by fieldworkers. The anthropologist
plays many subroles within the limitations of his overall role as an in-
quisitive and usually agreeable stranger, so his activities and the reasons
for them seem especially confusing. Jeremy Boissevain describes in detail
his many daily contacts with shopkeepers, the parish priest, and neighbors.
It becomes clear that much of the most valuable data came from unplanned
casual contacts. Someone he met on the way to the priest's house, people
he met in local bars, others in church, casual contacts in the shops—
these provided essential data that cannot be acquired through more formal
planned activities. This is one of the truly satisfying aspects of the field
experience, but it is also anxiety-arousing since one never knows from

day to day and moment to moment whether one will be able to make productive contacts or where they will lead once made. But Boissevain does not neglect the other means for gathering relevant information. The use of current documents, archival resources, photography, direct interviews, genealogies, and census-taking are discussed. And finally, data processing and write-ups are treated, both of which are very instrumental in determining the shape of the case study that students and colleagues will read.

The Author

London-born Jeremy Boissevain is Professor of Social Anthropology in the University of Amsterdam, having previously taught at the Université de Montréal in Canada and the new University of Sussex in England. In a certain sense he is a late-comer to the field. After graduating in 1952 from Haverford College, where he studied romance languages, he served for almost six years as CARE mission chief in the Philippines, Japan, India, and finally Malta, resigning in 1958 to begin graduate work in social anthropology at the London School of Economics and Political Science. He obtained his Ph.D. in 1962 for his study of local-level politics in Malta (Boissevain, 1965). In addition, he has carried out field research in the Fezzan desert in Libya, in an isolated agro-town in Sicily, and among Italian Canadians in Montreal. The results of this last research have just been published (Boissevain 1970). At present he is working on a book about what he calls the neglected "nongroups" in the social sciences: networks and coalitions. This will be based partly on current research he is carrying out in Malta. He is married and has four daughters, two of whom were born in Malta.

He says:

The reason I became an anthropologist is because for the nearly six years I worked with CARE in developing countries, I was always an outsider looking in. In my work I was faced with a number of problems which I thought could be easily resolved if only I were able somehow to get on the inside to see what it was like.

In 1958 I made the break and decided to study social anthropology (on the advice of Professor Laurence Wylie, my former French teacher at Haverford). I am very happy with this decision although I realize that even an anthropologist can never become a complete part of the society he is examining, but it certainly is the next best thing to it.

G. D. S.

Preface

All anthropological research can be divided into four major phases: (1) the preparation for the field, (2) the actual fieldwork, (3) the analysis and writing up, and, last but not least, (4) a period of introspection and reanalysis after the first major work based on the fieldwork has left the researcher's hands. Personally I consider each of more or less equal importance. The preparation and formulation of the questions by the researcher before he sets out into the field influence the sort of data with which he will return. Even a talented researcher using the most sophisticated research techniques will only find the answers to the questions he asks. On the other hand, even if he has excellent data, unless he submits himself and the data to a rather rigid discipline, he will not be able to digest it. Moreover, once digested, it must then be set out clearly and simply so that the reader who knows little or nothing about the problem and area will be able to understand the exposition.

Phase 1 and especially phase 3 are generally given insufficient importance. Yet in terms of input, these demand an investment of at least three or four times as much time and energy as phase 2. I stress this because in this chapter I focus primarily on phase 2, the actual fieldwork. The reader should remember, however, that as far as I am concerned, all phases are of equal importance.

Preparation for the Field

Preparation for my fieldwork in Malta began an unusually long time ahead. It began in fact before I even studied anthropology, when I was still employed as Chief of the CARE[1] Mission to India. The first thing that I did when I learned that I was to be transferred there was to look Malta up in the *Encyclopedia Britannica*. I learned that Malta was in fact an archipelago consisting of four islands, with a total area of just over 120 square miles, situated between Europe and North Africa. Malta, the largest of the islands, is in fact only 17 miles long and 9 miles wide. Though it has been a port of call between the Christian and Moslem worlds for centuries, and its language is a Semitic dialect, the chief features of its culture are European and its people are fervently Roman Catholic. With a population of just under one third of a million, it is the most densely populated country in Europe, if not the world.

At the time Malta was a British Colony, and we met a number of persons in India who had served with the British Armed Services on the island. From them we learned that it was very rocky, hot in the summer, not particularly breath-

---

[1] CARE, The Cooperative for American Relief to Everywhere, Inc., is a nonprofit, nonsectarian, nonpolitical American welfare organization supplying food to large-scale feeding programs. It also provides critical supplies and equipment to technical assistance and community-development programs in various parts of the world.

taking as far as landscape was concerned, and that the people were extremely pleasant. After four and a half fascinating but hectic years in the East, my wife and I both looked forward to a tour of duty in Europe.

The twenty months I spent with CARE in Malta were important for my later

Jeremy Boissevain and the parish priest on the way to the farewell picnic.

research. Although I had learned not a word of the difficult language because nearly all Maltese with whom I came in contact spoke excellent English, I had made a host of extremely useful acquaintances. Moreover, I had learned a great deal about the formal and, to a lesser extent, the informal aspects of the religious, administrative, and political organizations, not to mention the competitive cocktail-party circuits. Moreover, as I discovered later, because of the nature of my work I had an enormous credit of goodwill on which I could draw. The Maltese were extremely grateful for the help that the American people had given them through CARE.

In September 1958 I began two years of intensive training in social anthropology at the London School of Economics and Political Science under Raymond Firth, Lucy Mair, Isaac Schapera, Maurice Freedman, and Paul Stirling. I spent two years there studying not only the principles of social anthropology, but also reading all I could find on Malta and Southern Europe, studying Maltese and formulating my research design and grant application. Reading up on Malta meant working for two days a week in the Colonial Office Library, where I found an excellent collection of books on Malta published in English, French, and Italian, as well as relevant government papers and reports. At the British Museum I was able to trace a lot of incidental references, especially in periodical literature.

My background knowledge on the Mediterranean area was less solid. In the late fifties there was very little sociologically relevant material on this area in print. Moreover, I lacked the time, training, and patience to get the most out of what there was, and my teachers, leading specialists in other areas of the world, were not at home in the literature relevant to this area.

Language was a different problem. It was one which with hard work and concentration I could hope to go a long way toward solving before I actually went into the field. By a stroke of good fortune I met a Maltese headmaster, Francis Chetcuti, studying in London. He lived near us and was prepared to help me with my Maltese for a few hours a week. The study of any language, by whatever means, is hard work. I estimate that I spent at least 320 hours studying Maltese that year. Nonetheless, when I arrived in Malta, I felt I had precious little to show for it. Although by June 1960 I had a vocabulary of somewhere over a thousand words, a fair grasp of the principles of the grammar, and a rudimentary reading knowledge, I had no practice in speaking or listening to it. Francis Chetcuti, in common with all educated Maltese, found it difficult to speak Maltese with a non-Maltese. What I did have, however, as I realized later, was a fairly solid framework on which I could build, and my knowledge of spoken and written Maltese progressed rapidly once we settled in Farrug.

The research problem I became interested in was village-level politics. In particular I had become intrigued through my own experience in Malta by the presence of two competing band clubs in a number of villages. As luck would have it, Francis Chetcuti had been headmaster in several of the southern villages in which this rivalry is particularly acute. One of these villages was Hal-Farrug. As well as my language teacher he became my first informant, and I spent many hours discussing aspects of Maltese society with him.

Hal-Farrug appeared to be ideal. It was small enough so that we could get to know everyone, it was divided by rival band clubs, and I had learned a good deal about it from a friend in Malta. Shortly after New Year 1960 I wrote to a

The parish church and square of Hal-Farrug on a Wednesday morning in November.

friend in Malta, Father Charles Vella, asking if through his network of contacts he could help us locate a house in Hal-Farrug, or in one of the small surrounding villages.

My application to the Colonial Social Science Research Council reflected my interest in local politics and the repercussions at the village level of the national turmoil that had divided all Malta at the time into two hostile camps. Thanks to the support I received from Trafford Smith, a former Lieutenant Governor of Malta then back at the Colonial Office in London, my teachers at the London School of Economics and, particularly from my supervisor, Dr. (now Professor) Lucy Mair, my application was successful.

Full of expectation my wife and I and our two daughters, aged six and four, left England for Malta in our Morris Minor station wagon on Monday, June 27, 1960, camping along the way.

Arrival and First Contacts

We arrived in Malta at dawn on Monday, July 18, 1960 after an overnight trip on one of the expensive and dilapidated little Italian ships that ply between Malta and Syracuse. We were welcomed by Father Charles Vella, and within two hours we were cleared through customs, our car had been unloaded, and we were having breakfast in the Meadowbank Hotel on the Sliema seafront. This was to be our home for the next three weeks.

The next two days were spent getting used to the idea of sleeping in clean sheets on soft beds and seeing to a deluge of official papers. On Wednesday I set out to see if I could find my way to Hal-Farrug. I had never been there before and, like most foreigners living in Malta, as well as a large number of Malta's town-dwelling elite, I did not know my way about the southern villages at all. An entry in my diary for that day reads as follows:

Went for a drive to Farrug. Got lost and passed through Mqabba. This is quite an interesting looking town. It has about the right "look." Then through to Safi, where a group of ten- to thirteen-year-olds surrounded my car and asked me why I wanted to go to Hal-Farrug, because people there were "savages." The children were friendly enough but tough; they hung about the car for quite a bit. They wanted me to come back and talk to them.

This was my first introduction to the good-natured rivalry between villages and the friendly but aggressive curiosity of village children. There is a Maltese proverb that eloquently sums up this character trait: "God protect us from wild bees and village children." After driving about a bit more I found my way to Hal-Farrug. The diary entry continues:

Farrug is a small town. It looked cosy. I stopped at a shop for a box of matches and an orangeade. A friendly lady making fishnet in the shop served me. Several boys dressed only in short trousers and undershirts came in to stare at me. I noticed a sign which said Farrug Stars Football Club.

These were the first impressions jotted down in haste and, as is evident, in not nearly enough detail, because those first impressions are extremely important. I had spent fifteen minutes drinking orangeade, smoking a cigarette, and trying my Maltese out on the lady of the shop. The shop turned out to be the football club in which I was later to spend many evenings. The first impressions of Farrug were very positive.

The day after I finally met Dun Gorg, the parish priest of Farrug, who, at Father Charles Vella's request, had located a house for us. The house belonged to Tereza Abela. It was the ground floor of a house in which her daughter Angela and son-in-law Leonard lived. It consisted of a room that opened onto the street, another behind that, and a small room with a sink, which opened onto a little courtyard at the other side of which was a third room which until very recently had been used as a stable. The house was very sparsely furnished and the courtyard was lined with an elaborate system of cages housing chickens and rabbits, and clouds of flies.

The next day I brought my wife along to see it, and we agreed that it had great possibilities. Tereza Abela, who had had some experience renting property she owned in a neighboring town to English Service families, said she would carry out the necessary changes. She promised to paint the stable, arrange for a shower, sink, and toilet, provide beds, a large working table, chairs, and some sort of a sideboard. Carmelo, her eldest son, a skilled electrician at the dockyard, arrived and I was able to discuss a number of technical details with him. Dun Gorg promised to keep an eye on things and assured me that if anyone in the village could, Tereza would see that her boys carried out the work in the fortnight promised. He would see to it that Tereza remained interested in encouraging her boys. We left well pleased at the prospects of finally being able to begin fieldwork in two weeks.

We spent the next twenty days settling down to life in Malta in general, filling in more documents, collecting our trunks, and shopping for the innumerable odds and ends of household equipment that we would need. The logistics of everyday living are in fact a great deal more complicated than those whose life has settled down into a comfortable pattern realize.

Another thing I did was to visit systematically a number of my old contacts with the government. This brought me into the Department of Social Welfare, Department of Information, Central Office of Statistics, University, Department of Agriculture, and law courts. I also made courtesy calls on the Governor and Lieutenant Governor.

I also decided to do something about the infestation of flies attracted to the house by Angela's rabbit and chicken cages. I went along to see the director of the Medical and Health Department, a former CARE contact, and explained the problem of the flies, asking if it would be possible to have the courtyard sprayed with a potent DDT solution. I called back in two days and learned that he had made an appointment for me with the district health inspector. When I met the inspector at our house I had certain misgivings. He was beautifully dressed in a spotless white linen suit and looked quite out of place in the dirty street and, later, in the chaotic house in which the Abela boys were hammering away. When I asked him where the DDT sprayer was, he replied that first he must inspect the house to see if it conformed to public health regulations. After peering in the newly constructed shower stall and into the dark little cupboard which housed the rather battered second-hand toilet, he asked Carmelo a few pointed questions in Maltese. I can still see the inspector, standing in the center of the little courtyard, with a mass of flies settling down densely on his white suit. He told me that the work Carmelo was doing was not only unauthorized, but it was against the regulations: the sinks, toilets, and shower were not properly connected with the sewage system. The landlord must bring the conversions in line with the regulations.

At this point I forgot about the flies and concentrated on getting the immaculate inspector out of the house as quickly as possible. The longer he remained, the slimmer would grow my chances of being allowed to remain in the house which had been found after so much trouble. I was not about to jeopardize my research for a few thousand flies. Fortunately the inspector was easily persuaded to have a cool drink in one of the bars in the village square. I did not ask about DDT anymore. Twenty minutes after he had condemned my house as a menace to public health, he was motoring out of Farrug. We had no more trouble with him. The house remained ours, as did all the flies. Later we had ample opportunity to remember his misgivings about the plumbing system.

Finally the great day arrived. On Saturday, August 6, 1960, at about five in the evening, we moved into our house. Before we knew it, our children were playing happily out on the street with neighboring children, and gazing in awe at the hundreds of goats and sheep streaming back to the houses at sunset. One of the Abela boys came in to ask how things were. He tried, without success, to get the kerosene refrigerator to run. He told us that the music we could hear came from the square. The Saint Martin Band Club was holding a rally to whip up enthusiasm for the coming centenary of their saint. He poked at the refrigerator several more times and then hurried to the square himself.

After tucking the children into their beds in the white-washed stable, which had now become their bedroom, I steeled myself to go to the square. For many months I had been nervously thinking about the moment when I would have to stride across the square in the full gaze of the whole village, and begin my fieldwork. In brief I had a very bad case of stage fright. Unfortunately I had not realized that there was absolutely nothing to be nervous about, for my fieldwork had in fact begun quite some time before.

A few steps beyond our front door I met Salvu, another of Tereza's Abela's sons, with a friend, and together we walked toward the music. The square in front of the Saint Martin's Club was milling with people. Music blared from a loudspeaker stuck in one of the windows. People were clapping and shouting slogans and poems in honor of Saint Martin. Though many were indeed staring at me, I found I did not mind: I was talking to Salvu and his friend. In front of the band club I saw another familiar face, Pietru Cardona, a local school teacher to whom Dun Gorg had introduced me on my first visit. He pulled me into the band club to admire his tape recorder, which was in fact producing the deafening music. Inside I met old Victor Azzopardi, the senior village school teacher, church sacristan and, at the time, treasurer of the Saint Martin Band Club. Though at first reserved, he loosened up at once when I told him I knew Francis Chetcuti, who a few years before had been headmaster in the village. An excited stream of words about band clubs, festa[1] music, different types of fireworks, and how you make them kept washing over me. After a bit I left Pietru and walked with Salvu Abela and his friend through

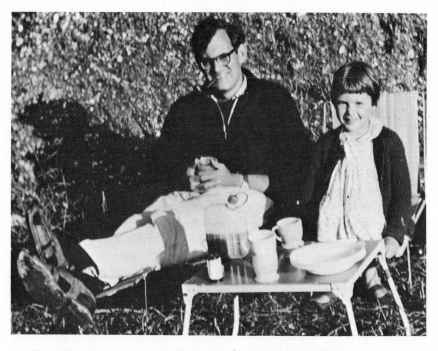

The author and his oldest daughter, Ieneke, relaxing during fieldwork in Malta.

the village. Though we attracted comments, they were good natured ones. They finally brought me back home. I nodded to Leonard, our upstairs neighbor, who was hiding in the shadow of his doorway listening to a furious quarrel between neighbors a little farther up the street. I learned later that one had hung an enormous picture of Dom Mintoff, the labor leader, over his door. His opposite neighbor objected violently. Fieldwork had begun. The beginning had been painless and pleasant.

[1] A festa is a celebration in honor of a saint. In short, it is the Maltese (and Italian) word for the *fiesta* of the Spanish speaking world.

Adjustment to Hal-Farrug

Although our adjustment to the way of life of our neighbors proceeded rapidly, it was not always without problems. There were basic household problems and new influences that affected our family customs. Besides these, we of course also faced the problem of learning new roles and modes of behavior.

The house was small, but it was reasonably comfortable. It was certainly much more comfortable than the tent in which we had camped for the three weeks previous to our arrival in Malta. Foolishly, we kept comparing, sometimes rather guiltily, our surroundings with the tents and mud huts which we imagined to be typical of anthropological housing in the field. What we forgot was that these would not have been ordinary mud huts placed at random, but the local equivalent of the town houses and mansions of the elite. Applying this principle to Hal-Farrug, we should have maintained a much higher living standard. The focus on peasants, villages, and slums in the sociological literature on southern Europe in general reflects the researchers' inability to keep up with the local elite. It may be possible to study peasants even if you live in a mansion, but if you live in a peasant house it is not possible to meet as an equal those who live in mansions.

Partly as a result of this error, and our recent camping experience, we did little to improve the comfort of our sparsely furnished quarters. The easy chairs remained those of our camping trip: ground-level folding stools. With a few pounds' worth of screening material I ended the constant invasion of flies that almost drove us to despair during the first forty-eight hours. The flies were now confined to the outside, where they continued to attack relentlessly, quickly spotting the laundry on the line and leaving indelible traces on the finish of our car.

The plumbing performed well for the first three weeks and then rebelled. I discovered this as I was having a shower and the neighbors above flushed their toilet. Suddenly I was ankle deep in rebellion. After this I arranged to have the mini-cesspit that served both our houses emptied weekly. In fact most of our neighbors had sewage troubles and the smell of sewage gas was with us everywhere in the village. Fortunately the village is today connected with the main sewage system of the island.

We, or rather my wife, quickly got used to the main problem of housekeeping: the fact that Maltese rise very early. We were anxious to buy as much as we could in the village in order not only to give the business to our neighbors, but also to establish contact. She soon learned to go shopping early, for most of the meat and fresh vegetables were bought up by the women at 5:00 in the morning on their way back from the first Mass. After her first shopping expedition at 8:30, when all she had been able to find were a few bits of meat and some wilted vegetables, she usually set out just before 7:00. It did not take long before she was shouting at the vegetable vendor just like our neighbors, and disdainfully flinging the produce about on his cart in order to get a good bargain. I sometimes think that Maltese vegetable vendors are among the most abused persons in the world. Whenever she had problems concerning shopping she always found a willing escort of women who showed her where she could buy what she wanted.

My new role as a researcher forced us to modify a number of our family customs. I felt obliged to be in the village as much as possible to see what was happening, but I could not always predict when important events would take place. This meant that my coming and going in the family circle was often irregular. My wife had to get used to seeing me disappear in the evening after I had read a story to the children in their stable, which now smelled sweetly of the esparto-grass stuffing their mattresses. Unlike Maltese women, she did not have the network of relatives in the village whom she could visit while her husband was away, though later she did make many friends.

The children made friends quickly with the children of a large farming family opposite us. They, too, had a lot to learn about customs. They especially had difficulty getting used to not accepting biscuits, sweets, and soft drinks eagerly as soon as they were offered. This is considered greedy. They soon learned to refuse politely several times before being convinced to accept the gift. In a short time too they learned songs in praise of the archibishop, and to make rude noises whenever the name of Dom Mintoff was mentioned. Some of their little playmates were rather conservative.

Another problem we had was what I call the two worlds of Malta: town and country. The way of life and the network of contacts that we were building in the villages were completely alien to our upper-class Maltese friends from the towns. But perhaps "problem" is too strong a word. After we moved to Farrug, we dropped out of the sight of many of the acquaintances we had among the town-dwelling elite. A few friends would come and visit us occasionally. Although they never said so directly, the contrast of our sparsely furnished village house with the sumptuous townhouse in which we had once lived was puzzling to most of our Maltese acquaintances. Most Maltese, and especially the competitive professional classes, are intensely materialistic. It was inconceivable to them that someone should *choose* to live in our present surroundings: a tragedy must have befallen us. We saw less and less of them. Maybe this was just as well. The arrival of doctors, lawyers, and ex-cabinet ministers to see us would have troubled the image we were trying to establish. Nonetheless, our very occasional sorties to a nobleman's reception or a formal luncheon with the governor, highlighted the cleavage between the way of life of the villagers and of the town-dwelling professional classes. Equally instructive were the patronizing and disdainful references to Hal-Farrug and villages like it, and to the people who lived there, by the Anglicized upper-classes we met at these functions. The women in particular cooed in their English-accented, Italianized

Maltese at the quaint, rustic way I spoke their language. Although we went to few such functions, those we attended taught us a great deal.

Bringing a large family into the field obviously creates certain problems of adaptation. A good deal of time and energy is invested in the simple logistics of everyday life. These unquestionably take time away from research and writing. Sometimes the combined pressure of the established roles of father and husband plus the new roles the anthropologist is learning and tentatively acting out becomes a considerable strain. Nonetheless the positive advantages gained from having a family in the field far outweigh these disadvantages. To begin with, a family provides an island which is part of another way of life. In Hal-Farrug certainly this prevented me from becoming completely absorbed in local events and helped to maintain a certain objectivity; it also provides companionship. Although the researcher can become close to his informants, he is always an outsider. Research can be a lonely business. Third, a family gives the researcher an adult status. In a society in which all adults are expected to marry, those who produce children (our third daughter was born shortly after we left Farrug!) are regarded as more complete persons. This means that you share this status and the experience that this brings with leaders of the community. Finally, through my wife and children I made a number of extra contacts with neighbors, and gained valuable insights into the world of women.

In short, though we had some problems of adjustment, none were insurmountable. That they were not was in no small measure due to two factors: the flexibility and willingness of the members of my own family to learn new customs and modify behavior and the extreme helpfulness and patience of the people of Hal-Farrug. Within a month or so after our arrival we were no longer *L-Ingliz* and *L-Ingliza*, the generic nicknames given to all foreigners; we became *Gerri* and *Gerrija*. We thus received personal nicknames derived from my Christian name from our neighbors. There were still, however, many problems of adujstment that I had to solve in my role as participant observer.

Participant Observation

The chief research technique of an anthropologist is very different from that of a sociologist. The sociologist works with informants in a research situation, and then retires from the scene. His contacts are generally short and not repeated over time. He knows his informant only in the role of informant. An anthropologist, on the other hand, must be able to get along with people well, for he remains in contact with his informants over a long period of time. He must play many roles before them: not only that of interviewer, but also that of husband, father, neighbor, friend, patron, client, clique-member, and so on. Many of these are new roles for him. Moreover, he must play these roles, whether old or new, in public. In small communities such as Hal-Farrug, the anthropologist, as the newcomer and representative of a foreign culture, is constantly at the center of the village stage. He is consciously acting. After a bit he is usually acting well and receiving compliments from his audience. This is a very heady mixture. The experience of course varies, but it is something that all anthropologists who have done fieldwork share, and in a certain measure it sets them apart from those who have not.

I enjoy fieldwork. Looking back on the work that I have done in my various occupations, it is the close and prolonged periods of contact with people in the field that stand out as high points in my life. Of these the most important was the first.

All anthropologists, I think, are faced with two conflicting roles as participant observers. In Hal-Farrug I felt this very strongly. On the one hand, I wished to construct as large and wide-ranging a network of contacts as possible. On the other, I needed to pursue specific bits of information from selected informants. Although much of the quality of the information I was able to get depended upon the friendships that I had been able to build, the techniques of building those friendships very often got in the way of the information I tried to collect. This is because informants see themselves not as informants but as friends. For the anthropologist they are both. In retrospect, it seems as though I spent many frustrating hours discussing world news with Pietru Cardona—especially the fate of Patrice Lumumba, for the time was 1960—when I would have preferred discussing the band club rivalry, political factions, and gossip relating to key figures I was studying. My relations with Pietru at this stage were not close enough to get this sort of information through prolonged direct questioning. I had to get it indirectly during many hours spent with him and, of course, others, doing things which interested them. With Pietru I discussed Lumumba, with others it was hunting or catching birds, with yet others it was football and drinking.

Later, after many hours of what one might call informant servicing, I developed a few key informants with whom I could retire in private to discuss matters which they did not want others to know they were telling me. I was able to get this information because of the time and energy invested in playing the role of friend and conversationalist. These, and I come back to this, are time-consuming activities. With experience a researcher can learn to be more economical with his time than I was. This depends in part upon his ability to formulate his problem extremely clearly. In no case can he dispense with investing much of his time playing the role of friend to his informants. The information he collects is directly related to his ability to make and maintain friendships among his informants.

There were other new roles that I had to learn to play. One was that of churchgoer. Although we are not Catholic I was determined to go to Mass regularly to hear what was said, to observe who came and where they sat and so forth. Consequently, at 5:45 A.M. on the Monday morning after our arrival, I went to the second of the two daily Masses. Remembering the Mass of the day before, which I had attended from the pavement outside because the church was so crowded, I arrived early to assure a vantage point. There was no one in the church when I arrived, and I sat on the right hand side of the nave, in the third row from the front. Hardly had I settled down when a horde of tittering girls arrived suddenly and surrounded me. I turned uncomfortably around and saw three nuns seated on the aisle. There appeared to be no one else in the church except those around me. It suddenly became apparent that I was sitting in the place traditionally occupied by the nuns and their numerous little charges. After an embarrassed half hour of being observed closely and giggled at intensely, I bolted. Later that day I met Dun Gorg. He discreetly suggested that I sit in one of the lateral apses where the men sat, because it was the custom for the women in the villages to sit in the central nave. I had learned this the hard way. By then I had decided to spend my mornings sleeping and to confine my church attendance to the crowded and important Sunday Mass. I had learned two valuable lessons: to conserve my energy and time as much as possible, and to try and get a description of how I should behave in a given situation before being confronted by it.

The people of Farrug also had adjustment problems. They had a stranger in their midst who was an enigma. I had a family yet I did not go to work like other men. I seemed to be always about, and I asked so many questions. At the outset I explained to the parish priest that I wanted to study all aspects of life in a typical village for my Ph.D. thesis. Yet this information did not circulate widely. When people asked him what I was doing he would try to explain. By no means did everyone ask him, and not all those who did understood his explanation. It soon became apparent that I was remarkably well informed about matters they thought no nonvillager could know. These were simply things such as village nicknames, where people lived, what they did, how many children they had, where they worked, and so on. I certainly did not make it apparent that I knew other more intimate details. There was one man in particular who was troubled. He had heard about me from other people, but never asked me directly what I was doing. He was convinced I was a spy. The problem he and some of his friends faced, as I learned later from Pietru, was to determine for which country I was spying. Because I was American, had studied in England, had a Swedish wife and one child born in Japan, another in Malta, it was not a straightforward matter. He decided finally that I must be a United Nations spy, and began spreading this information about. Pietru told me what was happening and who was responsible. I made a point of meeting the man in his bar. In the course of an evening's hard drinking, for he had an absolutely phenomenal capacity (which I do not), I convinced him that I enjoyed drinking, that I was a student on a very limited budget, that I was genuinely interested in Maltese villagers, that spies usually operate among the town folk, that I had to write a thesis for my teachers, and that he could help me a lot by telling me about his own experience as a leader in the Saint Martin Band Club. The following day I had a frightful hangover, for we had been drinking pint glasses containing a mixture of cheap local wine, beer, and lemonade—a grassroots shandy. I never heard any more about spying.

As participant observer I took part in a wide range of activities. I spent a good deal of the day talking to the shopkeepers and to old men sitting on their doorsteps, and in the evening with the younger men in their cafes, clubs, and on their doorsteps. I also went along on excursions, festas, pilgrimages, weddings, picnics, parties, and receptions in the various clubs. We had Dun Gorg

The author with the chief of the new St. Martin firework factory with the 1967 masterpieces. The one Jeremy Boissevain is holding weighs 20 kilograms.

in to dinner, and after he left the village I often took his successor to the neighboring airport for a drink, a change of scenery, and private conversation. I attended football matches, went hunting, spent a day clap-netting birds, photographed weddings and baptismal parties, went to the fields with farmers, and made the rounds with vendors. In short I saw a lot of the people of Farrug in the various roles they played.

I also systematically pursued a number of key informants: the parish priest, Pietru, old Victor Azzopardi, the sacristan, his brother Pawlu, the president of the Saint Rocco Band Club, the baker and many others. To get systematic information about political matters it was often necessary to see them in privacy. This presented a problem, for the people of Farrug live very close together, and Malta is overpopulated. Moreover Farrugin are reluctant to invite anyone but their closest relatives into their own houses regularly. Exceptions were the parish priest and the shopkeepers. Fortunately Pietru's unmarried sister ran a bazaar and we could talk there in English, which he spoke well. I often went with single informants on picnics or to festas in other villages. Sometimes I drove them into Valletta with me. Occasionally we would simply go for a drive to be alone. Some came to our house, but this gave rise to speculation among the neighbors and the informants were uneasy. In short, our car, brought to provide transportation, in fact also provided important isolation with key informants.

About a month after arrival I began to establish a routine. I got up at 6:00 or 6:30 every morning. Often I would spend a peaceful hour working on my notes before the rest of the family arose. After breakfast, at about 8:00, I left to pick up our car, which was garaged at Tereza Abela's farm on the edge of the village. Normally I went a roundabout way which took me past the parish church, the parish priest's house, the baker's shop, and Pietru Cardona's. It also took me past the main bus stop. All along the way I talked to people, and I always stopped for a chat with Pietru or his sister in her bazaar. This twenty- to thirty-minute swing through the village usually brought me up to date. I then brought the car to the house and my wife brought our eldest daughter to an English-language school in a neighboring town. In the beginning I studied Maltese in the mornings: later I used them to interview the older men who stayed in the village, or to work in the public library in Valletta. Noon was hectic because either my wife or I would have to drive to pick up our daughter for lunch and then return her an hour later, collecting her again at 3:30. In the afternoon I always stayed in the village to work on my notes, and, if the night before had been particularly grisly, I also took a short nap.

Except between 6:30 and 7:30, when I was at home eating and putting the children to bed, I was constantly busy with informants from 4:00 in the afternoon until the clubs and bars closed at about 10:30 or 11:00. After this I would get to work on my notes, first completing my diary and then writing up detailed notes of interviews and observations made during that day. Often I was too exhausted by 12:00 or 12:30 to continue, and would simply jot down an outline of subjects to write up the next day. Sometimes my day's work would end with some scribbled nonsense, an illegible scrawl or an ink blot when I fell asleep over my notes.

An illustration of a more or less average day will perhaps make clearer the rhythm of research. I will not say that it is a typical day, for every day was different. It does, however, illustrate the general attempt to establish and maintain a wide range of links, and to interview certain people more intensively.

Monday, September 19, 1960, started as usual. On the way to pick up the car I learned from Pietru that a number of Requiem Masses were to be held that day in memory of the nineteen-year-old boy electrocuted a year before in one of the quarries surrounding the village. After my wife and daughter left for school, I settled down to study Maltese. After an hour I got fed up and went out to practice it. I went first to the little bazaar of Pietru's sister, where I spent forty-five minutes talking to Pietru's two sisters, his mother, and three customers who came to the shop. I then crossed the street to talk to a farmer, who had come to get a drink in Pietru's cousin's bar. We spent the best part of an hour discussing his farming problems and, of particular importance to me, his reaction to the discussion of the parish priest in church the day before about the financial situation of the Saint Rocco Confraternity. Between 11:00 and 12:00 I worked intensively with the parish priest on my household card system. Dun Gorg liked to display his phenomenal memory and was dictating details of every family in the village: name, nickname, place of birth, age, occupation, band club allegiance and, in passing, choice bits of gossip as well as his personal likes and dislikes.

After lunch, I reviewed the household cards I had prepared with Dun Gorg in the morning, and wrote up the case histories and other information he had provided. (Much later I compared his data to the door-to-door census of my own, and found his to be amazingly accurate.) After my wife and daughter returned home at 3:45, I took the car to the garage to wash it. Carmelo Abela came home at about 4:30. After his tea he came and gave me a hand with the car. When he started to tell me how he had met his fiancée, I began to wax the car to have an excuse to stay with him. As soon as Carmelo left me for his fiancée, I returned home and wrote up the story of his courtship while the details were still fresh (Boissevain 1969: 35–36).

That evening at 8:00, I met Pietru accidentally in front of the parish priest's house. We decided to go for a walk outside the village to find some cool air. At about 9:00 we returned and sat in front of the school chatting. Pietru told me the story of his own courtship and the difficult time he had deciding to break his engagement. We also discussed at great length the evil eye; it had given him a fever the day before. At about 10:30 Pietru went home, and I stopped by his aunt's wine shop. Since only the duty policeman was there chatting to Pietru's cousin, and she obviously was anxious to go to bed herself, I left after fifteen minutes. Although I intended to write up my notes fully, when I got home I found that I was too tired. I simply filled in my diary for the day and outlined the topics to write up the following day. I went to bed at about midnight.

After five months in Farrug, I assumed that the villagers accepted me well enough to give information freely on the delicate matter of political and band club rivalry. In retrospect it was too short a time to assume that sort of confidence. I was still an outsider peering in at the private life of the village. There was still much that people did not care for me to learn. This was especially marked with regard to factional conflicts, which marred the image of village unity that they liked to project to outsiders. I discovered this clearly on Tuesday, 3 January, 1961. The village that day was buzzing with policemen who kept arriving and leaving on motorcycles. In the afternoon I went to Pietru's sister's bazaar to find out what had happened. I casually asked why there were so many policemen in the village. I saw Pietru and his sister exchange glances, and heard Pietru ask in rapidfire Maltese whether he should tell me. His sister shrugged and said I would find out anyway. I chimed in that I agreed, and suggested they tell me now to save time. They burst out laughing and remarked that my Maltese was now so good that they could not keep secrets from me. Pietru and his sister, who was better informed, told how Dun Gorg's coat of arms in the church had been replaced by that of the village sometime during the last two nights, probably on New Year's Eve. Dun Gorg, told about it by phone, had come to Hal-Farrug from his new parish early that morning to verify it, and then reported the damage to the police (Boissevain 1964:1283–1284; 1965:72–73; 1969:63).

To some extent collecting information, especially about matters which many people regard as private, always remains something of a cat-and-mouse game. I had this cat-and-mouse relationship with Pietru until I returned to Farrug the summer of 1967 and hired him as my research assistant. By then I had demonstrated through publications that I needed his help for scientific reasons, and he became much more cooperative.

Other Research Techniques

Besides the participant observation described in the preceding section, I employed a number of other research techniques to gather information on Hal-Farrug. At the public library I systematically went through years of newspapers and yearbooks in order to piece together the background. The newspapers in particular were a useful source of information. The Maltese have acquired from the British the habit of writing letters to the editor. If a village faction fight grows particularly bitter, the weaker party very often tries to wound its opponents by ridiculing them through a letter to the editor. This then gives rise to a furious polemic in which all sorts of fascinating data are made public. In this way I gathered a number of interesting tips on important clashes in Farrug's political past.

The problem of how much time to devote to archives of various sorts is a problem in countries with a long written history. I can offer no rule of thumb. I also consulted some of the parish archives to get vital statistics on deaths, marriages, baptisms. Through contacts established with CARE, I was able to study the police archives pertaining to the village for the past thirty-five years. In addition, I went through records at the Rationing Office, the Electoral Office, and with Rediffusion, the wired sound-broadcasting company. I also, unsuccessfully, advertised in the press and searched the libraries for diaries. It would obviously take me too far afield to discuss the type of information gleaned from the various sources and its relevance. The historical depth given in *Saints and*

Fireworks and *Hal-Farrug*, as limited as it is, would not have been possible without this search. On the other hand, I wasted much time on archives as I did not always know what I was looking for, especially in the beginning. In order to carry out such research economically I should have had a much more sharply formulated research design than I had.

In the beginning in Hal-Farrug I made extensive use of my camera to connect names to faces. I photographed many crowd scenes, and later asked informants to identify the persons. One of the most useful pictures in this respect was the portrait of the Saint Martin partisans posing proudly with the mountain of fireworks they prepared for the centenary of their Saint (Boissevain 1969:73). People would tip me off when interesting things were going to happen, and, if crowds were present, see that I got a ringside seat with a running commentary. Although there was also a keen photographer in the village who earned a bit of extra money with his hobby, we did not really compete. I only charged the cost price on my pictures, which for the most part were scenes in which he was not particularly interested. The camera also was a convenient means of getting me invited to intimate family celebrations, such as bethrothal parties, where a regular village photographer would have been an uncomfortably familiar figure. Although once an avid amateur photographer, I soon found that taking really good photographs is incompatible with being a good anthropologist. Both are full time occupations. Moreover the best angles are often far from informants.

Direct interviews of course were one of the chief techniques I used. I had interviews with the various village leaders, association officers, living former village parish priests and police officers, politicians who had canvassed in the village, and many more. Many of these interviews were formal in the sense that I had made appointments for them. Many were also accidental, such as the interviews with Carmelo Abela and Pietru Cardona described above. If I could, I always spent some time before an interview preparing it and thinking through the questions, making sure that I had them firmly in my head. Very often I would jot down key words with a ballpoint on my palm or, more usually, on a page in my pocket notebook. In the course of the interview I would elicit a date or an address which gave me an excuse to open the notebook so that I could jot down trigger words to remind me later of the subjects discussed. Once the notebook was open I could also unobtrusively check the prepared list of questions to make sure that I had covered all the planned subjects. An interview with untrained informants, especially if you are after information he is not too eager to part with, has a way of branching out along unforeseen paths. Later it is surprisingly difficult to remember the different topics discussed.

Genealogies were a help in learning how the villagers were related to each other. I collected ten extensive genealogies which were sufficient to place everyone in the village. Genealogical data I collected on the census provided further information. Because I was not particularly interested in kinship at that time, the genealogical data I have on Hal-Farrug is rather thin. Later, in the summer of 1968, I was to collect a giant genealogy from Pietru Cardona, who has over 400 living relatives of his generation. This, however, belongs to a later period of research.

I conducted the village census in the fourth month. For many days I procrastinated whether it would be worth the effort. Finally I decided it would be, and that I should do the work myself and not try to get someone else to do it. The data I collected related primarily to household composition, occupation, and membership in the various associations. Although I tried to get information on extra sources of cash income and land ownership, this made people suspicious. Since the economic data they then gave was extremely unreliable, I soon stopped asking for them, fearing that it would jeopardize my relations with the villagers. Even my neighbor Leonard, Tereza Abela's son-in-law, did not want me to note down that he supplemented his dock yard policeman's salary by buying and selling eggs and poultry.

It is important to remember that I was in Malta during a time of political crisis (1960–1961). Questions which were related to politics were difficult to pose. Many persons did not wish to disclose their true political sympathy for many reasons. Those who supported the Labour Party were afraid of being branded as communist heretics by the faithful; some were afraid of losing their jobs; yet others were afraid of generating conflict with family or neighbors. Another sensitive subject I have already mentioned was allegiance to a particular festa faction. For this reason I did not include direct questions relating to political or festa faction affiliation on the census. In this small community it was of course possible to get this information, as well as that on extra sources of income, indirectly.

Once I stopped asking about money, I was welcomed into most of the 244 households. The few exceptions were houses in which mentally disturbed members of the household were confined. The success of the census was in no small measure due to the way in which Dun Frangisk announced from the pulpit that I was going to every household to ask some harmless questions. In fact, in most of the houses where I called, the problem was not reserve but overfriendliness. Many thought of my visit as a social occasion and offered me the glass of whisky that good manners demanded. Moreover many gave me eggs, soft cheeses, and tomatoes. I often had to dash home to keep my pockets from bursting, and once I had raw egg slithering down the inside of my leg. The census took eleven days. By the second day I had developed a confidence and smoothness which made me feel a little silly about the hesitation I had had about carrying out the survey.

On the 8th of January we moved from Farrug to Kortin, where we lived until we left Malta in September. The object of the move was to gather comparative information on a larger village and one that was not divided by band club rivalry. Although I intended to return to Hal-Farrug after three months, the house was no longer available when we wanted to move back. Tereza Abela and her sons had moved into it, leaving her husband, with whom she had quarrelled, to look after the farm. Though I continued to visit Hal-Farrug regularly to attend a number of the important functions, including many weddings, participant observation in the village was obviously reduced to a minimum. Later a research assistant and I made short comparative studies of the general organization, leadership, and patterns of conflict in twelve other communities. Much later, during the summer of 1967, thanks to the generosity of the Wenner-Gren Foundation for Anthropological Research, I was able to revisit Hal-Farrug to bring myself up to date. Pietru provided me with very valuable assistance, as did a number of others, including the new parish priest. Some of the data I collected at this time found its way into *Hal-Farrug*.

Processing the Data

One of the most critical phases of fieldwork is processing the voluminous data collected. I received little systematic instruction on this during my graduate work. Though I heard vague descriptions of how anthropologists processed their data, the only "anthropologist's field notebook" I was actually able to touch and look at, and this only after many unsuccessful requests, was one of Malinowski's old field notebooks from the Department's museum. From Paul Stirling I heard how John Barnes kept his notes. Since this seemed an economical method I decided to adopt it myself.

I used a variety of notebooks. To begin with I had a little pocket notebook with a hard cover and a pencil, which I carried with me always. In this I jotted down odd bits of information during interviews, and more detailed outlines of the subjects discussed as soon as informants were out of sight. I also kept a second one in which I systematically put down the meaning of new words I heard; unfortunately I discontinued this after two months. I used a stenographer's notebook for formal interviews when I knew I could write, and for all genealogies, for copying data from the police records, and for rough notes from newspapers and other archives. Finally I had a series of much larger notebooks which I kept under lock and key in our house. Into these I wrote up in detail interviews and personal observations, some points of which I had usually jotted down in my pocket or stenographer's notebook. The lined pages were numbered consecutively and I ruled in a large margin on the left hand side. The entries were made chronologically. In the margin I wrote the headings under which the entry could be indexed. Following Paul Stirling's advice, I indicated as many possible headings as I could. These headings and subjects were consolidated in three central indexes at the back of each notebook: events and subjects peculiar to Hal-Farrug, names of people, and events and subjects of general importance. Every day I tried to bring this index up to date, cross-referencing where necessary. While in the field I did not allow myself enough time to do this properly. Besides these notebooks I also kept a daily diary into which I entered appointments and a rather terse summary of persons and places visited during the day. This was a chore which I did not do in great enough detail, but I did do it faithfully. The importance of this diary had rightly been stressed repeatedly at the field seminar in London. It provides a rough structure to the subject matter in the notebooks, as well as a record of how I spent my time, and whom I saw on what occasion. I had separate notebooks for Gozo, where I carried out a certain amount of research, and for the detailed notes which I took from library books. I indexed them all in the same way.

As already indicated, I developed a card system which provided data on household composition, occupation, nicknames, political allegiance, band club affiliation, and place of birth of each member. This card system, set up with the help of the parish priest at the end of the first month in Hal-Farrug, was invaluable, and I constantly drilled myself with the names, addresses, nicknames, and occupations of the village's 1300 inhabitants. Even today I still remember this information, and on return visits recently I have again, I fear, raised the spectre of the spy with it.

Besides notebooks and cards I had a system of folders for various activities, certain persons, genealogies, and subjects such as kinship, godparenthood, church organization, and so on. I placed these upright in a cardboard box. Into these I filed pamphlets, texts written by villagers, sheafs of notes, pictures and newspaper cuttings. I also had a growing collection of government departmental reports, pamphlets, statistical abstracts, and census reports to which I made constant reference in my comparative work.

Fortunately the Colonial Social Science Research Council required its research fellows to make an interim report after the first half year. I did this when I moved to Kortin. I began consolidating my notes on Friday, January 13. A month later I posted the report, a 14,000-word paper on local politics in Hal-Farrug, to the Colonial Office and to Dr. Lucy Mair, my supervisor at the London School of Economics. It had been a busy month. I first worked out the statistical results of the house to house census. This was a particularly time-consuming piece of work. I also indexed my notes, thought through a number of basic problems, and made plans for the rest of my research. I could not, however, work on the report continually: The sewage problem again arose and the plumbing could only be manipulated through the floor of the converted chicken house I was using as my study. There were also many more general problems of settling into a new village. Writing the report forced me to rethink basic problems and look at my material in terms of those problems. In doing so I discovered numerous shortcomings in my material. Moreover, because I now had a written piece, I was able to elicit valuable criticism and comments from my supervisor and her colleagues at the London School of Economics. This feedback was invaluable.

Two months later I again took time off from actual research and retired to a friend's summer house in Saint Paul's Bay for a week. Isolated from family, neighbors, and informants, I again indexed notes, read my material through, took stock of where I was, and where I still had to go. Unfortunately I did not write anything. Finally, I must mention that I had valuable discussions on many aspects of my fieldwork as well as some of my findings with friends and persons outside the villages. Most of these were what could be called, quasi-academics, that is, they were persons who had certain academic interests but who were not even part-time academics. They included a government secretary who was an expert on folklore, employees of the library who knew where the books I needed were placed (many were not cataloged!) and who had done considerable private research for Sunday supplement articles and pamphlets, a priest who was conducting pastoral research, a police sergeant interested in folklore, and many more. These, unlike most at the university, were keenly interested in my research and offered many insights, as well as access to their clipping files and records.

Foolishly, I did not show them my interim report, and thus missed the feedback this would have provided. The reason I did not show it is perhaps partly due to the way my research was sponsored. I was working with funds received from the British Government via the Colonial Social Science Research Council. As political relations between Malta and Britain at the time were very delicate, I felt most awkward about my sponsorship. I therefore did not disclose the exact source of funds unless I was pressed to do so, preferring merely to note that a British institution had sponsored me. Had the true nature of the source come out, I was sure, and still am, that my relations with Malta Labour Party officials would have been much less cordial than they were. Consequently, I had always the slightly embarrassed feeling that I was there under false colors. This of course was foolish, for the area of research and the problems on which I was working were completely those of my own choosing, not those of the British Government. Nonetheless, the feeling persisted, and I was not as forthright about my work as I should have been, and have since become.

Analysis and Writing Up

We returned to London by air in the middle of September 1961. I took with me my notebooks containing some 1500 pages, some 360,000 words of notes, plus the household cards of Hal-Farrug and Kortin. The rest of my data—pounds of books, papers, surveys, and cards—followed by ship. Fortunately we were able to move into a furnished house. This meant there were few settling in problems and I was able to begin work immediately.

The first task was of course to complete my indexing. I expanded certain sections of the index. Using these new categories I reread all my notes, indexing as I went along. This task, as I remember it, took about two weeks of intensive, tedious work. After that I began writing. I was determined to deliver my final report to the Colonial Office by the time my research grant ran out in the end of November.

Mondays through Saturdays, I worked flat out from 7:00 in the mornings to about 10:00 at night, with four hours off for meals and playing with the children. On Friday mornings, however, I went to Professor Raymond Firth's seminar at the London School of Economics, where in the course of the year I gave several papers. Since I did not have the resources to continue after the summer, my thesis had to be completed before August 1962. I could not afford the luxury of going to any of the other interesting research seminars at the L.S.E.

The third week in November I presented Dr. Mair with a 25,000-word typescript. She gave it very severe criticism, and I spent the next two weeks rewriting and editing it before I passed it on to the typist. With considerable satisfaction I delivered the required three copies to the Colonial Office around the middle of December. These apparently disappeared into the great maw of the dying colonial apparatus and, as far as I have been able to gather, were never looked at again by anyone. They apparently never reached Malta. A year later I had to lend my personal copy to Sir Maurice Dorman, the new Governor of Malta!

My supervisor's criticism of the final report, if anything, was even more severe than of the first draft. I took her pungent but most instructive marginal comments to heart and began work on my thesis. The first chapter required a good bit more historical research and I journeyed back and forth to the Colonial Office Library a number of times. That chapter gave me a good bit of trouble, and not surprisingly, it was rejected twice by Lucy Mair. I then worked methodically through each of the nine chapters, revising where necessary after sessions with my supervisor. I finished in the beginning of July, and in August left for a research post in Sicily, returning to London briefly in November for the examination of the thesis.

Hal-Farrug, of course, grew out of this initial research and my first book, though I did not return in my writing to Malta until 1967. During this period I carried out research in Sicily, prepared and taught my first courses at the Université de Montréal, moved from Canada to England, and from there to Holland. At the University of Amsterdam I lectured on Hal-Farrug from January to June 1967. That summer I returned to Malta to discuss certain points with friends and briefly to restudy the village. Using my lecture notes I then dictated the manuscript for *Hal-Farrug*. My secretary in Holland typed out the tapes. During the Christmas break I revised the manuscript, rewriting extensively. It was then stencilled and, in February, sent for comment to the Spindlers, who were in Europe at the time, and to friends in Holland, Malta, and England. The final manuscript was sent, together with pictures, diagrams, and maps, to the publisher the beginning of May 1968.

The Wisdom of Hindsight

If I were to carry out the research in Hal-Farrug again, would I set about it in the same way? Not completely in the same way, I think. To begin with, I would not try to divide my time over two villages. It could be argued that in terms of my objectives—a comparative study of village politics—this was not particularly unsatisfactory. The trouble was that I learned much about many villages but not enough about one.

Another shortcoming was that my research problem was not clearly enough formulated when I went into the field. Of course it is an open question whether an inexperienced researcher fresh from graduate school can ever hope to achieve the economy of action of an experienced researcher. Moreover, the theoretical apparatus available on village-level politics in the late fifties and early sixties was remarkably thin (Easton 1959). On the other hand, besides lacking clear concepts as to just what the political field was—and there were important books on the subject that I had not read—I naively expected to find groups within groups. My lack of critical attention to the basic theoretical premises concerning the nature of society postulated by social anthropologists, most of whom, following Evans-Pritchard (1940:262), saw the social structure as the "relations between groups of persons within a system of groups," ensured that I was ill-prepared to observe, let alone analyze, the networks and shifting coalitions of individuals I was in fact confronted with. The disproportionate amount of time I spent making the rounds of village associations and participating in their activities, in spite of the fact that their members represented but a fraction of the total population of the village, can be attributed partly to my misconception about the nature of society. I saw these associations as the formal groups which I had been trained to think would provide the key to the social structure. They did not. It took a long time to escape from the simplistic, group-dominated functionalist model I used as my primary analytical tool in 1960 (Boissevain 1968). *Hal-Farrug* therefore has a very different theoretical orientation than my first book.

I am sorry too that I did not spend more time systematically collecting local expressions and categories of thought. Because of this my knowledge of Maltese, while eminently serviceable for conversation and reading, remains rudimentary.

Since my first research in Hal-Farrug, I have developed another system of note-taking. Briefly, I type each entry in triplicate on a separate card, indexing not only the cards but various subjects covered. I now also spend much more time working out the notes. In Farrug I foolishly felt guilty about spending more than two or three hours a day on my notes; often I spent even less. I assumed that I had to be where the action was, not realizing that unless what is observed is digested thoroughly while in the field, it loses meaning and therefore value once you leave. You can only do this properly if you spend approximately one third of your time in the field processing your notes and writing.

Another shortcoming was that I did not do nearly enough writing. I should have been consolidating my data frequently in short reports. One of the reasons I spent more time on my interim report than I should have, was because my writing was rusty, and my data scattered and undigested. Yet this report remains the most valuable single exercise I carried out while I was in Malta. It is only when an anthropologist sets down his observations and analyses these clearly for himself and others that he becomes aware of the lacunae. If he does this in the field he can still do something about it. By consolidating his data at regular intervals, he will leave the field with much material already worked out and on paper. Much of this can be placed without alteration in the final report. A number of tables and sections I used in *Saints and Fireworks* and *Hal-Farrug* were lifted verbatim from the report to the Colonial Office that I prepared in my chickencoop in Kortin.

These then are some of the things that I think I have learned from my experience in Hal-Farrug, as well as elsewhere in the years since I carried out my research there. Nonetheless, in spite of my shortcomings and greenness, or perhaps because of them, the five months spent in Hal-Farrug will always stand out as my most important experience as a researcher.

References

Boissevain, Jeremy F., 1965, *Saints and Fireworks: Religion and Politics in Rural Malta*. London School of Economics Monographs on Social Anthropology No. 30. London: The Athlone Press (Revised paperback edition, 1969).

———, 1968, The place of non-groups in the social sciences. *Man* (N.S.) 3:542–556.

———, 1969, *Hal-Farrug: A Village in Malta*. New York: Holt, Rinehart and Winston, Inc.

———, 1970, *The Italians of Montreal: Social Adjustment in a Plural Society*. Ottawa: The Royal Commission on Bilingualism and Biculturalism.

Easton, David, 1959, Political Anthropology. In Bernard J. Siegel, ed., *Biennial Review of Anthropology*. Stanford, Calif.: Stanford University Press, pp. 210–262.

Evans-Pritchard, E. E., 1940, *The Nuer*. Oxford: The Clarendon Press.

4

LIVING AND WORKING WITH THE SEMAI

ROBERT K. DENTAN
State University of New York at Buffalo

Related Case Study: **The Semai: A Nonviolent People of Malaya**

In Robert Dentan's chapter one gets a particularly vivid impression of the personal meaning of fieldwork even though he pays consistent heed to the scientific objectives and methods of his fieldwork. The objectives of his research, the methods and equipment used, the problems of survival in an unhealthy location are discussed in such a way that they are treated both objectively and personally at the same time. The Dentans experienced severe physical privation and threat. Living in a totally alien world, they were beset by insects, a rain forest climate, and general discomfort. They were made ill by debilitating tropical diseases. But they acquired friends and experienced the satisfaction of being accepted, nearly as one of them, by the people they came to observe, and they had motivating them the drive to acquire new knowledge and insight into how the Semai lived and the mental organization behind their behavior. It is a strong tribute to the values of anthropology that they came away from their fieldwork experience with the desire to return not only to unanswered questions but to see the people once more. Robert Dentan feels for the Semai and their country "the bittersweet blend of nostalgia and homesickness the Semai call *rəniag.*"

The Author

Robert K. Dentan describes himself as follows:

I was born in New Haven, Connecticut, in 1936. This accident of birth practically doomed me to go to Yale where I got a B.A. in American Studies and a Ph.D. in Anthropology. I went from Yale to teach at Ohio State University where I was an Assistant Professor. I went to the State University of New York at Buffalo as an Associate Professor in the fall of 1969. My wife and I were divorced in early 1969, although we still continue to keep in touch with each other. Later that year I acquired a new wife and, as a bonus, a small agent of chaos. My main hobbies are listening to romantic and popular American folk music; reading science fiction and detective stories; and going to "class B" movies. Most of these might be summed up as a generalized hobby: trying to understand why Americans act like Americans. It is for this reason that my appointment at Buffalo is a "joint" one, in both Anthropology and American Studies.

G. D. S.

Introduction[1]

This chapter assumes the reader has some knowledge of the Semai, the Malayan people with whom I worked. Readers without such knowledge might glance through a short article on the Semai and related peoples (Dentan 1964) or read the case study, *The Semai* (Dentan 1968b).

At the outset, I want to make two points. First, the following account emphasizes our field experience more than our field techniques. Many cultural anthropologists tend to romanticize fieldwork to the point of making a fetish out of it, claiming that their field experience gives them insights into the nature of human society that no other discipline can provide. This insight, they contend, stems from the fact that anthropological fieldwork is an intensely personal experience. The difficulty they have in communicating the nature of this experience makes their colleagues in other fields rather suspicious of anthropology's claim to superior insight. I am suspicious of it myself. Nevertheless, I want to stress how intensely personal the fieldwork experience was for me and Ruth, then my wife.

[1] I want to thank Drs. Edwin S. Hall, Rodney Needham, and Thomas R. Williams, as well as a host of students and friends, for reading and commenting on this chapter.

Robert Dentan burning the fur off a monkey.

One reason fieldwork has this character, I think, is that, unlike other "social scientists," an anthropologist in a remote community is doing research all day, every day. This sort of total immersion is quite different from, say, getting some questionnaires filled out and then going home for a beer. For about a year and a half, our "home" was with the Semai, and there was no beer around. For much of that time, the only people we had to talk with were Semai. Communicating with them thus became a tremendous personal need. Our social life and our research were inextricably intertwined.

Another reason our fieldwork had this personal character was that, at first, we had a hard time just getting along from day to day among people in whose terms we were weird and barely comprehensible outsiders with the social and technical skills of a Semai four-year-old. This initial social situation produced in us a psychological condition anthropologists call "culture shock." We felt depressed, incompetent, unattractive, and very lonely. I can easily understand the response of the great anthropologist Malinowski (1967: 261) when he writes in his field diary that one trivial frustrating incident "drives me to a state of white rage and hatred of bronze-colored skin, combined with depression, a desire to 'sit down and cry,' and a furious longing '*to get out of this.*' For all that, I decide to resist and work today—'*business as usual,*' despite everything." Although Ruth and I were physiologically and emotionally adult, we were to the Semai socially children. We had to learn Semai ways in the manner that children in any society have to come to grips with the often incomprehensible demands and expectations of adults. We made the same sorts of *faux pas* and went through the same sorts of traumas that children do while growing up. In many ways we never did "grow up" in Semai terms. To take a simple instance, Ruth was never able to pound our clothes dry against a rock the way the other women did. The women washing clothes with her would almost always comment, "Oh, Ruth, you're doing that just like a child." After a while, that sort of remark gets pretty hard to take.

Since from the Semai point of view we were always rather inept, we could not help feeling very grateful and very affectionate toward them when they came to accept us as people much like other people. For example, Ruth, who normally prides herself on the excellence of her cooking, still recalls how delighted she was the first time someone said of one of her meals, "You know, this tastes just as if any other woman in the settlement had cooked it." Similarly, we were very moved on a visit to a ceremony in another settlement when a man from our home settlement explained to some wary "spirits" that we were perfectly acceptable people who "speak our language, eat our food and live in one of our houses. They are of our people," he said, "just like us."

In short, whether or not our fieldwork gave us superior insights, it did not *feel* like doing research in any of the disciplines related to anthropology. We think that we understand ourselves better as a result of living with the Semai.

We also feel that it left us changed people and that the change was for the better.

It is primarily this intensely personal impact of fieldwork that makes me regret not having kept a diary in the field. The long letters that Ruth and I wrote to our families are poor substitutes for a diary. As an anthropologist, I probably would have understood the Semai better and sooner if I had forced myself to analyze my responses to them on a daily basis. More importantly (to me), as a human being, I think that keeping a diary would have helped me

East Semai woman winnowing rice.

understand the things that were happening to and within me. My regret about this omission is deepened by reading Malinowski's diary. He attempts to deal consciously with the torment of trying to communicate with people of a wholly alien background. As one of the remarkably few perceptive reviews of his diary (Gallagher 1967:26) concludes, without this sort of torment one's results "are more than just possibly liable to be piffle."

This confession of one of my errors leads to the second point I want to make. I went into the field as a tyro. Mulling over the data Ruth and I collected, I recognize that we made mistakes, both of omission and commission. Although space does not permit my "confessions of ignorance and failure" to be as extensive as Malinowski's (1935 I:452–482), I mention some of these mistakes later on. I do so not out of masochism, but because ethnographers sometimes omit such a list of errors, thus inadvertently giving the unwary reader the impressions that their accounts are definitive, the results of perfect techniques perfectly applied.

I am a firm believer in the British pattern of fieldwork, in which one goes into the field, collects one's data, goes home to examine and think about these data, and then returns to the field with a clear knowledge of one's earlier mistakes and a resolve not to repeat them. In this sense, I am currently only halfway through studying the Semai. I really must go back.

In another sense, however, I have barely begun. Anthropologists often find themselves referring to a people among whom they have lived as "my people." To a large extent, the phrase is merely a sign of affection for the people who came to accept and like one, an affection made deeper by the initial experience of culture shock. For a few anthropologists, however, "my people" carries an ugly connotation of personal ownership. I think wanting to reserve for oneself all research on a given people stems from a fear that one's own observations or interpretations may be in error. Fortunately, most anthropologists, including myself, feel that a restudy of "their" people is vital precisely to uncover such errors, as well as to provide new data. Since coming back to the United States, Ruth and I have not only encouraged people who want to study the Semai but also have tried to recruit people to do such studies. I try to keep in fairly close touch with people who are working with Semai, so that I can learn more about the Semai and so that the people in the field can get from me information that I have not yet published. It seems to me that such activities are such a logical extension of our fieldwork that they might be called "fieldwork from afar" or "fieldwork by proxy."

Entering the Field

SELECTING A PEOPLE

The problem we set out to investigate was why people the world over fail to make continuous use of foods potentially available to them. Everywhere that I know of, people subject themselves to food taboos or regard some things as unfit for human consumption. Since we intended to do a statistical analysis of variations in these food avoidances, we need to find a people who had a wide assortment of potential foods from which to choose. This consideration suggested that the people should live in tropical rain forest, because that environment usually embraces a wide variety of plants and animals. For the same reason, we decided to live in two communities in order to find out what variations there might be in food avoidances between two settlements that had a common cultural background. Finally, we wanted to study a relatively isolated people, since we felt that food avoidances might be responses to local ecology, and we hoped to avoid the problem of avoidances introduced from outside that ecology.

Originally, we settled on Indonesia as the place for our work, mainly because we had several Indonesian friends who were willing to help us gain entrée into the area. Unfortunately, during the year I was taking an intensive course in the Indonesian language, official relations between Indonesia and the United States deteriorated to the point that the Indonesian Embassy refused to issue us visas for more than three months' residence. One of the many unpleasant aspects of the present nightmarish world situation is that, while all the major world nations are deliberately or inadvertently committing cultural genocide on the ethnic minorities within their borders, anthropologists are often forbidden entrance to record these vanishing and unique styles of human living.

At any rate, we then decided to try to get into Malaya (now part of the Federation of Malaysia), since the national language there is very similar to Indonesian. We received visas with no trouble, and, when it became clear that we would have to extend our stay, the renewal of the visas took only a few minutes. It seems appropriate to say here that many anthropological grants set aside funds for "emoluments" (read: "bribes"). We received as much cooperation from Malayan officials at every level of government as anyone could ask. In the entire course of our research the only person to indicate in any way the slightest interest in an "emolument" was an American in New York City, which was also the only place anything was stolen from us.

The next step was to write a grant proposal, which we submitted to the Ford Foundation. After being awarded the grant, I went to the American Museum of Natural History and to Peabody Museum at Yale University, where I was given funds to collect artifacts. Later on, both of the first two institutions renewed our grants.

I then tried to get in touch with anthropologists who had worked with Malayan aborigines. At first, it seemed that most of them were dead. Luckily, one of the living ones, Rodney Needham, was passing through New York at the time. He agreed to meet with me. We drank beer and talked about the various problems of doing fieldwork in Malaysia, the kind of equipment needed, and so forth. He also kindly gave me a list of people in Malaya and Singapore who might be helpful to us. We wrote these people, explaining our project, giving our estimated time of arrival, and asking if we could talk with them. Their responses were, as we came to expect in Malaya, uniformly positive.

PARTICIPANT OBSERVATION AND THE EQUIPMENT PROBLEM

To explain our decision to follow Dr. Needham's advice and take along as little equipment as possible requires jumping ahead a little and explaining our decision to use a field technique called "participant observation," that is, to live as much like the local people as possible. There are two main reasons we wanted to use this technique. One was that we hoped to "learn by doing," even when "doing" meant making mistakes. For example, I do not think that I would ever have understood the economics of food distribution among the Semai if we had not participated so fully in the system that I twice got into hot water for breaking its usually unspoken rules. In one case, a close Semai friend of mine named Stump had loaded himself down with supplies from our limited stock. I told him that I would appreciate his waiting a week or so before taking any more. For the next couple of months he refused to look at me, speak to me, or enter our house, although he would come up on the porch and, with his eyes averted from me, talk to Ruth. I finally figured out that my offense was in overtly calculating the amount of food my friend took, thus hurting him deeply and completely fouling up part of a system of exchanges where values are never explicitly calculated. Similarly, I reflexively said "Thank you," but informants had told me that saying "good!" (*bɔr*) was the Semai equivalent of saying "Thank you," and I made a point of using the word. Finally, after one of these "Thank you's," a friend moistened his thumb and made the ritual "rubbing away" gesture the Semai use to erase evil. "What's the matter with you?" he asked. "Aren't we friends?" My error in this case involved both acting as if I did not expect him to give me things whenever he could and also seeming to feel obligated to him. In a sense, I was violating his personal integrity by implying that he was making the gift in order to get a response from me instead of out of a simple desire to give me something. My response was incompatible with the traditional Semai exchange system, but I only found that out by virtue of the blunders I made trying to participate in it.

The other reason we wanted to do participant observation was that we wanted to fade into the background, so that people (1) would feel free to behave in front of us the way they did when no outsiders were present and (2) would confide in us as freely as in anyone else. We were afraid that if people thought of us as "outsiders" they would tell us whatever they thought we wanted to hear and would conceal anything intimate or anything of which they thought we might disapprove. It turned out that both these tendencies were especially strong among the Semai. They distrust outsiders (*mai*) so much that they use a special slang to conceal what they are talking about in the presence of an outsider who is familiar enough with them to have picked up a smattering of their language. They feel that most outsiders regard them as stupid savages, and they play "stupid savage" for an outsider, thus at one fell swoop giving the visitor what they think he expects, amusing themselves and each other, and exploiting his stereotype of them in order to avoid cooperating with him.

Finally, we hoped that participant observation would prevent people's thinking of us as "recorders." People tend to get a little nervous when they think their actions or words are being recorded. For example, at first, when we tried to take pictures, people would rush into their houses to put on their best clothes—shoes, bras, long pants, and other garments almost never worn in the normal course of affairs. They would then arrange themselves into a grim, stiff group, glowering at the camera the way people do in late Victorian family photographs. After a while, as people got more familiar with us and the camera, they began (with some encouragement from us) to ham it up in front of the camera. When at last we had finally faded into the background, we were able to get unposed shots. The difficulties we had with photographs illustrate the problem we faced in deciding what equipment to bring into the field.

Every piece of field equipment that is "exotic" from the viewpoint of the local people sets one off as an outsider and makes manifest one's role as an observer and recorder. Even such a relatively unobtrusive thing as a small notebook can cause difficulties. One time, for instance, we were recording a ceremony in which a man was serving as the vehicle through which "spirits" could speak. We were strangers to most of the people in the settlement, although we had several friends there who explained that we were really just like Semai. The rest of the people were too polite to voice their suspicion of us directly, but it was quite clear that the "spirits" were expressing the feelings of the general community when they asked, "If the hearts of these two people are so good, why are they always writing in those little books?"

We therefore took into the field only what we thought to be absolutely necessary recording equipment: notebooks, file cards, ballpoint pens, a variety of forms and questionnaires, a 35 mm. still camera, a tape recorder, and a 16 mm. movie camera. In retrospect, I think we took too much. The tape recorder was fun for us and the Semai, when it was working. It was never working very long, however, because small creatures would get into it to eat the rubber parts, and the internal mechanisms were always getting jammed up by the bodies of the cockroaches, which tried to make the machine their home. It is possible to get "tropicalized" tape recorders that are less vulnerable than ours was, but such machines are very expensive and, perhaps because I am neither a linguist nor a musicologist, I do not feel that the tapes we brought back are of much ethnographic significance.

While the tape recorder was, when working, a harmless toy, the movie camera and its supporting equipment (tripod, light meter, special dehumidifying containers, lenses, film) rapidly became instruments of sheer horror. Although Ruth and I knew how to use these things, neither of us were very adept at it. Setting up the tripod, taking a light reading, focusing the camera, and then trying to get someone to do something "spontaneous" for the record turned out to be a sweaty, annoying, and time-consuming process. I think it might have been worthwhile, however, if the heat had not made the metal swell so that we were never sure whether the camera was going to run or not.

The final blow came one day when I got up at 3:00 in the morning to film the yearly crop-planting ceremony. (There are some things that even the most loyal wife will not do, whatever blandishments one employs.) A group of people had agreed to take me upstream to the fields in a canoe. Now, the canoe is not an aboriginal Semai artifact, and it became obvious that this particular canoe had not been put together very skillfully when, just after we got out of sight of the settlement, it began to sink. I could not help bail it out, because I felt I had to keep all the movie equipment dry, even though it meant letting my notebook get soaked. To safeguard the equipment, then, I sat with the camera held high in one hand, the light meter in the other, the tripod balanced precariously on my knees and the icy waters of the Telom River gradually rising over my groin up to my waist, at which point we decided to beach the canoe and dump out the water. The rest of the trip to the fields went in short spurts of frenetic paddling, bailing, and trying to find places to beach the canoe in order to get the water out of it. By the time we had inched our soggy way upstream to the fields, the sun was up, and the day was getting very hot, although the water remained icy.

We landed in a swamp, in front of a vast barrier of fallen tree trunks and thorny brush left over from clearing the fields. Normally the Semai get over this sort of obstacle by running along the trunks of the topmost trees. Normally I got over them by clutching the trunks with hands and knees and hunching myself along inchworm style to the accompaniment of merry Semai laughter. A fall can be a very serious matter in Malaya, since so many plants have poisonous spines or bristles that a basic rule in falling is not to try to grab hold of anything. Near a field, there is also the possibility of falling on a piece of split bamboo, the edges of which are razor sharp. In fact, Williams-Hunt, the only person to work extensively with the Semai before we did, died as the result of such a fall. By the time I had managed to extricate myself and the movie equipment from the canoe, however, there was only one person left within hailing range, and it was clear that I would have to carry most of the things myself. The man nearby agreed to take the tripod, and, clutching the tree trunks with one hand, the movie camera with the other, the still camera slung around my neck, and the light meter between my teeth (my pockets were still too wet to store it there), I hunched slowly along to the fields. By the time I got there, of course, the ceremony was over. I was dripping with sweat and feeling like the Ancient Mariner on a bad day. Nevertheless, I decided to film the planting itself. Getting the tripod set up on the glass-slick, wet, 45-degree slopes of the field under a blazing sun was rather hard, but eventually I managed it. I took a light reading on the meter, got the scene in focus, pushed the button to start the camera and was rewarded with a single click. The thing was not running. Trying to shield the film from the sun with my none too ample body, I opened the camera, checked the wheels to make sure the film was wound correctly, pushed the button, and got a gratifying whirr as the wheels spun around. I closed the camera case, took another light reading, got the lens refocused, pushed the button, and got another single click. I repeated the whole process another couple of times, and then my temper blew. I addressed several well-chosen phrases in English to the camera, went on to a general diatribe about taking movies in the field, and concluded with a series of totally unjustifiable remarks about the American Museum of Natural History, which had been generous enough to lend us the camera in the first place. Fortunately, none of the Semai could understand what I was saying. Since I had been unable to keep the notebook from being soaked on the trip, all I could do was shoot a few still photographs of the planting. Normally I would have stayed to help out, but I was too tired physically and emotionally to think of anything but going home to bed. I managed to get back afoot largely by composing mental letters to the American Museum. I arrived with what turned out to be the incipient stages of acute pneumonitis and a firm resolve to send the movie equipment back on the next boat to come upriver with our supplies. In short, while I think movies can be of immense ethnographic value, there are situations in which they are not worth the effort required.

The rest of the recording equipment, however, was well worth taking. The still photographs illustrate many aspects of Semai life that would be very hard to describe in words. We kept one set for our own reference and gave another to the American Museum of Natural History, where copies are available to anyone interested enough to write for them.

We also used several sets of forms, including a few we made up in the field. From the point of view of our theoretical interests, the most important was the one on plants and animals. Most of the material we gathered remains to be published, but the reader can get some idea of the sort of information we collected by looking at three minor articles of mine (Dentan 1967, 1968a, 1968e). For material culture, we followed the format used by Osgood (1940), although we were able to be somewhat more detailed, since Semai society is still functioning, whereas Osgood's Ingalik society was not. The data we collected in this way are on file at the American Museum of Natural History and, people there say, constitute one of the most extensive, if not the most extensive, documentations of any collections they have.

For information about household composition and relationships between households, vital to an understanding of social organization, we asked the standard anthropological questions (for which, see, for example, Appell 1969). We also worked out in the field a schedule for inventorying household possessions. Unfortunately, much of our data on household composition, genealogy, and life histories were lost when our canoe tipped over during a tricky portage over a fallen log on our last trip downstream from the first settlement. Before we moved into the second settlement, Ruth Lim of the Malayan Institute for Medical Research supplied us with a modified version of a World Health Organization form which is used by investigators all over the world (for this form, see Thomson 1960: 36–42). We found this a better research tool than the ones we had been using, since it applied not only to household composition and possessions but to economics, health, and nutrition as well. Although there are several reasons it might not have been as useful in the first settlement, I regret not having known about it before.

We also took along a copy of the *Outline of Cultural Materials* (Murdock *et al.* 1961). This book lists the sorts of information an ethnography should contain and spurred us to collect data we might otherwise have ignored. It is also divided into convenient numbered categories that we used to label the cards on which we typed up our field notes every evening. Using this system makes it much easier, after one gets home, to find specific data one has collected, although I confess that despite an elaborate set of cross references, I sometimes have had the maddening experience of being unable to dig out information that I know is in the files. The bitter irony of the loss of our household census and genealogy notebook was that we thought it so well organized that there was no need to type it up. We did not make this error in the second settlement.

Finally, Ruth worked out a questionnaire that got at the problem of the age at which children acquired specific skills. Again, it would have been advantageous to have used this questionnaire in the first settlement, but, as Ruth freely admits, she did not really get the hang of "scientific" fieldwork until we got to the second settlement.

There are three reasons we used all these forms, the administering of which was often boring to us, the Semai, or to everyone involved. The first is that we wanted to be as systematic as possible in collecting data, in order to avoid finding embarrassing gaps in our information when we returned. I have found, and been frustrated by, several such gaps in data we gathered in more haphazard ways. The second reason was that we wanted to do statistical analyses of the data we gathered this way, in order to see whether patterns emerged of which we, and perhaps the Semai themselves, were unaware. Finally, most of these forms are constructed in such a way that the information on them can readily be translated into code numbers and punched onto IBM cards for computer analysis. So far we have cards only for plants and animals, but eventually I hope to get as much of our information encoded this way as possible.

We decided to buy as much of our living equipment in Malaya as possible, in order to seem as little "exotic" as we could. We therefore were able to arrive with one trunk and a gargantuan shoulder bag in which we kept all our essential papers and the like and which Ruth had to lug around whenever we were in town. The only "exotic" living equipment we brought into the field comprised a mattress, a flashlight, a kerosene stove, medicines, a pressure lantern, and a water filter. Of these things, the most satisfactory was the ordinary, cotton-filled mattress we used in the first settlement. In a moment of misguided inspiration, I decided that we would use inflatable rubber mattresses in the second settlement. After about a week, both began to leak, so that going to bed required inflating the mattresses, flinging ourselves on them immediately, and trying to get to sleep before they went completely flat.

Although the medicines probably kept us alive, they were, like the shots we took before going into the field, less than absolutely effective. For instance, we took prophylactic doses of chloroquine to keep from getting malaria—a disease which, incidentally, could have been wiped out several years before if the World Health Organization had been able to muster the necessary funds. Thanks partly to the Vietnam war, however, chloroquine-resistant strains of malaria have evolved, and Ruth contracted so-called "benign" tertian malaria. Her sickness not only brought us out of the field for a while, but also, when she had a relapse in New York City, we had to spend several days convincing her doctor that a New Yorker could really have malaria. Similarly, my typhoid and paratyphoid shots proved so ineffective that I found myself standing out in the rain with a typhoid-induced temperature of 106° recording a version of the ceremony that I had missed the year before because of the movie camera fiasco and felt I could not afford to miss again.

Our possession of medicines also put us into a personal dilemma involving professional goals and ordinary human decency. On the one hand, we had the resources to cure or at least alleviate the suffering that some of the people around us, many of them our friends, were undergoing. On the other hand, we were not medically trained, and there was always a possibility that the people we gave medicine to might die anyway. Just by giving out medicines, we were running the risk of alienating the local Semai curers. In the case of a death, moreover, we feared that people might hold us responsible because we had given the patient an "exotic" medicine. That kind of community response would, of course, completely ruin our rapport with the Semai and thus destroy the possibility of doing good fieldwork.

Fortunately, Semai curers are usually willing to try out anything that might benefit their patients (compare Bolton 1968:818–819 for a description of the readiness of Semai curers to complement their own techniques and medicines with Western medicines). In the first settlement, I was able to work out a deal with a prominent curer, whereby he would use our medicines in addition to his own curative techniques. So successful was this arrangement that, when I once complimented him on his skill in curing, he felt the success of this cure was due to the combination of his skills with my medicines. In the second settlement, however, I stupidly forgot to make this kind of arrangement. When the child of a close friend of mine there became very sick, I panicked and urged my friend to take the baby to a Euro-American-style clinic that was fairly nearby. The local Semai curer was miffed, quite understandably, since from his point of view I was completely unqualified to intervene in the course of treatment he had already prescribed. He therefore forbade taking the baby to the clinic on the grounds that mixing medicines would make it yet more sick. The baby died, and then two more infants sickened and died of the same ailment, without my being able to do anything. Finally, the curer's own grandchild began to develop the same symptoms, and, feeling that his previously proven techniques were no longer effective, he came to me to talk about alternatives. We agreed to try the clinic, supplemented by his own curative methods. The child lived. The point is that, by my ethnocentric failing to treat as a professional a man who was, in his own terms, a professional, I am partly responsible for the death of three human beings.

Except for the flashlight, the rest of the "exotic" living equipment we brought into the field was superfluous. Ruth soon found it easier to cook on a Semai hearth than on the kerosene stove, which we gave away quite early. I was always afraid of the pressure lantern in our extremely inflammable bamboo and thatch house. For a while, I pumped it up in front of the house, attracting a large group of giggling Semai onlookers. After a few weeks, this procedure made me feel so ridiculous that I gave the lantern away too, and we used the usual Semai kerosene "candles."

Finally, we used the water filter for the same reason that we did not eat fresh vegetables and did both boil and chlorinate our water. That is, we did not want to get sick. Given that we did want to do participant observation and that, perhaps naively, we chose two very unhealthy areas to work in, the goal of staying healthy was unrealistic. We had to eat out with other people like everyone else, especially since we wanted to observe eating rituals and to collect the nutritional data that were subsequently analysed for us by the Institute for Medical Research. For all our contention that we were so susceptible to "water spirits" that we could only drink the tea we brought with us, boiled, it is impossible for the Semai to keep their hands so antiseptic that they do not transmit disease when they hand one food. Furthermore, both the areas we lived in were so hot that, simply to cool off, we had to go sit in the river several times a day. The rivers of Malaya carry a fantastic set of nasty microorganisms. So, despite the filter, I managed to get a bad case of infectious hepatitis, which again forced us out of the field. The only people in Malaya with enough gamma globulin to prevent Ruth's catching the disease from me were the Peace Corps. After a good deal of pleading and cajolery from lower-echelon members, their high command graciously granted Ruth half the amount she needed to keep from falling sick, with the result that her stay in the hospital was shorter than mine. In fairness to the Peace Corps, I must say that their medical personnel at Kuala Lipis, the town from which we got our supplies, were far nicer to us than they had to be, although we could not help being amused by the fact that the town they regarded as a wilderness outpost was the place we came to be cured and to taste the delights of civilization.

There was one other disease we acquired as a result of participant observation, for all our water filter and chlorine tablets. (I am omitting from this account sicknesses due to my weak lungs and those that did not interfere seriously with fieldwork, like jungle rot and ordinary dysentery.) Amebiasis is a worldwide affliction (Chandler and Read 1961: 62–63), which is very hard to cure and which most anthropologists catch in the field. I was lucky enough to be one of the three out of four "sufferers" who show few symptoms until their livers start rotting, but Ruth got not only amebic dysentery but also the appendicitis that sometimes results from this disease. The appendicitis developed on the Dutch freighter we were taking back to America. While freighters provide the cheapest and most luxurious mode of travel available, they carry no doctors, and we discovered that an appendectomy would have to be performed by a totally untrained officer, in the notoriously choppy Indian Ocean, on the basis of instructions radioed from Holland. We and the crew, with the exception of the fourth mate who was to perform the operation and was looking forward to it, found this prospect frightening. Ruth and I did not have enough funds to forfeit our passage money, however, and we all spent several tense hours before the shipping company's agent agreed to grant us passage on another vessel so that Ruth could have her appendectomy in a hospital ashore.

Under the circumstances, it is unsurprising that much as she prepares for sleep in America by reading a few chapters in a murder mystery, Ruth used to spend the hour before bed in the field reading the *Merck Manual of Diagnosis and Therapy* (Lyght 1956) to see what diseases we might have contracted that day, although her diagnoses were almost always wildly astray. It is also not surprising that she contends she would not have gone into the field if she had known the sort of physical and psychological traumas that would befall her. And, finally, I think it says something about the nature of our fieldwork that she also asserts that she wants to go back.

MEETING THE SEMAI

After arriving in Singapore, a city with which we immediately fell in love, we contacted Dr. Burkill of the Singapore Botanic Gardens, who generously agreed to lend us plant presses and the services of a trained Malay plant collector so that we could get the plants the local people used identified and preserved. We spent the next couple of weeks visiting various groups of Malayan aborigines, with the guidance of Dr. Ivan Polunin of the University of Singapore; Dr. I. Y. Carey, head of the Department of Aborigines; Inche' Ruslan, then Protector of Aborigines in the State of Johore; and Inche' Badrillah, Protector of Aborigines in the State of Pahang. Most of the groups we visited seemed very acculturated. We were tempted to work with the Jah Hut, because of their warm hospitality and stated desire to have their way of life recorded. We did visit the Jah Hut when we were in Pahang recuperating from one of the diseases that occasionally brought us out of the field. We collected some ethnographic data and a few artifacts for the American Museum of Natural History. Nevertheless, when we left the Jah Hut for the last time, one man said accurately, though in a kind way, "You will come back. You have the skin of our way of life, but you do not have the meat."

Finally, Inche' Badrillah arranged for us to go up the Telom River to visit a relatively unacculturated group, the Semai. For the first time we had a close look at virgin tropical rain forest. Like an Arctic landscape, the forest has a beauty that is utterly inhuman. But, whereas the Arctic's inhumanity lies in the near absence of life, the forest's is due to the lush abundance of all sorts of life, each of which seems to be competing with all the rest for limited resources of sun, food, and survival. I was to come to feel that the primal forest was the "real world" in a way that tamed landscapes could never be. Wallace Stevens comes close to describing this sort of feeling in a poem called *Arrival at the Waldorf,* when he describes how, after seeing a Guatemalan rain forest, he finds life in New York both more human and more superficial, "After that alien, point-blank, green and actual Guatemala." [1] Probably my love-hate feeling about the forest was intensified by the fact that I came down with a severe bronchial disease after each of three day-long trips through it.

There were two reasons for picking the particular settlement of Semai we eventually chose, although it was in some ways atypical. First, it was right on the banks of the river, only a couple of hours' raft trip from a "jungle fort," a government outpost with a radio that we could use to summon help in an emergency. The feeling of security this gave us turned out to be somewhat illusory, since, like most mechanical equipment in a tropical rain forest, the radio was not always in working condition and since, when we did get through to Kuala Lipis, that town's limited number of motor canoes were usually out up some river other than the Telom. The result was that, when we fell seriously sick, we often had to wait about a week, gobbling antibiotics and trying to do ethnography, before the canoe came to take us to the hospital. The second reason for picking this settlement was that it was relatively large and just across the river from another settlement. This situation allowed us to observe and talk with a fair-sized number of people, thus lessening the chance that the information we collected would reflect the bias of individuals or small groups rather than general Semai opinion.

Inche' Ahmat, the government official who came with us, explained to the Semai that we wanted to live for a while in their settlement. He also tried, and failed, to explain what we were trying to do. After we had moved in, I also tried many times to explain what we were up to: "We're trying to write a book about your way of life so that people in America and your own children and grandchildren will know how you lived." For people most of whom had never seen a book, none of whom was literate, none of whom had ever heard of America (to the end, they were convinced we were British), and none of whom could see any reason for outsiders to be interested in how they lived, this explanation was not merely incomprehensible but also obviously some sort of cover story. I finally settled on: "We're writing a report for the government about

---

[1] From *Collected Poems of Wallace Stevens.* Copyright 1942 by Wallace Stevens. By permission of Alfred A. Knopf, Inc.

what you eat, to see if you have enough food." The second explanation was accepted, but it led to the tacit inference that we were government officials living on government supplies. When, after about six months, I caught on to this assumption and explained that we had to buy our supplies with our own money, people were quite surprised and moderated their demands for food and tobacco.

At any rate, Inche' Ahmat and the people picked out a small "deserted" house in which we could live. We promised to be back in a few days, after getting our supplies. The owner of the house returned a few months later but, despite our offers to move out, he went next door to live with some relatives. Fortunately, the Semai feel that there is a special affinity between people who have slept in the same sleeping place and thus breathed the fragrance of each other's bodies. The result of this feeling was that the owner and I quickly became good friends.

We made two major mistakes in this process of choosing and gaining entrée into this settlement. We avoided them when we went to the second settlement. First we picked the second settlement in an area where medical assistance was relatively easy to get. On the other hand, we also ignorantly picked the hottest and most humid area in hot, humid Malaya. Second, instead of having Malays bring us in, Dr. Bolton, the devoted head of the medical branch of the Department of Aborigines, kindly asked some of his Semai medical aides to introduce us to a settlement where they had relatives. At the first settlement, we did not initially realize the intensity of the suspicion the Semai feel toward Malays. Although both Inche' Ahmat and our plant collector were consistently polite and friendly to the Semai, their very presence with us made us suspicious characters. After a couple of weeks I realized this association was making rapport difficult. I had to send the Malay plant collector downstream and train a Semai one.

In the second settlement, we had the same pleasant experience with a "deserted" house that we had in the first. My pat "government report on food" explanation, however, fell flat. The man who was to become our adoptive father said that such a report might be useful. Nevertheless, he went on, what he would really like to see was a book about the Semai way of life, so that Americans and his own people's children and grandchildren would know how the Semai lived.

Living in the First Settlement ("East Semai")

THE FIRST DAY

When we returned with our supplies to the first settlement, we found that the people had added a porch to our house. They had also taken a hibiscus shrub from the jungle fort and planted it in front of the house, because, when they were interned during the communist uprising of the early 1950s, they had

The men have just finished covering a grave with banana leaves and are starting to build a shelter over it.

A seven-year-old East Semai girl with a cigar.

East Semai boy playing nose flute.

noticed that "pale people" camp commandants seemed to like flowers growing around their houses.

Although people were wary of me at first, their wariness was based on the fact that I was at least partially a known quantity: a "pale person," a *Tuan* (a respectful Malay title used for Englishmen), presumably somewhat like the British officers they had encountered during the communist insurgency. Most people in the first settlement called me Tuan throughout our stay, although a few good friends gave me affectionate or joking nicknames. Ruth, however, was another matter. No one I talked to about the matter had ever seen a female "pale person" before. A few people addressed her, hesitantly, as Tuan, but they seemed to feel, correctly, that the term did not properly apply to a woman. Ruth finally broke the ice by announcing in her faltering Malay that she wanted to learn to live like a Semai woman. A swarm of giggling and chattering women immediately gathered around her, swept her up the ladder into our house, stripped her naked, wrapped her in a sarong, stuck flowers into her hair, painted her face, put a machete into her hand, and took her off to collect firewood. She quickly became *Ua' Roi. Ua'* is the term for a young woman (compare our "Miss"), and *Roi*, the closest the Semai could come to pronouncing "Ruth," means "housefly."

Another large group of people were examining me, much as if I were a particularly bizarre museum specimen. Only four people did much talking to me. The titular headman, who was acting in his official capacity as group spokesman, was an old, cynical, shrewd, and manipulative man, at the time of our arrival primarily interested in what benefits our stay might bring him personally. He was a Semai-ized Temiar, and my impression is that the Temiar, at least in that settlement, are less timid and more greedy than the Semai. I never got to know him very well, partly because he became tired of living on the Telom and went back to the Jelai river basin, where he felt he belonged. Another Semai-ized Temiar, Rambutan, a grey-haired elderly man from across the river, was also friendly to me, but his remarks indicated that he also, albeit in a subtle way, was mainly interested in what he could get out of us. He later became one of my main informants but so delighted in putting me on that I feel I can rely on his information only when I have corroborative data from other sources. I doubt, for example, that he ever saw the baby dragons (*naga'*) whose habits he detailed from his "personal observations." Ours was to be a purely working relationship, modified by a little mutual kidding. The third man to do much talking was a prematurely balding local curer named, appropriately, Uproar. He was far more overtly opportunistic than the two Temiar. We later came to know and like each other well, and he was one of my best and most articulate informants. Our relationship remained on a joking level, however, and there was never any question that in his interaction with me, as in his dealings with other Semai, the thought uppermost in Uproar's mind was usually "What's in it for me?" I was later to develop a much warmer relationship with his much shyer and less-well-informed younger brother, a man about my age and almost as neurotic and intense as I am. The only other person to do much conversing was Stump, a sturdy man in his thirties, with a hot temper, a difficult personal characteristic for a Semai to live with. He and his wife, a woman who always wanted to gossip about sex with Ruth, became our best friends in the settlement. When Stump and Rambutan became involved in a dispute about whether Rambutan was responsible for the haunting of Stump's house by the ghosts of people Rambutan had buried, Stump moved out of the settlement, and Ruth and I used to trek the half hour or so upstream to Stump's new house just to chat, about once a week. (Of course, as I pointed out above, anthropologists rarely just chat. There is always in each chat information to be recorded.)

On the first day, naturally, no one emerged as a personality. We felt in a sea of undifferentiated, small, honey-colored people, who would sometimes help us by carrying and arranging things, sometimes hinder us by their sheer numbers as they packed into our tiny house. The crowd with me blended with the crowd that followed Ruth when she emerged, exhausted, hands covered with blisters, from the forest. No one left the house when Ruth suggested that she wanted to lie down and take a nap. There were still masses of bodies in the house when we wanted to cook supper. We knew we could not feed them all, we did not know that the Semai do not think it imperative to feed guests when one does not have enough food, and so we settled down grimly to outwait them before cooking. By 11 P.M. most of the people had gone home. Ruth prepared a meal for us, and the remaining half-dozen visitors ate gustily while making disparaging remarks about the caliber of Ruth's cooking. After they left, we collapsed into bed, only to notice that inside our mosquito net were small, moving streaks of light. A check with the flashlight revealed that the lights were luminous centipedes. Ruth insisted on a thorough check of bed and mosquito net, an exploration that uncovered a variety of small, unpleasant fauna. By the time we got to sleep that first night, we were well into culture shock and resolved to check the bed nightly.

Problems in Doing Fieldwork

PRIVACY

My purpose in sketching some of the personalities and relationships that eventually emerged from the undifferentiated mass of humanity we met the first day is to introduce two problems we encountered in the field: (1) the difficulty of getting any privacy without disrupting the good relationships upon which our anthropological work and emotional well being depended, and (2) the disruptive effect of having outsiders come to visit us. The notion of privacy is rather alien to the Semai, except insofar as people of opposite sexes are not supposed to spy in order to see each other's naked genitals. For us to tell a man with whom we had a good relationship that we did not want to see him at a certain time, simply because we wanted to be alone, would have been a gross, incomprehensible insult. He would have been put in a state of ritual danger, and, if he did not feel that we had terminated our relationship with him, he would almost certainly have broken it off himself. On the other hand, as bourgeois Americans, we were used to houses with thick-walled rooms that insulate an individual or couple from others, so that the inhabitants can be alone to think, read, write, or perform "intimate" biological activities. We found it inhibiting, for example, when trying to indulge in a little connubial bliss in our creaky house, when Uproar, our next door neighbor, would shout jokingly, "Hey, what are you two doing in there?"

Similarly, I found it hard to adapt to the fact that going to the river to defecate meant answering cries of "Where are you going?" The evasive answer, "To the river," merely led people to ask, "Why are you going to the river?" A mumbled "To defecate" brought a reply of either "Have a good defecation" or, sometimes, if the speaker was a man, "Hang on, I'll come with you." To reject his proffered companionship would have risked ruining our relationship.

Sometimes I could sneak off, but, since Semai women tend to be even more gregarious than the men, Ruth almost always had a few companions. As she once remarked, "We squat there in a row in the water, with our sarongs up, like a bunch of ducks." The day Ruth discovered the value of this gregariousness came when she managed to slip off alone and found on her way back a tiger between herself and the settlement. She ran upstream, tried to find another path to the settlement, lost the path, and at last decided that, if she had to die, she wanted to die in the water. On her return, fortunately, the tiger had gone, leaving only a few paw marks in the sand. After that, she preferred having the women accompany her.

Although gregariousness did have its advantages, and although our thirst for privacy was in part just a bit of "pale people" ethnocentrism that we had to cast off in order to live with Semai, nevertheless the lack of privacy impeded our fieldwork in two ways. First, we were working from 5 or 6 A.M. to 11 or 12 P.M. every day at jobs that were often intellectually, emotionally, and/or physically exhausting. We needed an occasional break just to keep going. After about a month, we hit on the idea of a weekly "taboo day," on which we were "ritually unable" to do much socializing unless something unusual happened or visitors came from another settlement. The Semai, knowing of the Malay sabbath, could understand this sort of ritual restriction. Although we were never able to have a completely uninterrupted "taboo day," we were able to get in a little reading, sleeping, and letter-writing.

The other difficulty with having a house full of people all the time was that the constant chatter tended to distract informants, especially if they found the topic under discussion complicated or boring. Since most of the adults spent at least part of the day working, children were the main problem. My solution was to give each child a pen and some file cards, asking him to draw pictures of people, houses, and trees. When the child was leaving, I collected the drawings; noted the artist's name, sex, and age; and later filed the pictures. Drawings of this kind correspond with the sort of material elicited by a certain psychological test. I distrust the reliability of such tests, especially when used cross-culturally and in this sort of haphazard way. Nevertheless, it is interesting that (1) the drawings are very much like those made by Black American children, presumably because both groups feel outside the dominant culture and (2) two psychiatrists, neither of whom had any previous knowledge of the Semai, independently induced from these drawings an idea of Semai personality that tends strongly to confirm my own ideas.

I regret not also having had both children and adults draw pictures of food organisms, since such drawings might have revealed what features of the organism they found most striking. These features in turn might have served as useful clues as to how the Semai classify organisms and why certain rituals focus on certain organisms. One reason this omission is so frustrating is that I failed to take advantage of several other chances to discover such distinguishing features. For instance, I could not get specimens of all the things the Semai eat. Hence I could not rely entirely on the good offices of the Singapore Botanic Gardens or the Zoology Department at the then University of Malaya for identifications. I therefore tried to get informants to give the Semai words for some organisms of which I had drawings or pictures. Although I tried to check this information by also getting the Malay name, usually the Semai did not know the Malay word. In most cases, informants also disagreed about the Semai name for the organism depicted. The intelligent thing would have been to take a group of Semai to the Singapore Botanic Gardens and to the zoological collection at the University of Malaya.

If I had not been so obsessed with identifying the organisms, however, I would have realized that there were at least three research possibilities opened up by this difficulty in getting Semai names for the organisms in the pictures. First, there may be real disagreements about the names for plants and animals of certain kinds. Unquestionably, people in different settlements often do use different terms for the same species (Dentan 1967b), a fact that may have something to do with Semai ecology and social structure (Gardner 1966). Some of the apparent Semai confusion, however, may have really been mine. Different people may have been giving me words that referred to categories of different levels of generality, as an American might call a certain animal a "dog" or a "spaniel" (Frake 1961). Although what I do know about Semai taxonomy makes me think this possibility unlikely in most cases, not investigating it was a mistake. The most interesting possibility, however, in terms of finding out what features of the organism the Semai find striking, is that different people responded to different features of the picture. All I had to ask was "What makes you think this is a picture of that?" None of these ideas occurred to me in the field.

VISITORS

Given the Semai attitude toward outsiders, non-Semai visitors posed a threat to our relationships with Semai. In both settlements we had to be somewhat standoffish toward Malays who came to meet us. The Semai helped us maintain this rather ungracious attitude by, for example, whispering in Semai slang, "Don't take the cigarette that Malay's offering you. It's probably poisoned." Since most of the "pale people" who came to visit us were those too insensitive to pick up our obvious reluctance to have visitors who as "pale people" were so clearly identified with us, we used to have to spend much of the time they were around explaining to the Semai why they acted so rudely. For us, although the incident did not disrupt our relationship with any Semai, the most upsetting visit was that of a buxom, young, female "pale person" about 5 feet 10 inches tall. We decided, rather maliciously, to maximize her exposure to the Semai by getting her a sleeping compartment in a longhouse. Unluckily, the compartment she got was that of Bah Chong, an adolescent boy about whom we felt very fond and protective, partly because he was an orphan and no woman in the settlement would sleep with him, since he was short (4 feet 6 inches), very dark skinned, and had a goiter so large that it tilted his sensitive face slightly to one side. I was unaware, at that time, of the Semai equation between sleeping place, body fragrance, and personal affinity. The upshot was that, while the other men in the settlement were making snide comments like, "Wah, she's big! *Ua' Roi* (Ruth) is fine, but this one's too much," Chong fell deeply in love with our visitor. For the rest of our stay, Chong was always talking about her, dreaming of her, and coming to our house to sleep because he could not face the day without her. She, of course, had gone off after a week with no idea of the emotional disaster she had created. My own feeling is that I will never visit any anthropologist in the field, and I hope that no one will visit me.

SOME PROBLEMS THAT DID NOT ARISE

One factor that we had feared might disrupt our relationships with the community was the fact that, to get the exhaustive data on food and ritual we wanted, we knew that we would have to disrupt the local economy and perhaps seem to be playing favorites. For example, we wanted to observe what people ate, since direct observation is more reliable than the "recall method" used in the WHO form.[2] In order not to bias our data, we could neither give nor accept

---

[2] In such tests informants are asked to recall what they had eaten over a given period of time.

food from members of the household under observation. Since one way the Semai demonstrate mutual good will is by exchanging food, we feared we might lose rapport with the people we were observing. Perhaps because we picked people with whom we already had good relationships and because we promised a bonus of food at the end of the two-week observational period, the people we worked with cooperated without losing any rapport.

A similar but potentially more serious problem was posed by the fact that we had to pay some people to do boring things like collecting specimens, making artifacts, and answering repetitive form questions about the specimens and artifacts. Fortunately, the Semai were as worried about their personal relationships as we were about ours. In both communities, our paid informants asked that we keep the fact that we were paying them a secret. We were delighted to do so, since knowledge of such payment again might have made people think we were playing favorites. I think most people in both settlements suspected that we were paying certain informants. The reason for this suspicion was not only that informants spent a lot more time with us and did more things for us than other people did, but also that the informants themselves were so caught up in the traditional economy that they eventually gave away many of the things we secretly bought for them out of their wages. The habit of giving was too hard to break. Nevertheless, almost everyone was willing to turn a blind eye to such facts, presumably because they did not want to upset their relationships with the paid informants and with us.

A PROBLEM THAT TURNED OUT TO BE HELPFUL

The list of personal and methodological difficulties we met could be indefinitely expanded. Given our positive feelings about our field experience, however, it seems fitting to conclude this section by describing an apparent problem that eventually helped us understand our data better. For each food the Semai ate I tried to find out, among other things, whether people should eat it during pregnancy, just after having a child, while menstruating, before reaching a certain age, and so forth. I also tried to find out why people thought they should refrain from eating these foods. Uproar, our first paid informant, gave what seemed to be dogmatic and unequivocal answers to these questions. Casual chatting with other people, however, revealed that, although they largely agreed with Uproar about which foods should be avoided at what times, they gave entirely different reasons for the avoidances. I then systematically spot-checked with other Semai about one in every dozen of the 500 odd foods Uproar and I had listed. I found the same pattern of fairly good agreement about the avoidances and the same disagreement about reasons. I used a wide variety of informants and did not say that I was trying to check up on Uproar's reliability, lest personal factors influence people's answers.

The results of this spot-check disturbed me, because I thought Uproar and I were good enough friends that he would not consistently mislead me. There was also a methodological problem. Most Semai dislike openly disagreeing with each other or being caught out in inconsistencies. I therefore could not confront Uproar directly with explanations that ran counter to his own. If the dissenter were absent, I knew Uproar would say, as he had about disagreements in the past, "Oh, him. He's a liar." If the dissenter were present, I would run the risk of precipitating a quarrel, which would make life in the settlement harder for everyone, including Ruth and myself. And I had already had the experience, when I asked someone to repeat information that he knew I had written down, of being told "Read back to me what I said, and I'll tell you whether you've got it right," with the clear implication that the informant was not about to risk contradicting what he had already said. How, then, was I to determine Uproar's reliability?

I eventually decided to rely on the sheer bulk of the material. Uproar could not be expected to remember whether he had already answered questions about a minor food item on the list. I therefore acted as if every new specimen someone brought us was one we had never discussed, whether or not we had. Uproar's answers were fairly consistent about the avoidances but totally inconsistent about the rationales. I next went over the entire list with Rambutan and then with Uproar's younger brother. Again, I found that they tended to agree with Uproar about the avoidances but disagreed with Uproar, other informants, each other, and (under the "forgetfulness test") themselves about why one should avoid a certain food at certain times. The crowning touch came when, eating with Uproar's younger brother, I noticed his pregnant wife eating rat, which he had just told me pregnant women should not eat. To my question, he replied, "That's right, I keep asking her not to, but she just doesn't care." Further investigation revealed that many people who had never had any problems during, say, pregnancy, tended to eat the foods they were supposed to avoid.

The point I want to make is that the very inconsistency of these facts is informative. First, it suggests that explanations for these food rituals may rest on idiosyncratic personal experience. I was able to find several cases in which specific individuals avoided certain foods on certain occasions because they had had something bad happen to them after eating those foods on a similar occasion. The personalism of these explanations fits in neatly with the apparently personalistic inconsistencies in naming animals. Second, people's responses indicated that they followed the rituals only when they felt in danger. In other words, the greater the anxiety, the greater the likelihood that the ritual will be performed—a point long debated in anthropology. Finally, the inconsistency of the rationales for the rituals suggest that the ritual is the important and prior thing, the explanation merely a subsequent rationalization of the ritual. If the Semai had codified these explanations, I might have been deluded into thinking that the explanations were supernatural sanctions for avoiding foods. Again, although the idea that ritual precedes belief is an old one (dating back at least to 1889; Robertson Smith 1956:21), anthropologists still argue about it. In short, the very incoherence of the Semai data, which really bothered me in the field, actually sheds some light on current anthropological interests.

Living in the Second Settlement ("West Semai")

INTRODUCTION

There are three reasons this section is shorter than the one on the first settlement. (1) We were faced with far fewer problems of adaptation to the people. We spoke Semai, albeit with an odd East Semai-American accent. We knew how to act Semai. Conversely, the Semai in the second settlement were more used to the oddities of "pale people," and because we had been introduced by Semai, they were more willing to accept us. (2) Logistically, we were much better off. For example, in the first settlement, our supplies came upriver once a month. For a while each month, therefore, we seemed to the people, who got their own food in small daily amounts, to be selfishly hoarding a huge surplus. In the west we could buy our food in small daily amounts at the local market, as many of the Semai themselves did. Moreover, since the traditional exchange system was breaking down, people made fewer demands on our supplies. Another advantage was that travel was so much easier that we could visit distant settlements where Semai friends had relatives. Such visits provided us with interesting comparative data. Finally, we were physically much more comfortable. (3) Most of the personal and methodological problems we faced were so much like those we faced in the east that we were able to counter them with solutions we had already worked out.

PERSONAL RELATIONSHIPS

Because mutual adaptation was easier, we were able to form personal relationships much more quickly than in the east. In general these relationships were much warmer and less beset by mutual misunderstanding. I still correspond occasionally with my adoptive father and with Daylight, my principle informant and a real intellectual. (An anthropologist currently at work in the same settlement writes that Daylight is so reliable that he tends to take Daylight's word over the statements of people actually involved in an incident.) I had hoped to dig out these letters for information, but they almost all follow this form:

No news here, only good news. Send a photograph of yourselves and your house. We miss you. When are you coming back? We wish you the best of everything.

Sometimes the writer will mention a death or a marriage, and once Daylight asked me to help finance his niece's wedding feast. Most of the time, however, our Semai correspondents seem to feel that letters are to transmit not information but affection.

One sign of the ease with which we slipped into the new community was the names people gave us. Names, for rather complex reasons, are very important to the Semai. I never had to fight the *Tuan* role but was at once *Bah Rab*. When people found out that we were both first-born children, they began sometimes calling us *Long*, that is, "first Born," with none of the East Semai hesitancy. People would also occasionally call Ruth "sterile," a nonpejorative name for a childless married woman who has been of child-bearing age for several years. Finally, when our father adopted us, I became *Bah* "obtain," since, he said, information flowed to me, "like rivers into the ocean, which is deep but never filled." Ruth became *Ua'* "success," because, "whatever she tries to do, she will succeed." Furthermore, as this instance indicates, we never had to prod the West Semai into forming fictive kin relationships with us, as we had had to prod the East Semai.

In short, although our stay in the east was more adventurous and exciting, our stay in the west was easier and more personally satisfying, with the result that our work went more smoothly and productively.

Conclusion

After leaving the second Semai settlement, we spent a month in Kuala Lumpur, the delightful capital of Malaya. With the gracious permission of the Department of Aborigines, we examined census records for all Semailand in order to find out the age and sex distribution of the population, household size, the times at which fields were cleared in various areas, the acreages cleared by specific bands, and so forth. I began writing up our data on the way back to America. Nevertheless, I do not feel that we have enough material on these complex and diverse people for me to be ready to write a full-scale ethnography. For this reason alone, I want to go back. But as should be clear by now, I also want to go back because I feel for the Semai and their country the bittersweet blend of nostalgia and homesickness that the Semai call *rəniag*.

References

Appell, G. N., 1969, Social anthropological census for cognatic societies and its application among the Rungus of northern Borneo. *Bijdragen tot de taal-, Land- en Volkenkunde* 125:80–93.

Bolton, J. M., 1968, Medical services to the aborigines in West Malaysia. *British Medical Journal* 2:818–823.

Chandler, A. C., and *C. P. Read*, 1961, *Introduction to Parasitology*. 10th ed. New York: John Wiley.

Dentan, R. K., 1964, Senoi. In F. M. Lebar, G. C. Hickey, and J. K. Musgreave, eds., *Ethnic Groups of Mainland Southeast Asia*. New Haven, Conn.: Human Relations Area Files.

————, 1967a, The response to intellectual impairment among the Semai. *American Journal of Mental Deficiency* 71:764–766.

————, 1967b, The mammalian taxonomy of the Senoi Semai. *Malayan Nature Journal* 20:100–106.

————, 1968a, Notes on Semai ethnoentomology. *Malayan Nature Journal* 21:17–28.

————, 1968b, *The Semai.* New York: Holt, Rinehart and Winston, Inc.

————, 1968c, The Semai response to mental aberration. *Bijdragen tot de Taal-, Land- en Volkenkunde* 124:135–58.

————, 1968d, Some problems in determining the conservation needs of the hill peoples of South East Asia. In *Conservation in Tropical South East Asia.* International Union for Conservation of Nature and Natural Resources n.s. Publication No. 10:89–92.

————, 1968e, Notes on Semai ethnomalacology. *Malacolgia.*

————, 1969, Prey size and food avoidance among the Semai. Paper read at the American Association for the Advancement of Science meetings, December 27 (mimeograph).

————, in press, Labels and rituals in Semai classification, *Ethnology* 9.

————, in press, Notes on Semai kinship terminology, *American Anthropologist* 72.

Frake, C. O., 1961, The diagnosis of disease among the Subanun of Mindanao, *American Anthropologist* 63:113–132.

Gallagher, P., 1967, Games Malinowski played. *The New Republic* 156 (24): 24–26.

Gardner, P., 1967, Symmetric respect and memorate knowledge: The structure and ecology of individualistic culture. *Southwestern Journal of Anthropology* 22:389–415.

Lyght, E., Ed., 1956, *The Merck Manual of Diagnosis and Therapy.* 9th ed. Rahway, N. J.: Merck and Co.

Malinowski, B., 1935, *Coral Gardens and Their Magic.* Bloomington: Indiana University Press.

————, 1967, *A Diary in the Strict Sense of the Term.* New York: Harcourt, Brace and World.

Murdock, G. P., et. al., 1961, *Outline of Cultural Materials.* New Haven, Conn.: Human Relations Area Files.

Osgood, C., 1940, *Ingalik Material Culture.* New Haven, Conn.: Yale University Publications in Anthropology No. 22.

Robertson Smith, W., 1956, *The Religion of the Semites.* New York: Meridian. Originally published in 1889.

Thomson, F. A., 1960, Child nutrition. A survey in the Parit District of Perak Federation of Malaya. Bulletin No. 10 from the Institute for Medical Research, Federation of Malaya.

5

FIELDWORK IN
A COMPLEX SOCIETY:
TAIWAN

NORMA DIAMOND
University of Michigan

Related Case Study: **K'un Shen: A Taiwan Village**

The processes and difficulties of interviewing and observing, the use of written records, the adaptation of a value orientation questionnaire and of projective tests, and the recording of field data are all discussed in Norma Diamond's chapter. But the central theme is her role adjustment in the village society, influenced as it was by the fact that she was a young woman, a female student, and a "modern youth." Her role definition was further complicated by the American presence in Taiwan and the large missionary contingent resettled from mainland China, as well as her status by Taiwanese standards as a rich American in a poor village. For some of the people of K'un Shen the alternatives for identification offered by these factors were reasons for suspicion. For other villagers they were reasons for expecting aid in obtaining funds and other forms of economic betterment. For still others the discrepancy between the villagers' image of America as an ideal democracy and the actual position of the United States Government in Taiwan affairs influenced the relationship with the anthropologist as a presumed representative of American society. What to do with a stranger in their midst who was in some way influenced by these various possible identifications became the problem of the people of K'un Shen. Norma Diamond's handling of the problems of relationship to the villagers in the light of these possible reference points for her activities in the minds of the people is instructive, for analagous circumstances are encountered by most fieldworkers.

The Author

Norma Diamond writes:

I grew up in the suburbs of New York, the only child of a middleclass professional family. Both of my parents had emigrated from Eastern Europe, my mother as a very young child together with her family, and my father as a young man. Still, it was a fairly Americanized household.

I attended the local public school and then Richmond Hill High School with an uneven and undistinguished academic record that made my parents despair of ever getting me into college. However, I read widely and omnivorously outside of class (and under the desk during class), and apparently learned enough to be admitted to Queens College on the basis of a placement test. There I

Norma Diamond on the porch of the Episcopalian Mission in K'un Shen.

metamorphized into a serious student, and after two years transferred to the University of Wisconsin. By then, I was committed to a career in anthropology, having run through several other interests including English literature, journalism, psychology, and social work. I stayed on at Wisconsin for a year and a half of graduate work in anthropology, supported by tuition scholarships, a teaching assistantship, and a stint at the local museum cataloging materials and helping excavate archeological sites.

In 1956 I moved to Cornell University to do work toward a Ph.D. I was drawn there not only by their anthropology program but also by their Far Eastern Studies Department and the opportunities for doing work on contemporary and traditional China. In 1959, I was awarded a language fellowship to Taiwan, and immediately after that a Ford Foreign Area Training Fellowship for fieldwork there. On my return in 1962, I spent a final year at Cornell, and then was appointed as assistant professor at the University of Michigan where I am currently working. In 1969–1970, I am returning to Taiwan for further research, this time focusing on problems of modernization.

G. D. S.

Introduction

This chapter deals with my first fieldwork experience, a project carried out in Taiwan, Republic of China between September 1960 and February 1962. For most of that time, I lived in a fishing village on the west coast of the island. The research was undertaken as part of my work for a doctoral degree at Cornell University. Funds for it came from the Ford Foundation Foreign Areas Fellowship Program.

The research had two main goals in view. I hoped, first, to get material for a general ethnography of a Chinese fishing village, a community different in type from those already described in the existing literature on republican and communist China. Secondly, I hoped to gather more detailed information on folk religion, ideology, and values of the peasantry. This second concern was sparked in part by intellectual curiosity for that topic in and of itself, and in part by practical concerns. A better understanding of peasant values and beliefs might well prove useful in planning for development and change in Taiwan, or for thinking about modernization in general. I did meet these goals to a large extent and also found myself doing various things I had not thought of before getting out into the field, but this is not to say that I was completely satisfied with my work.

A year and a half was not really long enough to prepare myself and complete a comprehensive field study. When I left Taiwan, I still had the feeling that there were gaps and contradictions in the data and that there remained many things I did not yet understand. I suspect that every fieldworker has this feeling of incompleteness, a nagging suspicion that his hard-won feelings of familiarity with another culture are but an illusion, and his interpretations but artificial constructs that worked well enough to allow him to make his way through the society, but that would sound bizarre or caricatured to those actually living in it.

Preparing for the Field

Traditionally, most anthropological studies have involved field research in preliterate societies. Until recently, academic training for aspiring anthropologists has consisted of intensive study in the subfields of the discipline itself, with possibly some added work in psychology, sociology, or linguistics. Linguistics especially could and did serve as a valuable technical subject, enabling a newly arrived researcher to grapple on his own with the intricacies of a hitherto unanalyzed language.

The growing concern with the peasantries of complex civilizations such as China, Japan, or India has forced an additional body of material into the desired intellectual baggage of an anthropologist who expects to work in subsystems of heterogeneous and complex nation states. He must become not only a student of anthropology but also something of an "area specialist," intelligently conversant with the history, philosophy, major religions, art, literature, economic problems, and political structures of the country, even though his immediate projected work will remain limited to the confines of a peasant village or an urban neighborhood. Moreover, he should not and need not postpone language learning until the day he arrives in the field. The universities that offer him multi-disciplinary courses in his geographical area of interest can usually also offer a grounding in speaking and reading the major language of the region.

This training, which stretches out the years of graduate study, is by no means frosting on the cake; it is part of the body of the cake itself. It adds depth to field findings and at the very least it provides shortcuts to understanding what is happening in the field situation. Moreover, in dealing with a complex culture, the anthropologist no longer has to rely solely on accounts by traders, missionaries, and colonial officials. A larger body of literature—interpretive, factual, or fictional—will allow him to come to grips with the culture early in his training, and to see it from an insider's point of view.

It is one thing to enter a relatively isolated preliterate community with admitted ignorance of its ways. There it is only expectable that the "stranger" will be completely in the dark about almost everything. To play the ignorant stranger in China, or in any society that prides itself on its written heritage, however, may be interpreted easily as disrespect and arrogance. Even illiterate peasants will react to such total ignorance by suggesting that you find a teacher, or that you go to one of their schools to learn. Being a foreigner is no excuse. They know that English-speaking residents of their own cities can teach you the language and the basics of the culture. They know that there are universities, books, and scholars outside the village. They know that there is a Great Tradition in which they themselves cannot instruct you but which they assume is what you want to know about. Chinese peasants are proud of the formal learning of their culture even if they know little about it directly, and at the same time they are deferent about their own ways of action and belief that deviate from the elite ideal. However, they are quite willing to open up to someone who already has some familiarity with the Great Tradition of the culture but who has deliberately chosen to learn more about the life of ordinary people and their problems.

My own academic training for work in Chinese society thus had to be fairly broad. In addition to courses in anthropology and related social sciences, I took work in modern Chinese history, literature, and philosophy, and had three years of language training both in Mandarin and in classical Chinese. In addition, I was able to spend nine months studying Chinese in Taipei, Taiwan's major city, before starting my research in the village. Most of that time, I lived with a family from North China whose hospitality gave me a very pleasant introduction to Chinese life. During the day, I worked with my various tutors on Mandarin, Taiwanese (Amoy dialect, which is the most commonly spoken in Taiwan), and read what I could on local customs and history. In these early months when I needed an occasional psychological retreat from the strains of living in a new milieu I could find it among the small American student community in Taipei.

Selecting a Village

Even before coming to Taiwan, I had determined to look for a fishing village in which to do my research. Several years earlier, Bernard Gallin had studied a farming village near Taichung, in the central part of the island. My year in

Mending nylon nets.

Taipei overlapped with the stay of another anthropologist, Arthur Wolf, who together with his wife Margery was studying child-training and socialization in a farming village near Taipei. Earlier community studies on the mainland of China had also been concerned with farming villages. Except for studies of the "boat people" of Hong Kong by Barbara Ward and a brief survey of a fishing village in northeastern Taiwan there were no materials on this form of peasant life.

In Taiwan, as in southeast China, fishing constitutes an important part of the economy. The coastline is dotted with small fishing villages, occasional harbor towns, and modern port cities. Around the northern tip of Taiwan, fishing is done from sampans and small motorized boats. Commercial trawlers operate from the east coast harbors and the major ports of Kaohsiung and Keelung. A third variety of fishing occurs in the villages along the west coast, where much fishing is still done from homemade bamboo rafts. Here, fish ponds are the secondary industry and there is little agriculture. These small villages have been less affected by modernization and it was from this group that I intended to make my choice. I hoped to find a community whose economic base was still relatively untouched by changes in technology and whose population would not exceed the research capacities of one person.

From time to time a pots-pans-and-brushes salesman visits the village.

Fishing villages tend to run larger in population than farming villages since a much smaller area of land is required to support the same number of people. On the west coast of Taiwan, fishing communities ranged all the way from 500 to 10,000 people, from hamlets that were offshoots of larger villages to modern harbors with a diversity of industries. In one instance, a community had reached its large size due to the recent resettlement of several thousand refugees from the offshore islands. My final choice, a village that I call K'un Shen, was a comparatively homogeneous community of about 3000 persons.

K'un Shen is within walking distance of two other fishing villages and one farming village. It is linked by bus to the city of Tainan, 8 miles away. Proximity to an urban center was another drawing point since I was interested in how much influence reached the village from the city and how much interaction there was between the two. Administratively K'un Shen is now a part of the city, and economically Tainan has long served as its marketing center. To some extent, Tainan is also a religious and cultural center for the village. Yet, because it was at the time of the study one of the more traditional of Taiwan's cities, it did not present the villagers with a sharply contrastive pattern of westernized urban living.

Though K'un Shen was ideal for my purposes, I did not select it by purely rational means. Rather, I was led to it somewhat by chance while taking a look at a number of villages in the same general area. I had gone to the Tainan Historical Museum in the hope of finding a map of the coastal area more detailed than those commercially available. There, I fell into conversation with one of the staff. While explaining my interest in a map, I became aware of a slightly shabby man who listened to us with great interest. As I was leaving, he approached and offered to accompany me and my interpreter to a nearby village where he had friends. With a trust that may someday be my undoing, I readily agreed, and the three of us set out by pedicab over a pot-holed dirt road. Several hours later, dust covered, cramped and shaken, and increasingly sure that we had fallen victims to a cruel hoax, we reached a village. Along one side of the road, fish ponds glimmered in the sun, and we could glimpse the blue-green waters of the Taiwan Straits. On the opposite side there was a cluster of houses. The cab turned in at a cobbled street that led shortly to an open square flanked by shops. Here we disembarked, and as I stretched my cramped legs I gazed with interest at the brightly decorated and ornate temple that filled one end of the square. Our volunteer guide hurried us down a narrow alleyway and into a house: it was not yet time for sightseeing.

Our friend's friend turned out to be a *li-chang*, administrative head of that section of the village. We were plied with soda pop and questions for an hour, and then proudly taken around the village to see its main sights—the village temple, the school, and the white sandy beach. We left with the definite impression that our presence in the village to "find out more about how people live in Taiwan" would be welcomed, not resented. That day, I really made the decision to return to K'un Shen, though for several weeks after I went through the formalities of visiting still other communities and weighing the advantages and disadvantages of each.

Adjusting to Village Life

As it turned out, I did not move immediately into the village to be greeted by eager informants. During my first few months of fieldwork I commuted from

The author, 1961, K'un Shen

Tainan. My reappearance to announce my intention to stay in K'un Shen, while still welcomed by the *li-chang*, did not meet with any expression of wild enthusiasm from his kinsmen, neighbors, and friends. Indeed, housing suddenly became very scarce. One family proved willing to rent me a sleeping room, but we could not find accommodations for my male interpreter or a work room at that time. We compromised by renting a small house in Tainan, commuting by bus or bicycle and sleeping overnight in the village only on occasion. Eventually, as people came to know us better, rooms became more available and we moved to the village. By then, I had acquired a female assistant as well, and a cook was eventually added to the staff.

This last addition could be interpreted, no doubt, as a sign of weakness. The original plan was that we would each take our meals on a regular basis with a different village family and pay board. Yet I became reluctantly aware that village meals were sparse and dull except at festivals. I was determined to bear with it, but was secretly relieved to find that my two assistants were also less than happy with the arrangement. In addition, we faced the problem of hosting others or entertaining unexpected visitors. Luck intervened again, this time in the form of a woman who had worked for me for a time in Tainan. Though a mainlander and from a large city, she proved willing to join us in the village. Overnight, our diet improved, as we explored the delights of Szechuanese, Shanghai, and Peking specialties, and our morale increased as mealtimes became times for recreation rather than work.

The village diet was, I suppose, one of the chief sources of culture shock for me. The village raised sweet potatoes as a staple (little else would grow in its marginal soils) and even the better-off households ate sweet potatoes at ordinary meals, mixed with rice. This, together with some limp vegetables through which one searched with varying degrees of success for a sliver of meat, constituted the average meal. During fishing season, less marketable fish were served. Occasionally there was sausage, dried salted fish, or pickled bean curd for flavoring the rice and sweet potato mix. I was grateful that villagers concerned about my well-being would ask "Can you eat Taiwanese food?" rather than "Do you like Taiwanese food?" Except for the dishes served at festivals, weddings, and funerals, I would have been hard put to give a convincing "yes" to the second question.

Sanitation also presented problems at first. I was reconciled to outhouses, even to the Taiwan Japanese variant with its hole in the floor and swarming maggots. What bothered me more was the problem of trying to keep clean by sponge-bathing out of a tin basin in the privacy of the courtyard or sleeping room. Fortunately, I was able to persuade our landlord to build a bath house by offering to pay half the cost. In it, we installed a Japanese *ofuro*; a deep wooden tub heated by a charcoal burner. Twice weekly, my staff, the landlord's family, and I took our turns, scrubbing down with hot water and soap outside the tub and then, already clean by most standards, soaking for a while in steaming bath water up to our necks.

The mechanics of daily living were thus fairly easily solved. I did not regard my stay in the village as a form of physical hardship, either then or in retrospect. Psychologically, however, there was always some stress, in greater or lesser degree. It took a long time to adjust to the almost constant din of Chinese opera, popular songs, and emotional radio dramas in which half of the dialouge consisted of heart-rending sobs. Some of this was broadcast over a village public address system; most came from radios played much more loudly than Americans are accustomed to hearing. It seemed as if the owners of these marvelous machines felt compelled to share their offerings with their most distant friends. Then, too, for some two months a village orchestra rehearsed nightly in the courtyard of the house just behind mine. Over and over they played the same few pieces, with wailing of horns, clash of gongs, and shriek of Chinese violin. Other noise-makers were the well-meaning village youngsters, who had absorbed the idea, universal in Taiwanese children's culture, that Americans are delighted to have someone come up from behind and shout "Hello, O.K., Goodbye" at them, as loudly as possible.

Coping in another language, or rather languages, proved still another major source of strain. The school children all spoke Mandarin as a second language, though with a relatively limited vocabulary. My fluency matched theirs, or almost, but there is a limit on how much information anyone can get from children. My spoken Taiwanese was weak. Working with a tutor in Taipei and continuing with one in the field still did not provide the needed familiarity with the language. The only available textbooks, designed to aid missionaries in preaching the gospel, were excellent guides to grammar but in terms of vocabulary they fell short of the mark for my purposes. With time, my comprehension of man-in-the-street Taiwanese improved to a point where I was using my interpreter mainly as a check on my own comprehension, but I never really felt comfortable speaking and often had her translate my side of the conversation. In Taiwan, it did not matter if one spoke Mandarin with an "accent," since

Boys playing tops. Village temple and shops are visible in the background.

many Chinese there spoke with regional accents as noticeable and odd as any foreigner's. But rare indeed is the Taiwanese who has heard his mother-tongue spoken with an accent, and rarer still is the Taiwanese who does not find it hilarious or at least discomfiting. Only the youngsters seemed to be able to cut through my odd noises and inadvertent puns, and when adults looked baffled about something I had said, the children could repeat it for me with correct pronunciation, stress, and tones. (Taiwanese has nine tones and a complex system of tonal shifts. Tone is a crucial element of meaning, as important as phonemes: depending on tone, the sound "be" can mean to buy, to sell, a horse, unable, or to charm and fascinate.)

With language problems of this sort, my morale suffered. Occasionally I bordered on paranoia, convinced that no one wanted to understand me. In part, I had been spoiled by my Mandarin teachers who put us through a graded vocabulary and knew almost instinctively what we were trying to say, and who worked on the assumption that foreigners *would* speak badly as they struggled to learn the language. The Taiwanese had no such assumptions: Taiwanese was something you were born with, a natural ability rather than a painfully learned skill.

I felt a great deal of frustration at not being able to express myself well or comprehend things as completely and accurately as I might in English. On my periodic visits to the city, I would load up with books from the USIS library. I developed a passion for wordy authors. I savored every line of the overwritten Thomas Wolfe and cursed his editor for having sagaciously pruned his output by half. I rediscovered Dreiser, Melville, Henry James, Faulkner, and sat up reading till all hours. Some of the city bookstores sold "pirated" editions of American and European novels. I read to excess in an attempt to convince myself that I had not suffered brain damage, that I could still handle language. Then, I discovered the modern Chinese novels. Authors in Taiwan and Hong Kong are also wordy: often, they are paid by the line. Though these novels may not stand as great literature, they create for the newcomer to the language the illusion of control through the devices of repetition and overexplanation. Substituting these for English-language works provided greater confidence in understanding written Chinese, though not enough to send me boldly forth into the jungles of the Taiwanese vernacular.

Of course, I had some emotional support from my field assistants who were eager to practice their English during off-hours, and thus gave me a chance to act the part of a verbally skilled and intelligent human being. Then there were the village middle-school students who approached me with the bashful request that I help them with their English lessons once a week. I was more than glad to do this, partly as a way of reciprocating the cooperation given to me, and partly in response to the sheer flattery of being acknowledged as an expert in *some* language. I could also lick my wounds in the security of one of the city's Christian missions, comparing my problems with the experiences of a small group of English and American missionaries teaching at the local college.

Every five months or so, I journeyed to Taipei to visit friends in the American student community there, but they proved increasingly less a source of comfort as time went on. Immersed in language study, in their archival researches, in documents and footnotes, living in a very different kind of social world from mine, their problems were no longer my problems. With each visit, I felt a little more estranged from them. I jabbered about "my village" while they listened with strained politeness or occasional curiosity. But they could not share my life, and the Taiwan I knew was not theirs.

Women as Fieldworkers

Some problems arise when the fieldworker is a woman trying to do research in a culture that is strongly male-oriented and male-dominated. China is such a society, one in which sons are strongly preferred over daughters, and in which women have traditionally held low status. There is a common Chinese saying that in childhood a girl follows her father, in adulthood her husband, and in

Morning market; one of the few public roles for women.

old age her sons. With such an attitude toward women, one might reasonably expect considerable reserve, resistance, or open hostility toward a woman researcher. Her very presence in the community makes her a deviate from the feminine role, a personification of the fears of the more traditionally minded males, and, for better or worse, the model of what happens when women receive education and jobs, and gain independence from their families.

To be sure, the position of women in Taiwan has changed considerably over the past half century. By the late 1940s it was quite acceptable for girls to attend primary school and by the late 1950s only a few failed to complete the six-year course of study. In K'un Shen there were even some girls who went on to enroll in the middle schools (the equivalent of American junior and senior high school). Villagers were also aware of the presence of girl students in the provincial colleges. In fact, most of the village school teachers were women. A number of unmarried village girls worked in shops and factories in Tainan, though they continued to live at home and to remit most of their earnings to their parents. Usually, these earnings went toward their dowries. Also, because of economic pressures, most of the village women hired themselves out to do some form of wage work at home or around the village. Even so, women did not enjoy economic or political equality and traditional ideals for feminine behavior were still strongly encouraged.

In my case it proved difficult to separate the problems created by sex role from those rising from my age. Taiwan is also beginning to face the problems of the "generation gap." Within Taiwanese society, there is an increasing demand for more independence and involvement in decision-making by the young people, male *and* female. Major differences in values and attitudes have begun to develop between the generations. Still, ideally, people under forty are not expected to have much to say, nor are they given the chance to say it publicly. And I was usually considered to be less than forty, though estimates of my age varied widely, from sixteen to sixty depending on the criteria used.

As a self-confessed student, I was an example of modern youth. Technically, I should not have been a youth. Already in my midtwenties but still a student I was something of an anachronism. By normal Taiwanese standards, I should have been married five or six years before and had several children. Yet as a student, albeit an overly advanced one, I could not really be an adult, and I was obviously not a child or teenager.

Thus, on two counts I presented problems for definition and acceptance. Being a young woman closed off from me certain kinds of information and experiences. I could never, for example, be a sit-in participant at everyday informal gatherings where community matters were being discussed, gossip exchanged, and commentary made on events at large. Such gatherings, which usually took place in the evenings, were simply not attended by women. They stayed close to home after dark. The only possible compromise was to send my male field assistant to sit around the village shops in the evenings and act as my eyes and ears. No doubt people were aware that he relayed to me some parts of the conversations, but that did not seem to matter. People also passed on information and gossip to their wives when they came home, censoring out the dirty jokes or things that they did not regard as women's concerns.

Similarly, the need to conform to some of the minimum requirements of the female role prevented me from forming ties with males of my generation level.

This could easily have been interpreted as having sexual overtones. Interviews with males between roughly twenty and forty years of age I left to my assistant much of the time. However, I could talk freely with children, teenage boys, or elder men without causing raised eyebrows.

Still, there were occasions when my status as a *nu-shih* ("female scholar") or "student of Taiwanese culture" proved strong enough to override my sex-ascribed activities. Certainly I would not have been welcome at the equivalent of bull-sessions, gambling parties, and similar male activities. But I was accepted into some situations where females could not normally be present. When one of the young village men got married, for example, his uncle insisted that I take part in a visit to his new in-laws. Customarily, the day after the bride is brought to her new home, the groom and his wife, friends, and male kinsmen pay a visit to the bride's house, there to be treated to a feast and formally introduced to her kinsmen. Female relatives of the groom do not attend, nor do female friends of the family. However, with the uncle's backing I became an acceptable member of the party. On another occasion, I was invited to join the local temple committee in an all-night meeting at which rituals for the well being of the village were carried out. Again, women do not participate in this ceremony, nor do ordinary members of the village community. The ritual is performed by a closed group of hired priests and elected members of the temple committee.

In both instances, there were leading members of the community who thought it important that I be present if I were to understand local ways of doing things. My sex role then became neuter. In similar fashion, my role as outsider-observer overrode my sex role in gathering certain other kinds of information. What I learned about the fishing industry had to be learned from men. The details of raft building, use of fishing gear, costs, fishing lore, and so on are not women's knowledge, but the men were patient in explaining to me the workings of the fishing industry and its problems. The same attitude helped me in collecting material on religious beliefs and practices. With backing from members of the temple committee I was even given access to more esoteric materials such as the texts of chants used in religious ceremonies, which is not at all women's business.

Thus, while being female hampered me in some social relationships and re-stricted participation in some groupings, it was not a serious barrier in dealing with village men as a group or in learning about the male side of the culture. One explanation of this may be the high esteem in which scholarship is held in China, although I would not lean too heavily on that as a reason since in the village itself education beyond the sixth grade was not a goal, even for most boys. Besides, I was not operating as the villagers conceived a scholar should. The things I was interested in did not fall within the framework of traditional scholarship. Indeed, I was consciously evincing a respect and curiosity about a way of life that most traditionally oriented Chinese scholars would "put down." While I was still doing language work in Taipei, I showed up for a tutoring session carrying a monograph on a peasant village by a well-known Chinese sociologist. My tutor glanced through it and in great puzzlement asked me why *anyone* would bother to write a book about some unheard of and obviously unimportant village. It was much easier to convince my villagers that peasant life was important, and it was perhaps this, more than my scholarliness per se that enabled them to drop the normal standards for female behavior and topics of conversation. Besides, the men recognized how important their part of the culture was; in their eyes it was certainly more important that the kinds of things women could talk about. It would give a misleading picture of Taiwanese ways if these things went unmentioned just because the investigator was a woman.

Unfortunately, being a woman did not automatically open the doors to close friendships, confidences, and outpourings of information from village women. Those most receptive to me as a person fell into the same age groupings as my male informants. I was accepted most easily by the unmarried girls and by older women. Admittedly, older women whose children had already grown up and whose daughters had left home to be married had more leisure time and a need to talk. They were flattered at being asked for information and opinions and at being listened to seriously. Despite the fact that respect and care for the elderly is one of the values held in Taiwanese culture, the later years can be lonely and unsatisfying. Sons are busy with outside concerns and invest more of their emotions in their wives and children. Daughters-in-law often have neither the time nor the inclination to devote much attention to older women of the household. The anthropologist as sympathetic stranger becomes for them a sounding board for the value of traditional ways and the injustices and difficulties of present day existence.

For the young unmarried women, I represented something else—an extreme model of freedom and independence. Not that they would want to go half way around the world alone, to live in a strange village, but my doings made their own demands seem like reasonable compromises between traditional ways and the Taiwanese view of modern ways. However, the young married women seemed uncomfortable in my presence, despite their politeness and cordiality when talking with me. I was in their generation, but not of it. Some may have feared that too close an association with me would create dissension at home. Others may have felt that they were still too young to speak with any authority and that I should be instructed by the older men and women. Certainly they were more comfortable when interviewed by my female assistant alone, particularly when talking of such things as marriage and child-rearing. Perhaps they feared that I had set ideas on such things and would be critical of their opinions because of my foreign origins and "book learning," and they did not have the wisdom of years' experience to give them confidence.

Some Problems of Being an American

Anthropologists, until recently, have done much of their fieldwork under their own flag, in colonial territories, or among minorities in their own land. Such situations could be expected to create problems of identification and acceptance for the anthropologist. Taiwan is, of course, a sovereign state, the seat of the Republic of China since that government was forced off the mainland of China in the late 1940s. Prior to that time it had been a lost province of China, ceded as a colony to the Japanese in 1895, and not regained as Chinese territory until the end of the Second World War. However, it owes its continuance as the Republic of China at least in part to the vast amounts of economic and military aid provided by the United States. Without American military protection it would no doubt have long since been forcibly reclaimed by the mainland Chinese Government. There is a sizeable American military establishment in Taiwan, numerous air bases and missile installations jointly controlled by the American and Chinese military, and American military personnel are easily noticeable in the large cities, particularly Taipei and the port of Kaohsiung in southern Taiwan. In addition, there are numerous Americans present who are connected with the Embassy, the A.I.D. programs, and intelligence organizations. There is also a large missionary contingent; many of the missionaries who had worked in mainland China continued their work in Taiwan after 1949. Students and professors are a very tiny minority among the Americans present, and almost all of them confine their work to Taipei.

During my initial months in the village, people were somewhat at a loss in trying to identify me with one of the more familiar American categories despite my repeated reassurances that I was a student financed by a private educational organization. The thought that I had church connections was dispelled relatively rapidly. There are stereotypic expectations of missionary behavior, although the village itself has had very limited contact with missionaries. There had been, I was told, a missionary who came to the village and proceeded to preach to a baffled crowd from the steps of the temple. Their general nonreceptivity, expressed in a few well-aimed stones, had persuaded him to desist. Any such apprehensions about me were short lived; weeks went by and not once did I preach, publicly or privately. Moreover, I wore lipstick, smoked cigarettes, admitted to being able to dance, and when pressed to identify myself as Protestant or Catholic by more sophisticated informants emphatically denied being either.

These fears laid to rest, there lingered the thought that I was in the employ of some branch of the American government. One possibility was that I worked for an intelligence agency, an understandable concern, particularly for that branch of the Chinese government concerned with security matters. For the first half year of my research, I received periodic visits from a representative of the Taiwan Garrison Command, the military and internal security agency. The peculiar subject of his assignment seemed to discomfit him: I was clearly the first stray American female he had ever had to investigate. He questioned some of my informants to find out what sorts of things I discussed with them. In the end, he apparently decided I was mad but harmless, and even doing rather interesting work. On one occasion, he insisted on teaching me some folk songs he remembered from his childhood, so that I could incorporate them into my material on Chinese culture.

Less easily resolved were the hopes of some villagers that I had connections with A.I.D. or other development agencies and that I would be able to use my influence to obtain funds for the community and better their economic conditions. When I was conducting a survey of households in an attempt to get some idea of the range of occupations, incomes, and living costs, this subject was often raised by informants during the interview. Such an explanation could easily come to mind, as it provided an optimistic explanation of my interest in the local standard of living. The villagers, while not noticeably any less well off than peasants in farming villages nearby, felt that they were economically on the low end of the scale in relation to other groups in Taiwanese society and that there was considerable room for improvement. They had quickly adapted the innovations in fishing gear suggested by the Fishermen's Association, and hoped for further changes that would be to their advantage. One thing that had been offered to them in the past but had never seen light was the construction of harbor facilities. This would have permitted them to risk investment in motorized boats and thus to increase their efficiency in exploiting the fisheries. However the plans had been scrapped during the war years and were not resumed afterward. But they were still remembered, and mentioned to me with the hope that *I* could do something about them. Others simply hoped that my presence in the community signaled the beginning of an inflow of money, to be distributed as loans or grants to needy families. Some informants even went to great lengths to impress on me the extent of their poverty compared to others in the village, despite the loss of face this involved. For in K'un Shen, pride, independence, and the ability to manage without outside help are key values.

I reacted to these and similar appeals with feelings of guilt over my inability to do much of anything for the community or even for individual households. At one point I tried without any success to arrange with a medical missionary group for care of a village boy who had lost a hand in an industrial accident. The cost of an artificial hand and training in the use of it was far beyond what his family's spare money or the spare money in my field grant would cover. I became very depressed when I realized that my "influence" as an American could not bring about even this one small benefit to one village family. At another point, I entertained fantasies of playing "applied anthropologist," helping people to help themselves. The city government had decided to open a public swimming beach near the village. It seemed to me that here was a possible source of income for the community, one that could grow into something bigger. However, there were problems. City entrepreneurs had already appropriated the food and drink concessions, the renting of beach chairs and umbrellas, and bath house facilities. And most of the villagers viewed the construction of a swimming beach with negative feelings. Swimming is not a form of recreation or exercise in K'un Shen, and even the fishermen do not know how to swim. Children are strictly forbidden to experiment with the sport. No one goes into the ocean if they can help it. The sea is a place to work, not to have fun. Also, village puritanism could not approve the idea of young and almost naked men and women lolling around together. There are also religious feelings about the sea itself, including a belief in ocean gods who would be strongly angered by the frivolous use of these natural resources. There is fear of the spirits of the drowned, who become malevolent ghosts haunting the area where they met their untimely ends. There was also the precedent of a neighboring village that for a time had a swimming beach and was inundated by a tidal wave. The initial reaction of the people in K'un Shen was that they did not want to have anything to do with the swimming beach. However, over the years they have become reconciled to its presence, and a few villagers have even found employment there. During my stay, I had wild hopes that the villagers might become involved in the tourist trade as a way of continuing to use village resources in the face of growing competition in the fishing industry. I spun out fantasies of an overnight inn for visitors, the slow growth of a seaside resort town in which most of the profits would accrue to village members. The most I accomplished was that one of the people I pressed this on learned how to swim and got a job as a lifeguard at an established beach in order to find out what went on there. He probably showed better judgment than I.

In addition to guilt over my inability to work economic miracles, I also felt guilty about my affluence compared to that of the villagers. Despite my attempts to live close to the village style of living, I never approximated anything less than the standards of food, dress, and housing of the wealthier village households. As an affluent member of the community, I made contributions to the temple, and to the village school for books, prizes, and scholarships, but they were relatively paltry in terms of American wealth. I was always keenly aware of how much richer Americans are, even graduate students on small field grants, and my villagers thought of all Americans as being fabulously wealthy.

Indeed, my various informants had gleaned enough information about America from the various mass media to ask further questions about life in the States regarding salaries, welfare payments, commodity prices, and their frequency of occurrence. How many families had cars, television sets, record players, and the like? I felt compelled to answer honestly, and at the same time felt as if I were boasting about American affluence.

I was also uneasy discussing political questions that came up from time to time, although I tried consciously to keep off the subject of politics, both to protect my informants and myself. Politically, Taiwan is a strange place. The national government is strongly military in character and is understandably concerned with military and political security because of its proximity to a large communist state that claims Taiwan as its rightful territory. Civil liberties suffer as a result. There is censorship of newspapers, magazines, and books; there are arrests of persons suspected of sympathies with communist thought or of advocating Taiwan's independence; and there is a tendency to exercise extreme caution and conservatism in voicing social views of any kind. Reinforcing this caution is the bitter memory of the events of February 1947 when upwards of 10,000 Taiwanese were killed without trial as political suspects after an abortive uprising against the Kuomintang government and Army.

These events were brought to my attention from time to time, in connection with queries about American democracy at home and policies abroad. The United States is viewed by most Taiwanese as a truly democratic state, and there are many who find it difficult to understand why, with our power and influence, we do not exert some kind of pressure to make Taiwan conform more to the democratic model, more like the ideal America that they believe exists. I was amazed that this image of America held so strongly, despite the vituperative anti-American broadcasts from China that could be heard daily on the radio although the government did its best to jam them. To add to the irony, some of our own government personnel with whom I came into contact seemed to feel that the Taiwanese were deeply hostile to the United States and that only a strong watch-dog government kept Taiwan from a left-inspired rebellion. As a result, they could overlook or rationalize infringements of freedom as a necessity. Those who were made uncomfortable by them, and by anyone who questioned the underlying assumption, would of course argue that Taiwan was an independent sovereign country and the United States could not possibly interfere in its internal affairs. Meantime, put on the spot as a "representative" of my country, and probably the only American with whom these villagers would ever converse, I found myself at a complete loss in offering an adequate justification of my government's position or explanation of its role in Taiwan's affairs.

Field Assistants

Having gone into the field situation alone, it was very important that I find and train a field staff to assist me. During the initial five months of work, I had only one interpreter. He was introduced to me through the Joint Commission for Rural Reconstruction, a joint Sino-American agency for economic development. A native Taiwanese, he came from one of the modern fishing ports on the eastern coast and had been trained in economics at Taiwan National University. He served as an interpreter for me in my daily visits to the village (at this point I was still living in the house in the city) and worked with me translating Chinese and Japanese sources that we found in the local library collections. However, he was unable to stay through the course of the project: he received permission to leave the country for study abroad, and I began over again with another interpreter acquired from the same source.

This second venture was less successful. Though the young man came with high recommendations and abilities, his curriculum vitae omitted one vital point. He was a Hakka, a member of a linguistic and ethnic group found throughout southeastern China. Though long resident in Taiwan, the Hakka have not assimilated to the main body of Taiwanese society, but have remained a distinct ethnic group. For him, Hokkien was not the mother tongue but a second language. Moreover there is tension between Hakka and Hokkien groups, with the latter feeling themselves to be superior in all regards, and the Hakka no doubt feeling the same about themselves. To an outsider like myself, these differences were not apparent. The young man was obviously ill at ease working in the village, and my village informants seemed to be hostile to him in turn. I attributed this to his newness to the situation and perhaps to the villager's resentment that my previous assistant had been replaced. But as the weeks went by, things became more, not less, tense. The situation finally came to a head during an interview in which I was talking with someone about customs at the New Year. Suddenly, apropos of nothing, we were off on the topic of the Hakka. My informant was eager to tell me what was strange and unacceptable about them, and my interpreter was visibly flushed with anger. Terminating the interview as quickly as possible, I got us out of there, and in the ensuing conversation came to realize what the problem was. All I could see to differentiate this man from the villagers was his education, his class background, and his urban experiences, as had indeed been the case with my previous assistant. The villagers saw much more, the subtleties of which still escape me. By now, my assistant had developed a strong dislike for a number of my best informants, and the situation did not seem worth salvaging. By mutual agreement we parted company.

After interviewing several hopeful applicants who were sent to me by friends or who had responded to an advertisement placed at the USIS library, I finally decided on two replacements. One was an unmarried woman in her very early twenties, a middle-school graduate who had learned much of her English while working in an American military household. The experience of living with foreigners for two years had given her a measure of objectivity about her own culture (she came originally from a small farming village), but at the same time she was still strongly involved in it. Bright and eager to learn more, she became first my interpreter and eventually an independent interviewer and observer of village life.

The other newcomer to the project also came from a small farming village, but had studied for a number of years in Taipei. He had a Masters degree in political science and possessed a strong interest in sociology. Widely read in the social sciences, he was eager for the opportunity to take part in a field study on his own society. In his late twenties, and already married and the father of several sons, he was more easily able to move in adult circles in the community. Moreover, his academic training and reading enabled him to do a considerable amount of work on his own. Both of these Taiwanese assistants made valuable contributions to my work, and were able to direct my attention to things I would otherwise have overlooked or misunderstood. As might be expected, they did considerably better than I at forming friendships within the community. Both bore surnames that were common in the village, and they were regarded as possible distant kinsmen by many. Both had backgrounds that enabled them to feel comfortable in the village setting and to respond as individuals as well as outside observers.

In addition to this full-time staff that lived, worked, and socialized in the village, I had occasional part-time assistants. During the summer months, two young women who taught in a city middle school came to work for me. Together, they interviewed a sample of village women about child-training practices. One of them had taken anthropology as her major in college and was interested in getting fieldwork experience. Another source of assistance was my language tutor, also a middle-school teacher, who during the summer vacation came out to the village to help with an economic survey of village households.

Various key informants could also be regarded as field assistants. Several villagers were not only interested in the idea of trying to describe village life but after a time to take an active part in doing so. One such man, whom I came to know as a friend early in my fieldwork, was an active leader in the local Fishermen's Association and Farmers' Association, as well as being a member of the school board and temple committee. He was a natural leader, a man who had overcome his status as "adopted husband" to become an important voice in his wife's lineage group. Literate, "modern" in his attitudes toward technological innovations and education, and at the same time deeply concerned with the preservation of tradition, he stood as our informal sponsor and guarantor to the community at large. His enthusiasm for our work gained us entrance into village affairs and opened up a variety of contacts within the community. He had friends in all factions. And his home was always open to us for advice, for information, or for friendly talk. It was he who steered me through my first major religious celebration in the village, outlining for me in advance the various things that would occur and pointing out items of importance during the ceremonies, as well as answering questions about the things I "observed." He, and some others, made the tasks at hand much easier for me.

The Use of Written Records

During the initial months of fieldwork, while still feeling my way around the community, I almost despaired of ever being able to get an accurate picture of household composition, family complexity, data on age and sex distribution, and similar material. In a community so large, it would have taken all my energies just to find out the bare essentials of who was there. Fortunately, this work had already been done for me, in the form of household records collected and revised every few years through the local police station. Indeed, the maintenance of these records seemed to be the major task of the local police force. After negotiating with them and their superiors in the city, I obtained permission to use these materials, thus compressing a time-consuming task into a few short weeks of copying data onto my own forms. The records in question listed the members of each household, giving their age, sex, kin relation to the head, education, and major occupation. As they were arranged by building and neighborhood, it was even possible to take note of some of the family splits that had occurred. However, the records only covered a five-year period, with earlier records not available. As a precaution, we selected some households at random to check on our own, and found the police records highly accurate.

Documents of another sort provided us with time depth. From 1904 on, there were Japanese census reports for the village. Eighteenth- and nineteenth-century gazetteers for the area made occasional reference to the community. In local library collections we found two Japanese accounts of the community, one written in 1898 and the other dating from the early 1940s. Both of these gave indications of the changes in living style and economic base that occurred since that time.

One form of written records we did *not* have were lineage records or codes of conduct for lineage members such as are found in many areas of China and elsewhere in Taiwan. This was because the functions of the lineage were not elaborated in the community and the gentry model of lineage organization had never taken hold. Due to income and occupation level, the village had never produced that class of literate land owners who would have seen reason for keeping histories of their kin group, framing rules of behavior for members, and glorifying the deeds of the ancestors. Here, there were only the lists of constituent living households regarded as affiliated to the group, but no charting of the intricate linkages of relationship.

In our fieldwork, we could also make use of the villagers' literacy. For example, after we had collected considerable material on child-rearing and the adults' hopes and expectations for their children, I was curious to see what the children themselves thought about their future lives. With the cooperation of the school teachers, we collected essays from the children in the sixth grade on what they hoped to do after they finished school, what kinds of people they wanted to be, and what kinds of lives they foresaw for themselves. At another point, we enlisted the cooperation of several households at different income levels in keeping monthly budgets of income and expenditures. Informants in two of the musical groups were more than willing to write down the words and notations for pieces they performed. Educated older villagers could supply us with the written characters for the names of gods, religious objects, portions of ceremonies, items in the technology, species of fish commonly caught in village waters or raised in the ponds, and other such specialized terms not generally known. And as mentioned earlier, we had access to written versions of the religious chants performed at temple festivals and other religious celebrations.

Interviewing and Observing

During the initial months of the research, much of our work was unstructured. By that I mean that my main concern was to get the "feel" of the community and its various activities, to come to know a broad spectrum of people in various age groups and income groups, and to gain acceptance for myself and my staff in the community. Formal interviews and focusing attention on one line of inquiry did not seem to make sense at this time. It took at least six months before I felt that our presence was really accepted in the village. Then, there was a major religious festival held for the god of the main village temple, which coincided with the period of the New Year's holidays. Many people invited friends and relatives from outside the village to visit for the day. These new arrivals eyed me with intense curiosity as it became obvious that I was something other than an American tourist who had wandered in by accident. I was delighted to hear some of my informants explaining with cool sophistication that I was a student of Taiwanese customs who had chosen to live in K'un Shen because of its many advantages for learning such things. In short, some people now felt it a mark of distinction to have been selected in order to "typify" Taiwanese life, and with the arrival of outsiders, I, who had been the stranger par excellence for half a year, was suddenly transformed into a useful, nay prestigious, citizen. I had become a symbol of the importance of the village, despite the fact that I was inarticulate, uninformed, odd-looking, and occasionally quite tactless and mannerless.

During the early months I must have been an unavoidable nuisance. I wandered around the village, camera slung around my neck like an amulet, notebook tightly clutched in my hand, looking for conversation openers and asking simple-minded questions. I sat on the beach talking to the men at work refurbishing their rafts or mending nets and eagerly asked for information on fishing techniques, costs, incomes, and fishing lore. I smiled and greeted the women working outside their doorways at netweaving, laundering, food preparation, binding of brushwood, until sheer courtesy impelled them to invite me to join them and talk. Sometimes we spoke of things that seemed worth noting down, sometimes we just chatted at random or I answered myriad questions about what life was like in my own country. I was interviewed almost as much as I interviewed others.

Like the village youngsters, I hung around wherever something out of the ordinary seemed to be happening: a wedding, a funeral, a seance, a temple ceremony, a quarrel, or the visit of a traveling medicine show. In the search for things to do, I made a determined though not very accurate attempt to produce a map of the village. The police station had three maps, each of them unique, and my final product constituted a fourth variant of dubious value. However, that little exercise did provide side benefits in giving me an excuse for wandering very slowly around the village, poking up and down alleyways, until someone took pity on me and invited me to come sit in the shade for a while.

As I became a more familiar sight in the village and my purpose there became more widely known and accepted, it became less difficult to think of things to do. I surveyed households selected from the records at the police station, and worked through a list of questions concerned with internal organization, obligations to kinsmen living in other households, household finances, family relations. People generally knew enough about America to proceed on the assumption that things were indeed run differently there, and were incredibly patient in explaining to me how things were done in K'un Shen. Sometimes, the opportunity of having an outsider to talk to was sufficient to open the flood-gates of complaint and recrimination over the difference between ideal expectations and reality. There was the elderly widow supported alternately by each of her three sons and feeling wanted or respected by none of them, or the widow with two children living on her brother-in-law's grudging indulgence, and others in similar situations who welcomed the chance to give vent to their feelings without fear of upsetting the family's surface harmony.

One of the problems I felt in these early months was that I was prying, asking too much of people's time and goodwill to satisfy my own selfish purposes. Gradually, I realized that it was quite possible for people to shut me out politely but firmly if they did not want to be bothered. They were not, after all, under any coercion to tell me anything. What amazed me was that they *did* want to tell me something. Informants often elaborated their answers and pointed the way to new questions that had not occurred to me on my own. They were willing to answer what I regarded as personal questions and would volunteer information about themselves that I had not specifically asked for. Moreover, I was invited to participate in family events such as weddings, funerals, a feast commemorating an ancestor's death because people felt I should have the opportunity to see what was done at such times in contrast to whatever it was that was done at such times in America.

By the time that we had come to be accepted and well known in the village, my assistants also had acquired sufficient experience so they could be sent out on their own with lists of questions, some specific and some open-end. Our inquiries moved into areas that were somewhat more sensitive, such as attitudes toward traditional marriage arrangements and those based on "love" or choice by the young couple. We talked with people about birth control, sex, divorce, and the expectations people brought to marital relationships. We discussed the qualities that made a person good or bad and the tone of relationship that individuals maintained with their household members, kinsmen, friends, and neighbors: this was done in a more indirect manner of inquiry but many of our informants were quite specific in their answers. We also looked into such things as local political organization and attitudes toward the village school and modern education. We collected material on local medical practices, beliefs about health and sickness, and use of Western medicine.

One of the instruments we used was a revised version of a questionnaire originally designed for studying values in five cultures in the American southwest.[1] Each question set a situation and alternative solutions to it, and the informant was asked to rank the possible alternatives in terms of first and second preferences and to estimate which was most commonly favored by other members of the community. The question items were designed to uncover time orientation (whether the emphasis was on the past, present, or future), ideas about man's relationship to the environment (whether man lives in harmony with nature, is in struggle against it to overcome, or whether he is subordinated to it), the prevailing mode of interaction with other men (is it based on lineal authority, a collateral consensus of equals, or does it have an individualistic bent), and the orientation to activity (doing versus being).

With some minor reworkings of the questions to fit the Taiwanese cultural situation, we found this a useful instrument in which the items themselves served as motivation for further commentary and elaboration, including anecdotal exemplification of a chosen answer. The results also bore out some of our own intuitions about local values. We had already suspected, for example, that work relations and extension of aid to kinsmen were marked by a highly individualistic orientation. The frequency of household division, the frequency with which work mates were chosen on the basis of criteria other than kinship, the seeking of financial aid outside kin circles, all suggested that the value of individual responsibility was a guiding principle, and the responses to the test questions confirmed this. Only in the political sphere, where elections represented a recent introduction, did people still rely on consensus or even on the authority of older kinsmen in making their choice. But with that exception, the reality of K'un Shen peasant life did not accord with the picture often presented, which views the Chinese as deeply embedded within an authoritarian kinship system and both unable and unwilling to function as individuals.

Again, in the area of man's relationship to natural forces and his need for reliance on the supernatural, we found a high regard for science, a belief in man's ability to learn more and thus circumvent disasters, and little of the fatalism normally attributed to Asian peasantries. Only in the area of health and long life, where knowledge was weaker, was there more of a tendency to believe that these things were predetermined, and even here this did not preclude trying a number of medical cures before turning to supernatural aid. To our surprise, the people also lived in a time-orientation that emphasized the present and future, with little harking back to the past as a model for action.

---

[1] See Kluckhohn, F. R., and F. Strodtbeck, *Variations in Value Orientations.* Row, Peterson and Company, Evanston, Ill., 1961.

China's Great Tradition of Confucian thought does indeed place a high value on the past, but the "Little Tradition" of these peasants did not. To the residents of K'un Shen, the past meant poverty, low social status, and difficulties. They felt that their ancestors, though good people, had been poor and ignorant men who did not furnish a reliable model for survival in the present-day world. Finally, the responses showed a heavy emphasis on the importance of work, the use of one's time in fruitful (that is, money-earning) activity, and respect for hard work, including manual labor. Though Taiwanese folk-religion derives from Taoism and Buddhism, which emphasize a "being" orientation, this particular aspect of the two philosophical religious systems seems to have been rejected as nonfunctional.

The Use of Projective Tests

The use of projective tests to obtain deeper insights into another culture has been tried in many different societies. Tests such as the Rorschach and Thematic Apperception Test (TAT) were originally designed for clinical use, but in using them with a group of presumably normal subjects it is possible to derive an abstract of the modal personality type, areas of personal conflict that derive from the social setting, and the dominant modes for coping with them. I selected for use in the field a version of the TAT which had been redrawn for use with Chinese subjects: this version was provided to me by G. W. Skinner. Most of the cards followed the structure of the original Murray set.

The cards present one or more persons in various groupings of age and sex. However, the content and emotional tone is deliberately ambiguous. The subject is then asked to tell a story based on the picture, giving it a beginning, middle, and end. The interviewer plays a minimal directive role, giving instructions, presenting the cards, occasionally encouraging the subject to continue, but without leading the subject or being critical of the responses.

After a few trial runs, I found that the best way of conducting the test was to have my male assistant do the presentations without me present, since this seemed to distract the subjects or bias them toward giving what they conceived of as "American" responses. During the test, a tape recorder was kept running, and my assistant made notes on the nonverbal communications.

Our sample consisted of twenty-five children, between the ages of twelve and fourteen, taken at random from the fifth and sixth grades of the village school, and adult samples of twenty-five men and women from among adults we knew fairly well and regarded as representative of their age, sex, and class. The children were very cooperative, since they regarded the experience as a morning out of school in which they could play an interesting game. The adult males were also highly motivated and verbal. The women, however, tended to be much more reserved and reticent, and concerned with whether they were giving a "correct" answer. In part this reflected the style of women's responses generally, but it was also a reaction to a male interviewer.

After each set of test cards was answered, my two field assistants went over the tapes, line by line, transcribing them into character form following the Taiwanese construction (and occasionally having to create our own transcription for vernacular terms). We then worked together at translating into an English equivalent in content and emotional tone. Although time consuming, this procedure assured us of an accurate rendition of the subjects' response.

Recording Field Data

A word might be included here on the problems of note-taking and taping in this field situation. Most of our informants accepted the presence of the tape recorder during the TAT testing without question, though we did not use the machine in our fieldwork otherwise except to record musical performances. Informants were a little nervous about the machine at first, but seemed to forget its presence by the time they were into the second card. Most were curious to hear their voices and amused by the results. In only one instance was there refusal to talk with the machine running, in this case by a young woman who feared that it would "steal her soul." However, several days later she changed her mind and asked us to include her in the interview group.

Note-taking in the presence of informants presented greater problems, at least initially. As long as I was jotting down what people themselves defined as "information," for example a story about a god, a description of a festival sequence, fishing lore, and other things I would not be expected to know, I was rarely challenged. When I was, I would explain that I had a poor memory and thought it best to write things down so that I could review them and learn them. In time, people would tell me to write something down so that I would not forget it or be confused about it when I wrote my book about the village. However, items of gossip, personal revelations, observations of personal interactions could not be noted down at the time they occurred and I did not attempt to do so. I kept a field journal in my study, and wrote in it almost every day, praying for total recall of things that had occurred and comments made. When we worked with more structured interviews on specific topics, and obviously had a list of questions ourselves, there was no objection to answers being noted down during the interview.

Field data were typed in English onto simple key-sort punch cards which were made in duplicate. At intervals, I would send a batch of carbons back to my university, always keeping a full set of cards with me, so that I could review and check on information.

Evaluation of the Fieldwork

With the wisdom of hindsight, I realize that there are still many things I do not know about this village in which I lived for a year and a half. Missing from the data is any detailed information on immigration and emigration from the community during the past twenty years or so. Not till the end of my fieldwork did I become aware of the fact that there was a sizeable group of former villagers living in Tainan and elsewhere who still maintained significant ties to the village and who were considered to be under obligation to contribute to the temple, as if they were still resident in K'un Shen.

Similarly, through unawareness, and later through overcautiousness, I never did find out the bases for factionalism within the village and the composition and loyalties of the several political cliques in operation. Nor could I learn anything about secret societies.

Despite these and other gaps, I still found that I had more than enough material to work with when I returned from the field. My dissertation presented the data as an ethnography organized around key and variant values, and I reorganized some of this descriptive material into a case study a couple of years later.[2] A detailed analysis of the TAT materials is still in process, as are several working papers on economy and social structure.

In this sense, the field project was a success. I suppose it can also be counted a success in that I encountered no real hostility toward me or my purposes in the field, that I had cooperation from people, and that I rarely was blocked in my work by anything other than my own emotional hang-ups of the moment. Yet at the same time, I feel that there was always a distance between myself and my informants, even those whom I considered to be friends, and that my work lost something through the lack of really close emotional ties to individuals. I was almost always an observer, a transient sojourner, and whatever insights might have been lost through emotional blurring of perception would have been made up for in other ways.

[2] Diamond, Norma Joyce, *K'un Shen: A Taiwanese Fishing Village*, unpublished Ph.D. thesis, Cornell University, 1966; Diamond, Norma, *K'un Shen: A Taiwan Village*, Holt, Rinehart and Winston, Inc., New York, 1969.

6

FIELDWORK AMONG THE TIWI, 1928-1929

C. W. M. HART
University of Istanbul

Related Case Study: **The Tiwi of North Australia**

Few anthropologists have had the privilege of doing intensive fieldwork
with hunters and gatherers whose traditional way of life is intact. In
prewar Australia it was still possible and C. W. M. Hart ("Steve" to his
friends) took advantage of the opportunity. His tribe, the Tiwi, foraged
in an area more plentiful in game and water resources than the desert
country of people like the Arunta, yet living and traveling with them was
what most people would regard as hardship. Hart did fieldwork with the
Tiwi for about two years, and much of this time he spent traveling with
them with a minimum of personal equipment and no transportation other
than his two feet. But this experience in itself does not loom large in
Hart's chapter. What does loom large is how he found what seemed to
him to be the key to Tiwi social life, and what that was. Nothing better
illustrates the nature of the anthropologist's relationship to the field than
this. Hart had to live with his small group for some time before he began
to perceive this key, and still longer before he understood it. The intricate
system of betrothal deals and the meanings ascribed to them is a salient
feature of the Tiwi's social system, once perceived, but only prolonged
and intimate contact and many genealogies made it possible to see it in
principle and then understand it in full detail.

The Author

C. W. M. Hart was born in Melbourne, Australia, in 1905. He was already a law student at the University of Sydney when Radcliffe-Brown began teaching anthropology at Sydney in 1925 and Hart was among the first of the young Australians to become a full-time anthropology graduate student. The Tiwi, about whom little was then known, were given to him as his first fieldwork assignment and, as he recently said in a letter to the editor: "When I arrived on the Tiwi beach in April 1928 I was not an anthropologist but just a kid of twenty-three who had read a lot of anthropology books and listened to a lot of anthropological talk. When I left the Tiwi two years later I was an anthropologist."

In 1930, on a Rockefeller Traveling Fellowship, he spent a summer school at the University of Chicago with Edward Sapir and Robert Redfield, and then went on to the London School of Economics to work toward his doctorate with C. G. Seligman and B. Malinowski. Looking around for a job, in 1932, the darkest year of the Great Depression, the only teaching job in anthropology that was available in the whole British Empire (then at its height) was at the University of Toronto in Canada where he taught from 1932 to 1947. In the latter year he moved to the University of Wisconsin at Madison where he was Professor of Anthropology until 1959. In that year he took on the task of founding the first chair of Social Anthropology in the University of Istanbul and has been in Turkey for

Left: Steve Hart in 1947. Right: Hart in a Turkish village in 1968.

the past ten years. Through his Turkish students, of whom by now (1969) he has trained about fifty "first-rate fieldworkers," he has interviewed several thousand families in Istanbul alone and has drawn them from a wide range of social groups and institutions. In addition to this he has studied several Turkish villages.

Because no photograph of him (with or without beard) survives from Tiwi days, we reproduce one photograph of Hart taken in Madison on the Spindlers' front porch in 1947 and another taken in Turkey in 1968, with his Turkish student-interpreter and four Turkish villagers, which he suggests be captioned "Forty years a fieldworker and still going strong."

G. D. S.

Preliminary Note The Tiwi live on two islands, Melville and Bathurst Islands, which lie at the closest point about 25 miles from the Australian mainland. The fieldwork which is described here was done in 1928 and 1929. At that time there was a Roman Catholic Mission Station on the south end of Bathurst Island but no other white settlement. The total population was about 1100 and the total area of the two islands about 3000 square miles. A description of the culture, as Hart found it in those years and again as Pilling found it in 1953 and 1954 is to be found in *The Tiwi of North Australia*, by C. W. M. Hart and Arnold R. Pilling, first published in 1960. Some other references are given at the end of this chapter.

Getting Started

Fieldwork among the Tiwi in 1928–1929 was not difficult provided that the fieldworker was young, healthy, undemanding of personal comfort, and unmarried. (I suspect that these four conditions apply universally to fieldwork among the simpler peoples, but there is no space here to argue the point.) At

Mourning ceremony around carved and painted grave posts.

that date the Tiwi were still mostly nomadic, though the Sacred Heart Mission was nearly twenty years old and the Japanese pearling luggers had been coming to the beaches around Cape Keith long enough to cause the neighboring bands —the Yeimpi and Mandiimbula—to have almost abandoned hunting and gathering of their food and to depend instead almost entirely on the supplies provided by the Japanese captains in exchange for native women. I did not need the Yeimpi and Mandiimbula (except for their genealogies) and only visited them three times during my two years stay on the islands. On none of those occasions were they pleased to see me, since they feared that my presence in their camps might frighten away their Japanese friends so our mutual acquaintance was brief and noncommittal on both sides.

The Mission was a different matter. The only means of communication between Darwin and the islands was the Mission lugger, so one had to land at the Mission or not at all. Politeness required that one stay at the Mission on first arrival and indeed it was only after staying at the Mission for some time that one got to know the local conditions; for instance how much effect the Mission had had on the various bands. The missionaries were invariably kind and hospitable, but it soon became clear that I could not stay at the Mission indefinitely. Just as the Japanese pearlers represented a focus of power, so the Mission represented another focus of power. Both of them, by very different means, were engaged in changing the old native culture into something else and hence the tribe at large was divided into three factions, or if that word be too strong, three competing foci, the Japanese, the Mission, and the old, still unchanged, native culture. Of the nine bands into which the tribe was divided (see map), two were affected by the Japanese, three (the Tiklauila, the Rangwiland, the Mingwila) by the Mission, at least to some extent. Up to the north were the four bands who so far had not been affected by either Japanese or Mission and who could justly be called the real uncontaminated Tiwi. The Malauila occupied the northern section of Bathurst Island; the Munupula, Turupula, and Wilrangwila, the north-central and north-western sections of Melville Island. Clearly it was with them rather than at the Mission that I should spend most of my time. Moreover I became aware of another factor, which happens everywhere I think, and which should be carefully watched by every fieldworker. In another society, the anthropologist (stranger or outsider) is taken in and made welcome by one group or faction, who henceforward tend to monopolize him. He therefore becomes an object of suspicion or (at best) indifference to rival groups or factions. One has always to find a way to break away from one's original welcomers or sponsors.

This danger was exemplified by my relations with Mariano. I have already explained in detail in *The Sons of Turimpi* (Hart 1954) how I acquired Mariano, a Tiklauila, as my interpreter and chief guide, even before I left Darwin, and I arrived at the Mission more or less under his sponsorship. Looking back now, I cannot see that anybody else in the whole tribe would

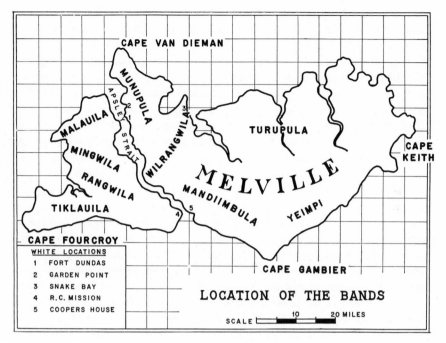

Tiwi Bands.

have been nearly so useful as he was. For intelligence, reliability, and capacity to objectively analyze and explain his own culture he could not be faulted. Moreover his pidgin English was far superior to that of any other man of the same age and seniority, and until I could learn the language for myself I simply had to keep him. The trouble was that he was a Tiklauila and one of the mission-affected faction; in fact he was one of the leaders of the faction. This of course did not mean that he was a Catholic; it merely meant that he confined himself to one wife (so far at least), allowed his children to attend the Mission school, and usually took the Mission side in the arguments and discussions among the tribesmen.

What was the Mission side? It is briefly described in *The Tiwi of North Australia* (Hart and Pilling 1960:102–103). Under prewhite conditions the Tiwi had been extremely polygynous, with older men having ten, fifteen, or more wives while younger men remained unmarried until the age of forty or more. As part of the same system, men obtained wives late in life, but girls were betrothed to their future husbands at birth and went to live in the camps of their husbands at puberty, that is, around fourteen or fifteen. Father Gsell, the founder and head of the Mission, being a good Catholic, hated the plural marriages and also hated the idea of young girls being married to very old men. He not only vehemently preached from his pulpit against both practices, but actively entered the marriage market himself by buying young girls (usually babies) from their fathers and their future husbands. By his payments of flour, tobacco, tea, and sugar to both the father of the girl and the man to whom the father had promised her, the priest recognized that both of them had rights in the child, and these rights he bought from them. The girl, if or when old enough, was then put into the convent at the Mission, brought up by nuns, and when she was seventeen or eighteen she was encouraged to choose her own husband from among the single young men; Father Gsell insisting however that the young man chosen solemnly promise that this would be his only wife, and that he would reject any further girls who might be bestowed upon him.

Thus Father Gsell had become himself a factor in the marriage-arranging and wife-trading that was so marked a feature of Tiwi culture. To the Tiwi there was not much difference in Father Gsell "bestowing" convent-bred girls on deserving young men and a Tiwi father bestowing his daughters on what *he* considered "deserving" young men. The young man selected by a Tiwi father as a son-in-law was expected to be grateful to his benefactor and become a satellite of the older man. In the same way the Tiwi expected that the young men who got their wives from Father Gsell would show their gratitude by becoming satellites of the priest. Mariano was one such man. He had obtained his wife from the convent, making the usual promise that he would accept no more wives from any source and so far he has kept his promise. But two fathers of baby girls had (independently of each other), bestowed these girls on Mariano and what he intended to do about these bestowals when they got older was anybody's guess. He told me he intended to sell them to the Mission when they were old enough to live in the convent, but this he could only do with the consent and cooperation of the two fathers. In this manner Father Gsell was in the marriage-business, through Father Gsell Mariano was in the marriage-business, and through Mariano I looked likely to become involved in the marriage business, or at least involved willy-nilly in tribal politics, much of which revolved around marriage deals and redeals.

To leave the Mission and go live with the northern bands was easy and desirable. The only trouble was the language. Around the Mission the younger men spoke pidgin English and some like Mariano spoke it well. But in the northern bands nobody spoke anything except Tiwi. So one had to compromise. I went to and joined the northern bands but I took Mariano with me. Otherwise I could not (at first) communicate with the northern bands. Once this decision had been made there was little problem. The pagan bands were glad to have us; with Mariano as interpreter and assorted members of the northern bands as teachers and helpers I could learn the language. I was no longer identified with the Mission nor with the Tiklauila, and in all sorts of small ways (by observing taboos for example) I could indicate my lack of sympathy for much of the Mission program. Away from the Tiklauila Mariano was not nearly so much a liability as I had expected; the traditional daily living under tribal con-

Applying body paint for a ceremony.

ditions was quite congenial to him; the Malauila and Munupula respected him even though they did not agree with him in his advocacy of monogamy, and in fact questions concerning the Mission rarely came up for discussion.

In the meantime I was able to learn the language. It did not come easily, but at least it came. I suppose there are places in the world where it is possible to do fieldwork without knowing the language or by working through interpreters; but surely much is missed by working under such conditions. By the time I left the islands I think I spoke reasonably good Tiwi, understood it better than I spoke it, and was never ashamed to ask that something I did not understand be explained or repeated in another way. The biggest factor in facilitating my learning was of course the isolation from other English-speakers that living in Munupi or Malau provided. If I had remained at the Mission I would have been speaking English every day to the priests and nuns, and would probably never have learned Tiwi. But in Malau or Munupi nobody spoke any English (except Mariano and he only spoke pidgin), so I either spoke Tiwi or did not speak at all.

Living with the Malauila and Munupula meant, of course, living pretty close to nature. In *The Tiwi of North Australia* there is a chapter called Daily Life, and for much of my two years with the Tiwi the daily life of the natives was my daily life too. That is, I went where they went, stopped when they stopped, ate what they ate, slept when they slept, and generally was interested and concerned about whatever they were interested and concerned about. It surprised me, who had no boy-scout background, how little in the way of manufactured objects one needed. Since the Tiwi establishments (collections of households) are always moving, and one moves easiest if one moves light, it was instructive to find out how light the baggage could be made. Sneakers, a hat, and a pair of shorts were all the clothing necessary; a shotgun to kill wallaby and wild fowl and plenty of shells for it; pencils and notebooks; soap and toothbrush (even towels were optional); pipe and tobacco; a camera and plenty of film. These seemed to be the only essentials, except that for an Australian, tea and sugar had to be added; and as luxuries, only because they were light in weight, salt, pepper, and Worcestershire Sauce, since Tiwi cooking is very tasteless without condiments. For the natives, stores had to include a few simple medicines like iodine (the "burning medicine" which they loved and demanded to have applied raw to all simple cuts), aspirin, and Epsom Salts. And lastly, the heaviest and bulkiest item of all, an endless supply of native twist tobacco, a currency that took one everywhere and opened all doors. Everything else was parked at the Mission and except for the shotgun, all the above items could be carried in one or two small sacks. Blankets were not necessary; the Tiwi on chilly nights sleep between two small fires which can be kept burning all night with twigs that you take to bed with you, and provided you do not roll, the fires give warmth and keep the mosquitoes away. The native food was perfectly adequate and usually abundant, and by lending my shotgun to a native hunter I was able on most days to contribute my share to the total food production of the household with which I was living. One of the objects thankfully left behind was a razor, since beards were prestige symbols for the Tiwi. Older and important men carried luxuriant beards, the bushier the more admired; only "kids" were beardless, and though I never achieved as bushy a beard as that of Father Gsell (an Alsatian by birth), mine was at least as bushy as that of Father McGrath, his second-in-command. Incidentally but importantly, the Tiwi sign of intense anger is to put the right hand behind the beard, sweep it into the mouth and chomp hard on it, a most convincing indication of fury. How can one uphold one's dignity or indicate one's anger in such a culture if one is clean-shaven?

This beard business is, I think, part of the day-by-day fieldwork tactics that fieldworkers in any culture have to be thinking about constantly, and the better they know their culture the better their tactics will be. Tact and tactics seem to have the same derivation as words. For a man without a beard to expect to be taken seriously in Tiwi culture was quite simply tactless or a gaucherie, and anthropologists should avoid gaucheries, otherwise they are no different from tourists. Tourists are usually tactless not through ill-will but through ignorance of the local culture; anthropologists thinking out tactics are merely striving to be more tactful as their knowledge of the culture improves.

Getting into the Kinship System

In my travels about the two islands I frequently met groups of natives who had never seen me before. Such groups invariably addressed three questions to the men I was with. "How old is he?" "Is he married?" "What clan does he belong to?" As I was only about twenty-three at the time (and, of course, unmarried), no Tiwi was likely to take me very seriously if told the truth, since, as I said in *The Tiwi of North Australia* (p. 54), "The men between 21 and 30 were the group which the elders were just beginning to take seriously . . . the younger members of this group were almost indistinguishable from the "kids" (that is, the under twenty-year-old group)." But with a beard I looked much older than 24 and in response to such questions my companions could easily up my age to over thirty without provoking disbelief, and my state of unmarriedness could easily be excused as being due to white men having different customs. All of which goes to show that in a culture such as Tiwi, with its great contempt for male youthfulness, an anthropologist of twenty-three was at a great disadvantage but at least I was well aware of it and constantly trying to counteract it.

The third customary question—What is his clan?—was much more difficult to deal with. Like all students of Radcliffe-Brown I had been well grounded in the overall importance of the kinship system in all Australian tribes and of how anybody not in the kinship system was considered to be not quite human. One of Radcliffe-Brown's stories had told of how, when he was doing the research that led eventually to The *Three Tribes of Western Australia* (Radcliffe-Brown 1912), he had traveled along the Ninety Mile Beach accompanied by a native interpreter named Teacup. Whenever they approached a new group or a strange camp, it was Teacup's duty to go in first and establish some kin connection between himself and the new group. Until such connection was made, no intercourse was possible between them and the point of the story was how on one occasion, Radcliffe-Brown was awakened by Teacup crawling into his sleeping bag announcing that both of them were going to be killed, because after hours of effort, Teacup had been unable to find any kinship link between himself and the group they had just met. I knew the Tiwi were not going to kill me, but after a few weeks on the islands I also became aware that they were often uneasy with me because I had no kinship linkage to them. This was shown in many ways, among others in their dissatisfaction with the negative reply they always got to their third question, "What clan does he belong to?" Around the Mission, to answer it by saying "White men have no clans," was at least a possible answer, but among the pagan bands like the Malauila and Munupula such an answer was incomprehensible—to them everybody must have a clan, just as everybody must have an age. To answer their first question "How old is he?" by saying "White men don't have ages" would be nonsense. To them it was equally nonsense to answer their third question as we did. And by talking such apparent nonsense we made them uneasy, and by extension, hostile or at least unfriendly. If I had a clan I would be inside the kinship system, everybody would know how to act toward me, I would know how to act toward everybody else, and life would be easier and smoother for all.

How to get myself into the clan and kinship system was however quite a problem. Even Mariano, while admitting the desirability, saw no way of getting me in. "These Malauila and Munupula are just wild men," he said privately, "they just can't understand that white people don't have clans and don't use kinship terms when talking to each other and about each other." In common with my generation of "new anthropologists" (1930 vintage), I had laughed derisively when I had heard or read the accounts of late nineteenth-century travelers and amateur anthropologists who claimed that they had been "fully initiated" into some tribe or other, and anyhow it was not initiation that I felt I needed but merely a place in the kinship system.

There did not seem much hope and then suddenly the problem was solved entirely by a lucky accident and solved so easily that it showed how right I had been in feeling the problem to be there. I was in a camp where there was an old woman who had been making herself a terrible nuisance. Toothless, almost blind, withered, and stumbling around, she was physically quite revolting and mentally rather senile. She kept hanging round me asking for tobacco, whining, wheedling, snivelling, until I got thoroughly fed-up with her. As I had by now learned the Tiwi equivalents of "Go to hell" and "Get lost," I rather enjoyed being rude to her and telling her where she ought to go. Listening to my swearing in Tiwi, the rest of the camp thought it a great joke and no doubt egged her on so that they could listen to my attempts to get rid of her. This had been going on for some time when one day the old hag used a new approach. "Oh, my son," she said, "please give me tobacco." Unthinkingly I replied, "Oh, my mother, go jump in the ocean." Immediately a howl of delight arose from everybody within earshot and they all gathered round me patting me on the shoulder and calling me by a kinship term. She was my mother and I was her son. This gave a handle to everybody else to address me by a kinship term. Her other sons from then on called me brother (and I should call them brothers); her brothers called me "sister's son" (and I should call them mother's brother); her husband (and his brothers) called me son and I called each of them father and so on. I was now in the kinship system, my clan was Jabijabui (a bird) because my mother was Jabijabui and Tiwi clans were matrilineal.

From then on the change in the atmosphere between me and the tribe at large was remarkable. Strangers were now told that I was Jabijabui and that my mother was old so-and-so and when told this, stern old men would relax, smile and say "then you are my brother," (or my son, or my sister's son, or whatever category was appropriate) and I would struggle to respond properly by addressing them by the proper term. Actually it was usually quite easy because all I needed was the term reciprocal with the term he used for me. If he called me brother I called him brother, if he called me son I called him father, if he called me sister's son then I called him mother's brother. It got a little harder after that.

For the rest of my stay on the islands this framework persisted. Mariano, in his stubborn manner, continued to address me as "Boss" (to show his Europeanization) and a few sophisticates around the Mission persisted in addressing me as "Mistarti," but the average old man or old woman, especially in Munupi and Malau, addressed me by a kinship term, referred to me by a kinship term (for example, question put to Mariano: "When is my sister's son coming to visit me?") and I hope, if they thought about me at all, thought about me in kinship terms. As they certainly thought about everybody else in such context, I infer that they found it easier and more comfortable to think about me in such a context. And because they were more relaxed and comfortable using that context, my fieldwork was made much easier and relations were on a much more friendly and casual basis than before.

How seriously they took my presence in their kinship system is something I never will be sure about. They certainly did not expect me to change my behavior because of it. Though I was now a Jabijabui with numerous relatives, no pressure was put upon me to act like a true clansman of that clan. My fellow Jabijabui did not ask for special favors or for conduct from me that promoted their special clan interest. They called me brother and I called them brother, and except for occasionally bringing it up in order to get a little extra tobacco, that was all there was to it. It seemed that the primary purpose of a kinship system is to promote ease and prevent strain in everyday, face-to-face living, and the other aspects of kinship and clanship are secondary or subordinate to that primary purpose. That was fine with me and I presumed it was fine with them. However, toward the end of my time on the islands an incident occurred that surprised me because it suggested that some of them had been taking my presence in the kinship system much more seriously than I had thought. I was approached by a group of about eight or nine senior men all of whom I knew, drawn from several bands and when they arrived the only point in common that I recognized them as having was that they were all senior members of the Jabijabui clan, that is, I called them all brother or mother's brother. It turned out that they had come to me on a delicate errand. They were the senior members of the Jabijabui clan and they had decided among themselves that the time had come to get rid of the decrepit old woman who had first called me son and whom I now called mother. (Many of them called her mother too, and those who did not call her mother called her sister.) As I knew, they said, it was Tiwi custom, when an old woman became too feeble to look after herself, to "cover her up." This could only be done by her sons and her brothers and all of them had to agree beforehand, since once it was done they did not want any dissension among the brothers or clansmen, as that might lead to a feud. My "mother" was now completely blind, she was constantly falling over logs or into fires, and they, her senior clansmen were in agreement that she would be better out of the way. Did I agree also? I already knew about "covering up." The Tiwi, like many other hunting and gathering peoples, sometimes got rid of their ancient and decrepit females. The method was to dig a hole in the ground in some lonely place, put the old woman in the hole and fill it in with earth until only her head was showing. Everybody went away for a day or two and then went back to the hole to discover, to their great surprise, that the old woman was dead, having been too feeble to raise her arms from the earth. Nobody had "killed" her, her death in Tiwi eyes was a natural one. She had been alive when her relatives last saw her. I had never seen it done, though I knew it was the custom, so I asked my brothers if it was necessary for me to attend the "covering up." They said no and they would do it, but only after they had my agreement. Of course I agreed, and a week or two later we heard in our camp that my "mother" was dead, and we all wailed and put on the trimmings of mourning. Mariano thoroughly disapproved and muttered darkly that the police in Darwin should be informed, but I soon told him that this was Jabijabui business and since he was not Jabijabui, it was none of his affair.

I have gone into some detail about my "mother" because the whole affair shows the all-pervasiveness of the kinship system and how every action, even the choice of a term by which to address me or the getting rid of a decrepit old woman, had to be handled along kinship lines. Even my telling off of Mariano can be seen in that light. He was my friend, but in a crisis I rejected his advice and acted in concert with my brothers and mother's brothers. The lines of friendship (and there were plenty of them in Tiwi) always dissolved or broke at the call of the kinfolk or clan. In times of crisis a Tiwi did not have friends, he only had brothers and mother's brothers and sisters' sons.

So by the end of July 1928 I was away from the Mission, caught up in the kinship system, learning the language, going round from camp to camp in Malau and Munupi, and more or less reconciled to life in the bush. Sleeping on the ground, washing in the creek or waterhole (if any), eating with one's fingers, some days walking from sunrise till sunset and camping (after dark) in an ant's nest, at other times camping for weeks at a time in the same spot, where food and water were plentiful. It was all rather dirty but apart from that very pleasant indeed and certainly helped, I think, to make my point that the role of an anthropologist and that of a missionary were quite different. As a guest I did whatever my Tiwi hosts wanted me to do; if they wanted to move I moved too; if they wanted to stay where they were I stayed too. Never in my life, before or since, have I been so submissive to the will of others, and never before had the Tiwi seen or heard of a white man who was so undemanding.

Time on My Hands

And therein lay the germ of the next difficulty. I had too much time on my hands. Evans-Pritchard was to tell me, years later, that he had found the same thing when working with the Azande of the Sudan and had only been able to combat it by a rigid determination to take notes, about something, no matter how boring or trivial, every single day he was in the field. But the Azande are a very numerous tribe and there is always something going on in an Azande village or cattle-camp. But as is explained at length in *The Tiwi of North Australia* (*passim* but especially pp. 44–45), Tiwi households (numbering ten, fifteen, twenty people) spent something like forty out of every fifty-two weeks of the year living by themselves with only minimal contact with other households. Frequently households were combined into what I called establishments and of these there were seven in Malau and about nine in Munupi in 1928. But more than half of them were of little use to me since they contained mostly young or middle-aged people who did not have much to add to my general store of anthropological information, and who, in any case, were expected to work all day. During the day only the babies and one or maybe two old wives to look after them would be left in the camp; the rest would be scattered through the bush, the women and children gathering wild fruits, vegetables and nuts, the men hunting. Only at sundown would they all come in and the brief period between sundown and bedtime would be busily taken up by cooking, gossiping, and eating. Encamped with such a household, what was I supposed to do all day? The hunters did not want me. I made too much noise and frightened the game away. The women did not want me since their gathering habits were all business and in any case unmarried men were supposed to stay away from them. Apparently the only daytime activity for me was to stay in camp and help the old women in charge of the babies, but such a role had little appeal.

In bigger establishments, which were those of the older and more prestigeful men, the old men did not hunt but stayed in camp all day, doing very little on most days except eat and sleep. Some of them did a little work like carving ceremonial grave-posts or, like Timalarua, making canoes or carving spears, but as a group these Munupula and Malauila elders were not particularly good informants, except for their memories of historical occurrences. On most matters none of these old men was as good an informant as Mariano. They did not have the somewhat detached objective attitude toward their own culture that he had acquired through his contacts with the missionaries and other white men. As the behavior of my Jabijabui brothers was later to show, the senior men of the northern bands were rather naive about their own culture, in the sense that they accepted its logics as self-evident without being able to explain or analyze them. None of the sophisticated Tiklauila around the Mission would have thought for a moment that I might start a blood feud against them if they

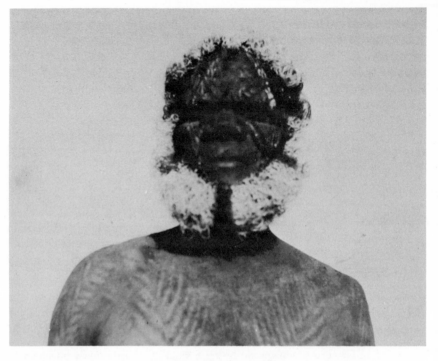

Timalarua, the canoe maker.

"covered up" my mother without my knowledge or consent; the more naive Malauila and Munupula thought it likely because that was the only logic of such a situation they knew. That was "the Tiwi way" and they knew no other way to handle it. The white policeman logic which Mariano immediately raised as an alternative logic for me to follow never occurred to them because it was not a Tiwi logic. From which I conclude that the best informants in still functioning native societies are rarely likely to be the pure unsullied primitive old pagans (the "noble savages") but are much more likely to be men who, through contact with another culture, usually European, have been shaken a little in their acceptance of their own culture to the point where they have "to explain it," even to themselves and who, when explaining it to outsiders are therefore able to bring out logics and interconnections that their more primitive seniors are incapable of putting into words.

This, of course, does not imply that I depended on Mariano for everything. Ceremonies came and went, mourning ceremonies and initiation and naming ceremonies, and there I could make my own descriptions and talk to the ceremonial leaders (Tuntalumi, Enquirio, Kewnayua) about the meaning and history and the symbolism of the rituals. Folklore and tribal legends any old man could give me but they did not vary much in their stories and I did not see much point in listening to and recording the same legend for the fifth or sixth time. Technology bored me. All the young functionalists of those early days had a profound contempt for the type of anthropology book that contained dozens of pages of descriptions of how the people made pots or baskets or cut digging sticks, a contempt which Radcliffe-Brown (and later, after I left the

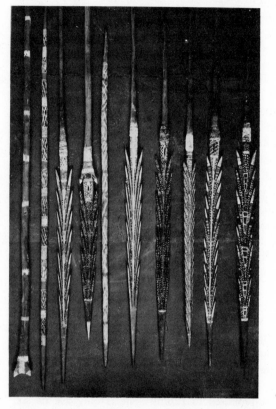

Carved Tiwi spears.

Tiwi, Malinowski) did much to encourage. What else in the culture was there that would or might occupy my abundant spare time? Pondering this question I came to my next moment of truth.

Some Unanswered Questions about Kinship

I had learned my kinship systems of Australia from Radcliffe-Brown (and there never was a better teacher) and had accompanied Lloyd Warner (as a "learner") on his trip in early 1928 to the Roper River where he gathered up kinship systems (at the rate of six or seven a day) for the tribes on the periphery of his Murngin area. As a result I thought of a kinship system as a diagram of vertical and horizontal lines usually 4 by 5 spaces in size with the native name of Father's Father at the top left hand corner and the native name for Daughter's Daughter at the bottom right hand corner. Tacked on in front of the middle line was a character named Ego, and you really needed two such charts for each tribe, one for Ego (male) and the other for Ego (female). (See Radcliffe-Brown 1912 for such charts.) In this sense I had "got" my Tiwi kinship system even before I left Darwin to go to the islands. Following Warner's methods, a half-hour's discussion with a few Tiwi who happened to be in Darwin at the time, made it clear that the Tiwi system was of the usual Kareira type (Type I in Radcliffe-Brown's classification), with a few special or unusual features added. Nothing to it: Type I with modifications. After arriving in the islands I had been using it for terms of address and of course after my adoption by my old mother was expected to use it for terms of reference also. There did not seem to be much more work to do on that section of the culture.

And yet things kept cropping up that were clearly matters of kinship, but which I did not at all understand. "She is promised to Padimo" somebody would say, pointing to a little girl of five or six. I did not remember anything in class concerning what "promising" a wife meant, or of who had the right to "promise" one. This was a matrilineal society and I already knew that in it sisters, brothers, mothers, and mother's brothers were very close to one another.

Well then, "Who promised her to Padimo? Her brothers?" Loud laughter. "Of course not. Her father. Only the father has the right to promise a girl to her future husband."

"But suppose the father dies. Does his disposition of the girl take place as he wished?"

"Certainly. The new father has to carry out the wishes of the previous father."

"Can the brothers promise their sister?"

"No, because they are too young."

"What do you mean, because they are too young? They are not always too young."

"Well, look at this little girl promised to Padimo. She is only five or six. Her only brother is about two years older than her, that is about seven. How could he promise anything to anybody. He's not dry behind the ears."

"Well, when he grows up can he promise her to somebody?"

"No, because she's already promised to Padimo."

"Look here, I know Padimo, he's a man of about thity-six. Twenty-five years from now this little girl will still only be around thirty and her little brother will be about thirty-two. But Padimo by that time may well be dead. What then will happen?"

"Well, you can't tell. When Padimo dies her mother will marry again and her new father will rename the little girl."

"Wait a minute, there are two points there. Suppose her mother does not remarry when Padimo dies. What then?"

"Oh, she has to. All women must have a husband all the time."

"Well, well, I didn't know that. No matter how old she is?"

"No matter how old and no matter how young. All Tiwi females have husbands."

"And secondly, what's all this about renaming the child?"

"Well, a father names all his children, but if he dies his widow must marry again, and then her new husband renames all her children."

"And if the second husband also dies?"

"Then she must get a third husband and he will rename all her children."

"And what happens to the old names?"

"They all become taboo."

"I see."

Of course, in the early days I did not see at all, but there was enough in the above dialogue and many like it to convince me that I really knew nothing about how Australian kinship systems really worked and that there seemed to be a great deal to the Tiwi system that was not even mentioned in the *Three Tribes of Western Australia*. Combing my memory, I could not remember anywhere in the Australian literature any discussion of decision-making in marriage arrangement, that is who decided which girl would marry which man. Apparently as long as a man married his mother's brother's daughter (in Kareira), or his mother's mother's brother's daughter's daughter (in Arunta), there were no other relevant considerations. (Later research when I got back to the libraries showed that my memory was right. Nowhere in the classic literature on Australian tribes does any writer explore the mechanics of how the decision is made by which this particular girl marries this particular man.) This conclusion of mine, is, on the whole, confirmed by a recent treatment of the same matter, apparently stimulated by the 1960 Tiwi publication, by one of the younger Australianists, Dr. L. R. Hiatt (Hiatt 1967).

The conversation reported above, and others like it, reveal an extraordinary number of new leads, all of them unexpected. The compulsory marriage for all females, the naming and renaming rules, the discrepancy in age between Padimo and his child bride of five or six, the implication that while a little boy of seven could have no say in the disposition of his sister he might have some say by the time he was thity-two, the intriguing question of how ancient widows of sixty or more got new husbands, all of these questions clearly needed intensive research. But one could not explore such questions very far on a general or abstract level. The discussions kept going around in circles because all the things mentioned and others not brought out yet were interconnected. For instance, I now want to ask why the father of the little girl promised her to Padimo in the first place. And I also want to know how on earth a man (or woman) ever gets a permanent name if their names are always changed after their mother remarries. And I now see dimly that if all first marriages of girls are of the

Padimo type, to a man thirty or more years older than the girls, then Tiwi women as a group are likely to be widowed many times during their lives and will therefore each bear children to quite a number of different husbands. What I needed most to sort out the jumble were some detailed, concrete cases.

If the reader wants to know how all these things and many others work out and tie together into a logical and orderly system he will have to read *The Tiwi of North Australia* for himself. Here, I am only concerned to explain how I came slowly to understand it all and to put it together as a cultural system. Discussed or explored with the Tiwi at the level of discussion exemplified above, which is what I call the abstract level of discussion, there are too many loose ends or places where the informants could say (indeed had to say), "Maybe" or "We can't tell," or "Perhaps that will happen, perhaps not." Only by getting hold of some complete details of actual marriages and promises and remarriages of widows could I hope to unscramble the jigsaw. And that meant genealogies.

Answers in Genealogies

I have always liked genealogies, and still do. There is something clean and structural about them, like blueprints. Rivers had used them extensively when writing *The Todas* (1906), and in some ways my problem was similar to that which he had faced when he discovered that the Todas were practicing both polygyny and polyandry at the same time. Though I was not yet sure what the things were, the Tiwi marriage system seemed to include many different things at the same time. Many years later, Ward Goodenough, studying the Trukese of Micronesia was confronted by another similar problem, that of understanding the complicated land-tenure system of the island of Truk, where inheritance follows several different patterns simultaneously, and like Rivers and me, Goodenough also found that tracing actual cases through genealogies was the only road to understanding (Goodenough 1960). In all three cases, my own judgment is that the genealogical method was not just useful but absolutely essential for the anthropologist concerned to understand his culture. Which makes one wonder why it is not used more often. The interminable disputes about the Murngin, for instance, might readily be settled if Warner had only given us some complete and detailed genealogies. Barnes has recently written a very elegant and stimulating analysis of the place of genealogies in fieldwork (Barnes 1967).

In any case, as soon as I showed interest in collecting genealogies, it turned out that "the time on my hands" problem was solved. The experts on genealogical matters were the old women, the older the better, since their memories went back further. And it was just these old veterans who had the most spare time. In the camps of the important men, they were the ones who stayed around the camp all day, keeping an eye on the babies, and attending to the wants of the old men. Their gathering days were past and though they might accompany the younger women into the bush, it was to act as watchdogs over the younger women rather than as energetic participants in the food quest. In practice they enjoyed a great deal of independence and if I asked some of them to stay in camp and supply me with genealogies, they did not have to ask anybody's permission to do so. Some old women, like my "mother" for instance, were quite stupid and senile, but there were plenty whom I could use, and whose memory of long-ago marriages could be checked against each other. So I had my task for all my spare time, the genealogies, and I had my task force, the older women in any camp that I came to. From then on I was always busy.

For the Tiwi genealogies must be the most complicated genealogies that any anthropologist ever sought to collect. Every older woman had at least four and sometimes six or seven husbands in the course of her lifetime, bearing children to at least three of them. Every old man had or had had a number of wives, some now dead, some still living and some bestowed upon him but not yet in residence in his camp. In *The Tiwi of North Australia* (p. 64) I gave a detailed breakdown of the twenty-one wives of Ki-in-kumi, an elderly Malauila, and he was by no means exceptional. Many of these wives had been married to other men before marrying him and hence their children had to be shown not only in Ki-in-kumi's genealogy but also in the genealogies of their real fathers (now dead), who often were not Malauila at all, and therefore would not only be on a different page but in a different volume. All bestowals and rebestowals and most, if not all, widow-remarriages were parts of deals, and somehow the nature of the deal had to be found and noted in the genealogies. As deals were often begun years before my arrival and the pay-off (or part of it) was only taking place now, it was necessary to get as much genealogical information as possible, not only about the living, but also about the dead. Old Ki-in-kumi had gotten started on his accumulation of twenty-one wives in his early thirties, which meant in the 1890s, and those deals of the 1890s were themselves the results or partly the results of deals which took place thirty years before that, and now in 1928, Ki-in-kumi, as an old man, was still making deals (that is, bestowing his daughters) according to the commitments of both those earlier sets of deals. (This point is well brought out by the footnote on p. 51 of *The Tiwi of North Australia*.)

The Age Factor

In addition to these Byzantine complexities of marriage and descent, the age factor was of great importance. All Tiwi young men started their careers by being or seeking to be what I have called "satellites" of older men. But, at some later stage of their lives many of them stopped being satellites and instead tried to attract satellites of their own. The formal kinship relationship of two men would not change with age, but their relationship as partners or rivals in marriage deals would change often. Therefore in making their genealogies, one had to watch carefully for changing ages. The genealogy of Inglis and Tomitari given in *The Tiwi of North Australia* (p. 74) would be meaningless if the ages of the people concerned were not given. Tomitari was the sister's son of Inglis throughout his life, as much in 1914 as in 1928. But their relationship as participants in a series of marriage deals changed drastically between 1914 and 1928, and the reason for the drastic change was that they were both fourteen years older in 1928. This incidentally is a good example of why the formal kinship system of 4 by 5 kinship terms plus Ego was so useless in understanding Tiwi marriage arrangements.

Thus there had to be included in all genealogies, as far as it could be established, the age when a bestowal or remarriage took place of (1) the male partner, (2) the female partner, (3) the bestowing agent (such as the father), or agents (such as a group of brothers) and (4) any satellites or stand-ins who might have been used by any of the parties.

In addition to all these complexities, there were always the dreadful and constant confusions introduced into the genealogies by the endless changing of peoples' names. The personal names of people changed whenever their mother remarried, which was often. Hence a man might appear in one genealogy at the age of three, under one name; then under a quite different name he would appear in another genealogy at the age of fifteen; then somewhere else under another name at the age of thirty, and finally in his own genealogy under the name I knew him by as a senior man. This was often good for a laugh. Getting the genealogy of a man of the last generation I would be told for instance that he had three sons, A, B, and (let us say) Timalamdemiri. "How many of them are still alive?" "Is A still living?" "No, he's dead." "Is B still living?" "No, he's dead." "Is Timalamdemiri still living?" Shouts of laughter. "You went hunting with him last week! He's now called Pingirimini."

So the genealogy project involved not only the collection of the genealogies of everyone in the tribe still living, but also as many of the dead as the old women could remember. It also involved the much more formidable task of editing them, sorting them, sifting them, correcting the people who appeared under different names in different genealogies, and finally cross-indexing them. Much of this could not be done in the field, especially the cross-indexing, but had to wait for my return to civilization where there were electric lights and I could work at night. The whole effort was well worthwhile. Without the genealogies, I could never have written the chapter entitled "The Prestige and Influence Systems" in *The Tiwi of North Australia*, and even there I only used the genealogies of the Malauila, preferring to stick to one band and cover that band completely rather than jump around from one band to another for random illustrations.

Lament

I was very fortunate indeed to have had the chance to do fieldwork under the conditions described above. The Tiwi no longer live their wandering life in the bush, but have now gathered permanently around the Mission Station or the new Government Stations, which have been set up on the islands. All over the world the same thing is happening. The true hunting and gathering tribes no longer hunt and gather. Levi-Strauss laments that in South America the lonely savannahs are becoming more lonely as man disappears from them. In 1928–1929 the savannahs of the Tiwi country were indeed far from being lonely places, and I remain most grateful to the Tiwi for having given me the opportunity to discover what it was like to live their type of life. If only they were still in their savannahs and I were thirty years younger, I would love to do it all over again. But alas, nowadays the Tiwi are monogamous, go to Mass every Sunday, and wear pants. Such is progress. How sad and how dull.

References

Barnes, J. A., 1967, Genealogies. In A. L. Epstein, ed., *The Craft of Social Anthropology.* London: Tavistock Publications.

Goodenough, Ward, 1960, *Property, Kin and Community on Truk.* New Haven, Conn.: Yale Publications in Anthropology, No. 46.

Hart, C. W. M., 1954, The Sons of Turimpi. *American Anthropologist* 56:247–261.

Hart, C. W. M., and *Arnold R. Pilling*, 1960, *The Tiwi of North Australia.* New York: Holt, Rinehart and Winston, Inc.

Hiatt, L. R., 1967, Authority and reciprocity in Australian aboriginal marriage arrangements. *Mankind* 6:486–474.

Radcliffe-Brown, A. R., 1912, Three tribes of western Australia. *J.A.I.* LXIII: 143–194.

Rivers, W. H. R., 1906, *The Todas.* London: Macmillan & Co., Ltd.

7

FIELDWORK IN
GURKHA COUNTRY

JOHN T. HITCHCOCK
University of Wisconsin at Madison

Related Case Study: **The Magars of Banyan Hill**

Nothing is more shocking to neophyte fieldworkers than to find there are no cultures, social structures, kinship systems, roles, statuses, or ecological systems in the field. There are only people acting, events occurring, man-made forms, and nature. Only in thought and in the light of concepts and theory do we more fully categorize, classify and analyze. Some of this thinking about field experience occurs afterwards at home, much of course in the field, and some well beforehand—witness John Hitchcock's statement of his research project in the Appendix to this paper. But fieldwork is much more than an encounter between a disembodied mind and a people. It also is emotion because it includes total persons with all their sensitivities, their deepest feelings, and needs.

In the final write-up for his colleagues only a small part of the anthropologist's reasoning and his long working and reworking of concepts remains; and even less of his feelings. Although this chapter is set within a context of search for an answer to a problem in anthropological theory, the author's intended emphasis is on dimensions of the field experience that such final accounts usually omit. That is why "Fieldwork in Gurkha Country" cannot be read in the usual way we read papers on field methods. Seldom far from the immediacy of emotion, the logic of its progression is not primarily in the working out of solutions to such problems as the ordering of society through the use of social science concepts, or the testing of a theory to explain differences in two ways of life. More fundamentally, the movement is to be understood in terms such as progressive frustration and disenchantment ending with an account of what transcended both. In keeping with his approach the author does not attempt rationally to justify his continued fieldwork to himself. He reveals instead what made it emotionally acceptable.

The Author

John T. Hitchcock writes:

A fellow graduate student at the University of Chicago, where I was studying English literature, first made me aware of a social science other than history and economics. We shared a rooming house and I was impressed by the completeness of his descriptions of life styles and values of people I knew, beginning with only a hint or two. (Years later I realized why he seemed omniscient about families in Newburyport, Massachusetts, and vicinity.) At that time his determinist, Durkheimian worldview struck a responsive chord. Strongly pacifist as an undergraduate at Amherst College, by early 1941 I was combining graduate work with flying lessons, to assure acceptance in the Navy pilot training program. The turnabout gave me an uneasy sense of being pushed by unfathomed forces. It seldom left and when it intensified some years after the war, during a strike at a school where I was teaching, I sought enlightenment in new academic direc-

The author, working up notes in the Monal headman's goatshed.

tions, turning first to sociology and finally to anthropology (Ph.D., Cornell, 1956).

Prior to the Ph.D. I had done fieldwork among the Ute Indians (Summer 1952) and wrote my thesis on material collected in North India on a Ford Foundation grant (1953–1955). While in India my wife and I had made two treks into the Himalayas and hoped we would sometime be fortunate enough to return. When a National Science Foundation grant made it possible (1960–1962), we went to Nepal. It provided terrain and people suited to the research design, but had in addition the special attraction of being at that time almost *terra incognita*, at least to Westerners.

Now Professor of Anthropology at the University of Wisconsin, I have taught previously at Amherst, Berkeley, and UCLA. During 1967 I was in Nepal on a National Institute of Mental Health grant studying shamans and their healing practices.

G. D. S.

Hem Bahadur and John Hitchcock interviewing a Monal family.

Prologue

Whatever else he may be, an anthropologist is a Theseus of sorts. Or perhaps a good Greek, because Greeks other than Theseus had the quality. It appears in the contrast between the Greek and Beowulf. Both plunged into the darkness of a foreign culture both came home with a tale and with proof. But it is Ariadne's ball of twine that makes the difference. Theseus not only got in and out and did the deed; he made it plausible. His deed goes beyond the Saxon's; it transcends the strength and courage, the flailing in a bloody sea. For it is both discovery and shareable method, it enters the realm of reason.

At the outset I ask the reader to accept my allegiance to the value epitomized by Theseus' ball of twine. In the fieldwork discussed here it was of pervasive concern. If it nevertheless appears as muted background, it is from the difficulty of doing justice in brief space to two things—to it and to facets of the experience that seemed to weigh more heavily considering our editors' request to tell it like it was.

With these other aspects it was a matter of coming to terms with emotion, not the least of which was disenchantment with the enterprise, including discovery, reasoned discourse, plausible method, the whole ball of twine. What was left? Why go on? This was the question and in answering I found myself finally in a realm beyond or prior to reason, a realm best expressed in story or symbol.

One final point about exclusion. Just as I have slighted normal preoccupations of the craft by stressing emotion, I have also stressed some emotions to the exclusion of others. In this essay I fear that "misery, as the sea, swells above all the hilles." Surely there is nothing of that contrary vision of grandeur flaming from a nature never spent—hard indeed not to feel in such a setting. Nor, another omission—anything of those good days with incomparable companions— "bravest of the brave, most generous of the generous"—many of the best neither named nor alluded to.

The region of the fieldwork, including the home of *The Magars of Banyan Hill* (Hitchcock 1966), forms a kind of lopsided mountain enclosure. On one side, beginning with Ulleri, a tiny spatter of village high on a southern flank of Annapurna, is a line that extends 40 miles southeast. Halfway, or two days' walk, lies the bazaar town of Pokhara, a mountain boom town, with a natural airstrip on packed river gravels. At the end of the line is Banyan Hill. From Ulleri the land slopes gradually downward, from high, harsh slopes to still mountainous, yet tropical and well-watered lushness. The second side of the enclosure runs west and north 70 miles, again rising into the foothills of the great Himalayan chain, this time close to Dhaulagiri. Here near the head of a narrow valley, with terraces scratched into its precipitous sides, is Monal, a tinier village than Ulleri; and beyond it a day's walk to the north, on the other

The author's two daughters and son on reconnaissance to Ulleri.

side of a 9000 foot pass, lies a broad meadow called Dhorpattan. A region of marshy summer pasturage and meandering streams, Dhorpattan is ringed by mountains whose conifer and hardwood forests give way to alpine grasses. To the north and rising to 15,000 feet the mountains become stone barrens, either white with snow, or black and grey, depending on the season. The final line, about 50 miles long, or five or six days' walk, returns east from Dhorpattan to Ulleri. It crosses the swift Kali, the river that has sliced Annapurna from Dhaulagiri to form a natural link between Nepal and Tibet.

I owe much to Julian Steward, but it was Marshall Sahlins' *Social Stratification in Polynesia* (1958) that stirred the specific idea for the project.[1] Assuming that Polynesia had been settled by peoples from the same cultural source, Sahlins asked what had happened to the original culture as it adapted to environments differing as much as high volcanic islands and low atolls that barely rose above the sea. With environment as the independent variable, and tradition as well as effects of diffusion from other areas outside Polynesia held constant, he believed that over time a natural experiment had occurred, only waiting for someone to record the results. This was the kind of situation I hoped to duplicate.

[1] For a description of the research project design see the Appendix to this paper, The Research Project.

In Nepal there are a number of Tibeto-Burman-speaking tribes living on the southern slopes of the Himalayas. Their speech and Mongoloid features make it reasonable to suppose that centuries ago they crossed the mountains from Tibet or China. I expected to find a tribe or subtribe whose members were living close to one another but at markedly different altitudes. My aim was to be able to say: clearly these are a people from a single cultural source but some have adapted to conditions at high altitudes, others to conditions at low. Being near one another, each group, whether high or low, has been aware of the same influences from the outside, whether ideological, economic, or governmental.

December and January (1960–1961)

Finding that work in the tribe I considered most satisfactory would have been impolitic because already, as it was put, they had "an Anthropologist King," I began research with Magars, a group that was more dispersed and chose Ulleri for a preliminary survey. By making inquiries in Pokhara I learned that Ulleri and many other villages in the vicinity were settled by Magars who probably belonged to a singe subtribe (Pun) and were living at a fairly wide range of altitudes. Since the second basic requirement was a difference in subsistence patterns, I wanted at the onset a Pun village situated too high for growing paddy rice, a village that was furthermore dependent upon summer grazing, with pastures at least a day distant, so that a portion of the village would have to shift their summer residence to tend the livestock. The contrasting low Pun village, which I hoped to find later would grow paddy rice but would be completely sedentary. Livestock would be stall fed or grazed in nearby pastures. In brief, nonrice-growing, near transhumance, was to be compared to rice-growing sedentariness.

Aided by informants in Ulleri and one other village, I was able to survey subsistence patterns in about forty surrounding villages. It turned out that the area had been settled by Magars of a single subtribe and this was heartening. But there were disadvantages. As a whole the area was one of relative poverty, so that differences between paddy-growing and nonpaddy-growing villages were slight. Moreover, the summer grazing pattern did not require much mobility, since most of the pastures were close. I found too, that it was the exceptional and not the typical paddy-growing village that was sedentary. In this region almost all Magar villages depended on a summer grazing pattern.

These considerations had brought me to the verge of leaving Ulleri when a decision on this score became irrelevant. My daughters, ten and eight, and my wife and I had decided to try fieldwork as a family. Experience in India made it seem feasible even with our son Ben, eighteen months. Aside from its apparent research advantages, at least as a place from which to begin a preliminary survey, we had decided on Ulleri because in an emergency a child could have been carried from there to the mission hospital in Pokhara in about 12 hours. My interpreter and assistant was Hem Bahadur ("the brave") Thapa, one of the few Magars who knew the hills well and spoke English. Krishna, also a Magar but unschooled, was our cook and general helper. He had heard about the job possibility and had come to us in Ulleri one evening, having run a distance in a single day it would have taken even a hillman two days to walk. Faced with our unexpected ménage, which was camped in a tent under a cattle-shed roofed with bamboo matting, and the next morning with an undiplomatic request to help with the diapers, he immediately decided to make the return trip. Hem saved him for us—not from any trace of affection then, but from fear of Hem's father, who was an influential figure in Krishna's home region. Less than two weeks after this crisis, barely long enough for Krishna to have found some pleasure in most, if not every aspect of babyhood, Ben died in his sleep. We did not know it until my daughter went into the tent that morning to see why he was so long in waking up.

Pat and I did not return to Ulleri until the end of our fieldwork. We then were on our way back from Monal and Dhorpattan and came by way of the

John Hitchcock and his son, Ben, on a reconnaissance trip to Ulleri.

village so that we could build a stone trailside resting platform called a *chautara*. They are common in Nepal and since they frequently are made as memorials, one sometimes can find on them a remnant at least of the original incised piece of slate noting why they were built, when, and by whom. We built Ben's *chautara*—not near his grave, which is in the forest with the other children's and unmarked—at the end of a steep climb above the village, beneath the only trailside shade tree there was. We found a man who could inscribe a stone with a date, January 17, 1961, "Ben Bahadur" in Nepali and under that, in English:

> Once, sweet, bright joy
> Like their lost children
> An Ulleri child.

March through December (1961)

During the month Pat and I and the girls were in Kathmandu (they eventually enrolled in a Nepali girls' Catholic boarding school, where they remained when we returned to the field), Hem was questioning hillmen and traders in the busy Pokhara bazaars to find out whether there were high villages near Pokhara or further west settled by Magars of the same subtribes as those in and around his own village, Banyan Hill. This village was a good example of the low, rice-growing sedentary type, and Hem's father had replied favorably to a letter explaining the work and asking if he would want us to live there and would help us. The Banyan Hill subtribes were Thapa and Rana, and Ales lived nearby. The question was whether we later could find high near-transhumant villages also settled by members of one or another of these subtribes. Since Hem's researches in Pokhara had made this seem probable, and the prospects of being able to begin work quickly were attractive, I decided to go to Banyan Hill.

In Ulleri where he knew no one and was among Magars who scarcely seemed like Magars to him, Hem was so shy and diffident I worried whether I could get through to people well enough to get any work done. Once among men like the Pokhara traders who knew his father, or among people from his own home region, the metamorphosis was remarkable. An example was the first meal on arriving near the outskirts of Banyan Hill. Hem strode into the courtyard of an orange-plastered thatched house. When he addressed a wiry man in a crushed white cotton skull cap who stepped from the verandah as "grandfather," I knew he was a Brahman; and when Hem introduced me as a schoolmaster in a "big high school where the teaching was done in English," I thought we had been brought here to pay respects to one of the region's learned priests. I was not prepared when Hem said, "Grandfather, we'd like some rice." Nor for the alacrity with which the request was met. My inquiries about whether we should stop here to eat were put aside by Hem's saying he often did and the man would have been hurt if we did not. So, seated rajah-like on a small round open-sided platform with a thatched roof—the scene some months before of a seven-day Hindu ceremony—we soon were enjoying large brass trays of boiled rice, with brass side dishes of spiced, buttery split peas and radish pickle. I know now that Hem's father either had given this man an expensive gift during an occasion when he was spending profusely to honor Brahmans, had loaned him money, or helped him in a court case, as he might do, or not do again. Our research had begun, as it would continue, under the aegis of a strong headman and his clients.

The terraced rice fields of Banyan Hill.

There were great advantages in entering Banyan Hill with Hem's father's support. We could appreciate this because we had begun work in a village where we had not had such help. When we left Ulleri we still were trying, unsuccessfully, to assemble the important men in order to explain the project, discuss the possibility of our providing a school teacher for the village children, and inquire about living in an abandoned village house. The day after our arrival in Banyan Hill, Hem's father had sent messengers to all quarters of the multivillage community where Banyan Hill was located, and on the following day a large gathering had appeared and listened while Hem and I explained why we were there.

To be sure, there was some resistance, especially among members of the

Banyan Hill subtribe of Rana. When we first began interviewing, Shri Ram of Chepte was the most difficult, but also the most important to win over, as he was the eldest. Knowing I could not understand Magarkura, the home language of the villagers, he used it during most of our first visit and many times subsequently. But the termination of these discussions was always the same: "Bhadai (WiBrSo), you are one of us. If you say it is all right, we believe you."

I could not be in Banyan Hill for a whole year, so that production figures needed for the comparison of cultural cores[2] had to be based on estimates rather than on measurements at the time of harvest. Error was inevitable, but within the shortcomings of the method, it was minimal. People knew that Hem would know—and if not Hem, his father—when estimates were very far off. It was the same with debts, usually a most difficult item. Here we were assured of much accuracy because Hem's father was the principal money lender. When I look back from the perspective of Monal, I realize how comparatively easy it was to obtain information in Banyan Hill.

Our most serious problem was the obverse of our advantage. Helpful as my association with Hem was, there were some kinds of information that were impossible to obtain through him. A prime example was labor given his father, a traditional levy exacted by headmen. This topic became especially sensitive when Pat returned from Kathmandu with a Magar young man to help her. It was difficult to find any Magar who spoke English and wanted to live in the hills. Hence a choice according to subtribe was not possible and instead of belonging to the headman's subtribe (Thapa), he belonged to the subtribe of the poorer Banyan Hill group (Rana). Since this group provided much labor for the headman, our new assistant began to hear complaints about the amount of free labor exacted. He was discreet, but one soon learns that no amount of discretion completely walls out the intuitive ambience of village awareness. The gradual stiffening between him and Hem began to become uncomfortable and I was relieved when he had to return to Kathmandu.

I kept a journal, though not with conscientious regularity. Like a pressure dome in a hydraulic system, it functioned only to take up slamming in the pipes. When reading it now I notice the research problem of most concern in Banyan Hill was the headman. I was disappointed he had not wanted to help us more in areas such as law where he was expert. This raised questions about my attitude toward him and reasons for failure to win his more willing and complete cooperation. Shared interest in his religion would have opened doors between us, but much as I would liked to have pursued this I did not have time. But then why this need to "cultivate" a satisfactory relationship when with others it came so much more easily? From his point of view, of course, I could see many reasons. Reform was in the air. In Kathmandu, laws and even governments were being rapidly changed. It was easy to perceive me as part of the new order,

---

[2] See Appendix for explanation of "cultural cores."

especially when I asked about labor dues (now forbidden), terms of share-cropping (now less for the landlord), and interest on loans (now fixed at 10 percent). On the other hand, I also could recognize in myself some feelings that were relevant. Structurally he was part of a caste system giving him great economic, political, and psychological advantage over many of the Untouchable families in the region. It was easy to transfer to him personally my unexpressed objections to the system, since he derived such conspicuous benefits from it, and he may well have sensed this. Some of my journal entries tell me that authority figures generally, especially when somewhat pompous, bother me more than they reasonably should. This too he may have sensed. Whatever the reasons it is clear enough he needed me much less than I needed him, and that to him I was much less interesting than he to me.

Hem had profound respect for his father, a respect normally induced in this culture, but further strengthened in his case by his father's position and qualities. This made it difficult for him to ask for his father's cooperation if it were not voluntarily forthcoming. A critical juncture was reached in the final days of the research when we still had not been able to get an estimate from him

Pat Hitchcock with camera in the courtyard of Hem's uncle, Banyan Hill. The Hitch-cocks lived above the horseshed in the background.

about the extent of his landholdings and loans. I would have been very reluctant to press the matter if I had not brought it up in our letter of query and had not explained at the outset why we had to ask everyone for the same information. Hem suffered, caught between a sense of obligation and dread. It became worse when his father, whose days were full, kept putting us off—surely, Hem thought, because he did not want to discuss the matter. I find the pressure I exerted on Hem to get his father to give us this information—which he did finally—a most unpleasant memory of Banyan Hill.

But at least with Hem's father we had made an agreement; with his paternal uncles we had none and unlike others in the village, these wealthy men had no reason to fear the headman. With two of them friendship carried us as far in the research as we needed to go. But with the third, who had begun to revolve in an orbit of his own apart from his brothers, we gradually met impenetrable resistance. As I reread some of our interviews with him I wonder at the compulsion that sent us back to his house again and again. Our relations were always good humored and bantering but the answers we got, like Jonathan Wild, never deviated into honesty. What we learned about this farm we learned by asking elsewhere. I never could discover where the trouble between us lay but suspect it arose because we were living with the brother he liked least, possibly as a result of religious differences described in *The Magars of Banyan Hill*.

Under the influence of Julian Steward's method of cultural ecology, the focus for all research in Banyan Hill, and later in Monal, was the subsistence pattern. In deciding what to study I began with relations between farmsteads and the physical environment. Although every family obtained goods from kinsmen in the form of gifts or from stores in the form of purchases, I placed prime emphasis on what they obtained from the land and from livestock. Beginning with numbers of livestock, estimated land areas and yields, I inquired about techniques of production. I found it useful in this connection to envisage processes being carried out by invisible persons. Wherever possible I quantified, selecting, for example, as one presumably important variable the time taken from various houses to reach the most distant tillage, forest, fodder trees, and water sources, using as measure the time it took me to walk to these places and back, a method that took account of slope.

Once techno-environmental processes had been described and if possible quantified, the second step was to ask what individuals, as socially defined persons, engaged in these activities. The invisible became visible and one began to form conceptions of statuses and groups, or kinds of organization based not only on social structure but on factors such as neighborliness and friendship.

One advantage of the approach was stringency. Our time in the field had been greatly reduced. Having a minimum of information to be obtained, no matter what else had to go by the board, gave fairly clear priorities and by making something at least seem feasible reduced the sense of haplessness.

For deciding what to study beyond this minimum I used a number of hypotheses derived from such basic assumptions as higher yields leading to a greater density of population and in turn to a higher degree of stratification. One of these hypotheses was that specialists in the low area would derive less income from their own land than from their caste occupation, since they would be more dependent on caste-determined, nonagricultural skills. Testing of the hypothesis led to an investigation of all caste specialists serving Banyan Hill to determine amount of land used and relative yearly income from it.

Mainly I worked with interview guides, indicating what information was needed for required comparisons while inviting flexible exploration of the topic. Hem and I made almost daily rounds of the village talking with whoever was free and amenable. I carried a clipboard with legal-size sheets interspersed with carbons and on them entered numbered paragraphs corresponding to the topics in the interview guides. Much that we learned was picked up fortuitously—for example, when we happened on groups performing domestic sacrifices. For recording this kind of information I carried a notebook, with a carbon for insertion between pages. Duplicate pages of the notebooks were cut out and kept separately with carbons of reports based on the interview guides. Whenever possible these copies were sent to Kathmandu for safekeeping. Toward the end of the stay I made a series of "clean up" questionnaire guides, covering gaps encountered when reviewing all material. One of the final tasks was a survey of nearby villages, to determine whether or not they were similar to Banyan Hill in respects relevant for the research and to get an estimate of population density.

On balance, as I have said, it was a boon to have well-defined research objectives and easily drawn lines between relevance and irrelevance. Yet the situation was not without paradox. The same design that was guide and support in Banyan Hill could become a demon rider, driving me up and down and across the "mountain enclosure" in fruitless search for a companion village to Banyan Hill, and I railed at it during days of fever or nights of bedbugs. Nor did it free me as much as I thought from concerns that according to its strict canons were irrelevant. As I realized when writing *The Magars of Banyan Hill*, it did not truly lay to rest a conscience enhanced if not derived from written exposure to eminences like Boas. I may have attended a wedding in a spirit of moral holiday, but if I had made any notes at all, it had been difficult, in the end, under those exacting Boasian eyes, to let it go at that. The communal live sacrifice at the fortress described in *The Magars of Banyan Hill* could not have been written without notes that from the point of view of the research design did not seem strictly relevant.

Although we carried a Leica for color transparencies and a Rolleiflex for 2 by 2 black and white and Kodacolor, our major aim in photography was to make a motion picture of Magar family life. When we moved to Hem's Second Uncle's courtyard, to live in an open-sided loft above his horsestall and to cook in his buffalo shed, we had an ideal vantage point for filming his family's daily routine—a family that included two wives (one elderly and the other very young) and the daughter of an absent third. The young, simple-minded teenage son of an ex-slave, formerly the property of this family, frequently came with his mother to help the elderly man, and additional help was provided by a member of the metalworker caste who worked as a plowman. We were impressed by the relaxed but intricate intermeshing of daily tasks with which this polygynous family and its helpers carried out the many chores of the farmstead, and eventually shot a sequence (using a Bell and Howell) showing a day in their lives. It included sound taped on a Midgetape recorder (which performed well here but failed later, at a most crucial time during the filming of a shaman). The family was cooperative and we felt we had made a film catching something of its uniqueness, with something said too about the tenor of life in all of Banyan Hill. When we reached the States and could view the footage we found we had been qualified to join a society whose most eminent member is an ornithologist who took many hundreds of feet of film on the long-sought Alaska nesting place of the golden plover. Our footage, though hardly to be compared with his, which was totally unexposed, nevertheless qualified, since a lab mistake had turned much of it a deep pink.

We had reached Banyan Hill in February, and in May, before the rains began, we had started our search for the next village, one to be inhabited by Magars belonging to the same subtribes as were found in and around Banyan Hill (Thapa, Rana, or Ale), and not only too high to grow rice but also near-transhumant. Both during the period when we were working in Banyan Hill and for some time after leaving it, this search occupied a total of almost three months of trekking. Occasionally traveling alone, or in varying combinations, with Hem, a second assistant, Krishna, Pat, and porters, I became, or so it seemed, a Don Quixote, addled not by cloudy symbols of chivalry but by hearsay. The last, most plausible and consequential of incidents can stand for many. Through Christmas the search had taken us further and further north. My second assistant (Bihari, on leave from the government to study anthropological methods), a porter, Hem, and I were three days from a bazaar town we had selected as base for this final search. As we traveled from village to village, sleeping on temple or farmhouse porches or in newly built, one-room schools, we had encountered a medley of Magars but none to specification. Having reached the agreed upon end of the foray, we had cooked a lunch of boiled corn maize beside a brook. Afterwards Hem and Bihari had gone to see if they could persuade a housewife to part with a chicken and out of curiosity I had gone over a rise and a little further along the trail. An elderly man approached. He wore a homespun wool blanket, a *khukuri* was thrust into a dyed many-layered wool cummerbund, and four curving musk deer teeth hung from a cord around his neck. Both of us stopped to appreciate each other's strangeness. He accepted a cigarette and we sat on a wall to talk. When I learned he was a Magar, and from three days to the north, I asked the crucial question.

What kind of Magar?
Thapa.
True word, brother?
True word, *sahib*.

But I remained unconvinced even after Hem, himself a Thapa, joined us, questioned the man at length and said he could certify to his Thapahood—even to his being a member of Hem's own clan, the Ramjalis. My skepticism remained strong because we had heard similar claims before, though not with as much corroborative detail. The reason for claiming to be a Thapa or Rana when one was not was that recruiters for the Gurkha Brigade were known to prefer Magars from these subtribes. In addition, these subtribes, possibly because they were concentrated in the rice-growing and more prosperous south where people were more Hinduized, had vaguely higher status. Our questioning continued over cigarettes. We told him we were not recruiters, we all but pleaded with him to admit he was in truth a Bura, Gharti, or Pun. But he insisted he was not and with so much sincerity that I finally began to believe him, a belief encouraged by desire, for he described in detail the Thapa riceless villages of his valley and how livestock from these villages were driven north into the mountains for summer grazing, sometimes two, and even three days away to a place called Dhorpattan.

We left him to begin the trek back to the bazaar town, and thought we had come as close as ever before to the end of our search. Even so there had to be more assurance, because a commitment now was a point of no return. The journey would take a week or more. If we did have to come back, as much as a month would have been lost and only a few months remained before we had to leave the hills. We began with inquiries in a tax office and learned there were Ranas and Thapas in the general vicinity but it was not clear exactly where. Finally we found an official who had lived in the region for a number of months and he assured us there was transhumance and said he knew personally some Rana and Thapa Magars. On the basis of this information, the best available, we decided to go.

Since we knew the area where we wanted to live would be riceless we purchased 160 pounds of it. The rest of the gear included sleeping bags, a two-man tent, ground cloths, camera equipment, stationery supplies, Banyan Hill notes, a portable typewriter, tape-recorder, dried apricots and raisins, sugar, cooking utensils, medical supplies, changes of clothing, some hard candy, and a couple of lanterns. We needed 14 porters.

The last night before Dhorpattan we all slept in a forest at about 10,000 feet. It was January (1962) and the temperature fell to below zero. We lay around a fire that was more truly a constantly reinvigorated conflagration. In the middle of that night of shivering one of the porters remarked loudly, "I am going to tell my sons, and I am going to tell my grandsons, *never* to come to Dhorpattan in January." A loud laugh went round the sleepless circle and the rest of that night the remark was repeated again and again for whatever warmth even diminishing laughter might bring.

Two days later, leaving Pat and Bihari in a cattleshed in the Dhorpattan meadow, Hem, Krishna, and I went down a valley to the south, past Monal, which we did not know then was the village where we soon would be living. The people we met were Gharti and Pun Magars, but they said further south a couple of hours and another hour up the side of the valley there were Ranas. On reaching the place late in the day we learned that a Rana family once lived there but had long ago departed.

The following day, after a night in a small bazaar at the lower end of the valley, we learned that other than a scattered family or two, there were neither Thapas or Ranas in the whole region that used Dhorpattan. We had come to live among Puns, Buras, and Ghartis. A most important experimental control had evaporated.

January through May (1962)

Banyan Hill was like a formal garden. Landscapes had been tamed to men's uses and the forests no longer were an intimate part of people's lives. The upper part of the Bhuji Valley, the valley where Monal was located and where we settled, still was part of the forest. Though the people had cleared village sites, men still could remember when their fathers were cutting the trees, and in the uppermost part of the valley and along the mountaintops people still were making new clearings. A Monal man bore claw marks of a leopard that had leapt on him, and leopards often came in the night, forced their way between layers of the bamboo matting that walled the cattlesheds or scooped underneath with their paws to try and hook a sheep or goat. To guard against them every farm kept dogs that wore clanking bells around their necks and were let loose to roam around the cattlesheds all night, where they kept up such a din of constant barking that some were hoarse. These dogs also helped drive away bears that came when the maize was ripe, though a constant beating on pans was a more effective method. Other dogs were used for coursing deer and an occasional wild boar, for hunting was a popular male pastime and although the matchlock was most common, one still could see an occasional hunter with the ancient bow and arrow. Pitchpine splinters illuminated the hearths, and forest spirits possessed the shamanas when they beat on drums of mountain goatskin and danced in costumes hung with the skins of mountain pheasants.

An incident with an old man, the only grandfather in Monal, made clear how precipitous, narrow, and difficult for farming the upper Bhuji was. We were climbing together over a mountain to another valley to attend a funeral feast in the village of his deceased wife. Near the top we met his daughter who had come from another village and also was going to the funeral. As we sat and smoked and ate some of the food she carried in her basket, he prepared me for the valley we were about to see. The sides of Bhuji, he said, hung down like a buffalo's tail, but in this valley the sides were as wide and flat as her back in the summer. When we left the forest and stood looking down at the broad fields, green with winter wheat and barley, the old man stretched out both his arms, and breathed a long ah! "*Kasto ramro!* (Would you believe it!)" he muttered and turned to us for confirmation of the wonder.

We entered Bhuji Valley as complete strangers. Though we carried a paper giving us permission to be in the hills and saying any assistance rendered would be appreciated, we realized after showing it a few times that it meant very little. For a time we were wrongly associated with a foreigner who had reported to the government that the traditional and heavily used grazing grounds in Dhorpattan were not occupied except for a few "squatters" and some believed a soldier on leave from the Indian army who reported that we were spies. But even when these misapprehensions were cleared up, most people remained somewhat aloof. These hillmen did not go out of their way to make friends with strangers and foreigners, nor find them of much interest simply because they were strange and foreign.

Our eventual decision to move to the village of Monal began with futile attempts by Hem and me to find a community that would allow us to live in it and ask questions in return for giving daily lessons to all the village children. (With the coming of a more liberal government in 1951, schools were encouraged, but at that time none were in operation in the Bhuji Valley.) At first we found no takers but did find a man who allowed us to store our gear in his house, and he then sent us to a Magar through whom we met the headman of Monal. With a daughter and son in their teens, the headman was interested in a school. Calling a village meeting, he helped us win assent to the idea and school began the next day, on a terrace, with Hem as a teacher. The only equipment was wooden writing boards, blackened with charcoal, and a kind of soapstone for chalk. Invited by the headman to live in his empty goatshed, we found room enough inside for Bihari's, Krishna's, and Hem's bedrolls. In one corner we made a fireplace for cooking, and with a tarp hung over the wide doorway the shed was warm and comfortable. Overhead was a small loft, entered from the outside on a notched pole, and it served as storage place for most of our boxes. Pat and I slept in the tent that we pitched beside the goatshed.

The staple in Monal was cornmeal mush and we had it in the morning with raisins and apricots boiled in sugar and water. We also had it at noon and sometimes at night, since we had to use our rice sparingly. There were few chickens and they were expensive. We tried buffalo and goat, both fresh and cut into strips and dried, but none of us liked it much. What we appreciated most— aside from the rare chicken or snared pheasant—was a leg of the small barking deer. For this we had a standard purchase order and received at least half a dozen. The money we paid made it possible for the hunters to purchase powder,

The headman's house, goatshed, and the Hitchcocks' tent in Monal.

caps, and balls for their muzzle loaders. There were no vegetables during the spring and early summer. Aside from meat, tea, and some hard candies, variety in our diet came from parched soybeans, boiled potatoes, two varieties of popped maize, including ordinary field maize, on which I broke two teeth.

Research in Monal was difficult. A major problem was the people's mobility—something I had looked for and received in good measure. Not only did Monal people go into the high pastures of Dhorpattan, taking cattle a distance it took them two or three days to cover, but they also had tillage on the 9000 foot mountain behind the village, as well as at various locations going north along the valley floor. Even during the winter months, people often were away from the village, going up the mountainside to graze cows, goats, and sheep, or to get fodder for their buffaloes, a task requiring a half day trip up the mountain and back. They also went there to cut wood, which then was sent leaping and thudding down long slides on the valley face. Thus in contrast to Banyan Hill, where many people always were about, Monal—except for a few elderly women and our school children—often was empty.

As best we could we followed the men, but it often was difficult to interview them at their work. I wanted very much, for example, to talk with a man whose son was going to be married and though he told me he did not see how it would be possible, I tried it while he herded his sheep at the top of the mountain. I imagined his work would be somewhat like what I had seen in Scotland, where shepherds sit puffing their pipes. There was little similarity. Fearing leopards, he had to keep moving round and round the flock, shouting at his dogs and constantly whistling or slashing off at angles after strays.

One morning we went to a farmstead to check on a question and found the whole family had already departed, along with all their livestock and all the bamboo matting of their cattleshed. Some members had gone to Dhorpattan to plow potato fields, the rest to maize fields at the head of the valley.

Two of our most difficult problems were crop yields and areas of tillage. The headman himself and two others were cooperative and from them we learned enough to know our information from others was very inaccurate. The headman did not have anything like the influence of Hem's father, nor did we think we should ask him to intervene in our behalf. To solve the problem we had to secure the assistance of a young man from another village and caste who gradually became part of our project. We found by checking against information we trusted that his approximations would be as good as we could expect.

As in Banyan Hill, loans and debts were a sensitive topic, and except for a few families I had only fair confidence in our data. The headman made the most loans but we had little reason to expect he would want to discuss them with us. We did not approach him about the subject until just before he was going to Dhorpattan. He said he would talk to us before going, but we missed him, because he left from his cattleshed at the top of the mountain without returning to his house—a not entirely surprising development. Still since we had been fortunate enough to obtain good information from Hem's father, with whom we wanted to make a comparison, I thought it worthwhile to take two days to go to Dhorpattan and try to persuade the headman to reveal the information. It was a long hike in the rain to his cattle camp, which was some distance up a draw. It was misting heavily and it was not until we came quite close that we saw his blanketed back just as it disappeared over a hillock. He had seen us before we saw him. We next met him when we were packing to leave and it was a time for giving presents, not for asking untoward questions.

The nadir of the stay in Monal came in the first month. It was a combination of things. An important feature of the design had been shot down, our status still was precarious, it was cold, damp, and muddy. Just before our arrival two young people, a boy and a girl and the only children in one of the village families, had died and there was a boy in the father's brother's family who was so seriously ill he could not talk. We had been settled a week when a boy on a trading trip fell sick and was brought to the headman's cattleshed. He died there and I helped bury him. Krishna cut himself and the cut became badly infected, Pat developed a fever and heavy chest, and throughout those days the men in the village angrily kept coming to insist that the grave of the young stranger be opened. The body, they said, had been cannibalized by Tibetans staying in a nearby stone resthouse. I kept trying to persuade them they were mistaken, but finally late one night when they had been drinking they prevailed on me to come to the grave as witness. On close inspection it was clear the burial had been disturbed, which accounted for the men's certainty on that score, but only to steal the blanket in which the body had been wrapped. This act, so much more understandable than the imagined one, was accepted with equanimity and the matter was dropped.

Journal

That boy could have been saved if we had given him our medicine and left. And there would not have been that other final tucking in with stones if we had never gone to Ulleri (though that "we" places the burden falsely, for I should have gone alone). What is this I am doing?

What do I say I am doing? Many of my countrymen have heard of your country; many served with you in the war and admired you. But few know anything about you really. I have come to learn so that I can tell them. Other people in Nepal like the Chhetri are known and have a history. The Magars have none. Your children will know nothing about their forefathers and how they lived.

The answers: Why should your countrymen or our children want to know how we live? Our children should be glad to forget it.

This all-will-be-lost approach, were it not for you and me, is honest, but it is not viable.

Once it was enough to argue that what I am doing will help prevent war. The response in one respect is ambivalent. No hillman likes war, getting killed, or injured. But many are glad to have had a chance to serve and earn a pension; many want to enlist. Even if there had been outright dislike for the military, the idea that by telling me how many fried breads they put into a basket for a wedding exchange they are helping prevent war must seem pretty stupid.

To the government: The more you know about your people's problems, the better you will be able to help them. The more you can learn about your enemy, the more successful your campaign. To the people: The government wants to help you, but unless they know what your problems are, they will not be able to.

The answers: The government knows what we want. If they wanted to help they could do it. We have been telling the government for a decade we want a dispensary, a school, some water pipes, a new bridge, a jeepable road. They do not need you to tell them these things.

They are very clear why I am here. To earn money. I can remember few men I have talked with who did not eventually want to know my salary, and when I say it is not much, they do not believe it, though they may add, to cover any conceivable insufficiency, that it must also be for "name." How not admit this?

What might be fair exchange? No one could do more good than a physician. Ease people in, through, and out. I cannot think of anything better. Anything learned would be just return for something they really want.

Next best would be entertainment. If not Flaherty's charm, then Wiser's violin.

The school. It is at least something, but not much and soon to be discontinued, though by then the government schools may be in operation.

"You're welcome because you're interested and listen well and we're proud of our way of life." Those are the cultures other people write about.

Except for the school, we are here because there is power in "maybe." Maybe we will do something, not clear just what, for the headman and his family, for others—a job in Kathmandu, a recommendation, a big loan, a trip to America. The power remains despite denials.

So, I provide a school, and without intending to, false hopes about "maybe." What they most want is health and wealth, and I give neither. On the other hand, they help give me wealth and "name." Considered simply on the basis of values exchanged this is exploitation.

And it is exploitation compounded. Compounded by pressure. I work too fast to move innocuously in and out of a community, letting friendships grow as they will. Persons become means. If the headman (Hem's father) had not been a means, I would not have pushed Hem to get those loans. It is compounded by an attitude I would quail at if it were not made respectable by being called "getting rapport," "finding the person behind the persona," and the like.

But is not this being overly nice? What about feedback, mankind, applied anthropology? Perhaps there is a little pressure, a little exploitation, a little "using" of persons. Small ill for great good. The momentary smart of iodine on the cut. I may make my bit, the publisher his, the university its, but in the end, and on and on. They simply know not well the subtle ways I keep and pass and turn again.

But just how does it turn and pass? Collecting in the academic attic where we sit like spiders digesting culture and graduate students? As a society we are not prepared to send the doctors needed. They need ten years' training. All or nothing, not to mention the danger of letting competition reduce prestige and salaries at home. And out of the thousands that are fully trained and making three or four times what anyone needs to live in decency, how many are ready to give money or time? And so on. If medicine is the easiest met of the greatest needs here, the greatest injustice is the caste system and are we a society that can do much about that?

When I wrote that journal entry the river all day and every night was telling of the rush of everything to waste. There was no question of leaving, but the research did have to be rethought. These people were too unlike those in Banyan Hill to believe the difference could be accounted for mainly by a single variable—adaptation to differing environments. They spoke a Tibeto-Burman tongue Hem could not understand and even their Nepali was so different that Hem and Bihari had difficulty with it sometimes. Another of the bedrock assumptions I had wanted to make was that the different Magar groups studied would be aware of one another's ideas. Even this assumption was shaken when I saw how surprised and shocked both Hem and Krishna were to discover that these people would eat a cow if it had died a natural death. After a journal entry trying to think through the implications of these changes for the research—changes that seemed to convert "doing science" as I then conceived it to "doing art"—I wrote:

> It's a return to Benedict's Zuni and the structuralists' Aranda, a Prospero's world whose cultures once touched to life revolve timelessly on inner intricacies of pattern or moral imperative; worlds, each of them, with their own single suns. What's lost is the sense of this one sun felt now on my back, generative of all becoming; and a chance perhaps to glimpse in a mountain instance some single one of its replicate ways.

In concluding now, should I move beyond this nadir winter? What followed was not unimportant. Of some of it we made a film. It records other encounters with village personalities, other research techniques, and the progression from these first days of finding entrance to the village and starting the school to the final early summer days when we were accepted and made welcome in many spheres of village life. Yet I hesitate to leave the winter because what followed was implied in it, as anything one does or thinks is implied by what is beyond question. This was a time of waste once again and to spare; and if it was for me to find something other than self-pity and total indictment, I had not cared to take the responsibility. That there were a few things unsought that found me out gives them meaning beyond anything they otherwise could have. They provide no metaphysic, new or worn, Eastern or Western, resolving guilt, moral ambiguity, the world's recalcitrance, grief; only three incidents found in my notes and lodged in memory, yet asserting still, as then, their unarguable and distinct reality in the face of weakness and disenchantment. Narpati, happily tipsy, alone, and barefoot in the slippery mud of the courtyard, soaked by a rain half snow, dancing to the drums and whine of the marriage band sheltered on the porch. The grandfather, naked for warmth in a common blanket with his sick grandson, sleeping with him on the ground in the cattleshed, and throughout the many nights getting up to hold the boy, retching and squirting with diarrhea over the manure pile, shielding him as best he could from the cold. And the headman's wife, the *mukhini*. I know no way to convey the meaning of my scattered notes on her except in this story, as true as my understanding can make it.

> "*Mukhini!*" A voice came through the low latticed window across from the firepit, the only window in the house. "*Mukhini!*" it called again. "He is struggling."
>
> "Lo, Kabi, we are coming," she said, addressing the little window with its

barely visible squares of light. She stood up and took the pot from the tripod. "Here, take these," she said to Indra Bahadur, her nephew.

Getting to his feet the boy swung his blanket to one side and the *mukhini* poured some of the hot beans into the linen-like garment that hung from his back. Setting the pot on the floor, she placed a very dirty towel, with a blue decorative band, over her head. The towel was a gift from her son when he had come home on leave from army service in India. The *mukhini* pulled it tight about her deeply wrinkled face with one hand, stooped to pick up the pot, and followed her nephew through the low doorway and out onto the mud porch of the house. Kabi, the cowherd was crouched by the window, his blanket drawn completely about him. His bare feet, his eyes, and his torn black cap were all that showed.

"Here, Kabi, you have some." The *mukhini* emptied the rest of the beans into the portion of the blanket he proferred. Setting the pot down she stepped quickly off the porch and made her way across the muddy courtyard, followed by her nephew and the cowherd.

Though it was only midafternoon, it was almost dark. There was no wind and the low clouds seemed to deaden all sound except the steady hushed roar of the river beneath them. Moving quickly along the rocky path that their bare feet knew by heart, the three descended toward a lower terrace where there was a long, low cattleshed, with walls and a curved roof of bamboo matting. At the center of the shed one of the bamboo mats had been pulled aside a little to make a doorway. The *mukhini* and her nephew slipped inside. The cowherd squatted at the entrance.

At each end of the dark shed, cows and buffaloes were tethered, leaving only a small space in the center. Here, to one side of a smouldering log, on an unravelling dirty straw mat, lay a boy, partially covered by a homespun grey blanket. He lay stretched out, sprawled on his back, his shoulders and chest bare, one arm beside him, the other flung out toward the log. A round woolen skull cap, made of the same material as his blanket, had fallen back from his head and lay under it.

The *mukhini* squatted down beside him, pulling her skirt away from the smoking log and tucking it between her thigh and leg. Her nephew stood behind her. She reached for the arm flung toward the fire, then drew back her hand. The boy seemed dead and the soul of a person who died away from home became a fearsome spirit, the *ganse dokh*.

Quickly glancing back at her nephew, she asked him to get her some liquor, and by pointing to it with her lips, indicated a wooden flask that hung from one of the beams. Stepping warily around the boy he gave her the flask and she poured a little of the contents into the boy's parted lips. He made no move and the liquor ran down the side of his face.

"He is dead," the cowherd spoke from the doorway, barely audible through the blanket he held over his mouth. "See how white his nose is."

The *mukhini* hoped her nephew would stoop and feel for the boy's pulse. But he remained standing, afraid. When finally she made herself take the wrist, searching for even a whisper, it still was warm, but the pulse had gone.

"Indra Bahadur, you and Kabi must call the lineage brothers."

*The wife of the Monal head-
man, the* mukhini, *with a ball
of wool.*

Indra Bahadur, happy for this chance to get away, hurried out the entrance,
and he and the cowherd disappeared up the trail.

Crouched beside the dead stranger, the *mukhini* was trying to order her
thoughts, to remember what must be done. There were the mustard seeds, which
should be scattered where the *ganse dokh* might come, so that one's soul—if
attacked—might hide beneath them and escape capture. And she would need a
coin, a half rupee, to put in the stranger's mouth. She would like to have provided a new white cloth for a grave sheet but she had none, and knew she could
not get one from the brothers.

Walking back toward her house, she thought of something else. She must get
some maize, for a grave gift, and the thought of the maize reminded her of the
day the three men had come. She had been sitting on the porch, with a long
bamboo stick beside her, which she used to drive away the old hen and her two
chicks when they got into the maize drying in the courtyard on a bamboo mat.
She was spinning a hank of wool she held under her right arm. Samundra was
sitting on the ground, just beside the mat of grain, the strap of the loom around
her back. She was just beginning to weave a wool blanket for her father.

The dog had rushed snarling from the porch and she heard a man call from
the far edge of the terrace just below the house. She had swatted at the dog
with the bamboo stick and when he cowered, she had squatted over his head,
holding him by the fur of his neck. When they knew the dog was held, three
men had climbed up over the terrace wall and had come into the courtyard. She
knew right away they were Magars from the west. She recognized the dark grey
color of their blankets and knew too that they were from the large group that

had camped that night below the village by the river on their way back from Butwal, seven days' walk to the south near the Indian border. They had gone to sell butter and purchase a year's supply of salt and cloth, plus a variety of trinkets, mostly for the women and children. With a kick and a shout at the dog to drive him off she invited them to come and sit on the porch and took down a straw mat from under the porch roof for them to sit on.

They had asked for the *mukhiya* but spoke to her of their business when they learned he had gone to the forest for the day. One of the men, the eldest and spokesman, said he was the son of the brother of a ritual brother of the *mukhiya*. He had come in the name of this close relationship. As soon as she heard this, the *mukhini* knew what village these men were from—a village two long days' walk from the high pass at the head of the valley. The *mukhiya* and the spokesman's brother had become ritual brothers when herding sheep together as young men in the high pastures of Dhorpattan.

The old man said twenty-five from his village and a few from neighboring villages had started the trek south almost a month ago. The price of butter in Butwal had been so low they all had decided to wait there, hoping to do better. When they finally agreed to sell, a boy in the party had fallen ill. He had pain in his chest and found it difficult to breathe so they waited a few more days hoping he would get better. Instead he had seemed to get worse. When they left he had been able to walk with them but they had had to travel more slowly. They should have been home by now, but had only been able to get this far. Last night they had run out of food.

The *mukhini* had gone into the house and measured out maize enough for the midmorning meal of all twenty-five. Then she had told the three men to come back after they had eaten and get what they needed for the rest of the trip home.

In the afternoon when they returned two women were with them. After she had measured out the maize, the two younger men went away, leaving only the elder and the women. One of them was middle-aged, the other young.

"*Mukhini*," the man had said, "I think the boy I told you about this morning is too sick to go any further."

"He is very sick," said the older woman. On her threadbare maroon satin blouse she wore a heavy necklace of silver coins, the old Indian rupees with good silver in them.

The *mukhini* sensed immediately what they wanted. The low clouds threatened snow and snow would close the pass, close it perhaps for as long as a month. They were desperate to get back to their village. With the boy too sick to travel they wanted to leave him here, with her.

"You have called a shaman?"

"Two are with us," the man had replied. "It is the Huntress, and perhaps also the Grave Spirit of his father."

"And which of you will stay with him?"

The man spoke with some embarrassment. "I am from the same village but a different clan. None of his lineage brothers came with us. His line has almost died out. At home he has only a mother and a small brother."

The *mukhini* looked at the two women.

"They are wife to the boy and mother-in-law," said the man. "The mother-in-law lives in a different village."

"Ah, *mukhini*," the mother-in-law broke out, "it's not that we don't want to stay. But if the snow blocks the pass it may be another month. I'm a widow and have had to ask neighbors to cut leaf fodder for my cattle and to feed my small son and daughter. It's too much to ask from those who aren't family members."

"When you gave your daughter to him, he became your son. You shouldn't leave him now."

The mother-in-law held her hands palm to palm in the gesture of supplication. "Out of your religious duty please care for him."

"It will be my responsibility if he dies here. His death will be on me."

"No, *mukhini*. It is his fate."

"People will say he died here."

"No, they will say he died because it was fated."

The *mukhini* turned in anger on the wife. "And you, why aren't you staying? It's a sin for you to leave your husband."

The girl didn't look up. The *mukhini* waited and finally the girl barely murmured, "I also must go."

The *mukhini* sensed now that the boy was too sick to live. The young wife was afraid to be alone with death among strangers.

"Take him please," pleaded the mother-in-law, again folding her hands before her face.

They were relatives of a ritual friend of her husband; she was the wife of a *mukhiya*, mistress of a proud and hospitable house. She knew she could not refuse.

When the man and the two women had left, she had gone to the cattleshed and gathered up her utensils. She had been cooking there because in this season it was a warmer and more pleasant place to be than the house. Only at night had she and her son and daughter come back to the house to sleep, leaving the *mukhiya* and the cowherd to watch the shed. But now she would feel better to cook in the house and to have her husband sleep there too. During the night Kabi, who also was a Magar from the west, could be with the boy and look after his needs.

Back at the cattleshed after returning the load of utensils, she had been in time to meet the man who had come with the boy's basket. He moved slowly, leaning into the tumpline of woven cord. It was a heavy load. When he reached the cowshed, he turned, squatted down, leaned back, and rested the full basket against the post by the entrance. The *mukhini* steadied it for him as he lifted the tumpline from his forehead.

"The boy carried it himself all the way from Butwal." The man spoke in admiration. The *mukhini* knew he would have had to carry it, for everyone else would have been carrying all they could manage.

A little later the boy appeared, preceded by the man who had acted as spokesman. He walked very slowly, his blanket over his shoulders, head down, looking at the path. He was followed by his wife and mother-in-law. The *mukhini* had opened the entrance wider and he had moved inside and let himself down in front of the fire. He sat looking at it dully. He breathed with difficulty and each shallow breath wheezed.

The *mukhini* asked the men to bring the boy's load inside and set it in the back of the room against one of the posts. The boy looked up as it was being brought in.

"Is the sugar there?" he asked in a husky whisper.

The mother-in-law and wife were standing at the entrance and the mother-in-law said, "It's there. No one has taken it." It was as if he had accused her.

Without looking at the women, the boy turned toward the man who was setting down the load. "Show me," he whispered.

The man untied the withes that held a piece of cloth over the top of the basket so that the contents would not spill out and the rain would be kept from the salt. He reached inside and felt about until he found a small sack made of birch bark, tied up with a piece of grass. He held it up for the boy to see, and the boy then turned back toward the fire, closed his eyes, and rested his head on his knees.

The *mukhini* remembered this day as she made her way back again to the cattleshed with the maize, the mustard seeds, and the coin. And she remembered other days during the week that had passed since the boy had come. She remembered especially how she had tried to get him to eat. She had tried to tempt him with rice boiled in milk, with her best liquor and beer, with fried breads, and every day with milk. But the boy always said he was not hungry. One day a man with a reputation for a knowledge of herbs and medicines had told her that the best thing for a boy as weak as he was, and with such terrible pains across his shoulders, was sugar. She did not have any but remembered that the boy had had some in his pack. She went down to the cattleshed. It was the third day after his arrival, the only sunny day there had been. She had persuaded him to go and sit in the sun, and she and Kabi had helped him outside. He was sitting sleeping against the bamboo wall when she got there. She sat and waited until he woke up and then she tried to persuade him to eat some of the sugar he had in his basket.

"No," he had whispered. "It's for my younger brother."

"But for your health," the *mukhini* had urged him.

The boy shook his head.

The *mukhini* entered the cattleshed and squatted by the fire to wait for the men. Her nephew was the first one back. She handed him the mustard seeds. "You throw them."

Taking from her the bit of cloth in which they were tied, he undid it, and started to hum a spell and to blow on the seeds. When he had finished, he took some of them and tossed them over the boy, a protection against the evil he harbored.

They heard voices and in a moment four lineage brothers had pushed their way through the opening and stood around the fire.

"He just sat up and told me he wanted to fight you all," said the nephew.

The eldest brother laughed. "He'll not be fighting anyone when we get him tied up."

"Wait," said the *mukhini*. "The coin." She bent over the boy and tried to put the half rupee in his mouth but she could not open it. She laid it instead on his chest.

"There's the maize." The *mukhini* gestured toward a small wicker container with four short wooden legs.

One of the brothers, who was fat with a thin droopy moustache, took the cloth from the top of the boy's basket. He spread it on the ground and emptied the maize into it; then knotted it together and placed it on the boy's chest, over the coin. "May no such fate ever come to us," he said quietly.

"His wife committed a great sin by not staying with him." It was the youngest of the brothers, a tall, slow-moving boy.

"Then your wife is a great sinner," said the eldest brother and all the others laughed, for a year ago the boy's wife had gone home to her parents and had been staying there ever since.

As two of the brothers worked loose a pole from the roof of the cattleshed, the eldest commented, "Everything has to be thrown in the river." He looked about the shed, indicating each item with puckered lips and a little jerk of his head: "basket, gear, walking stick, everything."

The brother standing beside him, the one wearing a large loosely wrapped turban concurred. "Otherwise the *ganse dokh* will come here."

"And when the mother and brother come in the spring?" The *mukhini*'s question only traced a thought; it was not dissent.

The men asked for some rope and while they and her nephew all were intent on wrapping the body in the blanket and lashing it to the pole, the *mukhini*, who was standing beside the boy's basket, reached inside and took out the sugar in its container of birch bark. Turning her back, she tucked it inside a fold of the long cummerbund that was wound many times around her waist.

When the lashings were made fast, two of the brothers lifted the pole and its underslung burden to their shoulders. The brother with the turban sat with his back to the boy's basket, adjusted the tumpline, and with the *mukhini*'s help lurched the load forward, rolled to his knees, and stood up. She handed him the walking stick and he and the rest moved to the door. As her nephew was leaving, the *mukhini* asked him for the mustard seeds and he handed her the small cloth bundle.

After they had gone she stood alone in the cattleshed for a moment and then went outside into the near darkness, stopping at the entrance to scatter some of the magic seeds. She walked over to the edge of the terrace where the path led down to the rushing river. From there she could just make out the men as they wound down the hillside into the gloom. Watching them, she emptied the last of the seeds into the path.

References

Boas, Franz, 1911, *The Mind of Primitive Man*. New York: The Free Press.

Benedict, Ruth, 1928, Psychological types in the culture of the southwest. *Proceedings of the Twenty-Third Congress of Americanists*, 572–581.

Forde, C. Daryll, 1934, *Habitat, Economy and Society*. London: Harcourt, Brace and World.
Hitchcock, John T., 1966, *The Magars of Banyan Hill*. New York: Holt, Rinehart and Winston, Inc.
Malinowski, B., 1935, *Coral Gardens and Their Magic*. London: Indiana University Press.
Sahlins, Marshall D., 1958, *Social Stratification in Polynesia*. Seattle: University of Washington Press.
Steward, Julian H., 1955, *Theory of Culture Change*. Urbana, Ill.: University of Illinois Press.

Films

Hitchcock, John T. and Patricia Hitchcock, 1967.

On Banyan Hill
Himalayan Shaman of Southern Nepal

On Monal
Himalayan Farmer
Himalayan Shaman of Northern Nepal

On Banyan Hill and Monal
Gurkha Country: Some Aspects of Fieldwork
in Social Anthropology

Appendix

THE RESEARCH PROJECT

The area of the research described here is the mountainous region of west central Nepal. The town of Pokhara marks its eastern edge and can be reached by plane from Kathmandu, by DC-3 a flight of about forty-five minutes. To the north rise the Annapurna (26,503 feet) and Dhaulagiri (26,826 feet) massifs and to the south the lower Mahabharat and Churia ranges, beyond which lie swampy lowlands merging into the plains of India.

Besides wanting to contribute to the ethnography of one of the Tibeto-Burman-speaking tribes in this part of Nepal, my major research aim was to make an *ex post facto* or retrospective experiment in adaptive variation.

In reaction to nineteenth-century racial, economic, and environmental determinists that contained their conclusions within their problems, many anthropologists (for example, Boas 1911) emphasized the role of history and diffusion in explaining the way of life of various groups and regarded the physical environment as prohibitive or permissive, but not creative. Admitting that cultures develop in unlike ways, these anthropologists have related their divergencies to overall distinctive and selective patterns (for example, Benedict 1928). The provenience of these patterns, however, is pushed back in time and is not explained (Forde 1949:465).

Other anthropologists, in reaction to a view of culture as accidental agglomerations of diffused and unrelated traits, have emphasized their holistic nature and the interdependency of all their features (for example, Malinowski 1935).

Steward (1955) tends to disagree with both points of view. With regard to the first, he assigns environment a "creative" role in the formation of cultures; and with regard to the second, emphasizes differences in degrees and kinds of interdependency among features of cultural wholes. In order to test these assumptions he proposes the method of cultural ecology, a method consisting of three steps: (1) analysis of the interrelationship of exploitative or productive technology and environment; (2) analysis of the behavior patterns involved in the exploitation of a particular area by means of a particular technology; and (3) determination of the extent to which these behavior patterns affect other aspects of the culture. The constellation of features which appear when the last step has been carried out he terms a "cultural core."

The research was to be guided by the method of cultural ecology and its specific aim, as stated in my proposal, was:

to test the hypothesis that two (or more) divergent cultural cores will be found to vary functionally with two (or more) types of environment. Environment is defined simply in terms of altitude bands. It is assumed that divergence in cultural cores will be related to four major variables: (1) cultural genesis of the group; (2) cultural features "offered" by diffusion both in the present and during the course of the communities' history; (3) internal innovations; and (4) environment. Pending investigation on the spot (which may prove the assumption of cultural unigenesis untenable) control of the first variable is effected by taking a single small tribe as the unit of investigation. Control of the second is effected both by selecting communities which share the history of the same isolated region, and by selecting communities which at present all are roughly equidistant from important foci of "outside" influences. Throughout their history, for example, each of the communities probably will have been presented with much the same array of technological devices and arrangements. Control over the third variable, internal innovation, is effected by choice of communities which always have been in fairly intimate contact with each other. . . . If the research supports the assumption that these three variables can be controlled, it will be possible by means of a paired comparison to sort out cultural differences between a highland and a nearby lowland community, and having done so to feel some assurance that these differences reflect variation in environment and are indeed cultural cores.

8

THE HUTTERITES
Fieldwork in a North American Communal Society

JOHN A. HOSTETLER
Temple University

GERTRUDE ENDERS HUNTINGTON
Ann Arbor, Michigan

Related Case Study: **The Hutterites in North America**

The difference between participant and nonparticipant observation becomes strikingly clear in this chapter as John Hostetler and Gertrude Huntington describe their roles in interaction with Hutterites and in the communal colonies where their field research was carried out. The full cooperation and support of the people in the colonies was secured because the authors respected Hutterite norms for demeanor and behavior. John Hostetler, with his Amish background, was accepted as akin to the Hutterites in general cultural and personality orientation. Gertrude Huntington and her family conformed, in nearly every detail, to Hutterite norms, and lived and worked within the role definitions appropriate to a family of no particular distinction within the colony.

From her description of her and her family's roles, the compressive quality of life in a tightly organized communal society, as seen by an outsider, becomes vividly clear. The rewards are sufficiently high so that the community keeps its membership, and it is efficient as a productive unit so that its economic base is sound. The "cost accounting" of the cultural system is in sharp limitation of individual freedom, independence, and individualism in general. The gains are security, both economic and personal. The Hutterite colonies, like Zuni Pueblos, are at one extreme of communalism. North American society, in terms of its dominant ethos, is at another extreme of individualism.

This chapter helps us to understand not only how anthropological field-work can take place in a tightly organized communal society but also the nature of that society.

The Authors

John A. Hostetler is Professor of Anthropology and Sociology at Temple University. His fieldwork in cultural anthropology has taken him to the Old Order Amish, the Hutterian Brethren, and the Mennonites. He is the author of *Amish Society, The Sociology of Mennonite Evangelism,* and coauthor with Gertrude Huntington of *The Hutterites in North America.* After receiving his Ph.D. at The Pennsylvania State University he spent a year as a Fulbright scholar in Germany researching sixteenth-century communitarian movements. He has taught at The Pennsylvania State University, the University of Alberta at Edmonton, and has held research awards from The Canada Council, The Social Science Research Council, the American Philosophical Society, and the United States Office of Education. His teaching and research interests combine the areas of cultural anthropology and socialization. He is currently directing a research

John A. Hostetler (left) with colony members at "coffee time" in Hutterite apartment at prayer before eating.

project on the life style of the culturally different child in American culture.

He was born near Belleville, Pennsylvania, and grew up with a farm background in Pennsylvania and Iowa. He is married to Beulah Stauffer Hostetler, who is an editor. The Hostetlers have three girls.

His reply to the question, "How did you happen to come into anthropology?" follows:

I turned from an early career in poultry judging and poultry husbandry to a career in understanding man because I decided that people were more interesting and more in need of understanding than turkeys. I knew nothing of anthropology until I entered graduate training. Once having been exposed to some of its principles and the fervent honesty of my teachers, I took all the courses my schools offered. This, combined with fieldwork in American communities, including my mother-culture (Old Order Amish), has helped me to understand from culture "how modern man got that way" and why traditional man has not.

Gertrude Enders Huntington, born at Wooster, Ohio, is married to David Huntington who teaches art history at the University of Michigan in Ann Arbor. With their three children the Huntingtons participated in the field study of the Hutterites described in this chapter. She obtained her A.B. from Swarthmore College with a major in zoology. After attending Oberlin College and Rochester University where she studied human genetics with Curt Stern, she taught at the Amerikan Kiz Koleji in Istanbul. On her return to the United States she studied anthropology and conservation at Yale University where she obtained M.S. and Ph.D. degrees. She is coauthor of *The Hutterites in North America* and articles by her have appeared in *Genetics* and *Yale Conservation Studies.*

Her reply to the editor's question, "Why and how did you come into anthropology?" follows:

My inclination toward anthropology probably began in my childhood. When I was ten years old I visited the Cuna Indians off the coast of Panama with a shipload of tourists. I was the first white female child most of the women had seen. They fingered my hair and clothes pulling the decorations and buttons off my dress, and gave me presents of necklaces and hen's eggs. When French and English children lived in our house during the second world war we argued the merits of differing conventions—American, English, French, and even African.

After a year of graduate training in genetics and some research on twinning, I worked in a predominantly Morman region of Wyoming, and then taught school in Turkey for two years. Visiting the homes of my students and traveling extensively in the Middle East I learned another way of life. The eroded hills and small villages along rutted dirt roads, contrasting with ruins of ancient gymnasiums, large amphitheaters, and paved marble avenues made a deep impression upon me, so I returned to Yale to study the conservation of natural resources.

*Gertrude Huntington with her
two boys and a Hutterite baby.*

While earning my M.S. degree I realized I was interested more in how people developed attitudes toward their physical environment than in specific techniques of land utilization. This led me to the discovery of a people who, while their neighbors had "mined the land" or "worn out several farms," maintained excellent productivity from ordinary acres. These people were the Old Order Amish who formed the basis for my Ph.D. dissertation.

G. D. S.

Preface

The Hutterian Brethren or Hutterites are an Anabaptist communal group living in the northern Great Plains of the United States and Canada. They are smaller and less well known than the Old Order Amish or the Mennonites, who also stem from the Anabaptist movement. The Hutterites originated in 1528 during the Protestant Reformation in the Austrian Tyrol and Moravia. For over four centuries the group has demonstrated a remarkable ability to survive changing political, social, and technological developments. By living on large acreages of communally owned land, each *Bruderhof* or colony is able to maintain limited geographic and social isolation. The number of persons living in a colony varies from about 70 to 140. Their everyday speech is an Austro-Bavarian dialect, but Hutterites also speak English. High German is used in their religious services. The Hutterites think of themselves as a people who honor God properly by living communally. Private ownership of wealth is forbidden. They are noted for successful large-scale agriculture, large families, and effective training of the young. They are the largest connubial communal society in North America. All Hutterites immigrated to the United States in 1874–1879 and located in South Dakota. Through natural increase, the 443 persons who settled in colonies at that time now number more than 17,000 persons. Their 170 or more colonies are located in South Dakota, Montana, and the three prairie provinces of Canada.

A Hutterite Bruderhof, or colony.

This chapter is an account of how we set about designing the research and obtaining the data for the case study, *The Hutterites in North America*. Use of the personal pronoun refers to the senior author except for the section on "Living with the Colony People," which is written by Gertrude Huntington.

Establishing Contact

The anthropologist who is aware of his own uniquenesses, his peculiar training, language skills, background, and niche will utilize his experience and personal resources. There are certain peculiarities and circumstances that made it natural for me to study the Hutterites. I could speak conversational German and Pennsylvania German for I was reared in the Amish culture. I had studied the Old Order Amish (Hostetler 1963), and I was familiar with the history, traditions, and literature of the Amish and Hutterites. Soon after my family was situated in a small faculty apartment in Edmonton, we were visited by five strong bearded men. They were Hutterite elders who had come to the provincial capitol on important legislative business. They explained that the law (Hostetler 1961) which had restricted them from buying land in Alberta was to be

Hutterite shoemaker displaying a pair of women's shoes (photograph by Larry Porteous).

changed, possibly to be made more stringent for Hutterites. Having heard that a professor from Pennsylvania had moved into their province, they had sought me out for they hoped that I could find a German language printer for them. This initial contact by the Hutterite leaders was mutually fortunate. I had not sought contact with them, but they had come to see me which was important in maintaining the rapport that was to follow.

At that time I was teaching a class in minority groups, so I took my students to the capitol building to observe the legislative hearing. We found not five Hutterite elders, but 26 bearded apostles seated before the Alberta Legislature. Hostile statements were exchanged on the floor of the meeting, and those who opposed the Hutterites wanted to see them "put in their place." During the week of hearings, I met many other Hutterite elders. Intuitively I realized the elders were accepting me as one of them. This acceptance was balanced by obligations to be their host and chauffeur in a strange city. I answered their questions about my background and about the Old Order Amish in the United States. I indulged in late night discussions and exposed myself to constant subzero weather. The result was my coming down with pneumonia. I did not regret the time lost for it was well spent in making contacts. The risks in this fieldwork did not involve poisonous snakes or amebic dysentery, but normal unromantic hazards. Following my recovery, I visited as many colonies as I could. In a short time my identity was established with virtually all colonies.

A Period of Evaluation and Incubation

Before beginning work on a major research project, I spent two years assessing the various possibilities for research. I made exploratory contacts with not only different Hutterite colonies, but also with government agencies, real estate agents, lawyers, salesmen, and neighbors of the Hutterites. I kept asking myself what in the Hutterite culture was significant for social science or instructive for the modern world. With a small grant from the university I made limited investigations of population change, migration, and mortality patterns. From this exploratory work it became clear that here was an opportunity for basic research. The confidence placed in me by the colony leaders assured me of almost unlimited access to data of all types. Getting to the colonies for fieldwork was no major problem, for the colonies were within easy driving distance. Short trips were possible over weekends during the academic year and over longer periods during the holiday seasons. All of these factors were necessary considerations in thinking about what and how to undertake a research project that would have value.

The literature on the Hutterites was abundant, although most was in German. The printed materials pertaining to their history and religion had been published with the aid of sympathetic outsiders, such as university professors who already in the nineteenth century had gathered much of this material. The two large chronicles that the group had preserved had become the object of study by historians and philologists (Wolkan 1923; Zieglschmid 1947). Much of the material relevant to a cultural analysis was in manuscript form, written in Gothic script by the Hutterites themselves and handed down from generation to generation. Persons who could gain the confidence of the people and read the German material would have ready access to the data.

Delineating the Research Problem

Nonanthropological approaches to the study of Hutterites had to be distinguished from the anthropological approach in defining the research problem. What we wanted was a total picture of the culture so that insights could be secured that would apply inside or outside of the Hutterite culture. We were not interested in a manipulative study. We found interest, for example, among government agencies in a study of "the Hutterite problem" as it was called, but not from the perspective of basic social science research. Farm organizations passed amendments and resolutions at their annual meetings asking the government to do something about "the Hutterite problem." There were repeated references in area newspapers to "the Hutterite problem" with emotionally loaded phrases such as "spreading across Canada like locusts," "threaten the social and economic fibre of Alberta," "parasites," and "amoeba-like growth." "The Hutterite Investigation Committee" (Province of Alberta 1959) had issued a report with recommendations soon after I arrived in Alberta. I attempted to interest these groups in a well-designed, long-range research project, but in this I failed. There was little support on the part of the provincial government or its agencies for research that promised no solutions to immediate problems. With no prospect of funds in Canada, I turned to sources in the United States who were interested in supporting basic research. I found such a source in the United States Office of Education, which provided funds for the study of socialization in various cultures.

After surveying the literature, assessing the availability of data, the probable cooperation of the colonies, and an adequate source of funds, the most promising research problem appeared to be a study of socialization. There were no systematic studies of Hutterite child-rearing practices and in fact no anthropological analysis of the culture as a whole. It was clear that the group had achieved a remarkable record of survival through periods of internal disruption and external pressure. Hutterites were reputed to have great success in training their young to live communally. Few persons deserted colony life. Previous publications provided clues that led me to believe that an investigation of communal socialization patterns would be a basic contribution to knowledge. A few such clues are given below. In the seventeenth century a novelist said of the colonists: "There was no anger, no jealousy, no vengeful spirit, no envy, no concern about temporal things, no pride, no gambling, no remorse," and there was

Mother and child (courtesy National Film Board of Canada).

"altogether a lovely harmony" (Grimmelshausen 1668). A Russian government official who visited the colonies in 1818 reported that after the birth of a child the mothers are assigned to separate quarters, and are separated from their spouses for a year and one half (Zieglschmid 1947: 420). The first sociologist who did fieldwork among the colonies stated that "the educational methods used by the Hutterites are training of the emotions rather than the intellect" and that "within each community a battle is being waged on an educational front between two widely different social orders, their own and ours" (Deets 1939: 39, 45). Eaton (1955: 41) reported unusual stability of the population and a low rate of desertion. Kaplan (1956: 104) concluded that the motivations that are built into the individual during socialization insure ihat the Hutterite "will want to do what he has to do."

The Research Design

The central purpose as stated in the research design was to acquire a knowledge of the methods of socialization (and indoctrination) in a highly collectivistically oriented society. Answers were sought to two fundamental questions: (1) Under what conditions and by what methods are moral values transmitted to children in a communal society?; (2) Under what conditions does the person who is trained for communal living deviate from the moral teachings of his society? In short, we wanted to know how individuals were equipped to live in a communal society, under what conditions individuals deviated from the norms of the society, and if they deserted the community, what adjustments were necessary to go from a communal society to one that was individualistic, as in modern industrialized society.

The research design incorporated what we believed to be the most relevant aspects of the culture: the formulation of the value orientation, the socialization activity in the community, and deviancy patterns. Within these areas of penetration we spelled out the different phases of the investigation—the problem, the method, personnel, and the budget.

The value orientation We wanted an explicit account of the moral postulates of Hutterite culture. What was needed was the "charter" of the society that Malinowski (1944: 140, 162) called "the traditionally established values, programs, and principles of organized (institutional) behavior," or "the recognized purpose of the group." To understand socialization we wanted to know the goals individuals were trained to accept and to live by. We wanted to know the traditional charter (from their date of origins) and how contemporary Hutterites interpreted the meaning of the charter. We wanted to analyze the existing documents in the original language and to translate relevant sections into English.

The socialization patterns in the community We wanted a knowledge of the environment within which learning takes place. We planned to make a field guide that would yield data on a wide range of subjects: maps of roads, buildings, entrances, and the like; topography, temperature, flora, and fauna; unusual environmental conditions such as hail, epidemics, droughts, pests; productivity of crops, livestock raising, and so forth. We wanted to distinguish between the "ideal" and "real" aspects of the community with respect to physical environment and to major social groupings, family and kinship patterns, leadership and authority, and patterns of interaction with outsiders. The field guide was prepared so that each subject had two parts: part A consisted of observed data by the fieldworker and part B consisted of the preferred pattern. For example, once we had a map of the roads and dwellings (observed data) we would ask the Hutterite informants what changes would be desirable or "What would you do differently if you had to do it over again?" By this method we were able to compare the "observed" with the "preferred" patterns of culture and thereby acquire a knowledge of any gaps between "ideal" and "real" aspects of culture. Various guides for investigating socialization patterns from infancy to adulthood were planned. Formal and informal learning were to be observed. We wanted to ascertain the amount of exposure to non-Hutterite sources of knowledge, and to administer achievement tests where appropriate. Attention would be directed toward learning that was not specifically stated in the charter and to individuals who take seriously those beliefs that are not a part of the traditional values. To accomplish this work I wanted to have trained persons, ideally husband-wife teams, located in three colonies.

Deviancy patterns   In addition to observing deviancy patterns within the community, we planned to interview persons who had left the colonies, those who had left permanently as well as persons who had been away and returned. On the basis of previous studies we believed that several dozen such persons could be found. We wanted to discover both the factors that attracted persons to the outside world and factors that repulsed persons from their Hutterite training and background. Depth interviews were planned (with an interview guide) to gather the necessary data. The data would reveal to what extent the deserters still evidenced the communally oriented morality, and what Hutterite attitudes toward property, religious values, and family relationships were maintained in the life of these persons after they were assimilated into the American culture.

Entering the Community

The first step after funds were approved for a research period of three and one half years was to secure a panel of consultants and bring them to Edmonton for the initial overall planning. This panel was made up of persons representing various disciplines in the social sciences.[1] One of the consultants had participated in an earlier study of the mental health of the Hutterites. The panel gave valuable aid in improving the research design and in preparing the field guides. I met periodically with the panel during the operative period of the research to review the progress of the fieldwork.

In hiring fieldworkers I sought professionally trained persons rather than students, and married rather than single persons, preferably with competence in the German language. They had to be socially mature and in good health. Persons were needed who would be the least offensive to Hutterites and who would also be willing to reside in a Hutterite colony for several months at a time. My thought was that either the wife or the husband might teach in the colony school while the other would devote major time to recording the observations. Fieldworkers would have to exercise great facility in accommodating to the Hutterite mode of living. Although I wanted persons who were sympathetic to Hutterite religion, I could not use persons who were inclined to be either too sympathetic or too argumentative. Since smoking is taboo, I could not hire fieldworkers who smoked. One of the reasons for choosing married persons is that among Hutterites, marriage is a mark of maturity and I wanted to make sure

---

[1] The panel of consultants were Laura Thompson, anthropology; Calvin Redekop, sociology; Joseph H. Britton, family and child development; Bert Kaplan, psychology; Dale B. Harris, psychological testing; and Robert Friedmann, history.

that we were admitted to the life styles of both male and female. A male field-worker, for example, is decidedly limited in observing the life style of women in the colony.

The three colonies we chose for intensive observation were selected on the basis of their affiliation, geographic area, size, age, and willingness to cooperate. The objective was to observe the basic unit, which was a relatively small number of persons. The largest of the three sample colonies had eighteen married pairs and the smallest had eight. The combined population in the three colonies was 280 persons. We preferred maximum geographic and social distance between the communities so that there would be virtually no interaction among the colonies we observed. The colonies were located respectively in Manitoba, Alberta, and Montana. It was important that the colonies be "normal" rather than atypical. The Hutterite leaders gave courteous advice to us in this respect.

Contact with the Hutterites was maintained on several levels at the same time. There was the level of the principal investigator who secured the needed cooperation and maintained contact with the leadership, the fieldworkers who established a residence and a living relationship with the colonies, and persons who went in and out of the colonies obtaining specific data such as interviewing certain individuals. The fieldworkers who interviewed ex-Hutterites were not the same persons who established residence in the colonies. Each of us, it turned out, established rapport with different persons. Hutterite inclinations for making friends with outsiders varied greatly. The differences in the quality of the relationships established between investigators and informants varied with their personalities and roles. Each fieldworker became aware of those persons in the colony with whom he could establish least rapport. The principal investigator was usually engulfed by the preachers so that he often had limited freedom to talk with the younger people or to move about from one social category to another.

Before placing the professionally trained persons in the colonies, we assigned one fieldworker to visit all three colonies to secure certain kinds of records and information. Her task was to obtain a complete colony census, births, deaths, number of persons in various social categories, copies of school instructional materials, and the like. She remained one month in each of the three colonies, and the data obtained was then shared with the professionally trained fieldworkers prior to their taking up residence in the colony. Although this fieldworker was neither married nor trained professionally she had all the needed qualifications to establish instantaneous friendships with Hutterite women. She was German speaking, middle-aged, heavy rather than slender, had been in Europe over a span of several years in resettlement work, was adept at following copious instructions, and was willing to brave subzero weather with her Volkswagen. Her genuine friendliness and short stay in each of the colonies did much to establish an attitude of cooperation.

The principal fieldwork was done by Gertrude Huntington, who was trained as an anthropologist and who has had experience in relating to ethnic minorities. Of special significance was the involvement of her whole family in the fieldwork: her husband, David, who was a participant for the last part of the summer; their three children: Caleb, aged two and one half; Daniel, aged five; and Abigail, aged nine; and her mother, Abbie Enders, who was a child psychologist and kindergarten teacher in Swarthmore, Pennsylvania, for many years. They established residence in the Alberta colony in the little house used by the teacher during the school year. The resident fieldworkers in the two other colonies were male school teachers, their wives, and children. The following section, "Living with the Colony People," is told by Gertrude Huntington.

Living with the Colony People

Before my initial trip to the community, I met with other members of the research team, read available material on the Hutterites, obtained detailed data on the geology, climate, and soil—the physical properties of the immediate region, and familiarized myself with the names, ages, and relationships of the members of the colony. To be a full adult by Hutterite standards a person must be married and have children. However, even when this status had been achieved, a woman is never completely adult in that she is not really independent. Even though she has children, she is always to be under the guidance of her husband or if she is not with him, she is usually visiting her mother, who then supervises her. Therefore, I arranged it so that I was always with my mother or my husband as well as with our three children during the period of participant observation. Only as a visitor did I go to a colony alone. I attempted to fill the role of a typical Hutterite woman of my age—a woman whose husband held no outstanding community position and a woman who did not have a special leadership role assigned to her. My mother, as the oldest woman in the community, was called "grandmother" by everyone and did only the work expected of older women. If she did not do some task because she was caring for our children or doing something related to the study, nothing was said for women over fifty have this prerogative. However, I had to do all the expected colony work or I was sent for. Women of my age are excused only for illness or childbirth. Our three children were each of a different Hutterite age stage. The youngest, Caleb, was a "house child" and was treated as such by all the members of the community. We carried his food from the kitchen and fed him in the house as was done for all the house children. Daniel was a "kindergartener." However, he was sent to the kindergarten only when my mother went too, to help or observe. The kindergarten was run on alternate days by the second and third oldest women in the community, so it was natural for my mother to visit. Abigail was nine and was, therefore, a "school child." She participated fully in the program for the school children, remaining under the direction of the German teacher for virtually all her waking hours. She ate her meals with the

Kindergarten scene.

school children and did the community work required of them. The only part of the program she did not participate fully in was the memorizing of the long German verses and answering questions on the Sunday sermon. She attended all the meetings of the school children, all the religious services, and worked mornings for one of the families who did not have a girl old enough to clean and wax the floors. Because of our family structure we were able to participate in every age level within the colony except that of the adolescents. We were able to establish rapport with the adolescents both because we were not part of the adult hierarchy and we were sympathetic and discrete. Our daughter, Abigail, was sometimes admitted to the fringes of adolescent activities. When my husband joined us later in the summer, he participated in the general (in contrast to specialized or administrative) colony work of the adult men. Due to the structure of Hutterite society, our roles were determined by our age, sex, and marital status. Our task was to carry them out properly by Hutterite standards.

Our integration into the community was achieved in a series of steps. The first two days we were guests and visitors. The Hutterite children made a great fuss over our children and were very attentive and kind to them. During this brief period we learned the physical layout of the central portion of the colony:

the location of the long houses and small houses in which the different families lived, the school house that also served as the church, the kitchen complex that contained the dining room, the laundry, bath house, and the pump house from which we carried our water. We ate all our meals in the communal dining hall sitting in our assigned seats that were determined by our age, sex, and family relationship. The adults ate at one sitting, the school children at another, the kindergarteners ate in the kindergarten house or at home with the house children. We never ate as a family unit. We did our laundry at the assigned day and hour in the communal laundry and bathed at the accustomed time, waiting our turn at the community bath tub. We attended church each day with the adults and the school children sitting in our assigned places.

As soon as it became evident that we were really trying to participate in the colony life rather than merely visiting or working on the fringes, we were urged to put away our "ugly" clothes and dress in correct Hutterite costume. Some of the women brought us used clothes that did not fit their children or that they were not wearing. Some was given to us, some was lent to us. Several of the better seamstresses offered to make us clothes for church and for Sunday if we would buy the material and the thread.

Among the Hutterites one's dress is extremely important as an emblem of classification. First, it signifies that one is a Hutterite; secondly, it proclaims the wearer's sex; thirdly, it indicates the type of activity the wearer will be engaged in, and finally, for women it signifies her acceptance of her position as subservient to men. The details of the costume also proclaim to the practiced eye the docility of the wearer in accepting the rules of his colony. In order to participate as Hutterites we had to learn the details of grooming that would enable any Hutterite to classify us correctly.

Once we were really accepted, as signified by our dressing Hutterite, we felt all the pressures of the colony to conform. The degree of conformity required is difficult for an American to appreciate, for it affects virtually every detail of one's daily life, all one's actions, and almost every expression of one's thinking. Any evidence of individuality on our part was immediately resisted. When my mother found many of the small regulations, especially those pertaining to the lower status of women irksome, the fellow colonists would imply that perhaps she was forgetful of them because she was so old. This was an effective means of soliciting conformity from one who is professionally competent as a school teacher and a child psychologist. With me they would imply that the colony work was perhaps too demanding. As status is closely tied to one's ability to work hard, long, and fast, I tended to shape-up and conform. Two of our three children were completely responsive to colony pressures and learned very quickly what was acceptable behavior.

After only a few days our two and one-half year old was observed to hit another toddler and then lean over and kiss him. Caleb already had learned that if you immediately kiss the child you hit, punishment is avoided at the hands of the baby-sitters or adults. The first Hutterite word he learned was "kiss." He played happily with the other house children and enjoyed the solicitious attention of the adults. By the end of the summer he never spoke above a whisper in the presence of nonfamily adults. Our school child, Abigail, quickly internalized the rules of dress and conduct and corrected us privately if we deviated in the slightest degree from the excepted pattern. "Grandmother, that *vanic* (overblouse) is not right to wear on Saturday afternoon." "Mother, yesterday you laughed when you were talking to Leonard and Fred (adult Hutterite men)." She learned to act shy in the presence of adults and to show no other emotion unless she was alone with the children joining in their rough and boistrous games.

The only member of our family who did not respond to social pressure was Daniel, our five-year-old boy, who was protected from full colony participation by keeping him out of the kindergarten and discouraging other adults from administering physical punishment. This is the age when "the stubborn will is broken" and by modifying the impact of the culture upon him he was able to maintain a degree of independence. This remained something of a problem throughout the period of participant observation, but it also enabled us to learn more about methods of child-training and peer-group pressure. Public opinion affected Daniel little, and the crueler his peers were to him the harder he fought back. He responded to teasing with anger, which is not tolerated in Hutterite children, and on several occasions he yelled, which is also not sanctioned. The first Hutterite words he learned were expletive words, calling another child a dog or a pig, prefaced with a suitable adjective. His closest colony friend was a boy two years older than he who was also somewhat excluded by the other children and who probably profited by Daniel's presence as a target for the other children's teasing and hostility.

Participant observation required complete acceptance of the colony time schedule. The day is broken up into small units with a constant change of activity. The speed with which a job is started and completed is stressed. Thus, dinner for the colony adults is eaten in seven to ten minutes, the dining room and kitchen are cleaned and the dishes for the dinner washed and put away in another seven minutes. One's activity is scheduled from the rising bell in the morning (at about 6:15) until after supper (about 7:00 unless there is extra work like haying or harvesting, or ducks to pluck).

At first my mother, I, and even my husband had difficulty finishing our meal in the allotted time and our school-age child often ate some of her brothers' food at home for she had not learned to eat fast enough to satisfy her hunger in the allotted time. The food was delicious, primarily of Russian peasant origin, with some unusual dishes. The heads were considered a choice part of the meat. Only the men were served the steer heads, but the women and the children were given duck heads, which we split and ate.

Families slept in their own apartment. We had a tiny house with two double beds for the five of us. At first we shared an outhouse with another family, but later they built one for us. There were no locks on the apartment doors and it was not the custom to knock before entering. We had a constant stream of people in and out from before breakfast in the morning, until about 11:00 at night. Whether or not we were in the house made little difference, for colony members are free to go around as they wish. However, there are personal friendships and not everyone visits everyone else and some do not enter another's apartment if no family member is at home. We had a little trouble adjusting

Hutterite youth in a bedroom apartment (photograph by Kryn Taconis).

to the complete lack of privacy, but the preacher explained to us: "You are fortunate to be living in the colony, for here there are always one hundred eyes watching you." He went on to point out that this protected us from any chance deviation from the accepted pattern of behavior. Later when I visited without my family I was greeted as a relative and during the three days was never alone. I slept with one of the girls and even on trips to the outhouse someone always generously accompanied me.

Personal needs could be indulged only within the system. Thus, we bought extra food and ate it or occasionally served it to fellow colonists late on a summer evening. Nice toilet soap to take to the community bath house instead of using the brown homemade soap for the Saturday afternoon bath became a type of personal luxury that was acceptable within the system. No one could leave the colony without the preacher's permission and in this way too we conformed, for had we had freedom of movement we would have been too privileged. The only time during a seven-week stay that our family was outside the colony as a unit, our school-age child begged, "Drive slowly, it is so easy to breathe out here." The detailed time schedule, the constant surveillance, and pressure to conform kept us always busy.

As participant observers we were careful not to be innovators. We attempted to support and adjust to the system as fully as we were able. Thus, I did not bring a radio or a camera with me (both forbidden possessions although widely used in secret by adolescents). However, at the end of our stay, my husband brought his camera and surreptitiously took a few pictures. We made an effort not to suggest alternative ways of doing things and not to introduce new activities or new ideas. Because a fairly large number of individuals were involved in the study it was possible for different investigators to have completely different roles. The person who gathered the census data and specific information from interviews was never in the colony at the same time that we were and was not identified with our family. Photographs were obtained from other sources so that we would not betray their trust by breaking an important taboo. We attempted to be as inconspicuous as possible and largely succeeded so that visitors to the colony never realized that we were not Hutterite. The only time I was recognized as non-Hutterite was after we had left our "home" colony and were on our way back to the States. Because we would be visiting other colonies on the way we were still dressed Hutterite. I took our youngest child who had bronchitis to the doctor. During the examination I asked him about one of the ailing colony members and he answered using his best medical jargon. Without thinking I responded with similar vocabulary. For the first time he really looked at me and asked, "Who are you? You don't talk like a Hutterite woman."

On one occasion I stepped completely out of character as a submissive Hutterite woman, although even then I was careful to determine colony consensus before I acted. A lovely nineteen-year-old girl who was cooking for the colony became ill with boils. The one in the middle of her forehead swelled until her eyes shut and she had red streaks running towards her eye. She had a fever and was obviously very sick. This same day the three highest ranking men in the colony, those who give permission to leave the colony for any reason, were away on business. The girl was becoming sicker in front of our eyes. Everyone visited her, clucked over her condition, and told her about people they knew who had died from boils. The feeling began to grow that she should be taken to the hospital, but the highest ranking man left in the colony was opposed. He did not believe in doctors. Everyone was critical of every possible course of action and no one was able to reach a decision or to do anything. Finally, with her mother's permission, and the backing of the women, I took her to the nearest hospital. She was admitted immediately. By the time I returned the leaders were back and everyone was relieved that the girl was safely in the hospital.

One can master the schedule of the day and the details of grooming more easily than the patterns of thought. I constantly came up against the fact that there was little cause and effect in the world. Newton, Descartes, and subsequent scientists have had little influence on the Hutterite world view. Everything happens according to God's plan. One day an adult Hutterite man who was in town was approached by a stranger who said, "I'm a religious man, but I don't belong to a church."

"That's too bad," said the Hutterite. "If you are a religious man you should support a church."

"No, no. I can't take that Virgin Mary stuff," replied the stranger."

"Do you believe that God created the universe?" asked the Hutterite.

"Of course, I believe that God created the world."

The Hutterite replied: "If God created the whole world, then one virgin birth shouldn't be too difficult."

Once their premises are accepted, the Hutterites have an answer or a proverb for every question.

In the northern plains where this colony was located there is a constant threat of hail. Three times the colony had suffered severe hail damage, and it was always a race to get the grain harvested in time. This had been a good growing season, the crop was heavy and ripe. The combines were ready and finally they cut one trial swath around a single field. The decision was to begin combining the following day. But next morning we awakened to rain. My husband and I were distressed; the colonists had worked hard all summer, yet everyone seemed calm. The second day we woke to continued rain. We said to the preacher, "Aren't you worried? It's raining." He smiled gently and said, shrugging his shoulders, "What can you do?" The third day the rain continued, it was cold and damp. In contrast to the colonists, we were quite frantic. "It is still raining" we announced in rather critical tones. The minister turned to us and said severely, "You know Who makes it rain." On another occasion I had been the last woman to wash and before my clothes were dry it began to rain. The woman closest to me in age, who had washed early came to help me take them off the clothes line and bring them in. As I hurriedly snatched them down, I commented, "I don't see why it has to rain every Monday." "To teach us patience," she quietly answered. The major problem I had was not in adjusting to any of the details of life or work different or difficult as they might be, but to base my actions on the concept, so central to Hutterite colony life, of *Gelassenheit,* or full resignation. It is very difficult for someone raised in our individualistic American culture to think and act as a passive instrument, to renounce all self-will, exchanging it for patience and self-surrender to the colony. Yet, this is necessary if the participant is to experience the joys as well as the tribulations of colony life and if he is to understand the deep satisfaction of the Hutterite way of life.

Full participation in a Hutterite colony demands about eighteen hours a day, seven days a week, so there was very little time for writing while in the field. I kept a series of 8 by 5 spiral notebooks: one journal on food, recipes and home remedies, one on women's work and activities, one on men's work and activities (kept largely by my husband), one on movement to and from the colony, and three miscellaneous notebooks. Every moment of privacy I used to talk into a tape-recorder, which was always set up except that I kept the tape hidden so that it could not be listened to in my absence. As soon as a tape was filled it was mailed off. My mother, husband, and the children also recounted incidents into the tape-recorder. This material averaged about fifty typed pages a week. There was always the feeling that had there been more hours in the day more material could have been recorded more fully.

There is not room in a Hutterite colony for a long-term visitor, and Hutterites dislike prying questions even when asked by fellow members. Their contacts with "outsiders" are stylized and frequently superficial. Therefore, if one is to study such things as the total culture—life styles, child-rearing, the role of women—one must really participate. Only on the physical, working-living level can real relationships be built and meanings and feelings that are never verbalized, be observed. The anthropologist needs to know enough about the culture in advance and be sensitive when he first arrives, if he is to find an acceptable role. The great advantage to be gained from having a whole family enter a community, must be weighed against the demands the researcher's family makes on him and the effect of a number of people entering the community. Children are excellent observers and reporters, but one must consider both the long- and short-term effect of the experience on one's own children. In his interest and excitement to learn about culture the anthropologist must remember that individuals are more than cultural representations or sources of information. In the final analysis we are working with the real lives of real people and we must not "use" either our own families or members of the host culture primarily as "tools" to further an abstraction. The individuals, the society, or the culture should not be destroyed or painfully injured by our study.

Making the Documentary Film

For seven years the National Film Board of Canada, a government filmmaking agency, had sought permission from colony leaders to make a documentary film. Early in the period of our fieldwork their producer, Colin Low, asked me about the advisability of exploring again the feasibility of making a film on Hutterite life. To obtain permission from the leaders was in my judgment impossible, but I agreed to "consider methods of approaching the problem and of bringing gentle and considerate influence to bear on the problem." The making of a documentary film was not a part of the research design, but I realized that a good documentary film would supplement the analysis and is therefore recommended in our book (Hostetler and Huntington 1967:119). Initially, I agreed to serve as consultant for the film board and eventually as liaison person for the Hutterites. We include a discussion of the filming here for it illustrates several techniques of fieldwork: how we gained entry for a specific purpose, how we managed a temporary suspension of the taboo against photography, and how a nonparticipating observer functions in contrast to the participant observer.

My task as consultant was to bring the right influences to bear on a colony that would be receptive to the idea of making a film, and to protect the colony from the censure of other colonies. This I had to do without jeopardizing the rapport I had already established with the Hutterites. After seeing several of the National Film Board films and talking with Colin Low, I was convinced that the film board would do their best to make an expert educational film. They were sensitive to the religious convictions of the Hutterites and they would not attempt to film anything on the colony without permission. The filming could all be done in one colony but it would be necessary for two or three people to be in residence for a minimum of one month without major shooting restrictions.

If a film could be made, its members would have to be persuaded to suspend temporarily the taboo against photography. The preacher-assembly, consisting of all colony leaders, would obviously not approve nor even discuss such a proposal. The colonies I knew that would permit photography under certain conditions, had factional elements within them. To make a film of a colony that had internal problems would be unrepresentative. I sought wider support for the idea by conferring with the legal counsel for the Hutterites, a former member of Alberta's Parliament and a man highly respected by the Hutterites, for he had assisted them with their land and tax problems. He favored the making of a film and felt that a film would dispel many unfounded fears and prejudices against the Hutterites. Together we agreed upon a colony that should be approached. In the colony we selected, the preacher and I had become confidants. Among Hutterites he was highly respected, and his colony was small, fairly well isolated from others, and he had good rapport with all of his members. Isolation was desirable to keep visits from other colonies at a minimum.

I decided to share with the preacher the letter I had received from the National Film Board of Canada that outlined the purpose and the conditions necessary for making a film on Hutterite life. With a cover letter of my own, I mailed it to the colony, stating that we might discuss it on my next visit. During the same week the lawyer for the Hutterites sent a letter to the same colony urging them to consider seriously the proposition. Suspension of a taboo required informal consensus, and for this reason it was important that the colony read the proposal for making a film and discuss it among themselves. After a few days I visited the colony to ascertain what reactions there had been to the letters. The reactions were not entirely negative, and the colony agreed to an exploratory meeting with Colin Low and myself.

After a few weeks, Colin Low and I were driving by automobile far into the plains of Alberta to keep the appointment with the colony. In the trunk was a movie projector and several of the best films the National Film Board of Canada had produced. The selection consisted of films on Canadian natural history, its people and early settlers. Colin Low thought that if the colony showed interest in the proposal we should show them some of these films.

At the colony we were greeted as usual and ushered into the preacher's apartment. As we were seated around the room in the presence of many adults and children, we explained our mission.

"We don't want any picture taking," said the preacher. "Let me ask you just one question. Would Jesus Christ let himself be filmed for a movie? No! We cannot do it either." About that time a large Hutterite man, whom we understood was the "boss," came into the room. There was a gust of odor from what must have been the pig barn. After exchanging introductions he pointed his finger at Colin: "Your name sounds Mormon, Mr. Low. Mormons are the enemies of the Hutterites."

Our hopes for filming were virtually shattered, even though I had known the preacher and his colony for many months. We were confronted with seemingly insurmountable barriers and rigid ethnocentric patterns. From my earlier contacts, I had learned that the colony people have a need to assert their basic premise before discussing a significant problem or proposition. Their discussions, therefore, generally begin with asserting the superiority of God and of communal life as the right way for mankind to live. Once they had expressed their basic premises, the discussions of filming got underway. We explained that after all, the film board had no connection with Hollywood. No one was to make a profit from the film, for it would be made by the government and not by a private corporation. It would not be sold commercially for showing in theatres. I pointed out that when the government asks for a favor, they should give serious consideration. Colin Low said that Hutterites were greatly misunderstood, which they well knew, and the film would help to break down hostility and create better relations. We explained that Colin Low was no longer a Mormon of Alberta, having left his community as a young man. We acknowledged the Hutterite contention that the Mormon church owned even larger blocks of land in Alberta than did Hutterites and that Mormon influence in the legislature had helped to form restrictive laws against Hutterites.

Six hours later we left the colony with the tentative promise that the filming could proceed in the spring. The colony agreed to house the filmers over a period of several weeks while the photographic work was being done. Everything could be filmed except for the religious services. The films and movie projector we had brought to show the colony, remained untouched in the trunk of the automobile. Colin Low discovered, as I had suspected, that the colony would not permit the showing of any movies to their members.

The total time spent in colony residence by the filming crew was five weeks. The crew consisted of the producer, the camera man, and myself as liaison person, and during the final three weeks, a soundman. All agreements were oral. The colony was to be compensated for electricity, for any equipment that the photographers used, and for meals and lodging. The film crew ate their meals in the colony dining hall. I usually ate with the preachers in the apartment where we could discuss schedule and any problems. The producer requested that the colony function normally so that there would be no interference and a true documentary would be the result. The Hutterites also wanted a minimum of interference with colony work. Even though there were ground rules from the start, several points of tension developed that needed periodic discussion and clarification. Among other things the filmers agreed not to take any boys along to town without the permission of the colony. The lighter moments during midafternoon and midafternoon coffee breaks fostered personal rapport between the Hutterites and the film crew. Colony members showed great interest in the successful outcome of the film. Every evening the films were taken to the post office for prompt shipment to the film "boss" in Montreal, who promptly processed the film and sent telegrams, frequently with lauditory comments. Highly favorable reports had a positive effect on the colony members. Sympathy was evoked for the camera man when he was kicked in the face by a pig so that filming had to be suspended for two days. The cooperation of the colony members exceeded all expectations of the producer and virtually no colony member was camera-shy, nor was there any interference from onlookers.

After two weeks of work the producer was faced with a complex problem he seemed unable to solve. The despondency of Colin Low was noticeable to the colony members. The girls asked me one day: "What's the matter with Mr. Low, John? Is he homesick for his family, or what's wrong with him?" Others thought he was under religious conviction and was about to renounce the world and consider living in a colony. The problem for Colin Low was that there was nothing of tension or excitement in the photography. We shared the predicament with the preacher. "Everything is too peaceful and too wonderful in the colony life; if we show this to the outside world they will not believe it," Colin explained to the preacher. We could not introduce any scenes showing dissident elements, colony tensions, family factions, or dissenters. To stage any such situations was impossible. The problem was partially resolved by having a direct interview with the preacher on a variety of pointed questions about Hutterite beliefs and by the conversation between a hitchhiker and the occupants of the egg truck. Other elements of excitement that gave a sense of movement in the film were cattle branding and a coyote chase.

The major complaint of the colony was that the filming group stayed too long. After three weeks, colony foremen began to hint strongly that they should leave. This was understandable, since the colony was engaging in an activity that if divulged to other colonies could evoke severe censure or possibly excommunication. Colony members rationalized their stay by saying: "They take their time because they work for the government, and the government is always slow and can afford to take time." The preacher said: "Get those people out of here John; we don't want to get in trouble with our elders." The young executive-type son of the preacher said: "Dad, we will have to make a confession after it's all over." Other colonies did indeed find out about the filming and the news spread. At the next assembly of preachers, the colony was confronted by the presiding elder and was asked to make apologies and not let it happen again.

Twenty-eight thousand feet of film had been shot. The Hutterites did not allow the film to be shown on the colony, nor did they want to censor it. They were firm in their request that I see the film before it was released. The few Hutterites who have seen the film on television at neighboring farms have made favorable comments. A Manitoba Hutterite who saw the film said: "The coyote was too slow in running, it must have been a tame one."

Relations were cordial with the colony after the filming was over. The colony held no one responsible for the suspension of the photographic taboo except themselves. I realized afterward that from their point of view the colony permitted the filming not for any of the reasons we had advocated but out of respect for me as a close friend and to their attorney. Even to this day the value of the film is downgraded by the colony. After the filming, I found it necessary to protect the colony from vicious gossip of other Hutterites and from outsiders who wanted to take more photographs. I counteracted rumors from other colonies that the preacher was offered an exorbitant sum of money for giving permission to film the colony. The traffic of visitors increased as a consequence of the film and newspaper photographers wanted to take additional pictures. The colony firmly refused permission to let other persons take additional photographs or movies. Now that the film had been taken (during a temporary suspension of an important taboo by a single colony) I assured the colony there would be no need for additional picture-taking for many years. Even though the colony permitted the filming there was no change in basic attitude or belief. The colony was not disrupted, weakened, or changed in any way.

Concluding Observations

We have discussed some of the special problems encountered in doing fieldwork among the Hutterites. It is not suggested that our work among the Hutterites is representative of the kind of problems the anthropologist would encounter in other ethnic groups. Some of the methods we have used can be applied to the study of other cultures, but the details of relating anthropologically to each culture will vary. Effective fieldwork involves not only learning all one can from the discipline, but also adapting one's personal resources, uniquenesses, and individual experiences. We will conclude with some general observations on fieldwork, terminating the research, interpreting the findings, and maintaining contacts with the society.

The role of the participant observer and the nonparticipating observer differ greatly. The latter is illustrated by the producer and camera man while residing in the colony. The filming group did not emulate the roles, colony functions, and its schedule; they were amiable onlookers who were accommodated somewhat uneasily for a specified period. The nonparticipating observer comes in contact with the culture for a limited time usually to obtain information on a specific aspect of the group: its economic and agricultural practices, its origins, old books and manuscripts, or perhaps to obtain blood samples. The anthropologist who is interested in the total culture will become a participant in the work and inner life of the community. Participation is possible insofar as the individual is acceptable to the group. Hutterites, like the Old Order Amish and other ethnic groups, are very quickly able to judge the motives and sincerity of the prospective participant. Once the participant observer has accepted the roles and the work responsibility of the colony he is obligated to help support the traditions and the taboos of his age set. The nonparticipating observer can often flout the taboos because he is presumed ignorant of the colony standards. The colony can only accommodate him for a brief period, for an extended stay would introduce disruptive elements into the culture. Since Hutterites are interested in gaining converts, they are perhaps less suspicious and more receptive to outsiders than some ethnic groups. Some individuals tried to persuade us to join the colony and some offered to assist us in organizing a "colony" in our home communities. The degree of openness to outsiders varied greatly among colonies.

The time spent in analyzing the findings and preparing the research report (Hostetler 1965) for the granting agency was more than three times that spent doing fieldwork. Our task was to organize the findings in relation to the research design and the specifications supplied by the granting agency. The required number of copies were lithographed and bound in hard cover. After the research report was completed we proceeded to outline and write the case study. Return trips to the colonies were advantageous. Observing a colony when it is newly founded and again at later stages when its population and its prosperity has increased yielded still additional insights.

Termination of the fieldwork presented no major problems. Many personal relationships had been formed during the course of fieldwork, which now had to be physically terminated but not altogether severed, for return visits were anticipated and communication by letter is possible. We were careful not to make others dependent upon us, but also to reward the colony in ways that were approved by the culture. Many exchanges were reciprocal. We typed colony letters or documents and occasionally obtained old or rare German books they wanted. The colony was especially inclined to give us gifts of produce, chicken, duck, bread, vegetables, braided rugs, pillows, and also small articles they had bought in stores.

Our fieldwork is formally terminated, but our relationships and ties with the Hutterites will never terminate. As participants we gained their friendships and invested a great deal of ourselves. They are a part of our lives. Just as they are always ready to take back their few stray members who have left the colonies, so also they are ready to take us back. On leaving the colony we were told, "When you come back we will greet you as a relative."

References

Alberta, Province of, 1949, *Report of the Hutterite Investigation Committee.* Edmonton, Alberta, Canada. September 1959.

Deets, Lee Emerson, 1939, *The Hutterites: A Study in Social Cohesion.* Gettysburg, Pa.: Times and News Publishing Co. A doctoral dissertation at Columbia University, Faculty of Political Science.

Eaton, Joseph, and *R. J. Weil,* 1955, *Culture and Mental Disorders.* New York: The Free Press.

Grimmelshausen, Hans J. C., 1668, Simplizissimus, Book V, Chapter 19.

Hostetler, John A., 1961, The communal property act of Alberta. University of Toronto Law Journal 14:125–128.

———, 1963, *Amish Society.* Baltimore, Md.: Johns Hopkins Press. (Revised 1968.)

———, 1965, *Education and Marginality in the Communal Society of the Hutterites.* University Park, Pa.: Pennsylvania State University.

Hostetler, John A., and *Gertrude Enders Huntington,* 1967, *The Hutterites in North America.* New York: Holt, Rinehart and Winston, Inc.

Kaplan, Bert and *Thomas F. A. Plaut,* 1956, *Personality in a Communal Society.* Lawrence, Kansas: University of Kansas Publications.

Malinowski, Bronislaw, 1944, *A Scientific Theory of Culture and Other Essays.* Chapel Hill, North Carolina: University of North Carolina Press.

Wolkan, Rudolf, 1923, *Geschicht-Buch der Hutterischen Brüder.* Vienna, Austria, and Standoff Colony, Alberta.

Zieglschmid, A. J. F., 1947, *Das Klein-Geschiechtsbuch der Hutterischen Brüder.* Philadelphia: Carl Schurz Memorial Foundation.

Film Note

The film *The Hutterites* was produced by the National Film Board of Canada, Montreal, Quebec. It is black and white, 16 mm., and lasts 28 minutes. It is available in the United States for purchase through Sterling Educational Films, Inc., 241 East 34th St., New York, N.Y.; 614 Davis St., Evanston, Illinois; and 1211 Polk St., San Francisco, California.

9

FIELDWORK AMONG THE VICE LORDS OF CHICAGO

R. LINCOLN KEISER
Wesleyan University

Relevant Case Study: **The Vice Lords:**
Warriors of the Streets

In the chapter following Lincoln Keiser shows how the urban ghetto situation and racism affected his field research. These pervasive factors are apparent in his getting introduced to the leadership of the Vice Lords, establishing residence in the ghetto, gaining entrée to the fighting club, and in the special problems of participant observation in the organization. In the ghetto environment, a White among Blacks, his role was complex. Although he got on the inside, he remained an outsider and racism in some form was always present as a barrier even with his best friends. That he and his friends among the Vice Lords surmounted this barrier sufficiently to permit the research to be done at all, is an indication that this barrier need not prevent some degree of effective mutual understanding.

He also deals with the influence of his own theoretical orientation on his fieldwork, showing how it was a factor determining what he observed, how he asked questions, and how he interpreted what he saw and heard.

The Author

Besides writing a case study of the Vice Lords, Lincoln Keiser has edited *Hustler! the Autobiography of a Thief* (1965). In 1968 he went to Afghanistan to conduct research on the social structure of mountain societies of the Hindu-Kush, and wrote his Ph.D. thesis on a comparison of the problems of social control in two such groups. At present he is teaching at Wesleyan University. Born in Janesville, Wisconsin, in 1937, he is one of eight children, three of whom are step siblings.

He says of himself,

As a boy I lived in several different parts of the country since my father, a Congregational minister, changed positions a number of times during my childhood. While I was in grammar school my family lived in New York State and

R. *Lincoln Keiser.*

during trips to New York City I spent a lot of time in the American Museum of Natural History. Wandering through the halls of the museum and observing the exhibitions of cultures and societies from all parts of the world aroused my interest in anthropology. This interest continued through high school and as an undergraduate at Lawrence College I decided to become an anthropologist. I entered graduate school at Northwestern University, received an M.A. degree in anthropology in 1964, and continued studying for the Ph.D. degree in social anthropology at the University of Rochester, specializing in urban and in political anthropology. For relaxation I read science fiction. I also enjoy skiing as well as a variety of other sports.

G. D. S.

Introduction

For some time many anthropologists and sociologists have felt that the particular research techniques developed through the study of small-scale societies had limited, if any, value for research in modern industrial urban communities. Michael Banton has said, for example, "The relatively simple life of a tribal village can perhaps be adequately described in purely verbal terms but the uniformities found in urban life can for the most part be expressed only statistically. In the town few generalizations of any validity can be obtained without

In Vice Lord territory.

the use of social survey techniques . . ." (1957: xv). Sociologists have expressed similar views concerning the use of anthropological methods in studying urban phenomena. "When studying an entire primitive society in this way [using anthropological methods] one can be fairly certain of having witnessed the full range of behavior that members of that society hold in high regard, given the relatively constant constraints of the physical environment. However, when this method is applied to subcultures contained within a single society, it is apt to lead to fallacious results . . ." (Short and Strodtbeck 1965:75).

Recently, however, a significant number of anthropologists have begun to go into the city, and have taken with them basic ways of studying human behavior that were developed through the analysis of peasant and tribal groups. But cities are quite different from the kinds of places where anthropologists have traditionally worked, and this difference generates different problems, both of a practical and theoretical kind. In this chapter I will explore some of the problems that I encountered and the ways I tried to solve them in my research with the Vice Lords, a Black street gang located in the Lawndale area of Chicago's West Side ghetto. I shall discuss problems that derive from approaching the study of human behavior from a particular anthropological orientation, as well as problems that are related to the particular nature of cities.

There is another important factor that is not directly related to the urban setting as such. This derives from the racial situation in the United States. I was a White working in a Black ghetto area, and this had definite effects on my research. Some of these effects will be discussed in this chapter.

There are certain kinds of problems that almost all anthropologists face when undertaking any piece of field research. It will be helpful here to enumerate some of these briefly. Later in the chapter each will be discussed in terms specific to my research. In undertaking a field research project, one must first pick out an area in which to do research and choose what will be studied. Then there is the problem of getting established. This involves settling physically in the area; becoming adjusted to living in an alien environment; and establishing the necessary social relationships so that one can begin gathering data. Data gathering itself presents problems. On one level this involves data-gathering techniques, but on another level there is the problem of what, out of the almost infinite array of human behavioral aspects, one chooses to record in the first place. Although the latter is related to the explicit purposes the researcher has in undertaking the study, it is also related to the anthropologist's basic theoretical orientation, for this generates ideas concerning what is problematical in human behavior, and, therefore, what is to be recorded. The anthropologist is not always conscious of this orientation while he is actively involved in field research, and thus he is not always aware of how it is affecting what he records. The anthropologist's emotional reactions to the social and cultural setting in which he is working is another source of problems. Having to interact in social situations where one does not know the cultural significance of various actions places a tremendous emotional strain on the individual, and affects his relationships with the people he is studying. Also, although the anthropologist tries to approach his work as dispassionately as possible, he is a human being, and he reacts to situations in terms of his own values and ideas. How the anthropologist handles these feelings is one of the most serious problems of field research. Finally, after the research has been completed, there is the problem of writing up the material into some kind of coherent account.

Picking an Area and Topic

The choice of an area and a research topic can be made in several ways. One may be primarily interested in a particular geographic area and then develop a research topic appropriate to that area. In other cases one's primary interest may lie in a particular topic, say for example, political anthropology, and the geographic area is chosen for its special relevance to the topical interest. In both these situations, however, the choice of one's first fieldwork project usually stems from reading and other work done in the course of undergraduate and graduate training.

My choice of a Black gang (or "club," as it is known in the ghetto) for a research topic came about a little differently. In 1963, while I was a graduate student at Northwestern University, I had a part time job as a waiter in the dining room of a luxurious retirement home located in Evanston, a suburb of Chicago. Blacks were hired as kitchen help by the company who ran the dining room, while Whites did the work that involved contact with the patrons. Most of the Black workers were women, but there were a few men my age who worked as dishwashers. Part of my job consisted of clearing the tables after a meal and taking the dirty dishes to the counter in front of the dishwasher. Thus I got to know Jesse and Al, the two dishwashers. We never became really close friends, but I did get to know them well enough so that my presence did not interrupt their normal conversation. Often I would sit with them during a break, and linger at the dishwasher to exchange a few words. Al had grown up in a neighborhood in Chicago that had no fighting clubs. He had met a girl in a bar, and wanted to see her again. But she lived in the neighborhood of a subgroup of the Egyptian Cobras. Jesse was from that neighborhood, had been a member of the Cobras, and knew that this girl was considered by the Cobras to be the "old lady" of one of the group's important members. He considered it his duty to "run it down" (explain it) to Al. Thus the Cobras were a constant conversation topic. I heard bits and snatches of the conversation—enough to be aware that here, in the world of the fighting clubs, was a highly interesting cultural and social system in operation.

My interest was aroused because I was involved in anthropology and reading about how cultural and social systems worked, but my initial contact with the world of the fighting clubs had nothing to do with my anthropological background. My initial contact was primarily related to two factors—the nature of cities, and the operation of racism in the United States. Cities are, among other things, huge conglomerates of people, few of whom know one another. In small-scale societies, those in close spatial proximity usually have many kinds of social interrelationships, for example, kinship relationships, economic relationships, and political relationships. Another way of putting this is that in small-scale societies there are few, if any, strangers. Everyone knows everyone else, and knows them in a variety of social contexts. There are lines of potential social interaction laid out at birth among almost everyone, and individuals activate these at particular times. This is not the case in the city. Many people who are in close spatial proximity have no social relationships, for example, passengers on a bus or subway car. Others who do have social relationships have highly contextualized ones, that is, they relate to one another in a single, or at best, a few contexts only. An individual may relate to one set of people at his job, another set in his home, and yet another set in his club. In the city the process of laying out lines of potential social interaction has an importance lacking in small-scale societies. Another way of putting this is that in the city most people are strangers, and making friends out of strangers is an important and continual social process. Friends are made out of strangers through the interaction that takes place in particular social contexts. For example, a person gets to know others by interacting with them in his job, or at his church, or at parties, or in the classroom. My initial contact with Black fighting clubs was a result of a process of making friends out of strangers that is an integral part of urban social systems.

It is here that racism became important. My initial contact with the world of Black fighting gangs resulted from establishing social relationships with individuals who were a part of this world. That this occurred in the context of a job is related to racism. There were no gang members in any of my anthropology classes at Northwestern; there were no gang members at any of the student parties I attended. In our society at the time I met Jesse and Al, Whites who formed relationships with Blacks, usually, although not always, did so in the context of a job. Middle-class Whites who formed relationships with lower-class Blacks, almost always formed them in the job context. Racism limited the kinds of jobs open to Blacks, and thus limited the kinds of jobs in which I could have met and gotten to know ghetto-dwelling Blacks. Working as a low-paid dishwasher was a job poorly educated Black men could get. If Al and Jesse could have gotten better jobs, quite possibly I never would have met them, and never have made contact with the world of Black fighting clubs.

My job at the retirement home ended, and I lost contact with Jesse and Al. By then I had become interested in fighting clubs. I now knew that certain fighting clubs were not composed of a small number of young men as I had originally thought, but had quite large memberships which were internally organized in complex ways. I had heard references made to Juniors, Seniors, and Midgets; to K-Town Cobras, Jew-Town Cobras, and King Cobras; and to war counselors, supreme war couselors, and presidents. I had heard it said that people had "heart" and "reps." How did this all work? What was the nature of the subgroups? How were they differentiated, and how did they connect with one another? What were the social identities, and how were they connected to form social roles? What were the beliefs, concepts, and values which the members of the clubs held, and how did they fit with the set of social groups and social identities? In short, the question that came to my mind was, what is the nature of this social and cultural system and how does it work? I felt that indeed, here was an area well worth future research.

Getting Established

The next problem was getting established, that is, establishing relationships with members of a particular group; settling in some kind of residence; and adjusting to living in a different environment. Establishing relationships was difficult. No one, much less a White, can go into an area inhabited by a club and initiate a research project. Very careful and time-consuming ground work has to be done. It is necessary to make contact with influential members of the group and to gain their trust before one can begin serious work. I approached this problem again through the means of a job. I was offered employment with the Social Service Department of what was then the Municipal Court of Chicago, and was assigned as a court caseworker to Boys' Court North. Boys' Court North handled cases of boys seventeen through twenty years old. Its spatial jurisdiction included the Lawndale area of Chicago's west side Black ghetto, and the court dealt with members of three large fighting clubs—the Egyptian Cobras, the Roman Saints, and the Vice Lords. The court caseworker's job consisted of counseling individuals referred by the court; thus I became acquainted with members of these three groups.

The Social Service Department was interested in learning about the nature of fighting clubs, and I was given permission to question persons referred to me by the court about features of club life. This posed problems. My role as caseworker conflicted in some ways with my role as anthropologist. As a caseworker my primary purpose was to help the people referred to me make the kind of adjustment to the urban world that would prevent their coming into conflict with the rules and enforcement agencies of predominantly White, middle-class Chicago. This meant I was trying to change behavior in terms of my own value system. As an anthropologist, however, it was crucial to try not to judge behavior relative to my own values, much less to change it. Since my primary responsibility was to the role of caseworker, I was seriously limited in the use of my "clients" as anthropological informants. Further, because I was connected with the court, many boys were reticent to give information about their club. In spite of these difficulties, I was able to gather some basic material. The people most willing to talk about their group were Vice Lords, and, therefore, most of my information was about that club.

In order to conduct further research, I had to establish relationships outside the court context. I accomplished this, however, through my involvement with the court. While talking with a "client" referred by the court, I was told about a woman who had taught in a West Side school, and who had become close friends with several Vice Lords. I contacted her, and she agreed to introduce me to Sonny, one of the Vice Lords she knew. At the time I met Sonny, I also met another Lord called Goliath. In the next year Sonny, Goliath, and I went to parties together, met in bars, and visited each other's homes. During this time I also met a few other members of the club and collected several life histories. It happened that Goliath and I got along especially well, and in the course of the year became quite good friends. In the fall of 1965 I returned to graduate school, and in the summer of 1966 initiated full-scale research.

At the beginning of the summer I approached Goliath with my plan. I would rent an apartment in the ghetto, and Goliath would live with me rent free. In return he would introduce me to the leaders of the Vice Lords, and give assurance that I was not a police spy. Goliath agreed, and the plan was initiated.

Finding an apartment proved more difficult than I had anticipated. Most of the apartments in Lawndale are owned by White absentee landlords, and they were highly suspicious of my motives for wanting to live in the ghetto. When I went to see about renting one apartment, the landlord said, "I'm sorry, we only rent to Whites." I looked at him and said, "Well . . .?" He gave me an embarrassed laugh and said, "Oh, I mean Negroes." Goliath ruled out other available apartments because they afforded too much opportunity for ambush attacks. Finally, after we were unable to find anything suitable in the area around 15th Street, we looked in the North Side ghetto, and found an apartment there. It would have been best to live within the 15th Street Lord's territory. But on the north side I was at least located in a Black neighborhood; I was able to question informants in surroundings that were relatively natural for them; and I was able to give "sets" (parties) for the Vice Lords that were not only useful in gaining rapport, but which also gave me an opportunity to observe behavior in this important social context.

At the beginning of the summer Goliath introduced me to Tex, Bat Man, and Shotgun, three of the most important leaders of the 15th Street Vice Lords. The 15th Street Lords was a section of the City Lords (see Keiser 1969 for a discussion of Vice Lord sections and branches), and I concentrated my research for the first half of the summer on 15th Street. About halfway through the summer Tex was arrested for strong armed robbery, and sentenced to prison. At about the same time, many of the older Vice Lords were released from prison and they decided to reorganize the club. Meetings of the "Nation" (the entire club is called the "Conservative Vice Lord Nation"), attended by members of all the subgroups, were reinstituted. Through Goliath I approached these older individuals who had become the leaders of the Nation. I explained that I wanted to write a book about the Vice Lords, and offered to share any royalties with the group. The proposal was put before the club in a meeting, and with the support of my friends in the 15th Street Lords, and some of the people I had known as a caseworker, the majority of members gave their approval. This legitimized my position in the eyes of the other club members, and the rest of the summer I concentrated my research on the corner of 16th and Lawndale, the meeting place for all the Lords in the branch known as Vice Lord City.

Adjusting to living conditions was nowhere near as difficult in my Vice Lord research as it was in my study of a mountain village in Afghanistan where conditions were similar to those usually encountered by anthropologists working in non-Western societies. I lived in an apartment that, although dingy, had hot and cold running water, a bathroom, and a stove and refrigerator; I bought my food in supermarkets and restaurants with money I was accustomed to using; and the language spoken was generally similar to my own. However, there were some differences that took some adjustment on my part. The greatest of these was getting accustomed to living with the possibility of robbery and ambush. Goliath took many precautions in choosing an apartment that had a well-lighted entrance and well-lighted hallways. We kept a .45 pistol in the apartment, along with several wooden clubs. Goliath always put a match in the door jam before we left so that he could tell if anyone had forced open the door while we were gone and might be hidden in the apartment when we came back. At night he put boards and empty cans in front of the windows and doors so that if someone tried to break in, he would make so much noise that we would be awakened. These were precautions that any sensible person took—like buckling your safety belt while driving in an automobile. Goliath no more dwelt on the possibility of someone attacking us, than I dwell on the possibility of being killed in an automobile accident. There are dangers, you take precautions, and go about living a normal life. It took a while for me to get used to taking these precautions without getting extremely nervous. It turned out they saved me possible trouble and injury. Early one morning a man forced his way into our apartment through a window. He knocked over the board we had set up and awakened me. I was waiting for him with a two-by-four (Goliath had spent the night with a girlfriend and had taken the .45 with him), and when he saw me, he turned around and went back out the window.

Gathering the Data

There are two aspects of the problem of gathering data. First, is the problem of methods. The ones I used are standard in anthropological fieldwork: I did participant observation and conducted interviews with informants. For me, participant observation consisted of observing behavior while hanging out on the streets, going to bars, attending parties, visiting friends and relatives, and simply driving about the West Side with members of the club. As a participant observer I was involved in the first stages of one actual gang fight, and was part of the preparations for another that never materialized. My presence in the neighborhood was legitimized by me being "the man who is writing the book." People knew what I was doing there, and why I was doing it. But I could never fully participate in the life of the streets. For one thing, not everyone accepted me to the same extent. For some, the fact that I was White seemed to cause little difficulty. In conversation, Vice Lords often call one another "nigger" in a joking manner. When "nigger" was used in conversation by a person who did not know me very well, often he would turn and say, "Oh, excuse me," as if he had insulted me. One time when this was said, a friend of mine answered, "That don't make no difference, Jack. The man's a nigger just like us, only he's white. He's a white nigger." Others had such strong antagonisms that they were unable to be friends with me. They tolerated my presence, but for the most part ignored me. Finally, there were some individuals who could not control their hatred toward Whites, and in a few instances it boiled into the open aimed at me. When this happened, I simply walked away.

But to an extent, I was always an outsider—even to my close friends. The history of Black-White hatred separated us. They, as well as I, felt the need to constantly verbalize that we were friends *in spite* of the racism that exists between Blacks and Whites. Cultural differences also underlined our separateness. I dressed in casual clothes—Levi's and a sport shirt—but these were different from the clothes worn by Vice Lords; I was not conversant in street slang; and I did not act properly in certain social situations. This last factor was especially important. For example, one evening I was in a bar with Sonny. We were standing together talking when three attractive girls walked by. Sonny shook his head slowly and said, "Foxes! Stone Foxes!" [A "fox" is an attractive girl. A "stone fox" is an extremely attractive girl.] I laughed and raised my hand to slap him on the shoulder. In the ghetto there is a particular way people express agreement. This is what I have called "hand slapping" in *The Vice Lords* and Blacks generally call it "slapping fine." This custom has now begun to diffuse to Whites, but at the time, it was not generally known outside the ghetto. If A says something felt by B to be worth emphasizing, B will raise his hand. A will then put out his hand palm up, and B will slap it. Now when I raised my hand to slap Sonny on the shoulder, I was initiating an action that was both very similar, if not identical, to the beginning moves of a hand-slapping episode, and occurred in a context that was grammatical for such an episode. Therefore, without thinking, Sonny put out his hand palm up. However, as soon as he did so, he realized that I was White, and did not customarily emphasize agreement in this manner. At the same time, I knew about hand slapping, and understood what Sonny was doing. For an instant we were staring at each other—Sonny with his hand out, but making motions to drop it, and me with my hand raised in the air. Sonny did not know whether to drop his hand or not, and I did not know if I should slap his hand or his shoulder. I decided to slap his hand at the same time he decided to put it down. We both laughed with embarrassment and shook our heads. But the ease of the moment had been lost, and the Black-White gulf that separated us was brought sharply into focus. Anthropologists often have experiences like this in their work with alien cultures, but in this case the incident had extra significance because of the history of Black-White relations in the United States. It emphasized that we were from two different cultures, but it also emphasized that we were from two groups of people who had a long history of hatred and suppression between them. Elliot Liebow in *Tally's Corner* uses the particularly apt metaphor of a linked fence to express this separation. According to Liebow, he and his Black informants could walk along together, see each other, and even occasionally touch, but the fence remained between them (Liebow 1967:250–251).

Ways of recording data are another facet of the methods problem. Each evening I wrote as much of my observations as could be remembered. It would have been best to have carried a small notebook with me so that I could have taken notes on the spot. Initially I did this, but it made most Vice Lords so uneasy for me to take out my notebook and write down something that I decided to stop. Further, much of the social interaction between Vice Lords that I observed occurred while individuals were riding in my car and could not be written in my notebook at the time. I attempted to remember as much as possible, but at the end of the day I always knew that much had been forgotten.

Interviews with various informants were another source of data. I conducted structured interviews and gathered life histories. A tape-recorder was used to record this material. There are difficulties in using a tape-recorder, but I felt the advantages easily outweighed the disadvantages. I was able to record highly detailed accounts of interviews that I could not have written by hand. Transcribing the tapes was the main difficulty. It took me months of steady work to finish the transcriptions. My research took three months of one summer and one month of another, but if it had taken an entire year—usually the minimum time an anthropologist spends in the field—the task of transcribing the tapes would have been monumental.

In recording life histories I simply asked the informant to tell about his life. The only questions asked were either those necessary to clarify something I did not understand or those necessary to get further amplification of an incident I felt was interesting and important. Structured interviews were organized around particular topics. These were derived primarily from my observations. If I thought something I had observed needed amplification, I focused on this in a structured interview. For example, I had heard Vice Lords refer to their "territory." References were made both to the territory of the branch, and to the territories of particular sections. This suggested the following questions: how are the territories of particular branches distinguished from one another, and from those of rival clubs; and what distinguishes the territories of sections? From putting together data gathered from observations, I was able to get an answer to the first question. I had no clue, however, to the way section territories were distinguished, and so I focused on this problem in a series of structured interviews.

It will be useful to include some of these interviews in this chapter because they illustrate one of the biggest difficulties in conducting structured interviews. This is the problem of framing the right questions to ask an informant. The anthropologist really has to know what kind of answers will be correct before he can think up questions that will elicit what he wants to know. In the example above, I wanted to know how section territories were distinguished. I thought that sections must hold different rights in particular parts of Vice Lord City and so I framed my questions in these terms. This idea was wrong. Therefore, the questions I asked failed to get me closer to understanding the basis for the distinction. My first interview was with a Vice Lord known as Duck. It went as follows:

R.L.K.   What's the territory of the Ridgeway Lords?

Duck   Ridgeway, all the way from 18th to Independence.

R.L.K.   Where do most of the Ridgeway Lords hang out?

Duck   On 16th Street. There be very few on Ridgeway.

R.L.K.   If they all hang out on 16th Street, why aren't they considered 16th Street Lords?

Duck   16th Street just a hang out for everybody.

R.L.K.   When you say that's the territory of the Ridgeway Lords, what do you mean? What does it mean that you have that territory?

Duck   Everybody got their little section where they hang out at. It's just different street names. They just go by street names, that's all.

R.L.K.   Well, is it because they live on that street, or is it because they hang out on that street?

Duck   They hang out on that street, and most of them live on the street, but you don't have to live on the street.

R.L.K.   O.K., suppose you live on Ridgeway, and you're in the Ridgeway Lords, and you move away, does that change your membership, or can you still belong?

Duck   You can still belong.

R.L.K.   But if you start hanging around with the group where you live now will that change your membership?

Duck   Not exactly. I keep telling you we all the same. You can belong to one group, but you can hang out wherever you want.

It was obvious I was no closer to understanding the basis for section territorial distinctions than before I started the interview. But I still failed to realize that my questions were based on an incorrect assumption about what the right answers might be, and in the next interview I worked from the same direction. Therefore, I not only missed an important clue, but also thought I found the basis for the distinction which was, in fact, not the case at all.

R.L.K.   As a member of the Ridgeway Lords, what is the difference between my territory and your territory?

Earl   They trying to keep the Roman Saints from falling down on us, and we trying to keep the Cobras from falling down on them. We got two different groups coming from two different ways. From the east it's the Roman Saints, and from the west it's the Cobras. We trying to hold the Cobras back far as we can so they won't get closer to 16th and Lawndale, 'cause 15th Street is the back door to the City.

R.L.K.   What I'm trying to get at is what difference having a particular territory means for individuals in different groups. Now I don't know if this is the case, but are there certain things that Ridgeway Lords can do in their territory that they can't do in your territory?

Earl   You right there. Like some of the 15th Street Lords might go over there— they ain't got no business jumping on no one over there, and they ain't got no business coming over to our hood and jumping on somebody.

The first answer should have given me a clue as to how Vice Lords distinguish between section territories, but because I assumed there must be differences in terms of rights, I failed to see its significance. When I asked Earl to give me an answer in terms of rights, he did. This simply led me further along a blind alley. It was not until the interview with Big Otis that I finally understood the basis for territorial distinctions between sections. I started this interview with the same assumption. Fortunately Goliath was present. He saw at once what I was trying to find out, and why I was getting nowhere. Goliath provided the right questions to ask as well as the right answers.

Goliath   What advantages do you have in your own territory?

Big Otis   We know all the gangways and rooftops, and we know just about everybody in the streets.

Goliath   Do you use your territory also like a meeting place? Like for instance, all the fellows get together to go someplace and take care of business (get together for a raid on an enemy club), could you all meet in this same area, could you get together right away, like could you contact everybody?

Big Otis   Yeah, you know where to find them at. You know where all the places they be at.

Goliath   In other words, you wouldn't have to worry about the Cobras coming down and whupping you in you territory.

Big Otis   No, we know it before they get down there.

R.L.K.   How is this different from the territory of the Ridgeway Lords?

Big Otis   It's no different.

R.L.K.   Why isn't the territory of the Ridgeway Lords your territory? What makes it different?

Goliath   See, everybody in one box, like for instance Tex and them, they be on 15th Street, so they make sure don't nobody come down Ridgeway that we don't know. This way you block off the whole area, and there always be somebody around. If you can't handle it, then you get help.

Big Otis   Yeah, if the Cobras coming from one end and the Saints coming from another, it's our job on 15th Street to stop the Cobras.

It is apparent that the distinction between section territories is based on differential responsibility rather than differential rights. Sections have the re-

A Vice Lord corner.

sponsibility for protecting particular parts of Vice Lord City from enemy attacks. A section's territory, therefore, is that part of Vice Lord City for which it is responsible in case of enemy attack. In order to fulfill this responsibility, section members must have good knowledge of how their territory is laid out— where gangways lead, how to gain access to rooftops, what alleys are deadends, and the like. It is advantageous, if not necessary, to have such knowledge when section members must actually defend their territory against enemy raids. While sections have the duty to defend a particular part of Vice Lord City, they have the right to assistance from other Vice Lord groups if they can not accomplish this alone. It is the duty, however, that is crucial in differentiating section territories.

Another aspect of the data-gathering problem stems from the theoretical orientation of the researcher. "Facts" are intimately connected with theory. What I saw as facts and therefore recorded, was directly related to my theoretical orientation. Because of my orientation, I did not record certain things that are undoubtedly important.

My theoretical orientation was that of a social anthropologist. In social anthropology human behavior is generally looked at from the perspective of social interaction. The concept of culture is important too, but is important primarily as it relates to social interaction. The basic postulate on which social anthropology rests is that social interaction is not random but has an order to it. In other words, social life forms a system. When looking at social interaction as a system, social anthropologists often employ the ideas of social groups, and social roles in getting at patterns and regularities. It is much more complicated than this, but what I have described is basic to what social anthropologists do. In any case, it was this orientation that directed my research; the questions that I asked and the data that I recorded were dictated by it.

But I did not ask other important questions and collect other important data. For example, I did not look at Vice Lord behavior in terms of social networks. After becoming acquainted with the network idea, it was evident that certain aspects of Vice Lord life would have made better sense if ordered in terms of this idea. I had not thought in terms of social networks, however, and therefore had not collected the necessary data.[1] Other anthropologists with different basic orientations would undoubtedly have asked yet again different questions, collected different data, and arrived at different pictures of Vice Lord life.

The Problem of Emotional Reactions

One of the greatest difficulties in my Vice Lord research was handling my emotional responses. On the streets of the ghetto I was functionally an infant, and like all infants, had to be taken care of. I did not know what was, and what was not, potentially dangerous; and I did not understand the significance of most actions and many words. For example, one afternoon while I was standing on 15th Street with a group of Vice Lords, a young man in his early twenties walked up and started yelling that he was a Roman Saint, and was going to "whup" every Vice Lord he found. It was obvious by the way he talked and acted that he was mentally deranged. One of the Vice Lords said, "The dude's crazy, Man! He ain't no Saint. Leave him alone." Suddenly a dead-pan look came over the young man's face. Abruptly he turned from us, and walked down an alley that was directly opposite from where we were standing. Very calmly, and with no show of speed, every Vice Lord in the group walked away, out of a line of possible fire. Suddenly I found myself standing alone, looking down the alley at this fellow. Tex came up and pulled me to the side. He said, "Man, the dude get to the end of the alley, he liable to get his jive together and burn you down (pull out his gun and shoot you)!" Besides feeling stupid, I did not know whether to be afraid or not. The fellow reached the end of the alley, turned the corner, and was gone. The extent of my helplessness had been made quite clear.

When you are an infant in age, it is one thing to be helpless, but when you

[1] Social networks are the web of social ties built up by individuals mainly on a personal basis. See "Theoretical Orientations in African Urban Studies" (Mitchell 1966), "The Significance of Quasi-Groups in the Study of Complex Societies" (Mayer 1966), and especially, "Networks and Political Process" (Barnes 1968) for a discussion in depth of the notion of social network, and its importance for urban research.

are twenty-nine years old, it is quite something else. This feeling of helplessness was very difficult for me to handle. In the early part of my research it often made me feel so nervous and anxious that the events occurring around me seemed to merge in a blur of meaningless action. I despaired of ever making any sense out of anything. Vice Lords sensed my feelings and I could see it made some people uncomfortable. This increased the difficulty of gaining the rapport necessary to carry out successful research.

The only solution to this problem was not to give up. Slowly the weeks passed, and as I became more familiar with the members of the club and the neighborhood, this feeling subsided. And then, suddenly I started understanding things. But although I may no longer have been an infant, I was still a child. Whenever I thought I was really "hip," that I really "knew what was happening," something would occur that brought home the extent of my ignorance. For example, on the very last night of my first summer's field work I mistook a challenge to fight for a friendly warning. A Vice Lord said to me, "Hey man, you better walk light!" Because a gang fight had taken place a few hours earlier, and because I had heard "walk light" used in previous contexts as a friendly warning, I completely misunderstood and responded most inappropriately, "Yeah, I'm hip." Actually I could not have been more unhip for "You walk light!" or "You better walk light!" is usually a challenge to fight, while simply "Walk light!" is used as a friendly warning. Because of the complete inappropriateness of my response, my would-be protagonist did not know how to proceed. He stood there for a minute, and then walked across the street and attempted to get other Vice Lords to support him in attacking me. Goliath, however, went over and started threatening him, and an argument ensued. Finally, after it was apparent that no one would follow him in "jumping on" me, and some would actively oppose him, he left the corner. I did not find out what had taken place until later when I asked Goliath what the argument across the street had been about.

I also had emotional responses to events that stemmed from my own value system. How to handle these responses was another source of difficulty. There were certain aspects of Vice Lord life—and I need not go into them—that I found personally distasteful. In the early part of my research, they made me upset and uneasy. Later, at times I found myself getting angry. Although intellectually I felt my values were not demonstrably superior, I still could not stop my emotional reactions. These reactions often made it difficult for me to retain objectivity. More important, I was never completely sure if Vice Lords sensed my reactions, and in turn reacted to them. Thus I was not always certain if my feelings affected the events I was trying to observe. Although I tried to control my responses as much as possible, I am still not sure how successful I was. Undoubtedly some bias crept into my observations, and probably certain events I was trying to observe were changed in subtle ways in response to my emotional reactions.

The Problem of Writing Up the Data

Writing up data into some kind of coherent account involves at least two problems. First, the anthropologist must decide on the data to be included in the work, and second, he must decide on the manner in which to organize and present the data that is included. The first problem is often difficult to solve because in writing an account it is necessary to describe living people, many of whom are close friends. This is especially difficult when the study may be read by members of the society in which it was carried out, as was the case with *The Vice Lords* (Keiser, 1969). I think most anthropologists feel an obligation to write nothing that could injure the people in the group in which they worked. On the other hand, the anthropologist wants to write the best possible account he can, and information that members of a society might not want known can be important for understanding how particular social and cultural systems work. If information was given in confidence, then the anthropologist has the moral obligation to keep that confidence. In other instances the anthropologist may have information not given in confidence that people still might not want others to know about. One obvious solution is to change names, dates, and places so that the description cannot be linked to particular people. Sometimes, however, changes such as these will not provide an adequate disguise. Then, in my opinion, the particular information should not be included if it is really injurious to the people involved. The difficulty comes in deciding whether something is really injurious. I do not think there is any simple, clear-cut answer to this problem. The anthropologist must be as sensitive as possible to the feelings and problems of the people he is describing, and write his account accordingly.

In trying to solve the second problem, that of organization and presentation, my theoretical orientation was as important as it was in gathering the data. The theoretical orientation provided a framework on which I tried to construct a coherent account. My main goal was to demonstrate the systematic nature of Vice Lord social life. In order to do this, however, it was necessary to take a cultural perspective as well, for aspects of culture related to patterns of social interaction in important ways. I started with definitions of the cultural and social systems. The social system was defined as the ordered system of on-going social interaction; and the cultural system as the ordered system of beliefs and values in terms of which social interaction takes place.

After an introductory chapter tracing out general lines of Vice Lord development, I described certain features of Vice Lord social structure. This included such things as the series of groups to which Vice Lords belong, the set of political offices that are held by particular members, and the way the club relates to physical space. It was necessary to describe these aspects first so the reader could follow the later argument. In the following two chapters I tried to show that part of the pattern and order in Vice Lord social life was in the systematic relationship of social groups and social roles to recurring sets of behavior recognized by Vice Lords as forming distinct social contexts. In these two chapters my argument was based on three crucial ideas—social groups, social roles, and social contexts. These ideas formed an important part of the framework around which I organized my material. The idea of social contexts was especially important since it was the relationship of groups and roles to particular social contexts that was patterned and ordered. Here is where the cultural system became crucial. The social contexts were differentiated from one another in terms of beliefs and values that formed part of the Vice Lord cultural system, and in the next chapter I discussed some of these. Thus the set of social contexts that gave order to social roles and social groups was in turn ordered by the beliefs and values of the Vice Lord cultural system. The final chapter was an edited version of a life history. It was included to give the reader a different perspective on Vice Lord life than the one provided by the more formal account of earlier chapters. I hoped by including all this material and organizing it in this manner that the reader would gain some idea of the nature of Vice Lord life.

References

Banton, Michael, 1957, *West African City*. London: Oxford University Press, for the International African Institute.

Barnes, J. A., 1968, Networks and Political Process. In Marc J. Swartz, ed., *Local-Level Politics*. Chicago: Aldine.

Keiser, R. Lincoln, 1969, *The Vice Lords: Warriors of the Streets*. New York: Holt, Rinehart and Winston, Inc.

Liebow, Elliot, 1967, *Tally's Corner*. Boston: Little, Brown and Company.

Mayer, Adrian C., 1966, The Significance of Quasi-Groups in the Study of Complex Societies. In Michael Banton, ed., *The Social Anthropology of Complex Societies*. A.S.A. Monographs No. 4. London: Tavistock.

Mitchell, J. Clyde, 1966, Theoretical Orientations in African Urban Studies. In Michael Banton, ed., *The Social Anthropology of Complex Societies*. A.S.A. Monographs No. 4. London: Tavistock.

Short, James F., Jr., and Fred L. Strodtbeck, 1965, *Group Process and Gang Delinquency*. Chicago: University of Chicago Press.

10

CHANGING JAPAN: FIELD RESEARCH

EDWARD NORBECK
Rice University

Related Case Study: **Changing Japan**

Like the other chapters in this book, "Changing Japan: Field Research"
is an intensely personal document, but Edward Norbeck, to the benefit of
his readers, makes this particularly explicit. He starts the chapter with a
brief autobiography and ends it with a telling report on the ways in which
Japanese society and culture is difficult for him. For a man born on a
wilderness farm in northern Saskatchewan there could be no greater dis-
continuity of experience. And yet he became, in some ways, culturally
Japanese and underwent a significant expansion of self and perception as
a result of prolonged and repeated field experience in Japan. His fieldwork
in Japan went, on the whole, smoothly as compared with the difficulties
experienced by others in their fields. His communities were responsive
and his informants generally friendly, supportive, and informed. But he
tends to minimize the difficulties. We find that he learned to speak both
standard Japanese and the local dialect and conducted his fieldwork without an interpreter. He takes this for granted, as anthropologists should,
but anyone who has learned and worked in a language foreign to his
childhood knows the commitment and diligence this required. We see
also the demands made upon him and his family in a foreign social
system and physical environment and can realize the adaptation was, as
it always must be, largely, though never exclusively, one sided. This

Edward Norbeck, 1951, with Ainu-Japanese informant, in Hokkaido.

chapter helps us to understand how Edward Norbeck collected his data. It also helps us to better understand the Japanese community that he studied.

The Author

Edward Norbeck is Professor of Anthropology and Chairman of the Department of Anthropology and Sociology at Rice University, Houston. Formerly Dean of Humanities and Social Sciences at Rice University, Dr. Norbeck holds other administrative appointments at his university and has for many years combined teaching, research, writing, lecturing, and university administrative work. He is the author of many scientific papers and the author or editor-contributor of several books on a wide range of anthropological interests including *Takashima, a Japanese Fishing Community* (1954), *Pineapple Town—Hawaii* (1959), *Religion in Primitive Society* (1961), *Prehistoric Man in the New World* (coeditor with J. D. Jennings, 1964), *Changing Japan* (1965), and *The Study of Personality: An Interdisciplinary Approach* (senior editor and contributor, 1968). One of his major research interests is Japanese culture about which he has published three books and many shorter writings.

Edward Norbeck says of himself,

I was born in Canada and came to the United States when I was eight years old. Before becoming an anthropologist I spent ten years in the business world in various administrative positions and forty-three months in military service. My doctorate in anthropology was received from the University of Michigan in 1952 after earlier degrees from the same university in oriental languages and oriental civilizations. My wife, Margaret Field Norbeck, was a doctoral candidate in anthropology at Columbia University at the time of our marriage. We have four children, three our own and one legal ward. My favorite avocation is trout fishing and camping in remote roadless wilderness areas in the mountains of the far west.

When asked why he became an anthropologist he replied,

Since childhood, I have been interested in all living things and less interested or uninterested in the inanimate and mechanical. My choosing to become an anthropologist reflects these interests, the genesis of which I cannot explain, and undoubtedly also my early experiences of participation in more than one culture, which aroused my curiosity about the range of human behavior.

G. D. S.

Background

What should an anthropologist say in an account of the field research upon which he has based a published work? He can and should tell when, how, and where the field research was done, giving attention to distinctive and unique features of the society and culture studied and to the problems encountered. He should also tell the reader something about himself, about his own cultural background and personal characteristics. Another kind of useful information that he might include is rarely mentioned in scholarly writings, and is known to us principally in a few remarkable novels. This is the effect that exposure to a foreign culture has had upon the researcher. As personal documents, testimonies of this kind are unavoidably subjective, but subjectivity does not imply lack of value. Thus far in its history, I shall note, anthropology has given curiously little attention or printed pages to either subjective or objective accounts of the effects of field research upon the researcher.

I shall try to do all of these things, beginning with a brief account of relevant personal information about myself, continuing with a more detailed recounting of when, where, and how field research was conducted, and concluding with some subjective statements of my personal reactions to first-hand experiences with Japanese ways of life and the seeming effects of these experiences on my own behavior.

I was born in 1915 on a homestead farm in the wilderness of Northern Saskatchewan, Canada, the sixth of nine children who grew to maturity. My father and mother were born and lived until young adulthood in Sweden. My father migrated because he was disinherited after a quarrel with his father, and my mother fled with the aid of neighbors to escape from an oppressive stepmother. During my early childhood, both of my parents retained much of their native Swedish culture. Until their deaths, both spoke English with pronounecd accents but, in my memory, they did not speak Swedish. If I had ever known any of the Swedish language, I had forgotten it by the age of four years, when our family moved to the town of Prince Albert, Saskatchewan. During the first four years of my life, I had little direct contact with people outside the family. Our way of life was nevertheless a composite of Swedish culture and the Canadian culture of the region, which was then principally of English tradition, differing in various ways from the culture of the United States to which I was later exposed. The Canadian manners, customs, and attitudes of the predominantly English stock living in Prince Albert at the time seemed to me proper, generally desirable, and even inviolable. The customs clashed in no disturbing degree with the fading Swedish customs of my parents, and I could easily put aside the Swedish ways when necessary. I was happy in Canada, but happiness ended in wounded shock at the age of eight, when our family moved to the United States, settling in St. Maries, Idaho, a town of about 3000 people near Spokane, Washington, where I lived until I finished high school.

A miniature boom town, economically dependent upon the logging industry, St. Maries was composed principally of old Americans from many parts of the United States, who set the tone of the community, and some Scandinavians. Part mill town and part frontier community, St. Maries was divided into an Old Town and a New Town. Old Town was truly alive only on weekends and consisted mostly of seedy frame buildings, stores, hotels, pool halls that were also illegal bars and gambling houses, and a few whorehouses. The establishments of Old Town attracted as clients principally lumberjacks, drawn from the logging camps in surrounding mountains for Saturdays, especially Saturday nights, of action and Sundays of regret. New Town, the major part of the town, was the habitat of the respectable but it, too, had a strong flavor of the frontier.

For this new life, everything about my brothers, sisters, and myself was wrong—our clothes, ideas, customs, etiquette, and especially our semi-British speech. We all suffered severely from cultural shock—words that had not been invented at that time—and for my brothers and myself the injuries were often physical as well as psychological. After two or three years of a series of reciprocal fisticuffs and nonreciprocal exposure to scabrous insults and every other form of social sanction of the world of children and adolescents, we were admitted to the society, partly because we had changed our ways somewhat and perhaps partly because our peers had grown accustomed to us. My interest in anthropology probably arises in some part from these experiences of the first decade of my life, which had brought exposure to three different cultures and a half-objective awareness that life could be ordered in many ways.

After leaving Idaho at the age of sixteen and before becoming a professional anthropologist, additional exposure, first-hand and vicarious, to still different cultures came to me in various ways—residence in several parts of the United States including Hawaii; residence in Germany; employment in administrative positions that included service as a personnel officer for a large construction firm; college instruction in foreign cultures; and the study at some time or another of seven foreign languages, three of which—Japanese, Chinese, and Polynesian—are not Indo-European. I had perforce already become in some degree an anthropologist before I ever consciously thought of doing so.

I am 5 feet 11 inches tall and, since adolescence, have weighed an unchanging 150 pounds. My hair is brown, my skin of medium color, and my eyes are blue. My wife, who is trained in anthropology and assisted me in my field research, also has hair and skin of medium color. Her eyes are brown. These words mean to say that, although we are instantly recognizable as Caucasians, little about our appearances is remarkably distinctive in Japan. Some Japanese have skins of shades similar to or lighter than ours; a few have brown hair; and many are of comparable height and weight. To be sure, the Japanese do not have blue eyes, but any observer is likely to be unconscious of the color of blue eyes unless some reflecting background brings out the color. Unlike Caucasians with physical features that stand out markedly in Japan, such as very pale skin and yellow or red hair, we presented no shock to the eyes. It seems certain that to our informants we soon became unremarkable in appearance. (We know of other Americans and Europeans who, because of their physical features, were always obtrusively outsiders. In rural communities where Caucasians are seldom seen, such distinctive features may in subtle ways be detrimental to field research.)

The observations, study, and field research upon which *Changing Japan* (Norbeck 1965) is based cover a period of nearly thirty years. Observations began in Hawaii before World War II, where my work of five years as an administrative employee of a pineapple corporation brought me into contact with many people born in Japan or of Japanese ancestry. My formal study of the language and culture of Japan began during the war while I served in the army as enlisted man and officer. After about two years of training in the army, received at universities and elsewhere, I served principally in the military intelligence as a translator of secret, coded, wireless messages between the home office and the various European embassies and consulates of the Japanese diplomatic corps. At the end of the war, anthropology seemed more attractive than the world of business, and I enrolled in university training for the doctorate in anthropology, specializing in Japanese culture. My first visit to Japan, during 1950–1951, was for the purpose of conducting field research for my doctoral dissertation.

But please take heart. It will not be possible in a few pages to compile a chronicle of all of the events and circumstances of my training and field research that relate to Japan. Much of the relevant training and one project of field research, a study conducted in 1956 of a company town of a pineapple corporation in Hawaii, did not, in fact, directly concern Japanese culture or society. These experiences have nevertheless indirectly been important in my study of Japan, especially for purposes of comparison. I shall here discuss only the field research up to the time of the publication of *Changing Japan* that relates most directly to the book. This consists of about one year of residence in Japan in 1950–1951, about nine months in 1958–1959, and one year in 1964–1965. This period of nearly three years was nearly evenly divided between the study of rural and urban life. At some time or another, I have visited at least briefly most of the prefectures and major cities of Japan and some of the byways, including Ainu communities in Hokkaido. I have conducted brief field research in several rural communities widely distributed throughout the nation. It is not possible to discuss all of these communities and my remarks will concern principally the rural community of Takashima and its neighboring city of Okayama, and the cities of Tokyo and Nishinomiya, communities in which I resided for considerable periods of time.

The Rural Community

Takashima is a hamlet (*buraku*) of Kojima City, Okayama Prefecture, about 125 miles south of Kobe. At the time of my first field research there, Takashima (in translation, High Island) was a community of 188 people on a small, beautiful island, lying in the Inland Sea about one-fourth mile from the mainland (the island of Honshu). Several years later, Takashima became a hilly promontory of the mainland as the result of a governmental project of filling in the expanse of water separating it from the mainland. Although administratively part of the small city of Kojima since 1948, Takashima in 1950–1951 retained much of the culture and social organization of the traditional rural community of Japan. The community was then remarkable in Japan in lacking electricity, which had not been provided because of the high cost of installation and the low return from such a small community. In other ways, Takashima was not backward, and electrical facilities were installed a few years later.

For livelihood, most of the people of Takashima depended in 1950–1951 upon fishing in the Inland Sea, principally with nets and small, motored watercraft. Household gardens and a few larger plots of cultivated soil were a secondary source of support, which provided little cash income but was important to nearly all families. The people of Takashima stemmed from a farming rather than a fishing tradition, and their culture represented a mixture of the two. In general, the culture of Takashima was fairly typical of small rural hamlets, and the community was chosen in large part for that reason.

By late 1964, life on Takashima had changed greatly. The city of Kojima, and especially the immediately neighboring city of Kurashiki, had grown as industrial centers, and employment in industry had become the main source of livelihood for residents of Takashima. The postwar modernization and industrialization of Japan had made Takashima into a residential community for industrial workers, put television into virtually every home, electrical and gas appliances into most homes, raised standards of education, and, as elsewhere in the nation, had brought about extensive changes in the family, religion, and almost every other aspect and element of the traditional culture. Among the losses brought by progress was the beauty of Takashima in earlier days. Progress had replaced the sea and beach with the spoils from dredging, on which industrial plants were to be constructed.

Choosing the Community

My wife and I arrived in Japan in June 1950 by slow freighter, armed with a small grant in aid of research from the Social Science Research Council. As was usual for the time, the sum was inadequate, but we had no feelings of deprivation and made shift with the aid of personal funds. I knew very little about rural Japan, on which only one sizeable anthropological study had ever been

The island and community of Takashima, 1951.

Part of the community of Takashima, looking toward the mainland.

published, John F. Embree's *Suye Mura* (1939). My preparations at the University of Michigan had included no formal training whatever in techniques of field research. The outcome of my project of making an ethnographic study a rural community seemed then to depend upon my own ability to sink or swim.

In 1950, Japan was still an occupied nation and, according to the regulations of the American military authorities, foreign scholars were required to secure housing and food in ways that were not disruptive to the Japanese economy. We were ordered to obtain our food from the United States, a policy which was followed fairly consistently for some time by the field station of the University of Michigan's Center for Japanese Studies, established in Okayama City in 1950, with which I was associated as a graduate student. When we arrived at the center in Okayama in 1950, the shops of the nation had little food or other commodities. Before we left in 1951, the shops were full of merchandise, and the rule about importing food was forgotten except for various foods that were not ordinarily in the Japanese diet.

In the company of several other American scholars, their wives, and a few children, my wife and I were provided with quarters at the Michigan center. These consisted of an unheated bedroom of Japanese style, with conventional rush matting on the floor. Our beds were two narrow air mattresses, fastened together insecurely by safety pins. For bedding we used Japanese quilts of cotton in warm weather and a combination of Japanese quilts and American electric blankets in cold weather. Facilities of the center consisted of two frame buildings that combined features of Western and Japanese architecture and decor, and included rooms for study, dining, and entertaining. The quarters were ugly and the facilities for bathing and for heating the center were poor, but most domestic tasks were done competently by a staff of Japanese servants and the scholars were free to devote their efforts to research.

All in all, living at the center was comfortable, and the families in residence had few dissatisfactions. There were, of course, mild cases of cabin fever from prolonged exposure to the idiosyncrasies of fellow human beings, and perhaps everyone suffered from the lack of privacy and the necessary regimentation of hours for meals, meetings, and the like. Okayama summers are oppressively hot and humid, and the mild winters seemed sometimes bitterly cold for lack of adequate heat in our living quarters.

My first field experience in Japan was an apprenticeship of about two weeks of study of the tiny farming community of Niiike, near Okayama, which various members of the center studied jointly over a period of several years. My work consisted of making an inventory of every article in the house of a Niiike family. I examined, asked questions about, and recorded descriptions of everything from pins, needles, and articles of clothing to the bathtub and kitchen stove. Meanwhile, consultation with perfectural officials about a fishing community suitable for the study I had planned yielded the names of several. These

I soon visited together with the director of the center and other scholars in residence. Takashima was finally chosen because it seemed a fairly typical community and because its location, some 20 miles from the Michigan center in Okayama, made it possible for me to commute between the community and the center. As time passed and the supply of food became more abundant in Japan, I was able to find both quarters and food in Takashima for my wife and myself, and either I alone or the two of us were able to stay in the community for lengthening periods of time without returning to the center.

Once Takashima had been selected, arrangements were made for a formal introduction to the entire community at which time I would request permission to conduct a study of the life of the community, for the honestly stated reason that little was known to the rest of the world about the ordinary, daily life of the people of Japan. Arrangements for the study were made through officials of the prefecture, who made contact with Kojima city officials and the elected head of the Takashima association of households, a formal organization composed of one representative of each household of the community that concerned itself with communal affairs. As a part of the formal introduction, I thought it useful to have influential farmers of the farming community of Niiike attest that the scholars of the center were people of honor who did not disrupt community life. Our party finally consisted of two obliging farmers from Niiike, dignified elderly men who acted with impressive assurance, the director and other scholars of the center, and myself. When we arrived, a large collection of residents of Takashima, male and female, were gathered in the communal meeting hall of the hamlet. After tea and confections had been served to all, I spoke in halting, formal Japanese, making my request, of which all Takashima residents had been informed beforehand.

The farmers from Niiike gave favorable testimony, and other members of our party had similarly favorable words to say. A response of consent, also formulated beforehand, came quickly from the head of the community association. The people understood the objectives of the study and found it worthy, he informed us. This response was expected since my request was unusual principally because it was the first such request made of Takashima and because it was made by a foreigner, a member of an erstwhile enemy nation. Subterfuge had been unnecessary in stating the goals of the study for these were not remarkable in Japan, where scholarship is held in high regard and where, even in tiny communities, some person is likely to be conducting a "study" of local history or something else of his own devising.

But, continued the head man, there was one stipulation. The members of the community would give consent only with the understanding that they and their community would not be regarded or described in print as if they were members of an uncivilized tribe with barbarous customs. I was easily able to assure the assembled people that no such thought entered my mind and that no such course of action could even be possible since everyone knew Japanese culture was ancient and well developed at the time when the ancestors of the Americans in the room were wild tribesmen.

Prospects for the future seemed good. No opposition or hostility whatever seemed evident on the part of the assembled people, and our petitioning party left with a feeling of success. After we had left the meeting hall, the Niiike elders generously observed that the people of Takashima seemed quite a decent lot "for fisherfolk."

Conducting the Research

I began research in Takashima the day after formal consent had been given, and for some weeks commuted daily by a jeep station wagon owned by the Michigan center, arriving early and often staying late so that my meals consisted of a hurried breakfast, sandwiches for lunch, and sometimes a dinner of left-overs eaten after the scheduled dinner hour at the center. The trip between Okayama and the pier for Takashima boats took over one hour and, because the road was extremely rough, narrow, and passed through several communities in which children at play would dart unexpectedly from alleys into the road, cautious driving was always necessary. At the pier, I could usually find someone who was willing to take me to Takashima, either a Takashima resident or someone from the community on the mainland shore where the pier was located. Later I rented a boat.

My first acts were to introduce myself to everyone, a process that took some weeks because fishermen sometimes set off for work early, returned very late, or stayed overnight on their boats. During this time I also collected genealogical information on the residents of the community, a task that is easy in rural communities of Japan. Introducing myself to municipal officials of Kojima City with advance notice, I requested and was immediately given access to the compilations of vital statistics maintained by the city for each of its subdivisions. It was a task of only a few days' work to copy the entire genealogical record and other vital statistics, which had been recorded for nearly a century. Later, I checked the individual genealogies and familial statistics with informants in Takashima and found that errors were few. Preparing a map of the island, including a map of the farm plots identified by the household of ownership, the cemetery and the identity of its remains, and the placement of all dwellings and other buildings was a much more formidable early task. This required photo-graphs, measurements, remeasurements, and a tiresome consultation with Takashima residents over matters that I knew were important but were never-theless irksome to someone who wanted most of all to know how life was lived.

Within six weeks all persons were clearly identified and much information about them was recorded. Thanks to the genealogical records, I had quickly learned the networks of kinship of the community, information which was valuable in many ways, including the suggestions it offered to guide my selection of informants.

It was my aim to obtain information on every possible aspect of the life of the residents of Takashima, and to interview all able-bodied adults as well as to talk less formally with children and adolescents. Every adult in the community was interviewed at least once. Selection of regular informants depended of course upon their availability, willingness, special knowledge as related to their sex, age, and occupations, seeming intelligence and reliability, and still other considerations. No informant was ever paid for his services.

One of these other considerations was the ease or difficulty of communication between informants and myself in the Japanese language. I spoke hesitatingly only the standard Japanese I had learned in the United States, a form of Japanese which differed from the customary speech of Takashima in ways analogous with the differences—in accent, vocabulary, grammar, and, notably, in elegance—between Cambridge and Cockney English. All Takashima people understood standard Japanese and all could understand me. Some Takashima people responded in standard Japanese and some responded with native speech that soon became comprehensible to me. Others were very difficult for me to understand. Women were at first easier to understand than men, because their roles as women traditionally demanded greater elegance and politeness in speech and thus conformed better with textbook Japanese than the "rougher" speech of men. For some men, the social ideal of masculine speech included poor articulation. At the end of my research, I was still unable to understand much of the speech of two men of the community, who were described laughingly by other informants as speakers of "pure Takashima dialect."

One other matter was very important in choosing informants. As a foreigner conducting a study of the whole community, it was permissible for me to associate with everyone. I was certain, however, that it would be harmful to become closely identified with any persons who were strongly disliked by others for moral or other reasons. Judgments of character and reputation at first had to be made by myself. Inquiring of informants at that early time was far too dangerous in a community composed of people with multiple ties of kinship and bonds of friendship that were as yet largely unknown to me. My judgments were based partly upon chance remarks of informants and upon observation of the apparent reactions of fondness, hostility, respect, and the like between people. Most of all at first, I depended upon my own reactions to individuals, and, doubtless because human behavior is much alike the world over, judgments made on this basis turned out to be correct.

I learned early that the community was divided on the basis of prestige into two groups, the larger of which was composed of people bearing a common surname who claimed descent from the original settlers of the island and who, although generally poor, had greater wealth and much greater social prestige. Relations between the two groups were cordial, but the elite mingled socially with their inferiors only when necessary and held them in mild contempt. I could associate with the outgroup, but I must avoid any appearance of intimacy with them and be careful not to bring them together with their superiors in any social context that implied intimacy.

At the time of my first interview with the head man of the community, I had suspected that he was generally disliked and I did not like him myself. He seemed arrogant, rude, and terribly contemptuous of his neighbors, telling me that the people of Takashima were stupid, ignorant, and unworthy of my atten-

Takashima, family group of three generations posed at entrance to their house, 1951.

tion. Most stupid of all, he had said, were the women; no amount of education could make them or any other women into intelligent beings. I noted that other adults of the community avoided him or acted constrained in his presence and that children were strangely quiet before him. Because of my own feelings toward this man and my observations of his apparent relations with others, I talked with him only often enough to meet the demands of etiquette, maintaining a relationship of cordiality replete with all the forms of speech that signal formal politeness. This course of action turned out to be fortunate. The eyes of the community, very experienced in judging matters of this sort, were always fastened on me, and busy tongues soon let everyone know that my relations with the head man were not close. More than anything else in the first months of fieldwork, this made me acceptable. I was later told "in confidence" repeatedly that the head man was disliked heartily but chosen for office as a necessary evil because of his wealth, power, and undeniable competence, which made him the best choice as a leader who must deal with the outside world (the city administration).

Other actions that helped gain the good will of informants were normal social behavior in any society. In return for any extraordinary kindness or service, we offered thanks in the form of gifts as well as verbally. These were sometimes American canned foods but more frequently gifts of merchandise manufactured in Japan, purchased by my wife or myself in the shops of Okayama, items that fell within the proper range of traditional gifts. Most gifts were inexpensive, but the total cost for the year was impressive. In 1950–1951 the people of Takashima were still very poor, and they were grateful for gifts of used clothing sent to us at our request by relatives of my wife in New York. By the end of our year of research, the women of Takashima were sometimes remarkably dressed in clothing from Fifth Avenue shops.

Photographs were particularly useful in gaining good will. I had not fully realized how much the people valued photographs of themselves until I became the object of censure of a ten-year-old boy, who for some days thrust his head around the corner of buildings to express his resentment of me by gesture, giving me the Japanese version of the evil eye. A friendly informant laughingly apologized for the naughty behavior of the boy and explained that he was angry because I had not taken his photograph. Two photographs of the boy in his best clothing, a baseball suit, converted him into a friend. Services in developing and printing photographs were excellent and cheap in Okayama, and the people of Takashima were photographed again and again, singly, in family groups, and in any other grouping desired. I became the unofficial and unpaid photographer of the community for weddings and all other events of importance.

As the weeks passed, several men and women became principal informants and personal friends with whom I continue today to maintain contact by letter. Two entire families composed of three generations were regular informants at whose homes I was always welcome. Their patience, interest, and kindness were heartwarming. Among these kindnesses was an invitation for my wife and me to stay in the home of one family to observe and take part in the wedding of their daughter. We witnessed the preparations the day before the wedding day and on the wedding day, including most of the process of dressing the bride— the elaborate procedures of facial makeup, the donning of a bridal wig, and the intricacies of encasing the bride in an elaborate bridal kimono. Honored guests at the wedding, we also were invited to remain the following day to watch the return to normal life. Since the bride was the only child and heir, Japanese custom required that her husband be adopted as male heir in the bride's family. Custom also called for the reversal of some of the events of the ordinary marriage of a woman to a male heir of a family, so that procedures of the wedding in various ways treated the groom as if he were the bride. No other wedding that I later attended was so interesting or so unusual.

As time passed, I became well acquainted with one of the intellectuals of the community, a widow then forty-five years of age, who made a bare living for her fourteen-year-old son and herself by farming a tiny plot of land and by making fishing nets for other families of the community. Minoru (her real name) had always been unusual in the community. Like other people of her age in Takashima, her formal education had been limited to the six years of public schooling required by law at the time of her youth. She had been the most outstanding student in her class and continued later to educate herself as time and circumstance allowed by reading such magazines and books as came her way. Despite her poverty, Minoru was held in esteem in the community. Minoru's husband had given up fishing during the war to take employment as a seaman on a deep-sea cargo vessel and had been killed when his ship was bombed somewhere in the Pacific by an American airplane. Minoru was then left with three children to raise alone. At the time I arrived on Takashima, she had already guided her two pretty daughters into successful marriages to men in neighboring communities. Minoru bore no rancor toward Americans for the death of her husband and had uncommonly objective understanding of the whys and wherefores of life on Takashima.

In many other ways, Minoru was also unconventional. Her preferred manner of speaking was thrifty, colorful, and—in a nation where oblique utterances were the mode—often wonderfully direct. Minoru's knowledge of local history, customs, and people was detailed—and she loved nothing better than to talk. She understood very well the etiquette and other customs of her community, offending no one, but she also understood when and how convention might be safely broken. She, and she only, maintained friendships made in school days with a few people in surrounding communities who were members of a local community of outcastes, pariahs ordinarily shunned by all other persons. Minoru's house, now in a shabby state of disrepair with weak spots here and there in the floor that one learned to step over to avoid the possibility of crashing through, was another example of her departure from the usual mold. Other dwellings were clustered tightly together in two groups, the larger of which was inhabited by the elite. Only Minoru's house stood apart, at a higher elevation than others, so that Minoru's family had privacy. Built at the time of her marriage, nearly twenty-five years earlier, the house had been placed at her urging in a position where, as she explained to me, she could see without being seen.

As a member of her society, Minoru was in a real sense marginal, and had a rich measure of the detachment that comes with self-chosen marginality. But

she was also a highly respected member of the community who actively participated in community affairs. These attributes added to high intelligence, keen
interest in my work, friendliness, and a great store of knowledge of the local
culture made Minoru my most valuable informant.

Minoru soon invited my wife and me to live with her and her son, a student
just beginning high school. We were happy to do so, occupying as our bedroom
the tiny parlor, separated from the other three rooms of the house by thin
sliding doors that scarcely served as barriers to the passage of sound. With a
satisfactory home base in the community, I was now in a much better position
to observe and to participate, and the collection of information proceeded
rapidly. I interviewed every adult and found that nearly all seemed to enjoy
their roles as informants. Naturally some were fine informants and a few
were very poor. An eighty-four-year-old man in such splendid health that others
said he did not know how to die, turned out to be the greatest disappointment.
Early in the course of my research, several long visits with him yielded almost no
information of value despite an apparent willingness to talk. Minoru then came
to the rescue, assuming an informal role as advisor, which she maintained to
the end. Always somehow knowing where I was and what I did whether or not
I had informed her, Minoru remarked casually, "You know, old Chōhei ought
to be a treasure chest of information, but, unfortunately, he has never been
bright." Other informants also assumed similar roles as guides and counselors.

Within the limits of seemly behavior, I asked about every subject I could
imagine, saw everything that was seeable, and participated in everyday and
special events including some activities, such as digging clams and cultivating
crops, that in Takashima were ordinarily women's work. The women seemed
pleased to have the company of the foreigner and the children also seemed
pleased when I joined them in games, explaining the rules with courtesy, care,
and sometimes with flurries of giggles. I was present at coming-of-age ceremonies, weddings, funerals, Buddhist commemorative services for the deceased,
and—my memory is now a little unsure—probably all religious and other events
of importance in community life during the year.

My most bizarre experience was as observer at a lengthy ceremony of faith
healing, an attempt by a male faith healer and a female assistant, both outsiders,
to cure an apathetic man dying of tuberculosis. Ritual was conducted in a
darkened room of the patient's house, and included sonorous incantations,
mystical movements of the hands, lengthy blowings of a conch shell, and the
building in the room of a fire of crisscrossed sticks of special wood. The fire,
together with a number of pieces of burning incense, filled the room with dense
smoke and put the tubercular patient into a fit of coughing, which the two
colorfully dressed faith healers, now scarcely visible to me, did not allow to
interrupt their invocations or the blowing of the conch shell. Throughout, the
patient's younger brother, who did not approve of faith healing, sat beside me
staring determinedly at the pages of a comic book.

Laughable strange experiences were plentiful. There was my adventure with the pirate cab driver, the name given to drivers of private cars without taxi licenses that sometimes operate in the entertainment area of the Ginza in Tokyo at the time when nightclubs and cabarets close. Together with two other Americans, I hailed a pirate cab and had the driver take us to two widely separated places in the city, instructing him to wait for us at the first stop. When we finally tried to pay the driver hours later, we found that he was not a pirate cab driver but simply a Japanese citizen too polite to deny our requests.

Best of all was my introduction to the emperor's famed white horse, in 1951, when Japan was still an occupied nation. Very few Americans were then given the privilege of visiting the imperial palace, and this was said to represent policy of the American military authorities. But distinguished Europeans were invited to do so from time to time. When two Swiss businessmen whom I knew received invitations, I went as an undeclared substitute for one who was unable to attend. The other Swiss, Mr. S, and I arrived at the proper gate of the palace at the proper time in a driving rain, and presented our invitations. We were then put in the custody of five Japanese interpreter-guides, who spoke excellent English and treated us with professional courtesy. Our trip began interestingly enough, but our guides maintained a cool stiffness of speech and manner that allowed us no responsive action except complementary formality. Our visit took us on foot from building to building in the rain and, after a time, to the imperial stables. The head interpreter, an aged and elegant man, announced that the emperor's white horse was on the left. This surprised and impressed us and we stopped for a closer view. Apparently overcome with respect, Mr. S expressed his feelings by suddenly sweeping off his hat and bowing. As he did so, a great splat of water sailed through the air from the brim of his hat and hit the horse. The guides were speechless but far from soundless. The elegant old man set the pattern. Mr. S had not only bowed to the horse's rear end, he had even anointed it. The five guides roared with laughter for some minutes, and from time to time later in the day burst into renewed laughter. The rest of our visit was full of euphoric good fellowship, and we said goodby to our hosts with the warmest of words from both sides.

The most pleasing experiences, growing lovelier in restrospect, were the times spent on the night fishing boats in the summer and early fall. Most often I went as the guest of one or another of three families, sometimes with a father and son only and, dependent upon the type of fishing, sometimes in the company of a wife or adult daughter also. We slept on the deck of the boat and prepared delicious meals of fresh fish over a small charcoal broiler. Often calm as a small lake, and studded with hundreds of pine-clad islands, the Inland Sea is at any time a place of the greatest beauty. At sunset, its beauty is beyond description.

Nets were lowered from the boats before darkness fell and were lifted at dawn. Night was a period of rest and friendly chatting, a time of peaceful happiness. The humid heat of the land was replaced by fresh breezes, and the

Takashima man and wife pulling in fishing nets.

gentle bobbing of the boat and splash of wavelets were a rocking lullaby. It was not hard to understand why most Takashima fishermen wanted to be nothing but fishermen.

Recording Information

The ways in which I recorded information varied with the occasion, but I always attempted to devote as little time as possible to writing while in the presence of informants. When the conversation concerned personal matters such as quarrels, the character of individuals, or "delicate" subjects such as sexual relations, I ordinarily recorded nothing while in the presence of informants. If the interview were long and I thought I could not remember all of the pertinent information, I excused myself often to go to the toilet, where I hastily jotted down in Gregg shorthand key words to jog my memory later. This practice of excusing myself so frequently led Minoru to inquire about the state of my health.

Once accustomed to me, many of the informants were willing to speak with utmost candor on almost any delicate subject provided no one else were present. I am thus the repository of a vast number of deep, dark secrets about moral failures—all less rare and probably less reprehensible than their speakers seemed to think. I made it a firm rule never to repeat the statements, secret or nonsecret, of any one informant to any other informant, a practice of which the people of the community became aware. For some people I then became a therapist, a channel for the safe expression of anger, resentment, guilt, and other invidious emotions.

My interviews also extended to people in neighboring communities that related in some way to Takashima, teachers and the principal of the school attended by Takashima children, Buddhist priests at nearby temples, city officials, and the like. These, for the most part, were formal interviews in which I could record notes as I talked.

Recording was also done abundantly by camera, principally by still photos in black and white or color. Movie photography was limited because of its high cost to a dozen five-minute rolls. Tape-recording of conversations was attempted but judged unsatisfactory for the kinds of information I was gathering. Informants sometimes became self-conscious; transcription was a lengthy, tedious task; and much of the recorded conversation was of very low grade. The tape recorder was, however, sometimes valuable to win the interest of informants. It was extremely valuable in recording folk music. With the aid of a specialist in folk music from the radio broadcasting station in Okayama, my wife and I were able to record about eight hours of folk music in various communities where accomplished but generally aged singers lived, music that probably could not be recorded today for lack of singers.

At the end of my research in Takashima, my handwritten field notes consisted of two very slim notebooks more or less filled with cryptic symbols. My typewritten notes consisted of a file of 5 by 8 inches equal to perhaps 2000 manuscript pages. The slim notebooks contained mostly brief memory joggers written in shorthand, which I used as the basis for typing lengthy accounts. For fear of forgetting, typing had to be done soon after notes were taken, and it was my custom to try to type notes daily, generally in the evening. Sometimes I returned to the center and did nothing but type notes for a day or two.

My wife, who does not speak Japanese, also recorded notes in shorthand, typing them later. Making use of a Japanese woman from Okayama City as an interpreter, she gathered information from Takashima women on child-rearing and other "women's affairs." We both found it necessary to verify carefully the information given by our informants, mostly because no two informants had quite the same experiences or views of the world. One aged informant described in detail an annual cycle of religious events that required many sheets of paper for typing—and, it turned out, included ceremonies observed during the informant's youth but now long obsolete. A middle-aged woman who had known only poverty and unremitting work declared, honestly enough from her own viewpoint, that the annual ceremonial calendar consisted of two events falling on two days of the year when she was able to rest and feel festive.

Some informants reported only ideal standards of behavior, as our attempts to verify their statements sometimes brought out. During one of the annual

Adults and children inside community shrine at Takashima toasting rice cakes at traditional ceremony on New Year's eve, 1950.

festivals when "all" people were said to visit the small Shinto shrine in the community, I kept a continual watch on the shrine and found the visitors totaled eleven people, young children accompanied by aged grandmothers.

By observation of gestures and other nonverbal forms of communication, my wife noted that her otherwise excellent interpreter omitted or altered to greater elegance any account of custom, such as some of the local practices of toilet training and weaning, that she as an educated woman raised in Tokyo thought barbaric. Much checking and rechecking of these subjects and others were done by use of multiple informants and observation. Some of the information supplied by my wife's interpreter had to be changed on the basis of interviews I later conducted.

According to rules of the Center for Japanese Studies, all data collected in the field were to become a part of center records. Accordingly, copies of all my typed notes were given to the center. For insurance against loss, an additional carbon copy was prepared and mailed to myself at an address in the United States. As a systematic way of putting topics in order, I used the subject guide of the Human Relations Area Files (1950), inventing a few titles myself when the guide was inadequate.

The birth of our first child was expected in early June 1951. At a tearful party held in the communal hall we took leave of the people of Takashima in

Takashima people at the shore seeing-off the ethnologist and his wife, 1951.

May so that the birth might be in the United States. Our child was born on June 18, 1951, somewhat behind schedule. At the time of our departure, all field notes had been typed, a project that sometimes required painful self-discipline. Thanks to the typing and ordering of data in the field, a 400-page draft of my dissertation was completed within a few weeks after that date.[1]

Urban Research

Changing Japan was written in the field in late 1964, mostly at night. My main research of the time concerned religious changes and their relationships to social and economic changes (Norbeck 1970). By the beginning of 1965, I had lived for fairly long periods of time in three Japanese cities, the provincial city of Okayama part of the time in 1950–1951, Tokyo in 1958–1959, and Nishinomiya in 1964–1965.

During my residence in Tokyo in 1958–1959, I was associated with Tokyo University, giving courses in anthropology there and also conducting field research in northeastern Japan, 200 to 300 miles from Tokyo, on postwar economic and social changes in rural communities (Norbeck 1961). My family, now increased by two additional children, and I lived in Tokyo in a part of the

---

[1] Later published as *Takashima, A Japanese Fishing Community* (Norbeck 1954).

city where we had no Americans or Europeans as neighbors. Our lone child of school age was taught school subjects by my wife with the aid of correspondence courses. During my field research in northeastern Japan, I stayed in inns and farmhouses in the company of a variable number of Japanese graduate students who served as my research assistants. At home in Tokyo, our quarters were first a cramped apartment, mostly Japanese in architecture and furnishings, and later a large house, old and decaying, in which the bedrooms were Japanese and other rooms were more or less of Western style. Baths, kitchens, and toilets in both places were strange blends of East and West. One competent Japanese maid, who lived in, aided in all domestic work.

As a professor at Tokyo University, I was one of the millions of commuters on trains and subways. In the normal course of my life I came into contact with many Japanese. Since it was my business as an anthropologist to do so, I sought contact with others, some of whom were beyond the boundaries of proper society. As a foreigner, and therefore presumably rich, I was ordinarily sought after by such people rather than seeking. One of Tokyo's rarest tenderloins of the time, a part of the district called Shinjuku, lay between our house and the most convenient train and subway stations. When, as was sometimes my custom, I walked through this area at night, invitations to linger and dally came at intervals of every few yards. Once these people of assorted ages and sexes—there were usually a few male transvestites who advertised their identity by having crew-cut hair—became accustomed to my passage through the narrow, neon-lit streets, I became to some of them an old acquaintance who was greeted cordially but not treated as a prospective client. On evenings when paying clients were few it was possible to stop for tea, coffee, or a drink of sake, beer, whiskey and a chat in the bars and nightclubs, many of which were either outright houses of prostitution or gathering places for prostitutes. As among more respectable people of Japanese society, I was generally treated with courtesy and found that my informants—as they had now become—were often willing and eager to talk about themselves with the greatest frankness provided no third person were listening.

The foreigner in Japan, and perhaps especially the foreign university professor, is the subject of attention from many Japanese whose motives are entirely honorable. Many people who are total strangers, especially college students, introduce themselves so that they may practice the English language. For me, these numerous encounters usually ended with the goals reversed. English faltered quickly and, as soon as it became known that I spoke Japanese, our conversation proceeded in that language. For the foreigner there are also many invitations from neighbors, student groups, civic organizations, and other social groups to give addresses, judge contests of competence in English, or otherwise participate in group activities. Through such channels the receptive foreigner may have much casual contact with Japanese culture. I was very receptive. Information used in *Changing Japan* that is derived from this stay in Tokyo in

1958–1959 cannot always be identified clearly. Many observations and impressions were recorded only in my memory.

My wife and I made a brief visit to Takashima in 1959, during which tears flowed freely from the eyes of many women and some men, tears of welcome and farewell, and tears evoked by telling me of those who had died. Among the dear departed, dying of old age and disease, was the magnificent, ancient pine tree that had spread its branches above the community hall and was said to be 300 years old. Communication by letter with Takashima people through the years had kept me informed of many events in the community. Minoru had moved to Osaka, taking employment there as a cook in a company boarding house so that her son could attend college. From time to time Minoru made brief trips to Takashima and she was well informed of events in the community. A visit with her in Osaka and a return visit from her to our house in Tokyo yielded much additional information.

During 1964–1965, my family and I lived in the city of Nishinomiya, which lies between, and equally distant from, Osaka and Kobe and is a suburb of both of these larger cities, twenty minutes from each by commuter train. As in 1958–1959, my research was sponsored by the National Science Foundation.

Most activities of the Japanese nation, including those related to my project of research on religious, social and economic changes, center on the city of Tokyo. For this reason, I spent about one week of each month in Tokyo, living in hotels there, where I interviewed religious professionals, religious converts, scholars, and businessmen. The choice of Nishinomiya as a place of residence was forced in part by lack of suitable housing in Tokyo at any price within our means. We lived in Nishinomiya on the campus of a Japanese university in a large, old house, mostly of Western style, that was owned by the Christian mission society which had many years earlier founded the university. Our children, now all of school age, attended an English language school in nearby Kobe, traveling by commuter train. Our immediate neighbors were Protestant missionaries, generally American, and Japanese faculty members of the university. My research took me to religious establishments in nearby Osaka, Kobe, Kyoto, and Nara as well as to establishments in Tokyo and elsewhere. These visits sometimes extended over a few days, when I was given lodging at the religious establishments. Since I was interested in economic changes, my work also took me to a number of the nation's large industrial concerns.

Even more than during our earlier stay in Tokyo, I was a commuter. Following the only procedures appropriate in Japan for such work, I made arrangements for appointments and interviews well in advance and generally through a number of Japanese scholars who served as intermediaries. During free time between appointments, I continued as in earlier visits to Japan to try to see everything, talk to everyone, and take photographs. The photograph appearing on the cover of *Changing Japan* is one of a large number taken at New Year's in 1965 in Osaka. By using a reflex camera held at waist level I was able to photograph people without their knowledge. I do not know the identities of the young people in the photograph, and I have sometimes wondered if my use of their photograph is entirely ethical. I do know without having inquired that they were dating and that they were very pleased with each other.

By the time I began research in 1964–1965 my acquaintance with Japanese scholars had become wide, and these men freely gave much aid. A trained research assistant in Tokyo and two professional aides in the Osaka-Kobe area helped in gathering needed information from published sources and in making arrangements for interviews. All interviewing was done by myself, as in earlier times recorded principally in shorthand as thriftily as possible and later transcribed and amplified from memory.

Another visit to Takashima in late 1964, even more tearful than our earlier visit, allowed me to see the changes there. Visits with Minoru in Osaka and return visits from her to our house rounded out my knowledge of modern Takashima.

Problems

My tale so far seems to be one of success that scarcely mentions problems, but the tale is incomplete. Of course there were problems, many of which were simply of the kinds that attend any human endeavor spanning a sizeable period of time. There were frustrating delays, some of them a reflection of the Japanese custom of proceeding slowly in many matters of life. Occasionally an assistant turned out to be incompetent. One, but only one, Japanese scholar briefly put obstacles in the way of my research. Interviews with dignitaries of the militant religious sect Soka Gakkai were never relaxed or pleasant. Rarely, fellow scholars from America brought momentary problems during my association with the Center for Japanese Studies in Okayama.

An unthinking director of the center once demanded that I cancel a full schedule of very special New Year's invitations in Takashima so that I might be present in Okayama to hear an address sponsored by the prefecture on the subject of whether or not the cultivation of olive trees were feasible in Okayama. The speaker concluded that olive culture was unfeasible, and I spent days apologizing to my Takashima hosts. Another director insisted that the rowboat I was to purchase with center funds be of Western style with a rounded bottom, a craft so dangerous for use in the sea that Takashima people would not enter it. After a few excitingly perilous trips in the boat, I secretly beached it and rented a more seaworthy boat. These and similar incidents were all trivial inconveniences that one might encounter at home.

And of course, I must have made mistakes, of procedure as well as in recording information. I am aware of only one error of importance and it was readily understood and forgiven. In Takashima I became hopelessly lost in a network of exchanges of gifts, thereby placing a distressing burden of guilt upon some people too poor to make, or to continue making, reciprocal gifts. As the months passed, many small gifts were made to me, some reciprocal and others not. The conventions of Japanese gift-giving are exceedingly complex. After a time I could not always remember the history of the exchanges and I made it a practice to give a return gift whenever I received one. After presenting such a gift at the entrance of a house one day, I said goodby but lingered by the house to make adjustments to my camera. From within the house I heard a pained voice say the English equivalent of "My God! He hasn't done it again, has he?" Thereafter, Minoru and other favorite informants served as counselors when I participated in exchanges of gifts.

Informants rarely presented problems of gaining rapport or cooperation. The Japanese are a literate, courteous people who understand and respect scholarly activities. If the aspiring researcher is professionally competent and understands the Japanese language, Japanese etiquette, and, especially, the use of the middle man and other indirect procedures customarily followed in conducting many activities, his work will ordinarily be successful. In both country and city it was sometimes difficult for me to be alone with a single informant, and various subjects could not be discussed satisfactorily otherwise. (It is curious that my interviews with officials of Soka Gakkai were almost always conducted in the presence of a second, monitoring official with whom I had not sought an interview.) There were, of course, variations in the competence and reliability of informants, but, as a whole, the Japanese must certainly be among the world's most cooperative subjects for the anthropologist.

I nevertheless experienced problems of adjustment that probably exist for all Western scholars working in Japan. Some of these problems were simple matters of physical comfort. Others stem from ethnocentric values that cannot easily be altered. Still other problems can be called psychic, and these probably inhere in some measure in field research in any society. A few are peculiar to Japan.

Adjustment to Japanese foods is very trying for most Westerners, but it is probably seldom a problem to the anthropologist committed to such an adjustment, and it was not a problem for me. All Japanese seem to have heard that Westerners greatly dislike most Japanese foods, and they are visibly pleased when a foreigner informs them and demonstrates that he likes their cuisine. A few foods particularly displeasing to Western sensibilities, such as baby bees and a species of grasshopper, will not ordinarily be served to a Westerner. These are, moreover, rather uncommon foods that are disliked by many Japanese. Western foods are available in all cities of Japan, and it is probable that most of the food served today in Japanese restaurants consists of Western dishes, often curiously Japanized. Many raw foods are, of course, quite the same as those of the West, and it is possible to maintain a diet of completely Western dishes. Few varieties of vegetables and fruits are available in winter months, and meals may then be monotonously repetitive. But there are gustatory compensations in superior seafoods, certain splendid fruits, and, after some acquaintance, in an agreeable adjustment to Japanese dishes that turns into great fondness. When on a wholly Japanese diet, I have sometimes suffered from the monotony of the meals in rural communities. After a time, I always suffer from hunger. Rice forms the main part of traditional Japanese meals, and I have never been able to consume as large a quantity of rice as is eaten by the average male Japanese. Snacks of canned fruit and other nutritious foods solve the problem.

Now and then excess consumption of alcoholic drinks has troubled me a little. Especially in rural Japan, the guest is urged repeatedly to drink heartily, and he cannot refuse toasts or exchanges of drinks with other guests. In rural communities of northeastern Japan I was expected to endure alcoholically as long as the most durable of the Japanese present at parties given in my honor. A mayor of an isolated mountain community there once left me, and himself, debilitated for days. When he finally collapsed into unconsciousness on the floor in the midst of a performance of a gay country dance, the hour was four in the morning. An American investigator visiting this community a year or two later informed me that I am known as the greatest consumer of the community's history. I am by preference a temperate drinker.

Mental commitment to adjust to Japanese life is not very helpful in allaying the discomforts of excessive humid heat and, especially, of cold. Traditional Japanese houses of most of Japan lack heating equipment except portable charcoal braziers over which one hovers, metal containers that are filled with hot water to serve as bed warmers, and a few other similarly small and ineffective devices. Small electric, gas, and kerosene heaters are common in the cities, but none of these devices ever seems satisfactory because of the flimsy construction of most dwellings. I have tried every expedient to ward off cold—long underwear and layers of clothing, pocket handwarmers, bed warmers, electric blankets, every available device for heating rooms, and very hot baths. None was ever truly adequate, and my memory of wintertime Japan is that a wide band of ice lies between my shoulderblades from November to May. Chilblains then transform my feet into swollen, itching torments, sometimes red and, at their worst, an apparently decomposing grey-black. Easily available medications for chilblains help but do not cure.

Other small creature discomforts are many. Baths are often too hot and, in inns and in family dwellings, one tub of water serves for many people. Standards of health are nevertheless high, and my illnesses in Japan have been confined to a mysterious brief fever, several cases of infected flea bites, an itching skin fungus that I think was gained in the communal bath of a country inn, and chilblains. Medical care is readily available. But rooms, doors, furniture, and sometimes even bathtubs are too small, so that the outsize foreigner, and the increasing number of tall Japanese, bump their heads and are otherwise uncomfortable. Public toilets are sinks of smelly despair that ordinarily lack toilet tissue, which one soon learns to carry with him. Some toilets are still co-educational, used by both sexes, but almost all foreigners seem to adjust quickly to this custom. The large toilet receptacles used in Takashima, pottery containers in which wastes were allowed to accumulate for long periods for later use as fertilizer for crops, became in the summer months the sites of tempests in pee-pots from seething waves of maggots.

Some other Western ideas of propriety must also be modified in Japan, although these are seldom trying. Cramped quarters required adjustment to the sight of nudeness or partial nudeness, which one does "not see," and one must become accustomed to female servants at inns entering the room at almost any time. In a backwoods inn I once bathed in the kitchen in an unscreened tub placed about 10 feet from the kitchen stove where the proprietor's wife was cooking dinner. Solicitous practices of some Takashima women during my wife's pregnancy included patting her on the abdomen to inquire how the child was getting along.

Except for suffering from cold, however, only a few of the Japanese customs and conditions of life relating to bodily comfort were really distressing to me. I suffer terribly from prolonged sitting on the floor in traditional Japanese fashion, and, after some days of protracted sitting, the suffering becomes mental. I desperately long for a chair. Other discomforts are more strongly psychological. I can endure but have never adjusted satisfactorily to the noisy and, from the viewpoint of a Westerner, greedy habits of eating of some Japanese men. Still more trying are the lack of privacy and the dense crowds of people.

My wife and I sought unsuccessfully dozens of times to be quite alone, out of sight and hearing of anyone. A long trip by rowboat to a barren rocky islet brought us face to face with a large troupe of Japanese picnickers, who streamed forth from a cave. On the apparently most deserted beach or mountaintop, people always appeared soon after our arrival. Only once were we successful in being alone, but our success entailed unusual extravagance. On a snowy day when sightseers were very few, we alone chartered a large bus to take us to the end of the road near the top of Mt. Aso, a famous volcano. While hiking through the snow to the lip of the crater and returning, we were alone at last.

The crowds on city streets, trains, and subways always exhaust me and, as the people swirl about, I become dizzy and think longingly of the summit of Mt. Everest, the Kalahari Desert, and soundproof vaults with locked steel doors. The behavior of Japanese crowds adds to the discomfort. In boarding and leaving trains and subways, the rule observed by many is every man for himself. I am often pushed about like an irregular piece of debris in a quixotic tide. Street crowds do not push so greatly, but they have other disturbing attributes. The margin of clearance allowed by a Japanese when passing, on foot or while driving a vehicle, is less than in the United States. Pedestrians do not seem to mind bumping each other or me and taxi drivers seem almost to shave other vehicles. What is most disturbing when I must be in crowds for a long period of time is a difference in the Japanese manner of walking. I am never in step and, although I do not collide with Japanese, I must maintain constant vigilance to prevent them from colliding with me. I am often unsuccessful.

Still worse as sources of psychological stress are two sets of circumstances, only one of which is peculiar to Japan, although both take distinctive form from features of Japanese culture. The first, an occupational ailment of anthropologists, might be called the fieldwork syndrome. The researcher working in Japan is at first bemused and captivated by what is beautiful, colorful, exotic, and charming. Much is indeed beautiful and charming. After a time he becomes accustomed to the different, jaded by the charm, and less moved by the beauty. He then realizes that his work is tedious, that some of his informants are inept, that the delays and necessary indirectness of many endeavors are rapidly consuming his time and frustrating him. He becomes increasingly aware of small bodily discomforts, and he grumbles about a country in which everything is two-thirds "normal" size. He loses appetite at the thought of entering a noisy, crowded restaurant, and the mere thought of careening taxis and jostling crowds makes him long for a career as a lone shepherd of the wilderness in a forest service lookout.

Worst of all for me is a kind of affect hunger, an alloy composed of a deficiency of my own and a trait of the Japanese people. I weary terribly of speaking and hearing Japanese, a language in which my competence allows me to come through in the gross but never in the fine. I crave conversation, a steady diet of conversation, in my own language, an unimpeded brook of flowing words filled with nuances of meaning. I long for a language in which my competence provides, by comparison, a surgical instrument rather than a thick, dull, and rusted meat cleaver. Closely related to this feeling of deprivation is another that stems from the nature of Japanese society. The Caucasian foreigner, and probably also the Mongoloid foreigner, is never incorporated into Japanese social groups. He remains forever a foreigner even if he is a Japanese national born and raised in Japan. The foreigner may have precious, close, and devoted Japanese friends, but his friendships with them are dyads, relationships of two, and they imply no real feeling of incorporation into any group. And in Japan, the group stands paramount. As this feeling of qualified rejection mounts, the researcher—and, of course, I am speaking for myself—infers from faces, voices, acts, and demeanor of all Japanese except close friends that he is in Japan on sufferance. It is then time to go home.

And now I shall be wholly subjective in saying how I think my experiences in Japan have affected my views of man and the universe. My visits to Japan have made me increasingly aware of both cultural differences and similarities. I see with greater clarity that there are many ways of doing things and that no single set of ways is necessarily or always superior to other ways. I see also that men everywhere are very much alike. These are anthropological truisms, but they become subjective truths only when the anthropologist somehow learns them from personal experience. I have also come to see rhyme and reason in Japanese behavior that once seemed inexplicable. But, again, this is a part of the anthropologist's work.

I believe that my Japanese experiences have never been personally harmful and that they have brought to me important benefits. The Japanese appreciation of aesthetics, for example, is both richer and more refined than that of my fellows in the United States. My own appreciation of aesthetics has been enlarged, refined, and made more rewarding as a result of my experiences in Japan. In other ways also I have become in some degree culturally Japanese, for which I am thankful. To my mind, the most important among these adjustments to Japanese life are changed views of what is appropriate in human relations. I have, of course, seen ugly emotions among the Japanese—anger, greed, selfishness and terrible jealousy. But I have also seen truly remarkable—and, I am very sure, self-rewarding—denial of the self for the benefit of others. I have seen, too, the remarkable strength and importance of the value placed in Japan upon the control of all emotions that might be disturbing to others, a value that is at the same time a quest for a feeling of harmony with other human beings and the entire universe. I think that I have learned something about patience and something about the obligations and rewards of association with one's fellow men. I think also that I have thereby gained some measure of inner peace. If these ideas are illusions, they seem none the less valuable.

References

Embree, John F., 1939, *Suye Mura, A Japanese Village.* Chicago: University of Chicago Press.

Norbeck, Edward, 1954, *Takashima, A Japanese Fishing Community.* Salt Lake City, Utah: University of Utah Press.

————, 1961, Postwar cultural continuity and change in northeastern Japan. *American Anthropologist* Vol. 63, No. 2, Pt. 1, 297–321.

————, 1965, *Changing Japan.* New York: Holt, Rinehart and Winston, Inc.

————, 1970, *Religion and Society in Modern Japan, Continuity and Change.* Houston: Rice University Studies.

Outline of Cultural Materials, 1950, 3d rev. ed. New Haven, Conn.: Human Relations Area Files, Inc.

11

FIELDWORK
AMONG THE MENOMINI

GEORGE AND LOUISE SPINDLER
Stanford University

Related Case Study: **Dreamers without Power:
The Menomini Indians**

In this chapter the Spindlers have tried to combine the anecdotal personal
background of field experience with discussion of certain field research
methods and techniques. The personal dimension looms large for that is
the focus of this book.

Fieldwork with the Menomini has played a most significant role in our
personal and family life. For years each spring our anticipation of leaving
for the field rose as departure day approached. Besides being exciting and
rewarding in itself, fieldwork meant living as we liked to live, camping,
close to nature and removed from urban conveniences, from early June
to late September. We chose to live this way, for indeed, Wisconsin is not
a remote wilderness and we could have lived in a house in town or a motel.

Our style of life in the field had certain advantages. We saw, during
these periods, virtually no Whites, for we were either alone or with
Menomini. We traveled with them to dances, went cherry picking with
them, participated in most of their affairs. This pattern was repeated each
summer for seven years, with occasional short visits in other seasons, and
since then intermittently. It is this long time span and the depth of our
personal involvement that makes the Menomini live for us now.

When we were not working we played.

Our style of life in the field and certain deep personal value orientations predispose us to certain biases. Partly because we enjoyed living as we did, we enjoyed fieldwork and liked the Menomini. The bias, however, goes further. Our style of life in the field brought us closer to the culturally conservative segments of the Menomini population, who were themselves living mostly in the woods nearby and close to nature, than to the most acculturated people who lived in regular houses in the towns of Neopit or Keshena in regular middle-class style. We established good rapport with a number of the latter, and count some among them today as long-term friends, but day in and day out our intensive and personally most meaningful interaction was with the members of the Medicine Lodge and Dream Dance groups, and with the Peyotists. Consequently our account of these groups in the case study is richer than of the others, and we have tended to stress cultural continuity and adaptation within a Menomini cultural framework more than we have current problems.

But the source of our bias goes deeper than our style of life in the field. In fact it may be said to be the cause of our style of life in the field. We both grew up in environments where direct enjoyment of nature was a positive and possible value, and where we both had largely rewarding

Drying-out day at camp.

contacts with people culturally different from ourselves. We were both born of parents in or past middle age, and we both spent more time alone than with peer groups as young children. These factors combined, for fairly complex reasons, to predispose us to philosophic and humanistic concerns more than practical ones, to value continuity more than change, cultural differences more than similarities, the past more than the future.

The "double bind" of being an anthropologist is apparent in our situation. Long-term, intimate personal involvement with a people results inevitably in personal bias—always selective, usually positive, sometimes negative. The development of this bias is related to antecedent life history experience as well as to situational factors. The biases thus developed enter into everything one does—in the field and afterwards in interpretation of data. And yet it is precisely this kind of personal involvement that makes much of the most significant data collectable, and some of the most significant interpretations possible.

We cannot eliminate the biases, for to do so we would have to become someone other than we are, or be devoid of human response in the field—an impossible bias. We think we have been able to adjust for some of our biases by acknowledging them to ourselves and examining our interpretation of data in this light.

The Authors

George Spindler   Born in Stevens Point, Wisconsin, a member of the WASP minority group in a predominantly Polish Catholic town, he learned about cultural differences early. He graduated from Central State, where his father had taught for thirty-two years. He taught in Wisconsin high schools for a time after graduation and met Mary Louise Schaubel at Park Falls, a northern town surrounded by semi-wilderness. Married in 1942, they spent the next two years traveling between Army posts until he was sent overseas. After the war he entered graduate school at the University of Wisconsin to which he had been attracted by a stimulating summer before the war through the teaching of Morris Opler. In the fall of 1948 the Spindlers moved to UCLA so that he could take Bruno Klopfer's projective techniques seminar, intending to return to finish the Ph.D. at Wisconsin. However, at UCLA he fell under the influence of Walter Goldschmidt in anthropology and Philip Selznick in sociology, as well as Klopfer in psychology, and consequently continued toward a Ph.D., combined out of the three fields, which he finally obtained in 1952.

The Spindlers came to Stanford in 1950 and have stayed. He is now Professor of Anthropology and Education and has been Chairman of the Department for one short and one long period. He has been editor of the *American Anthropologist* (1962–1966) and a Fellow at the Center for Advanced Study in the Behavioral Sciences (1956–1957). His publications include articles, many of them with Louise Spindler, on psychological anthropology, culture change, field methods, education as a cultural process, the military, peyotism, American Indians, and the American character; edited books, to which he also contributed as author, *Education and Anthropology, Education and Culture,* and *Education and Cultural Process*; and authored books; *Menomini Acculturation,* and *Culture in Process* (with A. Beals and L. Spindler), and *Dreamers without Power* (with L. Spindler). The Spindlers have done fieldwork with the Menomini, Blood, and Mistassini Cree Indians, and in urbanizing villages in Germany. George Spindler has also worked for several years intermittently in public schools in West Coast communities.

Louise Schaubel Spindler, born in Oak Park, Illinois, came to California at the age of three. She moved to Wisconsin after her father's death and finished undergraduate college at Carroll, graduating with strong interests in drama and literature. She taught in Wisconsin high schools for three years and attended graduate school in English literature summers. After she and George Spindler married, she and their daughter, Sue, born in 1943, became camp followers as George Spindler moved from pillar to post in various contingents of the U.S. Army, until finally he was sent overseas. After George Spindler entered graduate school she began her training in anthropology, studying part time as her other obligations permitted, at Wisconsin and UCLA. She took her Ph.D. at Stanford in 1956. She served as Assistant Editor for the *American Anthropologist* (1962–1966) and is a Fellow in the American Anthropological Association. She has published articles on witchcraft and acculturation, women's roles, and modal personality, a monograph, *Menomini Women and Culture Change*, and has coauthored a text in cultural anthropology with Alan Beals and her husband. She is coeditor, with George Spindler, of the Case Studies in Cultural Anthropology, Studies in Anthropological Method, and Case Studies in Education and Culture. She is now a Research Associate and Lecturer in the Department of Anthropology at Stanford.

She says of her professional interests:

When someone asked me for the first time: "Why did you become an anthropologist? and why do you like fieldwork?," certain feelings and impressions stood out sharply. Despite any ad hoc rationalizations, these are the "real" reasons. My father and mother both disliked routine. After I was born and my father was 65 years of age, they left Chicago to go "West" to recreate, on a very small scale, the drama of the early gold mining days. The long summers spent living with our family and a small crew of miners in a remote area of the Sierras where they were attempting to reactivate a once productive gold mine, were sheer adventure to me as a young child. It was not until George and I did fieldwork many years later that I experienced the same sense of challenge from both the people and the environment that I had experienced earlier. Other images that came to mind are those of my husband entering graduate school after World War II at Wisconsin as the first returnee in anthropology and introducing me to a most stimulating, idealistic, and inspiring anthropologist—the late H. Scudder Mekeel, with whom we spent many memorable hours. During this period, my background in romantic poetry seemed irrelevant. Later, when my husband and I (and daughter, Sue) went to the field together I found the challenge in attempting to study and understand a people who operate on different premises than ours a totally satisfying experience both in a scientific and in a personal sense.

G. D. S.

The Beginning

We began our fieldwork with the Menomini without any explicit training in methods or techniques of field research—as did most novitiates until very recently. C. W. M. Hart, then at Wisconsin, gave us useful advice. "Try to think of yourselves at first as newspaper reporters. Listen and watch, talk to

Louise takes a Rorschach.

people. Eventually patterns will begin to appear." We started doing just that during the summer of 1948.[1] We continued field work with the Menomini for several months each year after that through 1954, developing our methodology as we proceeded. We are still working intermittently and maintain contacts and

[1] In May 1950, J. S. Slotkin also began fieldwork with the Menomini, concentrating on the Dream Dance and Peyote Cult. He continued through July of that summer, and worked May–June in 1951. We operated entirely independently. His two major publications, *The Menomini Powwow* (1957), and *Menomini Peyotism* (1952) furnish important material on these organizations and the culture of the least acculturated segments of the Menomini population.

friendships with the people. Data collected during the major field period as well as since then are still being analyzed. The most recent publications are the case study (Spindler and Spindler 1970), and an analysis of witchcraft (L. Spindler 1970). We used a number of field research techniques, including a sociocultural index schedule, the Rorschach projective technique, structured and unstructured interviews, expressive autobiographic interviews, and the anthropologist's standby—participant observation.

Our research problem was defined, after our first summer of exploration, as an attempt to find out how psychological adaptation was related to social, economic and cultural adaptation (henceforth "sociocultural") in a rapidly acculturating, non-Western population. We cast the analysis as a whole into a framework we called an "experimental design" (Spindler and Goldschmidt 1952), meaning that we tried to keep our major variables separate (in this case the sociocultural as against the psychological adaptations of individuals), employ independent evidence as the basis for analysis of each, and use a control group—twelve white men who had married Menomini women and who lived on the reservation under conditions similar to those of the Menomini themselves.

It is not our purpose to detail the rationale for and application of the "experimental design" in our work. This is developed in other publications (G. Spindler 1952, 1955). It is a research stance that does force one to a certain rigor in the collection and use of data, but the term "experimental" both implies controls that no one can exercise in the field and a narrowness of conception that did not, in fact, operate as a constraint on our procedures. Being anthropologists, we spent much time and energy collecting data on the context of the defined variables. Nor are we concerned, in this chapter, with much exposition of the conceptual models or theory that guided our work or to which we hope it makes a contribution, though some conceptualization is necessary to make the use of research techniques sensible. What we are concerned with is how we arrived at a position where we could collect useful data, what we did to collect it, and how we analyzed some of it. We will start with gaining entrèe and rapport.

Entrée and Rapport

When, on June 5, 1948, we drove through Menomini country[2] on our first reconnaissance, it seemed impossible that we could ever penetrate far enough into the lives of the people, in enough different groupings and settlement areas, to make any sense out of the situation. There were nearly 400 square miles of

[2] Until May 1961, the Menomini lived on a reservation that became a county in the State of Wisconsin upon termination of federal protection and guarantees. The Menomini are now selling a part of their lands to Whites in order to increase the tax base.

forested land, bisected by two major highways with two major towns, several small settlements, scattered dwellings here and there in the woods and near the highways, and about 3000 people (Figure 11.4 shows the major outline of the area.) We stopped at gas stations, talked to some boys fishing at the dam in Neopit (the center of the lumbering industry that produces most Menomini income), drove around through the settlements, picked up a couple who wanted a ride. The people seemed casually friendly. We had already cleared our intentions with the superintendent, representing the Bureau of Indian Affairs, and had met a few office workers, including some Menomini, and a few

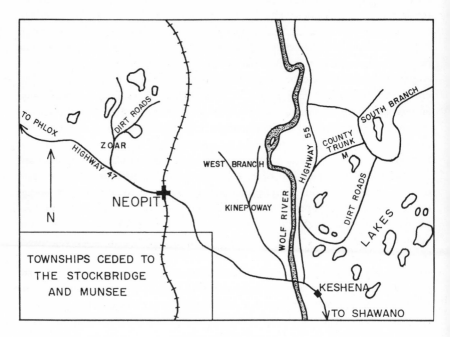

Menominee County.

members of the tribal council. Nothing seemed very clear that first day, nor did it for the next, or the next.

We stayed at first at one of the cabins for tourists near Rainbow Falls on the Wolf River. The proprietors were very kind to us, but after a few days we moved out. We could not remain tourists forever. We decided to camp on a lake nearby. We liked camping and it was much less expensive. We picked a lake just outside the northwest boundary of the reserve with the intention of moving onto Menomini land later. As it turned out, we stayed at this same lake, at the same camping place, for all of our summers of fieldwork. It had certain advantages, not the least of which was the fact that it was *not* on

Menomini land. We could not be accused of taking advantage of our role to use Menomini resources (hunting and fishing rights were jealously guarded), nor were we aligned residentially with any particular faction (and indeed there were factions!), and we had a desirable privacy. Yet our Menomini friends could come to see us when they felt like it. The lake shore was uninhabited and the Menomini felt at home there. They visited us often. Our location meant that our car became a second home, for every place we went we had to drive. But this, too, was a godsend, for our car became a place to interview people away from children, friends, and relatives; it became our study, where we could write up notes at intervals during the day; it became a means of escape, and there were times we needed to escape; and it became a constant means for reciprocating favors—we took individuals and groups all over the reserve, to other Indian enclaves, to the hospital, for groceries, to ceremonials. Our car was, in fact, a major factor in the first significant breakthrough in gaining entrèe.

After a few weeks we had come to appreciate that the Menomini were not one. There were not only political factions, formal associations, friendship groupings, but there were also categories of persons representing varying adaptations to the confrontation of the Menomini way of life and that of the surrounding American majority. Among the most significant of these were the conservatives termed "those Indians" by the Menomini we met in the agent's office, who lived mostly at a settlement called Zoar in the northwest sector of the forest nearest our camp, as well as scattered here and there in Neopit and in a general area called Crow Settlement near Keshena in the southeast sector. We wanted to gain entrèe into the conservative group as soon as possible, for we felt that this would allow us to develop a relevant cultural baseline, from which adaptive movement toward various segments of the dominant culture could be seen more clearly. We had also been told that it was exceedingly difficult to get into this group, or even to talk to the people. We puzzled over how to make the break. We did not feel that knocking on doors was the right approach.

But one day while traveling southeast on Highway 47 we picked up a lone woman hitchhiker. She said she was "dry" so we drove to a nearby rural village for a beer (no one bothered the Indians who went there for a drink, even though at the time it was illegal for Indians to buy alcoholic beverages). On our way back she suddenly said "Do you know Shumaysen? He's some kind of relative of mine. He's a real medicine man. He can tell what's gonna happen. If somebody is sick, he can find out what's causing it. He has some kind of power." Of course our anthropological tongues were hanging out by then. "Say, do yuh wanna meet him? He lives right by here." So we drove off the highway onto a single-track logging road and shortly arrived at a neatly kept rectangular shelter covered with roofing paper. Shumaysen was evidently at home, for smoke drifted out of the bucket of coals and rotted wood used to keep mosquitoes down and the door was open. We waited a bit and soon a slightly built old man dressed in neatly patched pants, with heavy galluses holding them up, faded red cotton flannel shirt, and work shoes, came toward us with a lively step. He had recognized his niece. We talked, or tried to, for awhile. He spoke little English, and Nellie was not interested in doing much interpreting. But we had acquired a few Menomini words and phrases, and with his sparse English we made out. He was very attracted to Louise Spindler—an admiration that continued throughout the rest of his life—and he smiled continually at our daughter, Sue, fair-haired and five at the time. After about an hour we left, feeling that we had made a good impression, but with the frustrating problem of how to follow up on this first contact.

The old man put on his costume and got out his Mitäwin *drum to show us how it worked.*

An opportunity was not long in coming. About two weeks later we spotted not far from Highway 47 an elongated frame of bent-over saplings covered by canvas that was apparently being used to house a *Mitäwin* ceremony—the Medicine Lodge—living proof that the traditional culture was very much alive. There were cars parked around it and a crowd of about a hundred adults and scores of children were hanging around outside. We pulled up, stopped our car, and listened to the muffled beat of the water drum[3] and the tight-throated

[3] A drum made of a wooden cask approximately 18 inches high, 11 inches wide at the base, with about 3 inches of water in it and a tautly drawn head of tanned buckskin.

The Medicine Lodge.

singing. No two more excited anthropologists ever sat listening to strange music. We wanted to get into the lodge. No one seemed to have the authority to let us in, or tell us whom to ask. George Spindler looked for the entrance, but none was visible. Finally, desperate to enter, he disregarded all rules of conduct for fieldworkers and slid in through a narrow slit between two sections of canvas, tripped, and fell into the midst of the action. To one side sat Shumaysen, who immediately motioned for him to come sit by him. The *mitäwok* (members) were dancing around the lodge in an orderly and solemn manner, apparently taking no notice of the intruder. Suddenly all the men and women, clutching their medicine bags made of whole otter, mink, badger, skunk, and snake skins, started shouting and danced vigorously about, shaking the snouts of their bags at each other to the accompaniment of grunting cries "Whe ho! ho! ho! uh! uh! uh!" We had read in the accounts by Alanson B. Skinner and Walter Hoffman of this high point in the ceremony when the *mitäwok* shot each other with the magical "megise" (small cowrie shell) kept in the stomach of each bag. It was believed that the *mitäwok* were protected against harm by their own powers, but that being shot could be fatal to the noninitiated. Suddenly a very large Winnebago woman who had been glaring at George Spindler swung her bag directly at him, hunched over it, and danced by, shooting him with it several times. Shumaysen looked worried but said nothing. No effects were immediately apparent, the meeting went on, and at intermission George left, feeling that he had been too forward, as indeed he had, and that his absence might be appreciated more than his presence.

We went on with interviews here and there, examined maps and census data, counted houses, visited the lumber mill, poked along the many trails through the woods, but really did not seem to be getting anywhere. Then George Spindler became ill and in a few days was hospitalized with a high fever of "undiagnosed origin." Penicillin and rest cleared it up in about a week, and we went back to work. But this was our break. We went back to Shumaysen, told him what had happened, and asked him if he could give us something to protect us from further harm. He told us to come back in four days. We did, and he

Inside the lodge the medicine bags were being used.

bestowed a packet, wrapped carefully in the directions for a Toni hair set and containing several herbs and dried fragments of the organs of animals, upon George with a brief ritual song and a tobacco sacrifice. George was to carry it with him at all times. He advised us that this would keep George from further harm.

From that event on we found it easy to make contact with members of the native-oriented group, the adults of which were all members of the *Mitäwin,* the *Neemihetwan*[4] (the Dream Dance Association, or "Pow-wow religion"), or both. Our implied acceptance of the native belief system in a critical area of belief was an important factor.

This raises an ethical question. Were we not deceiving Shumaysen and his cohorts, using a contrived anxiety and a spurious acceptance of his beliefs to gain entrèe? How far should the anthropologist go? Our explanation, to him and to others, was that we were not sure that the shooting by the medicine bag had made George ill, and that we did not know whether anything Shumaysen fixed up could protect one from harm. But apparently they believed that it worked. We were on their land, in their community, and while there would try to do things their way, so we would need to learn what those ways were. Further, we found it possible, as we became more and more deeply involved with the native-oriented group and their thinking, to accept what they did and believed on their terms without worrying about whether it was "true" or not. We came to regard their culture as a complex metaphor that was neither true nor false, just as we have come to regard our own. We think that some such position is essential in direct and prolonged participant observation.

Other means of gaining entrèe were utilized. As a family of three, young, quite poor (we were graduate students for the first three seasons), eager to learn whatever anyone would tell or show us, respectful of their customs and beliefs, we had a certain attraction for many Menomini. Most of the people in the native-oriented group, at least, had met only Whites who were trying to teach them, preach to them, sell to them, parcel out welfare, check on their sanitation, euchre them out of their slender funds, or put them in jail. We were something different. But it took some time for the people to decide what we were, what we really wanted, and whether or not we were to be trusted. People kept asking us what we were up to and we invariably told them more than they wanted to hear, but explanations of scientific intent do not help much.

Many anthropologists gain entrèe by asking for help in learning the language. This is considered a disarming approach, for rarely do people seem to mind teaching an agreeable stranger their language—especially people who have been taught by alien teachers and administrators that their language is no language at all and should be replaced as quickly as possible by a real one—English in this case. But though we were interested in learning as much Menomini as we could through normal contact and some study of such sources as Bloomfield's grammar and texts, we did not feel that we could afford to devote the enormous blocks of time to this task that it would require. The native tongue was rarely spoken excepting in the native-oriented group, and in this group all but the oldest people spoke reasonably good English. We never learned to speak

---

[4] We have not used the orthography employed in the case study in order to avoid typesetting problems in this book, where a different orthography might be required for each chapter.

Menomini, though we acquired some vocabulary and an ear for certain key phrases and words used in ceremonial speeches by the elders.

We had to have a regular and understandable task to perform. It was all very well to sit around, ride around, hang around, and talk to people, but this was not doing anything in their eyes.

The answer came the second summer of field work. We had decided, after the first summer, to go out to the University of California at Los Angeles to work under Bruno Klopfer's direction on the adaptation of projective techniques to anthropological research. These techniques, following the lead of A. I. Hallowell in his Ojibwa research, seemed to be the answer to our need for standardized but relatively culture-free procedures for defining the psychological variable. We had become involved, in the first place, with psychocultural problems through Scudder Mekeel, Hart's predecessor at Wisconsin. Dr. Klopfer was running a continuing training seminar at UCLA in the clinical use of these techniques. After a year of such training, George Spindler returned to the Menomini ready to apply them in the field. During the year at UCLA we also had the opportunity to develop further our research plans under the direction of Walter Goldschmidt, who with admirable decisiveness, forced us to recognize that we must separate our variables, develop some controls, and standardize our procedures. We returned to the field armed not only with projective techniques but also with a sociocultural index schedule, a set of hypotheses to test, and a determination to sample the whole range of acculturative adaptation existent on the Menomini reservation. We returned to UCLA after another summer of fieldwork with our initial sampling of males nearly completed, continued in the projective techniques seminar, partially analyzed the data, and returned again the next spring to the Menomini. George Spindler finished his dissertation the next year. The major monograph on the Menomini by him (1955) includes data gathering and analyses completed three years after the dissertation was finished. Meanwhile Louise Spindler had begun to work toward her dissertation, which she finished later. Fieldwork continued.

After initial experimentation with both the standard Murray Thematic Apperceptive test and a modification of it, we chose to work with only the Rorschach projective technique. We chose it because at that time we were more interested in abstract perceptual-cognitive organization than in specific interpersonal attitudes.

The Rorschach consists of ten inkblots, five achromatic, the rest colored. The respondent is asked to tell what each blot looks like to him, and what about the blot, or parts of it, made him think of that. The inkblots are culture free in the sense that they are not pictures of anything. The responses are never culture free. The same inkblots are administered each time the Rorschach is given, and in the same order, with the same instructions, so the elicitation procedure is standardized. The respondent presumably projects both his characteristic manner of perceiving and of organizing what he perceives, as well as his preoccupations, anxieties, and emotional controls. No psychological technique has received as much evaluation, as many tests of validity and reliability, and as much general criticism as the Rorschach. Despite the critical literature, the technique is still widely used in psychiatry and clinical psychology. It must be considered, however, controversial. The Rorschach seemed to work well for us, and allowed us to define some of the most significant aspects of our psychological variables with some precision. Perhaps it worked well for our purposes because we were interested more in the structural features of perception and cognitive organization in our various acculturative categories than in individual, qualitative, personality variations.

We will discuss our Rorschach strategy further but for now want to make a point concerning entrèe. The Rorschach gave us a reason to enter people's homes, request their close attention to our purpose for several hours at a time, and forced us to sample widely. It gave us something specific to do with a wide variety of people. It was like learning the language is for many anthropologists, but it was a better point of entrèe for us because it took us from person to person, from household to household, all over the Menomini community. A native-oriented man and his wife living well back in the woods in a shelter resembling a roofing-paper-covered wigwam could respond to it, as well as an individual living in a suburban house with two bathrooms and a two-stall garage. The people seemed to think it was perfectly reasonable that we should be interested in the way they "saw things" in the inkblots, if we were interested in the way people of different backgrounds and experience thought and felt, as we explained we were. We collected sixty-eight Rorschachs from males, sixty-one from females, all one-half Menomini or more, and all twenty-one years of age or older. We were refused only once. The people thought it was fun to look at the blots, called George Spindler "Doc Psyche," and cooperated willingly.

Our data collection did not stop with the Rorschach. This technique took from one to four hours to administer, sometimes longer. During this time we were usually in the car near the house, or on the stoop or porch (if there was one), or often inside. The normal activities of the household continued around us. While our respondent stared thoughtfully at the inkblots (Menomini, depending on degree of acculturation, take their time to figure things out), we stared thoughtfully at the other people and their activities, jotting down significant points and sometimes making a sketch of the house layout. It was often possible to do a fairly complete inventory of material household culture as well as its spatial distribution. Further, as the respondent warmed up to the novelty of talking to a White who took notes on what was said he began to talk about many things besides inkblots. Before we left we had often collected a full set of Rorschach responses, done a household inventory, collected numerous behavioral observations, and recorded a semi-structured but spontaneous interview containing autobiographic episodes, political opinions, gossip about other people, bits of personal philosophy, and some narrative history. And we always returned at least once, often many times, to each household where we had visited. This means that each of our 129 cases includes a substantial sampling of behavior, material household culture, and expression of sentiment, so that the file on each case is much more than a Rorschach protocol and a coded socio-cultural index. Each case is a case study. This was particularly true because there were always two observers present. While George was administering the Rorschach to his respondent, Louise would be engaging other members of the family in conversation and observing everything else that she could see or hear. And when Louise administered Rorschachs, George was observing. We were frequently aided by our daughter, who usually entered into the play of the

Sue and one of her best friends.

younger children, thus keeping them occupied and out of the respondent's or our hair. Children crawling all over one can be quite distracting, and it was useful to have a built in child-distractor along with us. Often such a visit was a full day's work, and by the time we had fully recorded our notes it would be midnight.

Sampling

Often anthropologists do not seem to worry much about sampling. After they have lived in a small village, or traveled with a nomadic band for months or years they come to feel that they know everyone. But the Menomini population was too big and too internally differentiated to permit us to take this stance.

There are essentially two strategies for sampling; a random sample and a proportionate stratified sample. In the first instance one draws, say, every third name from a file of all names and then makes every possible effort to interview, observe, or test that individual. In the second instance one decides what significant social strata, or categories of any sort exist, with approximate proportions of population, and then builds a sample that represents this profile. Of course one may randomize cases within defined strata or categories, but for some purposes individuals with known characteristics might be selected for study.

None of these strategies were possible for the initial sample of males. The Menomini do not stay in one place long enough to permit a true random sample to be collected. And we did not know at that time what strata or categories we would want represented in a proportionate stratified sample. We did know that there were a few people at the extremes of a posited acculturative continuum, from most traditional (least acculturated) to White middle class. We felt that we should try to collect relevant data from all of the adults in these two extreme groups and worry about what lay in between when we got that far.

This is essentially what we did. We collected Rorschachs, sociocultural index schedules, household observations, and semi-structured interviews from nearly all of the adult male members of what we came to call the native-oriented and the elite-acculturated groups that were in residence at the time of the study. Our "sample" of these extremes of the presumed acculturative continuum is virtually the universe. As we worked with the native-oriented we became acutely aware of the existence of the Peyote Cult, the Native American Church. The membership of the native-oriented group and the Peyote Cult were almost mutually exclusive, but many of the latter had been members of the native-oriented *Mitäwin* or *Nemiheetwan*, and a few of the native-oriented would go to an occasional peyote meeting. On the whole, however, the membership of the peyote group was distinctive from all other groupings and was perceived as deviant by nonmembers. We subsequently collected comparable case data from all of the adult peyotists. That is, all but one. One man who was one of our best informants on peyotism—the meaning of ritual, the ideology of the organization, as well as on other matters—simply refused to take the Rorschach. He would never tell us why.

We then had the virtual universes of what turned out to be three of five acculturative categories (see Figure 11.9). The other two categories, the transitional (culturally marginal), and lower-status acculturated (apparently fully adapted to white man culture but at a laboring class occupational and economic level) are less adequately sampled, for they constitute roughly 75 percent of the total population. We used the indigenous network of communications and friendships in order to secure new cases. This meant that by one or another means we made contacts with a few cases, usually through suggestions from

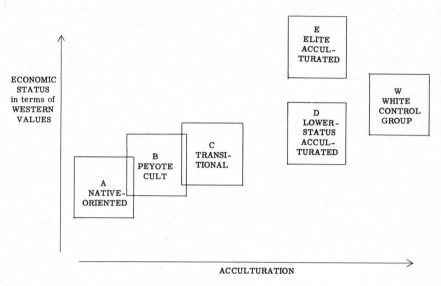

Acculturative categories.

established contacts in other groupings. After working with the new cases and determining that they did not fit into any of the established categories—native oriented, peyote, or elite acculturated—we obtained several suggestions from them for new contacts. We would follow up some but not all of these contacts, introducing ourselves as "sent by so and so," and "Jack looked at these cards (the Rorschach) and he's still healthy. He thought maybe you would look at them too." We would then obtain further references from our new case, and so on. There is, of course, the danger that by following along the existing social network we would tend to contact only persons within certain channels of communication. We usually tried to compensate for this by selecting only one of several cases suggested by our latest respondent, and by asking people to recommend others both "like" and "unlike" themselves. Our sampling of the transitionals and lower-status acculturated is not extensive enough to permit us to say that we tapped all significant types of adaptation, group membership, or personality contained within these large categories. Our case data do definitely indicate that the dispersion of both acculturative and psychological characteristics is greatest in these two categories, and especially in the transitional population. At least we were not led along restricted segments of the network by our method of sampling.

The sample of women, collected after that of the men was finished, was selected somewhat differently. By then we knew what our acculturative (not psychological) categories were. Because we wanted to match our male sample as closely as possible, as a means of establishing some control over acculturative variability (which we regarded as our antecedent variable), we secured women married to males in our sample, or residing in the same household, in 70 percent of the female sample.

Given the population of adults one half or more Menomini, we ended with a sample of approximately 22 percent of the total universe, with about the same sampling of households, but with the uneven distribution in acculturative categories described.

Sociocultural Index Schedule

By the end of our first summer of fieldwork we had an impressionistic grasp of the major dimensions of the sociocultural variable, but we had no defined categories. During the academic year at UCLA, as a part of our general preparation for the return to the field, we developed a sociocultural index schedule. This schedule contained 180 coded items under 18 major headings. These headings were: name (has or has not Indian name), age, "blood," location, marital status, education, subsistence (including income), home (including type, condition, sanitation, furnishings), automobile, political activity, language, type of reading, parental status ("blood," education, occupation, language, religion), religion, knowledge of native lore and belief, utilization of medical services, recreation, group membership (including ceremonial organizations and informal friendship groupings). The complete schedule can be found in G. Spindler (1955) and in L. Spindler (1962).

This schedule was filled out for every respondent, and became an essential part of the case data on each. Very often it could not be completely filled out until a second or third visit. Many items, such as an indoor toilet, lack of running water in the home, kind of heating and cooking facilities, condition and type of home and furnishings could be recorded on the basis of direct observation during the administration of the Rorschach. Other items, such as parental status, recreation, knowledge of native lore, income, participation in groups, could only be known by direct questioning or through prolonged acquaintance. We found it expedient to limit direct questioning very sharply, and in fact rarely did directly question anyone, though for some items it could not be avoided, but only after good rapport had been established.

The items themselves were selected to allow us to place individuals and households on the acculturation continuum that we surmised, through our first summer of work, to exist on the reservation. We also posited a socioeconomic differential for the acculturative categories within the continuum. The relationship is expressed in Figure 11.10. The schedule forced us to look at each case searchingly and to collect data that could be coded, then treated statistically. It also gave us a qualitative grasp of the sociocultural configuration characterizing each person in our sample.

Before the schedule data could be treated statistically to test the existence or

Some of the acculturated people live in new, modern homes.

lack of an acculturative continuum, some initial grouping of cases had to occur. We selected religious identification and group membership as points of entry. In effect we hypothesized that the native-oriented group, consisting of members of the two traditional ceremonial organizations still operating, would be least acculturated and of low socioeconomic status: that the Peyotists would be more acculturated and socioeconomically better off; that the people who had white collar and supervisory positions in the lumber industry and who were all Catholic would be most acculturated and socioeconomically best off; that people who earned their living by manual labor but who worked regularly, had no traditional religious affiliation and were Catholic would be no less acculturated but would be socioeconomically lower than the elites; and that the cases where there was some evidence of past experience with the traditional culture but no present affiliation, would be culturally and economically transitional, in between the acculturated and the rest. To test the validity of these hypotheses we applied three statistical procedures to our sociocultural indices. First we demonstrated that the tentative assignments of cases to sociocultural categories were broadly appropriate by showing that each sociocultural index was significantly (0.05 or more) differentially distributed throughout the five sociocultural categories, in order from native oriented, through peyote, transitional, lower-status acculturated, to elite acculturated on the basis of case assignments. To do this we applied the chi-square test. All indices excepting "blood" and drinking patterns proved to be distributed along the posited acculturative continuum to such a degree that the continuum as a whole could be considered confirmed.[5]

Next we demonstrated the degree of association for each item by applying the tetrachoric r, after satisfying ourselves that the conditions for its use were met. This produced correlations ranging from an insignificant 0.18 (drinking patterns) to 0.89 (knowledge of native lore and belief). The upper limit of r_t is 1.0, so 0.89 is a high correlation. In this instance it meant that knowledge of native lore was correlated very strongly with our posited assignment of individuals to acculturative categories. Finally, we applied chi-square tests to intercategory distributions, to find out at what points the various acculturative categories were distinguished from each other. This required testing every category against every other category, for 360 separate tests. The distribution of signifisant differences (G. Spindler 1955: 115) shows us clearly just where and how much our posited categories are differentiated from each other. For example, the extremes, the native oriented and the elite acculturated, are differentiated in almost every item, but the Peyote Cult group and the native oriented are differentiated in only three out of twenty-four items (knowledge of lore, type of furniture, heat in the house), and the native oriented and the transitionals are differentiated in respect to eleven of twenty-four items.

When we finished with this fairly complex analysis we were able to describe with confidence the nature of our sociocultural variable. The operation was also valuable from another viewpoint. We had to examine, time and time again, the distribution of every item. We hand winnowed all the data. Though this required many hours of detailed and, at times, exhausting labor, the payoff in comprehensive understanding of what our data were was very great. We also found that we had to abide rigorously to the rules of our own game. The statistical models kept us in line. We could have used a computer to advantage to perform the statistical calculations, but with the expert help of Sidney Siegel, then a graduate student in the Department of Psychology at Stanford, all phases of the operation went efficiently, if not painlessly.

The Rorschach

With our sociocultural dimension validated and explicated we now had to work out comparable ways of handling our Rorschach data. We had protocols from sixty-eight male Menomini and twelve Whites (the control group) to

[5] We have reinterpreted the significance of the Menomini sociocultural categories and the acculturative continuum which they constitute in the case study *Dreamers without Power* (1970) as "adaptive strategies"; as adaptations to the confrontation between discongruent cultural systems. This reinterpretation is too complex to cover in this chapter, and does not directly influence the *research* strategy we are describing.

begin with. Collection of the female sample and analysis of male-female differences came later.

A Rorschach protocol is a complex personal document. Respondents describe first what they see in the inkblots during the "performance" then, during the "inquiry" phase of administration, explain what about the blot made them think of this, and how they used the blot in the formation of the percept. The responses are qualitative, and usually include quite elaborate imagery loaded with potential symbolic meaning. For example, the following response to Card VI is taken from the protocol of a man in the transitional category. He was raised in a very traditional manner by grandparents, spoke no English until he was eight, then went off to boarding school, later the navy, then became a drifter, working here and there, finally to come back to the reservation. He lived alone, drank to oblivion frequently, dreamed about joining the *Mitäwin* and leading a resurgence of the traditional ways, read widely, wanted to write books about "my people," wanted to be an anthropologist, and did nothing. He was a casualty of the accuturation process. On Card VI he saw

". . . an old injun symbol. Like a totem pole. Yes sir, like a thunderbird totem pole, an old ancient one, driven into the ground. Yah, the pole looks like it was elaborately fixed up—like they had a lot of regard for the sacred past—like symbolic evidence. They seem to have marked each place with a symbol. To know them you'd need to understand some stories or . . . to me . . . seems like awful good . . . like in the center there's all the stories you would have gotten . . . and this all requires more than just a lot of thought. It sure seems to tell the story of a country. Them symbols are all up here (top). The rest of it down here (main body of blot) is all the people. They are all dead. It is like a dead planet. It seems to tell the story of a people once great who have lost . . . like something happened. All that's left is the symbol."

One could make much of this interpretively. In the context of his acutely transitional position the response appears to be a condensed and literal projection of his feelings about the past of his own people and their culture. Examination of his autobiography lends extensive support for this interpretation. The presence of this response and others like it in his protocol suggest the depth of his preoccupation with the extinction of traditional Menomini culture. In this frame of reference the Rorschach is a personal document that extends and further shapes our knowledge of this transitional man and the interpretation of his motivations, self-feelings, and phantasy. It is possible to go further in the interpretation, employing a more psychoanalytic stance, and hypothesize that the totem is a phallic symbol, and that the "dead planet" perception is an expression of concern with his sexual potency, as he himself grows older (he was just past 50 when the protocol was taken), debilitates himself by his drinking, and lives a solitary life. One could enter the other data collected from him with this hypothesis, with interesting results. Both of these interpretations as to the qualitative, symbolic "meaning" of the inkblot to him could be valid, simultaneously. Such interpretations are justified for some purposes—where we are concerned with individuals as such. The risks of misinterpretation and the overexercise of phantasy on the part of the anthropologist are considerable, but no greater than in similar interpretations of autobiographic content, folk tales or other forms of narrative culture, or reported dreams. But this was not our purpose. We wanted to discover in what manner and to what extent Rorschach responses, as formal indicators of adapting perceptual organization, were covariant with sociocultural adaptation, as we defined it. We wanted to treat the Rorschach data with rigor equal to that with which we had treated the sociocultural data.

We therefore turned to scoring the responses with codes that could be statistically treated. Scoring, following the methods developed by Bruno Klopfer and his associates, requires various scores for the use of form, movement, texture, dimensionality, and color in percept formation; a score for location of the percept in the inkblot and the extent to which various parts are combined or left separate in the percept; a content score (animal, human, object, symbolism, nature, and so forth); a score for widely used "popular" percepts; and a record of reaction time and response time. Various ratios between scores for movement, color, form, and texture are considered to be of special significance. The scoring procedure itself requires application of judgments, but the rules and basic principles are clearly stated and scoring reliability is not a problem when the scorers are equally well trained in the same procedures. Scoring the Rorschach responses is not any more risky than rating ethnographic descriptions of child training for severity or rating folk tales for indices of aggression.

The problem is the perennial one of meaning. What do the various scores or score combinations mean? The meaning of the various scores and score combinations has grown out of clinical practice and much of it is not well integrated by theory. In this respect the Rorschach is like most "personality tests." Some examples will help. The proportion of human movement responses (as in "It looks like two women in witches' costumes dancing around a pole" in Card II) in the total record is considered to be a possible index of self-projection and of perceived human relationships. It is more developed among adults than children. Whether this projection is positive or negative and whether it involves self-projection depends upon the content of the movement. Another example: the proportion of responses based upon form (outline and structure) alone, not enlivened by movement, texture, or color, is considered an index (along with a number of others) of possible constriction. Other interpretations are based upon the approach of the respondent to the intellectual problem of using the blots for percept formation. For example, a "combinatory whole" percept for Card X (one that integrates the salient features of the whole blot into one idea), with its variegated colors, unusual assemblage of forms, and spatially separated elements, is unusual. Percepts of this sort are considered indices of cognitive organization. Such an approach might be contrasted with one where tiny details on the edge of the inkblots would be used for percept formation. Value judgments as to which approach is "better" are irrelevant, but it seems reasonable to acknowledge that the styles of approach are quite different.

There are numerous complications, to be sure. For example the human movement hypothesis is confused among the native-oriented Menomini because many in this group are socialized to think of animal and human forms as interchangeable. Spirits appear in dreams and visions in either shape. Witches change from one to the other. Some animals, like the bear, are thought to have human characteristics. Therefore, the production of human versus animal movement in percepts in this group must be treated carefully. An examination of records, however, indicates that animals in human-like action are effectively equivalent to percepts of humans in human-like action. Allowance must be made for shifts in interpretation made necessary by cultural factors. It appears to us, however, that a number of the most parsimonious hypotheses are cross-culturally valid.[6]

In general, the basic procedural rule is to avoid over-interpretation. We tried to view the various score and score combinations parsimoniously, using hypotheses of the general type described above. A statement of the interpretive rules followed in the ascription of psychological meaning to the Rorschach scores in the Menomini research is available (G. Spindler 1955:21–24).

We also developed strategies for using the Rorschach responses as indices of significant perceptual shifts in the course of acculturative adaptation and as indices of significant differences between the sexes, without regard to ascribed meanings of scores. For certain purposes it did not matter what perceptual attributes were ascribable, as long as we could demonstrate that two groups were similar or different on the basis of statistical tests (L. and G. Spindler 1958). Our method for analysis of the initial sample of males was to define twenty-one indices of the type discussed above, then test the distribution of these indices among our defined acculturative categories to see if they were significantly differentiated. Chi-square was used, but supplemented by "exact probability" tests because of the small N in the various groupings. This method allowed us to make accurate statements about the extent to which each of the acculturative categories were differentiated from every other one. It became clear, for example, that the Peyote Cult membership was perceptually deviant from all other groupings in the Menomini sample. Both the extent and the nature of this deviation is congruent with the nature of Peyote belief, ritual, ideology, and behavior (G. Spindler 1955:139–147, 176–183; G. Spindler 1952; and G. and L. Spindler 1970; Chapter 3). The Rorschach data aids in

---

[6] Gardner Lindzey (1961) reviews the whole range of cross-cultural research utilizing projective techniques.

our understanding of the Peyote Cult because it shows us to what extent this cultural system is deviant at a psychological level as well as a manifest behavioral level in the Menomini population, the extent to which it is psychologically homogeneous and the degree to which ideology and ritual practice influence perception. The Rorschach data also made it possible to identify certain features of continuity in perceptual organization among transitionals that were shared with the native oriented, so that we could come to see the former as attenuated versions of the latter and as under special stresses resulting from their more marginal position. It also made it possible to evaluate more precisely than otherwise could have been the case the extent of the psychological as well as cultural break with the past represented by the elite acculturated.

The responses of the female sample were treated in the same manner as the male sample in the first stages of analysis. The female sample, however, proved to be internally more homogeneous than the male sample. We exploited this circumstance by developing an adaptation of Anthony Wallace's modal personality construct (Wallace 1952) in application first to the female sample, then to a comparison between males and females. We were able to demonstrate, through this analysis, that the acculturation process is disjunctive for males, that the modal adaptation is transitional-disturbed for them, and that the acculturative process permits maintenance of psychological continuity for Menomini females with a conservative (native-oriented) modal adaptation (G. and L. Spindler 1958; L. Spindler 1962).[7] We found it essential to separate the sexes for analytic purposes for they represent two quite different universes. Lumping them together would have confused the picture intolerably. The Rorschach helped greatly to clarify this issue.

The Rorschach seemed to serve us well. We have since then applied it to a comparable sample of Blood Indians, who occupy a large reservation in southern Alberta, and who like the Menomini have rich resources (cattle, wheat, and some oil) upon which decisive internal differentiations along economic lines are based. Our analysis to date indicates that the two populations are not only different from each other in distribution of Rorschach responses, but that their internal differentiation is quite divergent.[8]

In both the Blood and Menomini cases our purpose has been one that is shared with other workers using other research methods—to understand the perceptual and cognitive organization that must be considered a concomitant, if not an internal version, of the culture. If one takes an ideational view of culture —that culture is the mental organization that stands behind patterned behavior, but is not the behavior itself—then it is but one step from culture to

---

[7] See L. Spindler's dissertation (1956) for complete data on Rorschach and socio-cultural index samples and statistical applications. To conform to space limitations this material was left out of the 1962 memoir.

[8] For a fuller accounting of divergent adaptations see G. Spindler "Psychocultural Adaptation," 1968.

cognition. But this one step seems to be very difficult to take. Ethnoscientific methods have been used recently as a way of describing taxonomies of behavior and attributes of external conditions held by natives in various cultural systems. These taxonomies are often regarded as dimensions of cognitive structure. The Rorschach as we use it, is an attempt to use the individual's culturally patterned perceptions of contrived stimuli (inkblots), over which we can exercise some control for comparative purposes, to go to the cognitive structure "inside the head." The ethnoscientist's "Rorschach" is potentially all the things there are in the world, though any given research is usually confined to a single semantic domain, such as beer-making, firewood, diseases, or ways to get into a house, and the cognitive structure is regarded as being exhibited in regularities in speech patterns (Tyler 1969). Both attempts must be judged a mixed success, but to date, so are all other attempts.

One problem with Rorschach responses is that they are very cryptic. A respondent sees a "bear" in Card II. So do about one third of all respondents in cultural systems where bears are possible. We can be concerned with the blackness of the bear, the movement, the details used, the amount of attention to shading as texture ("fur"), to form, what the respondent does with the bright color on the card, but a bear is a bear for all that. As a response to our dissatisfaction with this cryptic quality, we developed a new technique which we have called the "Instrumental Activities Inventory." The instrument consists of a number of line drawings (usually twenty to thirty) representing activities that can be considered instrumental, within a given cultural system, to achievement of certain goals and life styles. Occupations as we understand them in Western culture are instrumental activities, but so is going to church, throwing cocktail parties, going skiing, getting an education, attacking the Establishment, dropping acid, and wearing long hair. In acculturation situations the range of instrumental activities reflects the confrontation of traditional and emergent or modern cultural systems, with their internally relevant instrumental activities. Being a medicine man among the traditional Blood is still an instrumental activity, but not for the young Blood. Holding a ghost feast after the death of a loved one is an instrumental activity among the native-oriented Menomini, but not for the acculturated. The choices people make of instrumental activities are a basic determinant of acculturative adaptation.

The series of line drawings can be shown to respondents with a minimum of instruction, letting the pictures serve as concrete stimuli, to be invested with meaning by the respondent, not the anthropologist. Respondents explain what the drawing represents and choose activities they would like to engage in, or see their children engage in, and ones they would not want to, and then explain their reasons for these choices. During the administration, various contrasts can be evoked by asking for responses to pairs or trios of the drawings. The responses may range very widely and be very rich. The content can be subjected to various forms of thematic and content analysis, to produce generalizations characterizing both cognitive style and specific rankings of values expressed in means-ends relationships. A formal ethnographic procedure of elicitation in successive frames could be utilized (Metzger and Williams 1963), though we have not done so. We have used the technique among the Blood, Mistassini Cree, and in a German village undergoing rapid urbanization (G. and L. Spindler 1965a, 1965b, 1970). We have not used it among the Menomini, but are fortunate to have the results of one of its antecedents, the picture technique for the study of values, applied by Robert Edgerton to our Menomini sample (Goldschmidt and Edgerton 1961). Though the value-choice framework employed by Edgerton is not identical in either its premises or application with the I.A.I., relevant data were produced.

Expressive Autobiographic Interview

After we had established our sample of males and females, with the sociocultural index, Rorschach, direct observation, and semi-structured interview materials collected for each of our 129 cases, we still felt the need to go deeper into the life adjustments of some. Rather than use another projective technique (we had tried the standard Thematic Apperception Technique and found it too culturally loaded), we used a technique that Louise Spindler developed and that she termed the "Expressive Autobiographic Interview" (henceforth E.A.I.).

The technique was chosen because it proved capable of revealing the kinds of adaptations taking place in role-playing, value orientations, and self concepts in the acculturative process.[9] Among the women, for example, the roles of mother, wife, and social participant were selected as foci, and the respondents, with gentle reinforcement, were able to express in their own words, in relation to their own lives, their concepts of these roles.

The E.A.I. is a cross between a structured interview and a chronological autobiography. The respondent is asked to tell the story of his or her life but intervention by the anthropologist at critical points as relevant to foci of the type mentioned above turns the autobiography to relevant considerations and permits an economy of time that is not possible with the full autobiography. As an initial impetus the respondent is asked to start with the very first thing she or he can remember that happened. The question seemed to intrigue most respondents and they were usually off to a good start. With subtle encouragement at crucial points the desired data seems to come forth quite easily. The emotional atmosphere established in the confidential framework of the life story seems

[9] The concept of "self" and "self-other" interaction is drawn from the work of George H. Mead (1934). See L. Spindler, 1962.

appropriate for questions of almost any type. The respondent introduces you to his or her family, reveals incidents cloaked with sentiment, touches upon the main areas of friction and conflict in his or her life, expresses attitudes towards parents, siblings, friends, and authority figures, and talks about such presumably inaccessible areas in traditional Menomini life as witchcraft and sex. For example, when a native-oriented woman told Louise Spindler during the course of relating important events in her life that a relative had died but gave no cause for death, Louise asked her if she was witched. This is a reasonable assumption in the traditional belief system, but ordinarily one would not ask such a question. Within the framework of the autobiographic interview the question was responded to as acceptable. "Yes. You could tell by the fingernails and toenails. They turn blue (when they're witched). You can see them (witches) coming in a big cloud of light, and you have to watch out. The person gets scairt like they was hypnotized. When this woman's baby (next door) died they watched around the house and graveyard but couldn't ever see it. It was slick work that time!" Further details are given about watching the graveyard so the witch will not rob the body of its heart or other organs, the taking of medicine (invested with power) to keep awake and for protection against sorcery, and so forth. After having read many accounts about how difficult it was to secure data on witchcraft from American Indian informants, and specifically the Menomini, it was rewarding to be able to secure responses like this relatively effortlessly. All of the women in Louise Spindler's E.A.I. sample (sixteen total) were asked about witchcraft, dreams, reactions to critical on-going events, predictions for the future, and sex, as well as about many other more prosaic areas such as roles as wife, mother, and social participant. The male respondents in George Spindler's E.A.I. sample (eight total) were less responsive in these culturally suppressed areas, but were quite able to go on freely and expressively (for typically constrained Menomini native-oriented males) about their personal involvements with ceremonial activities, vision experiences, and critical events.

Value orientations were explicitly revealed in both male and female E.A.I.s. For example, one woman, struggling to become middle class herself, said, "My grandparents believed in self-support: work from sunrise to sunset. They didn't believe in vacationing. If you don't work you can't eat, they said. I'm like that too: I feel these people around here weren't brought up right. My grandmother always believed in six days of work and one day to rest."

The conflicts in values suffered by a people in transition are also poignantly revealed. Another woman, torn between Whiteman and Menomini values said, "It always seemed kinda funny that my mother liked all those things—Indian dances and medicines, when my grandmother was a good Catholic. I don't know where I belong. I don't go to church and I use Indian cures for different things. I can't go to church now. If I should die I suppose I would be buried out in that potter's field! (a nondenominational cemetery)." Or the old man, Shumaysen, who concluded the first E.A.I. session with this: "When I think of his future (his grown son) . . . he is alone in the world with no understanding of life . . . of the old Menomini way. He is trying to make a poor copy of the White man's civilization. He'll never know anything himself, even if I was to teach him. He never contradicts me. That is all I can say about my son. It is as Skinner (Alanson B. Skinner, anthropologist) said. Now you come to talk to me, like Skinner did to my father. But sometime a man will come to my son and he will know nothing! Nahaw!"

The sample of individuals who responded to the E.A.I. was selected purpose-fully to represent both typical and deviant adaptations within each of the acculturative categories, with respect to both Rorschach and sociocultural indices. This enabled us to sample in qualitative depth both the unique and the modal, thus providing integration for relationships indexed for other individuals but relatively unexplored. For example, it developed that there were a number of individuals in the native-oriented male sample who had made prolonged forays out into the Whiteman's world or into transitional society, who had been re-jected in this attempt or themselves actively rejected what they encountered. By exploring this experience and its consequences in some depth with one individual it was possible to develop insight into what this meant in other cases similar to his, where we had relevant interview and observational material but relatively little life history depth.

The E.A.I. is a technique that is unlikely to be successful in the first stages of fieldwork. In our Menomini fieldwork we knew the people well before we asked if they would indulge us with their cooperation on the E.A.I. We also knew a great deal about the various cultural systems represented on the reserva-tion and could identify the key points around which to center inquiries. We regard the E.A.I. as a means of finding out more about something we already knew quite a bit about, but where certain relationships and content remained obscure until we applied the technique.

Participant Observation

Whatever the array of techniques the anthropologist employs in the field, his basic stance is usually that of participant observer. We have tried to demon-strate how other techniques were used in the Menomini research, and we have touched upon the role of participant observer in the section on entrèe and rapport. It is fitting that we should conclude this chapter with further discussion of the role of anthropologist as participant observer.

For the anthropologist, the role of participant observer implies continuous contact with the individuals being observed in all aspects of their daily life— feasts, births, deaths, marriages, accidents, and the like. This kind of participa-tion enables the anthropologist to see his people in a variety of roles. Thus, when we questioned a Menomini about his own activities or those of another, we could actually check later on the veracity of his statements or the discrepancy between the stated and the real behavior. This is of utmost importance. It is this kind of technique that gives the anthropologist an advantage over the researcher who must settle for data secured through questionnaires and interviews or limited observation. In the case of the Menomini, people told us that no one gossiped—that people were afraid to gossip for fear of being witched. We were then able to check later on who did gossip and under what circumstances, since we realized that the statement was the "ideal," what "ought to be," and would not fit reality. On one occasion a pious elderly man who sponsored Protestant revivalistic meetings in his yard lectured to us about the evils of drinking. A few weeks later, we encountered him in a tavern just off the reserve. He had

We attended a wide variety of affairs. Here the people get ready for a small Sunday afternoon "powwow."

been drinking quite heavily, but in order to escape blame, he pointed at us and in stentorian tones shouted, "I'm surprised." He continued to repeat the phrase, shaking his finger at us while he was being carried out. And we erased our check on our sociocultural indices in the nondrinking slot for him.

Playing the roles of participant and observer at the same time may seem an impossible task. But it is exactly what the anthropologist must train himself to do. When we were participating in a Peyote Cult meeting, a feast, a birth or death ritual, we were doing what all other participants with us were doing *and* we were sensitized to ingesting in great detail what was actually happening around us. The participant observer must be involved and detached at the same time—sympathetic and empathetic *and* objective. The task is made easier if the observer understands what happens to him and to others when they play roles and is trained to analyze the roles he himself takes in various situations. This task is no more difficult for him than it is for a good actor or actress. Shakespeare's Hamlet, in speaking of the function of dramatic art nearly describes the participant observer in recording and interpreting his observation of a particular culture:

> The purpose of playing (as Hamlet explains), both at the first and now, was and is, to hold, as 'twere, the mirror up to nature; to show virtues her own feature, scorn her own image, and the very age and body of the time his form and pressure.

And, as Bruyn, who quotes Hamlet (Bruyn, 1963), points out, the image of a passion is not the passion itself. The observers penetrate into the nature of the emotions in empathizing with the actors without direct personal involvement. It is these kinds of fine distinctions which the participant observer must learn to make.

Another difficult task which confronts the participant observer is that of role selection and change. The role of "Doc Psyche" was compatible and logical for George Spindler. In some ways the role of a female and wife seemed a little more complicated for Louise Spindler. While observing a Peyote Cult meeting with her husband she lay behind him along the outer border of the tent throughout the night, as did other wives (thus, incidentally, blocking the cold draft whistling underneath the edge of the Peyote tepee). On many occasions she was merely a "friend"; on other occasions she played a "nurse" role when persons were in need of medication or food. It seemed, as it does in our own culture, more important that the woman be dressed "properly" than the male. Thus, since the reservation encompassed a wide variety of persons in different socioeconomic statuses, this meant many changes in attire. For example, she might be observing a Menomini native-oriented ceremony in the morning in her camp clothes (skirt and tennis shoes). She might have a luncheon meeting with an elite acculturated woman which required nylon stockings and acceptable, middle-class clothes for this occasion. Then in the evening if there were a Peyote Cult meeting, which lasted all night in the drafty tepee, this would require wool stockings and durable warm clothes for lying on the ground (an old racoon coat from undergraduate days was ideal for this purpose).

It is the participant-observer role that eventually creates personal problems for the anthropologist as well as giving him the most important data he usually collects. The people become friends,[10] and he frequently becomes virtually a member of the family, so to speak. It is not always easy to write about one's friends, and more than one young anthropologist has come back from the field

An elite acculturated lady.

quite unable to write his dissertation at all for this reason. The antidote is the special kind of objectivity described. It is one of the reasons why the anthropologist must play a role. If successful, he is in truth friendly, in truth concerned with the welfare of his respondents, but in truth an observer. His job is to find out what the people think and feel as well as what they do. He must penetrate beyond the facade of rationalizations and diversions that all humans throw up around their activities and sentiments. But he must not become one of the people whom he is observing, though he may virtually seem to become one from the outside. He must keep his identity while he studies theirs. He may well observe himself in the sense of observing his own behavior as observer. This self-knowledge is necessary. When he loses this distance, between himself and his respondents, and between himself in the sense of his personal identity and in the sense of his role as participant observer, he has lost his usefulness as a field anthropologist.

---

[10] Some, of course, become enemies. Some anthropologists are able, they claim, to work effectively in a situation where most of the people are unfriendly. This would be impossible for us.

Husband and Wife in the Field

Many friends and students have asked us about our division of labor in the field, as well as more pointed questions directed at problems of competition, ego defense, and the like. We have already touched upon this in discussing how one of us would observe, while the other collected interview or projective test data. In this our working relationship has been complementary. In other ways, also, it has been so. For instance, Louise Spindler works with women respondents and in women's gatherings, especially where George Spindler would not be allowed, or would be suspected if he attempted interaction, though her work is not necessarily confined to women, or his to men. Perhaps this role division has called to our attention more sharply than is usually the case that males and females belong to different sociocultural and psychological universes, at least in the cultural systems in which we have worked. It seems to us that not enough is made of this in most ethnographies or other forms of field reports. As for the other aspects of our collaboration—we hesitate to make any seemingly prescriptive statements, for this is indeed a matter for individual mediation. In our case we have never competed with each other for the role of headman. No decisions are ever made without full discussion and mutual commitment. This has made it possible for both of us to achieve most of our personal goals in our fieldwork together. In writeup and analysis, we divide primary responsibility depending upon who collected the data on a given problem, and who has been working with it in greatest depth, but the other partner rewrites and critiques at length. The best part of it all is that we not only both want to do fieldwork but we never lack for something interesting to talk about.

Culture Shock

As a final note we should consider the phenomenon of culture shock, since it is a response that may have a decisive effect on one's ability to participate, observe, or write up the data after the field period. It is an occupational hazard and we have all suffered from it at one time or another. In our case, however, the only significant culture shock we have experienced has been upon return to the comforts and responsibilities of our own society. Every time we have returned from fieldwork, no matter where in the field, we have experienced feelings of futility, despondency, and a haze of indecisiveness. After a few weeks we adjust once more to the haunting, ever-present feeling that life is a crisis and to the inhumanity and sham so pervasive in our society. We do not feel this way when we start fieldwork.

To us, fieldwork is the stuff of anthropology—that and communicating what we found out and what insights we think this knowledge may give us about the human condition, including ours at home. It is not only, for us, the stuff of anthropology, but the fun of it. This is probably the reason that we have collected much more data than we have been able to analyze, write up, and publish, though we use all of it in our teaching. We never have had a truly bad time in the field, though we have not, to be sure, endured some of the extreme exigencies that our colleagues have. But we have fallen ill, been cold, wet, and insect-bitten, suffered from having to struggle along in somebody else's language, been rejected by the very people we wanted to know, harassed by children, repulsed by offensive sights and odors (given our own culturally conditioned sensibilities), our lives have been threatened by people and by impersonal forces. But it was all the very essence of living.

References

Bruyn, Severyn, 1963, The methodology of participant observation. *Human Organization* 22:224–235.

Goldschmidt, Walter, and *Robert Edgerton,* 1961, A picture technique for the study of values. *American Anthropologist* 63:26–47.

Lindzey, Gardner, 1961, *Projective Techniques and Cross-Cultural Research.* New York: Appleton-Century-Crofts, Inc.

Mead, George H., 1934, *Mind, Self and Society from the Standpoint of the Social Behaviorist.* Chicago: University of Chicago Press.

Metzgen, Duane, and *Gerald E. Williams,* 1963, A formal analysis of Tenejapa Ladino Weddings. *American Anthropologist* 65:1076–1101.

Slotkin, John S., 1952, Menomini Peyotism: A study of individual variation in a primary group with a homogeneous culture. *Transactions of the American Philosophical Society.* New series. Vol. 42, Part 4.

———, 1957, The Menomini Powwow. Milwaukee Public Museum Publications in Anthropology, No. 4.

Spindler, George D., 1955, Sociocultural and Psychological Processes in Menomini Acculturation. Vol. 5. *University of California Publications in Culture and Society.* Berkeley: University of California Press.

———, 1968, Psychocultural Adaptation. In *The Study of Personality: An Interdisciplinary Appraisal,* by Edward Norbeck and others, eds., New York: Holt, Rinehart and Winston, Inc.

Spindler, George D., and *Walter Goldschmidt,* 1952, Experimental design in the study of culture change. *Southwestern Journal of Anthropology* 8:68–83. Bobbs-Merrill Reprint A 210.

Spindler, Mary Louise, 1956, *Woman and Culture Change: A Case Study of the Menomini Indians.* Unpublished doctoral dissertation, Stanford University.

———, 1962, Menomini women and culture change. *Memoir 91,* American Anthropological Association, 64, Part 2.

———, 1970, Menomini Witchcraft. In Deward Walker, Jr., ed., Systems of

North American Indian Witchcraft and Sorcery. Moscow, Idaho: *Anthropological Monographs of the University of Idaho*, No. 1.

Spindler, Louise, and George Spindler, 1958, Male and female adaptations in culture change. *American Anthropologist* 60:217–233.

───── and ─────, 1965a, The instrumental activities inventory: a technique for the study of the psychology of acculturation. *Southwestern Journal of Anthropology* 21:1–23.

───── and ─────, 1965b, Researching the perception of cultural alternatives: the instrumental activities inventory. In Melford Spiro, ed., *Content and Meaning in Cultural Anthropology*. New York: The Free Press.

───── and ─────, 1970, *Dreamers without Power: The Menomini Indians. A Case Study in Cultural Anthropology*. New York: Holt, Rinehart and Winston, Inc.

Tyler, Stephen A., 1969, *Cognitive Anthropology*. New York: Holt, Rinehart and Winston, Inc.

Wallace, Anthony F. C., 1952, The Modal Personality Structure of the Tuscarora Indians. *Bureau of American Ethnology*, Bulletin 150. Washington, D.C.: Government Printing Office.

RECOMMENDED READING

Beattie, John, 1965, *Understanding an African Kingdom: Bunyoro*. Studies in Anthropological Method. New York: Holt, Rinehart and Winston, Inc.

This is the story of the fieldwork that stands behind *Bunyoro: An African Kingdom*, by John Beattie. The author deals with both the processes of participant observation and with various more formal techniques, such as questionnaires and use of official records.

Berreman, Gerald D., 1962, *Behind Many Masks; Ethnography and Impression Management in a Himalayan Village*. Ithaca, N.Y.: Society for Applied Anthropology, Monograph No. 4.

The author describes his interpersonal relations in an unfriendly North Indian village, and analyzes the ways in which various actors, including himself, caste groups in the village, and his interpreters tried to manage their behaviors so as to produce certain impressions upon each other.

Bowen, Elenore Smith, 1964, *Return to Laughter: An Anthropological Novel*. Garden City, N.Y.: Anchor Books, Doubleday and Company, Inc.

An introspective account of what it is like to be a fieldworker in a tribe in west Africa, cast in novel form. Originally published in 1954, this is the first account of its kind.

Bruyn, Severyn, 1966, *The Human Perspective in Sociology: The Methodology of Participant Observation*. Englewood Cliffs, N. J.: Prentice-Hall.

Whereas anthropologists take for granted the necessity of participant observation in field research, sociologists who want to use this approach must defend it. This self-consciousness has produced in this book a refined and sophisticated statement that deals with a much wider range of phenomena than those usually covered by the term "participant observation" as a field research technique. It is a challenge to the application of the scientific method developed out of the natural sciences to the analysis of human social life.

Golde, Peggy, ed., 1970, *Women in the Field*. Chicago: Aldine.

Twelve female anthropologists describe their experiences in the field with special attention to the problem of acceptable women's roles in the communities in which they worked.

Henry, Frances, and Satish Saberwal, eds., 1969, *Stress and Response in Fieldwork*. Studies in Anthropological Methods. New York: Holt, Rinehart and Winston, Inc.

Fieldwork in four different contexts ranging from Cree Indian to urban African, with emphasis on the ways in which the anthropologist in the field responds to various forms of personal, social, and political stress. The chapters are written by Ronald Wintrob, Peter Gutkind, Frances Henry, and Satish Saberwal.

Jongmans, D. G., and P. C. W. Gutkind, eds., 1967, *Anthropologists in the Field*. Assen, Holland: Van Gorcum & Company.

This volume, unlike most of the others in this recommended list, is concerned with nearly the whole range of field methods and techniques. It is cited because it engages, at several points, with contrasts between participant observation and surveys, between the outside and the inside view of the culture, and deals with some problems of great contemporary significance, such as various ethical problems, the restudy, and reliability and validity of social description.

Malinowski, Bronislaw, 1967, *A Diary in the Strict Sense of the Word*. Introduction by Raymond Firth. New York: Harcourt, Brace & World, Inc.

This diary has had a mixed reception by our colleagues. The reviewer for the *American Anthropologist* states that the volume has "no interest for anyone" (*AA* 70, 3, 1968, p. 575), and in the same issue the reviewer of another book refers to it as "private exuviae" (p. 574). Others claim that such comments miss the point. In any event, the Malinowski we meet in this diary is not the one we might be led to expect from reading his classic works on the Trobriands. It is indeed a private document.

Middleton, John, 1970, *The Study of the Lugbara: Expectation and Paradox in Anthropological Research*. Case Studies in Anthropological Methods. New York: Holt, Rinehart and Winston, Inc.

This is a straightforward account of how the anthropologist proceeded in the light of his research objectives. Like Beattie's, this account is related to a case study *The Lugbara of Uganda*. Throughout the book Middleton stresses the paradox of the anthropologist "having to live as a human being with other human beings yet also having to act as an objective observer."

Powdermaker, Hortense, 1966, *Stranger and Friend: The Way of an Anthropologist*. New York: W. W. Norton Company, Inc.

Written on the basis of personal experience in Lesu, Hollywood, the

Rhodesian copperbelt, and in Mississippi, this book provides illuminating discussion of problems encountered by most anthropologists in the field, particularly with respect to bias stemming from cultural and personal values that influence both observation and interpretation.

Williams, Thomas Rhys, 1967, *Field Methods in the Study of Culture.* Studies in Anthropological Method. New York: Holt, Rinehart and Winston, Inc. This slim volume covers a surprisingly wide range of topics relevant to fieldwork, including preparations for study, writing research proposals, entering the community, recording data, and choices of status and role in rel

DATE DUE